Who Needs College Anymore?

Work and Learning Series

Series edited by Robert B. Schwartz and Nancy Hoffman

Who Needs College Anymore?

*Imagining a Future Where
Degrees Won't Matter*

KATHLEEN DELASKI

HARVARD EDUCATION PRESS
CAMBRIDGE, MASSACHUSETTS

Paperback ISBN 9781682539521

Library of Congress Cataloging-in-Publication Data

Names: deLaski, Kathleen, author.
Title: Who needs college anymore? : imagining a future where degrees won't matter / Kathleen deLaski.
Description: Cambridge, Massachusetts : Harvard Education Press, [2025] | Includes bibliographical references and index.
Identifiers: LCCN 2024033441 | ISBN 9781682539521 (paperback)
Subjects: LCSH: Education, Higher—Social aspects—United States. | Labor supply—Effect of education on—United States. | Career education—United States. | Educational change—United States.
Classification: LCC LB2324.D455 2025 | DDC 306.43/20973—dc23/eng/20241210
LC record available at https://lccn.loc.gov/2024033441

Published by Harvard Education Press,
an imprint of the Harvard Education Publishing Group

Harvard Education Press
8 Story Street
Cambridge, MA 02138

Cover Design: Jackie Shepherd Design

The typefaces in this book are Minion Pro and ITC Stone Sans.

This book is dedicated to new majority learners,
for whom college was never designed.

Contents

Series Editor's Foreword

In 2011 the Harvard Graduate School of Education published a report I coauthored, *Pathways to Prosperity*. In that report, my coauthors and I challenged the growing "college for all" movement and called for a system of multiple pathways leading to postsecondary credentials of value alongside the dominant four-year college pathway.

Thirteen years later in a provocative new book, Kathleen deLaski takes this argument to a whole different level, asking, "Who needs college anymore?" While she concedes that there are four types of students for whom college will continue to be a good option, deLaski's view is that college as we know it will continue to lose market share and will become but one of three "doors" through which people will choose to acquire the skills and credentials they need to get launched on careers. As she observes, over the past decade the proportion of adults who say that college is not worth the cost has jumped from 42 percent to 56 percent, and 62 percent of respondents say they prefer short-term skills training and nondegree credentials to longer-term programs leading to degrees.

What would it take to move us *from* a world in which our labor market (and our politics) is sharply bifurcated between the 40 percent of adults with four-year college degrees or better and the 60 percent without such degrees *to* a world in which virtually all young people have the opportunity and support to acquire the skills and credentials to thrive in our rapidly changing economy? This is the question deLaski sets out to answer in this very lively, engaging book.

DeLaski herself has had an extraordinary career, and one of the reasons this book is so readable and compelling is that she interweaves stories from her own career journey and those of her children into her tour of the landscape of nontraditional education and training organizations. DeLaski began her career as a broadcast journalist, and a major strength of the book is that it draws on site visits and interviews she conducted over the past several years with educators, employers, researchers, and, most important, students. In 2013 she founded the Education Design Lab, an organization that brings design thinking to bear on the problem of how to better align education institutions to a rapidly changing world of work. One of the hallmarks of design thinking is to always have the perspective of the end user in mind as one designs solutions. That's why the voices of students are at the center of deLaski's narrative.

It's also critical to mention that the students we meet are almost universally "new majority learners," students from non-college-educated families. This is the population deLaski is focused on redesigning for and with, another thing that makes this such an unusual and essential book about higher education.

DeLaski is clear-eyed about the challenge of moving from a world in which most employers screen and hire for professional-level jobs based on degrees to one in which they hire based on skills. The good news is that surveys of employers tell us that many are ready to make this shift, and we can already point to some examples of major companies that have moved in this direction, most notably IBM. Five years ago, 90 percent of IBM's job postings required a four-year degree. Today only 50 percent do, and 20 percent of professional roles at IBM are now filled by non–college grads.

Nationally, however, despite the rhetorical support for skills-based hiring from CEOs, the evidence to date is that hiring managers still rely overwhelmingly on degrees. The challenge on the employer side is to develop what deLaski calls a "skills genome," a careful mapping, sector by sector, job by job, of the required skills. On the higher education side, there is a similar challenge: to move from broad learning outcomes to descriptions of the skills students are expected to acquire course by course. These are not trivial challenges.

A second major challenge is how to make early work experience an essential element of a redesigned "edu-training ecosystem" (deLaski's term). One of the most sobering findings from recent research is that over half of new college graduates are underemployed a year after graduation, meaning that they are working in jobs that don't really require a college degree. Even more disturbing is that ten years later, nearly half of these graduates are still underemployed. The headline finding: that first job really matters!

Survey after survey tells us that employers hire first on the basis of experience. This means that if you graduate college with no meaningful work experience on your résumé, you may be forced into a subprofessional job that didn't require a degree. There is no easy fix to this problem, but in deLaski's redesigned system we would lead with work, hence the attention she pays to apprenticeship.

This book is the tenth in a series Nancy Hoffman and I have been curating for Harvard Education Press on work and learning. One of the themes of the series has been that work and learning need to be much more integrated, beginning in high school, and to be seen as essential preparation for a lifetime in which continuous learning will be a core element of working life. No book in this series better illustrates this theme than *Who Needs College Anymore?* I'll end with deLaski's provocative redefinition of "college" as "any post–high school path that sets a learner up for a family-sustaining wage and opens their eyes to their own possibilities."

Robert B. Schwartz

A Note from the Author

This book draws from many interviews with learners and workers. To protect their privacy, I have used only first names for early-career workers and, in the case of minors, names have been changed.

Introduction

Who does need college anymore? I have put off answering this question in the twelve years since I started the Education Design Lab. Honestly, the new models of higher education that emerged over that decade, including our own pilots, have yet to become comparable alternatives to college, at least ones that we would recommend to our own children. And yet an alarming number of Americans are turning away from the college degree anyway, and policy folks have largely abandoned the "college for all" goal of the early 2000s.[1] Consumers are not waiting for evidence. They are voting with their feet, blindly. Which raises the question, Where are we headed? This gray zone of national ambivalence about the college degree is hurting us. It's causing stress for families, students, teachers, professors, employers, and policy makers. It's challenging our standing in the world and the future of our economy.

But we can fix this. I believe we are on the cusp of a new era in which college as we know it could become an umbrella descriptor for several proud paths to adultification, skilling, or confidence building. In today's fluid, do-it-yourself, just-in-time training culture, 62 percent of Americans are not earning a bachelor's degree. They are finding alternatives and work-arounds, many hacking their way to eventual economic sufficiency, a small number to lofty success.[2] But they are doing it without a national narrative or evidence to guide them. And many of them feel they have let their families or their futures down. There is no language for alternatives, except "trade school," and few recognized professional pathways as we move toward a skills economy. And it feels painful to see so many "alternative" learners I meet bounce around for years in their twenties, searching for life-changing education or training that only some eventually find, like reaching the end of a gamified maze or an Odyssean quest.

I have been fascinated by how the college degree has shaped us as a society, how it became both a class transporter and a class divider from the first days of colonial America. Now, after an impressive almost four-hundred-year run, the degree's status as the scaffold to the American Dream is breaking down. It's never been accessible for more than 50 percent of the population.[3] For the past one hundred years, we have fought that reality. Now we seem to be giving up, but it still worries us. One narrative tells us that "good" jobs require a degree, while the other tells us that college is too expensive or presents too much of a gamble as to whether you will finish or be underemployed. A major international survey, the 2024 Human Progress Report, tells us that US consumers are more pessimistic about higher education today than most other countries surveyed.[4]

I never expected to write a book. I am not a reflective person by nature. As a traditional journalist for the first fifteen years of my career, I was trained to report what other people thought. But one reason I became passionate about reimagining college was that I watched my own children grow up in the 1990s and early 2000s, as the college admissions process became a pressure cooker. Their road toward college was emotionally painful for our family. One child ended up going to community college and transferring to a four-year university. My other child opted for a different road, which I will describe later.

I don't think I realized how competitive college or the idea of going to college had become. I had only applied to one, Duke University, in the 1970s. In researching this book, I recently created a test account on one of those helpful college advising sites to see if I would have gotten into Duke today.[5] I entered my actual high school GPA, class rank, test scores, race, adjusted family income, and extracurricular activities. I mentioned that both my parents and my brother had gone to Duke. The assessment from the AI college acceptance simulator came back: "You have a 3% likelihood of getting into Duke." Ouch. And then it provided a helpful list of safety colleges.

As my own children struggled under the pressure of the system that called on them to be more competitive than I ever was, I now recall with embarrassment how I would encourage them some evenings. "If you don't do your homework, you'll end up flipping burgers at McDonald's." Cringeworthy. Why did I say that? At the time I was an executive at Sallie Mae, then the nation's largest student loan provider. Selling the "college is possible" dream was my day job. The choices perhaps were more binary then, as we'll hear in the book. The "college or bust" narrative was in full bloom, compared with now, when it seems that learners and employers are breaking the mold to demand other pathways to success and to finding professional workers.

When I set up Sallie Mae's foundation and then went on to assume other roles in philanthropy and build nonprofits, I was at first most interested in the K–12 education system and the zip-code destiny that linked your public school's quality with your college prospects and life outcomes. I spent most of that decade working to create more high-quality public charter schools in low-income neighborhoods. While there is much debate on the added value of charter schools, I feel it's safe to say public school advocates of the time believed that academic preparation was the thing holding students back and that college attainment was a key lever to break the generational cycle of poverty.

The college access movement I had joined in 2001 focused on getting students into college, and the movement made some progress. By 2010, college enrollment among Black and Hispanic students had improved meaningfully.[6] But at that point, we didn't have the data showing what happened to them once they got to college. Now we know that the statistics tell a somewhat hollow story. Of all students who start college, 40–50 percent fail to earn a degree.[7] And surveys began showing us that even many grads who got the degree were soon underemployed, underwater financially, or feeling like college had not been worth it.[8] The situation is exacerbated for students of color and lower-income students. They, as a group, found themselves more underemployed, with more debt, and with more of a feeling that college had failed them.[9] In that context, perhaps it is not surprising how many college access entrepreneurs have crossed over, like me, to work on the other side of the problem. Now some of us focus less on getting people into college. We push, instead, for college to be reimagined to meet their needs.

The story that emerges in this book, in my view, is not depressing. I hope it is practical and optimistic. It is based on 150 interviews with experts, entrepreneurs, researchers, counselors, college and high school administrators, teachers, and a lot of learners and employers. I also have borrowed from ten years of design thinking research at the Education Design Lab with learners, college administrators, faculty, and employers.

Like the Lab, this book approaches the question of who needs college using a human-centered design approach. That means being disciplined to look for solutions through the eyes of the end user. While all learners will benefit from a reimagining of college, I focus more in the book on "new majority learners"—that is, anyone for whom college was not originally designed.[10] The system labels them as nontraditional students, but new majority learners include lower- or moderate-income folks, people of color, children who are the first in their family to attend college, veterans, single moms, rural students, part-time attendees, neurodivergent students, just about everyone but white eighteen-to-twenty-four-year-olds who were driven to freshman orientation on a leafy campus in the family SUV, and even some of those students fit the nontraditional definition today. There is nothing "non" about new majority learners anymore; they form the majority of the market for education today, but they are not being well served, and the higher education system spits out nearly half of those who enter the gauntlet.[11]

The book is organized by stakeholder silos. Chapter 1 takes us on a quick romp beginning with the birth of our republic to show why we needed degrees in the first place and how we've now entered the dawn of a skills-first learning and hiring age. And there is a surprise discovery about my own family's connection to the origin story.

Chapter 2 analyzes the hype of the past decade through the story of the rise and fall of bootcamps to demonstrate how, even well before the pandemic, the pressure was building to unbundle degrees. Then the next four chapters look at the debate about who still needs college through the eyes of four key sets of stakeholders: employers, colleges, high schools, and finally learners themselves. The chapter on learners tries to break down which types of learners still do need a traditional college degree. Each of the chapters except chapter 1 ends with a summary of "user needs" related to education after high school. In human-centered design, such analysis is used to draw out end user needs from research to form insights about the essential barriers and then to translate those needs into ideas or solutions.

The final chapter of the book is boldly called "The Great College Reset." I encapsulate the top ten design principles drawn from user needs to consider how they are being met by today's colleges. That sets the stage for prognostications about the future and where the innovation is occurring. I predict that the silos between workforce training, college, and corporate training will essentially merge into one edu-training sector, but the umbrella may itself be called "college" and the degree may be one of many offerings in the array of learning and training products.

The goal of this book is to hasten the awareness and smart design of what comes next, and to organize thinking around the noble attempts not to throw the baby out with the bathwater. Speed is of the essence. And so is the narrative that reaches families. From an economic perspective, we can't have increasing numbers of adults opting out of professional career training at a moment when employers are desperate for more advanced skills. And from a civic perspective, we can't afford to lose the melting pot that at least exposes learners of all stripes and backgrounds to common education that fuels curiosity and provides life lessons for getting along with each other. And this conversation will only get hotter as our country's population growth stagnates and we depend more on immigrants to grow the workforce. Without new immigrants, zero population growth is expected by 2042.[12]

Without a commonly understood systemic approach, without language that refrains from stigmatizing, how will learners know their options to train for what we used to call "white-collar" jobs? Wealthier families will always be able to park their children on lovely campuses for four to six years after high school to "grow up," find themselves, and make lifelong friends and connections, but this option is becoming more elitist with each percentage point that tuition outpaces the cost of living.[13] Most of the rest of the emerging or retraining workforce can only hope to delight in soon-to-be normalized pathways that help them arrive at the same destinations.

Meanwhile, how will America navigate the downside of the technical skillification of learning, where we have no common view of "general education" after high school, no civic education, no mandatory classes in critical thinking? And, importantly, I'm as wistful as the next designer about what we give up as a country if we give in to "cheaper, (better?), faster" as the design criteria for the mid-twenty-first-century "college" experience. We've clearly put ourselves in this box by defunding public colleges at the state and federal levels, by being so smug as to lock the university door to keep out most learning programs that might smack of worker training. And so, many learners are looking elsewhere, and many of those who come to college leave complaining about the value, their return on investment.

Yet one reason I am optimistic is that I subscribe to both the "fix it" and "disrupt it" camps of social change. If we can fix college, by funding it as an entitlement; by making it more flexible, dynamic, and relevant; by building "work experience" into curriculum, college will weather the storm and regain its mojo. If we can also disrupt the degree and unbundle it into a stepladder model, with affordable high-touch and low-touch short-term micro-pathways, we can unleash a lifelong skills agility model that serves both workers and the nation's economy. I see signs that both of these movements, fix and disrupt, are underway.

I spend much of this book singing the praises of disruptors, of shortcuts to college, when I myself and most people I know have been huge beneficiaries of the "old" system. Perhaps this is the place to state that I hope we can preserve the supportive learning and network communities that many colleges have been able to create. I hope the book celebrates the "intrapreneurs" inside colleges who have worked to meet the needs of their students. I hope it celebrates the hundreds of social and business entrepreneurs working outside the system to create alternatives. I hope it celebrates all learners, but particularly new majority learners, who today are called on to be intrepid. Let's make their quests easier.

Part I
Getting Here

1

Why Did We Need Degrees?

By 2023, a clear majority, 56% of respondents, did not
believe college was worth the cost.

—WALL STREET JOURNAL CONSUMER SURVEY[1]

I learned in writing this book that I am a direct descendant of the first
person believed to have graduated from Harvard as the son of an indentured servant, in 1673.[2] I knew about my seventh-great-grandfather
because he became famous as the first minister imprisoned and barred
from the clergy for challenging British taxation over the colonies, almost one hundred years before the Boston Tea Party. He then wrote
books that sparked ideas used in the Declaration of Independence.[3] But
I had not known about his father's humble beginnings, making my ancestor, aptly named John Wise, one of the earliest success stories in the
American college access movement. I always wondered why I was drawn
to this field.

I was inspired to know more. Did John Wise need his college degree to
become an ordained minister in 1673? Was it his ticket to the colonial
American Dream? Apparently so. Harvard was originally established to
train ministers. An early Harvard marketing pamphlet, now etched in stone

at one of the entrance gates, stated the reason for establishing America's first college in 1635, a mere fifteen years after the *Mayflower* arrived: "to advance Learning and perpetuate it to Posterity; dreading to leave an illiterate Ministry to the Churches, when our present Ministers shall lie in the Dust."[4] Graduates were expected to read Latin, Greek, and Hebrew, to be Bible interpreters, historians, psychologists, and political commentators for their hardworking flocks.

Harvard was expensive by the standard of the day. We are not certain how John's father, who eventually ran a malthouse after his servitude, paid the fifty-five English pounds in tuition. Scholars surmise that he may have paid some of it in malt, as they have found records of him paying other debts that way, and it was acceptable at the time.[5] But he didn't have enough malt to send any of his other ten children to college. There was no degree market in those early colonial years for businessmen or farmers, anyway. John's Harvard class only had four students. In the next generation, three of John's five sons followed him to Harvard, and at least two of those became "eminent" members of their societies, so that in true legacy fashion, he demonstrated that the college degree—completely inaccessible to his poor forefathers in class-constrained England—could be a ticket to impressive social standing in one generation in colonial America.[6]

Surprisingly, after John's children, I can't find records of other family members attending college for the next three hundred years, until we come all the way down to my grandfather's generation in 1918. I can only imagine that the men did not need degrees for social standing they had already attained by family connections. Some of my better-remembered male ancestors had "professional" or what we later called "white-collar" careers: my great-great-grandfather was a doctor and a published naturalist in 1850s Maine. His son, Albert, after he ran away to sea at fifteen, came back and fought in the Fifty-Ninth Massachusetts Infantry Regiment in the Civil War and briefly became rich inventing methods to weave rubber into early automobile tires. But I could find no records indicating that he went to college to learn his chemistry.

DEGREE INFLATION

It wasn't until the early 1900s that jobs and professions, such as law and medicine, started "requiring" degrees. In the 1940s, college was a gift card for returning veterans as part of World War II's GI Bill, but we didn't see meaningful boosts in degree attainment until the 1960s. The percentage of people, mostly white men, with degrees remained under 10 percent until then.[7] By the 1960s, a managerial class emerged—manager roles increased in number as white-collar departments proliferated in business (finance, marketing, and research), and half of all management jobs required degrees.[8] "White collar" had a double meaning; it denoted the starched shirt you wore and, inferentially, the color of your skin. For white men, college became an elevator to the top floor or the corner office. But not for women, as my mother half joked. She said the objective of college in the 1950s and 1960s, for women, was often an MRS degree (MRS, or "Mrs.," being the old-fashioned moniker for wives), because so few jobs were open to them. Your best hope was to find the man who could take you with him on his elevator.

College didn't have a meteoric rise. There were periods of skepticism that coincided with economic downturns. "Who Needs College?" was a *Newsweek* magazine cover in 1976, at a time when *Time* and *Newsweek* covers telegraphed what was on America's collective mind.[9] It showed a picture of two white men in caps and gowns digging ditches and looking unhappy. The economy was struggling in the mid-1970s, and the implication was that this college thing might not actually give you a leg up in the hiring process in such a weak job market. Skills, such as manufacturing, could still be a more surefire track to economic security than that elitist designation "college educated."

In the 1970s, blue-collar manufacturing jobs were still providing families a good income, particularly in middle America, even when mom stayed home to watch the kids. So the question "Who needs college?" on the cover of *Newsweek* seemed valid. But it was also during this time that "blue-collar" jobs, particularly "trade" roles, such as plumbers and electricians, started becoming stigmatized by the growing percentage of families who sought college for their kids.

I was a senior in high school in 1976, living in a bubble like many teenagers. My parents were both college grads, but my dad was a self-employed accountant working out of our suburban basement, with my mom as his secretary. They were not helicopter parents. In fact, they were submarine parents when it came to planning my future. I can't remember a single conversation with them about my college plans. I was getting zero pressure on the home front, and Mom, as a typist, didn't seem to be using her degree.

I was really too busy to think much about it. I also held down a full-time job my senior year of high school as a can-can dancer. No joke. The show was Cole Porter's musical *Can-Can*. I snagged the role of Claudine, a French laundress by day, dancer by night at a racy Montmartre dance hall. In the dinner theater show, which ran six nights a week for several months, I was pursued by two older men, who were, offstage, dating each other but fighting all the time. I was sixteen. I still can't believe my parents let me "pursue my passion," but maybe it was because the money was good. I made $200 a week, plus tips waiting tables. I bought a red sports car. I left work at midnight and made it to 8 a.m. American Lit class, where Mrs. Smith sometimes let me sleep through her lectures.

In the middle of all this, my college applications were due. I don't think it occurred to me to mention the skills I was building outside high school. This was partly because SAT scores and grades were king in the 1970s. But also, the word *skills* then meant, and arguably still does, "things you could do with your hands." *Soft skills* was a term only being used in the army in the 1970s, to mean anything you were good at that didn't involve machinery.[10] I was good with a sewing machine, but that didn't feel any more relevant to squeeze into the small box permitted for the handwritten essay than my job at the theater. It didn't occur to me that my so-called soft skills might qualify me for entry-level roles that could start me on a meaningful career (outside of the performing arts). I had ruled out trying to make it using my "hard," or technical, skills in acting and dancing. I wasn't tall enough to be a Rockette at Radio City Music Hall. And I didn't believe I was very talented anyway.

It also didn't occur to me *not* to go to college, even though I liked working more than sitting in a classroom. I was vaguely aware that I was a very lucky member of the first generation of women who could aspire to a widening set of career options, that maybe I could take my own elevator to professional success, with or without a spouse. That was subliminally exhilarating. Plus, the term *student debt* was not on anybody's lips. So the college decision was easy—not even a decision—as the middle-class current of 1970s suburbia swept me along. Were there other paths? They were fuzzy to me. I had watched friends disappear around tenth grade, sent "out back" to what was then called the "VoTech" building, for auto shop or cosmetology, never to be seen again by us college-bound kids. But we'll meet the career and technical education students in later chapters.

AND THEN WE HAD SKILLS

As a can-can dancer in a dinner theater and a full-time student, I actually had built some skills that were not valued yet by college or corporate recruiters of the 1970s. I had become a rock star at multitasking, conflict resolution, oral communication, collaboration, customer service, deadlines, endurance (and surviving sleep deprivation).

What if I had had a "skills wallet" in 1976? And I could turn these skills into digital currency in the hiring marketplace? What if my skills dashboard could tell me how close I was to being a rocket scientist (not very), or arts administrator (sort of), or TV journalist (bingo)—which I became—to help me figure out my path, college or otherwise? What if there was a way to infer my skills, talents, and interests just based on my activities, my accomplishments, and my lived experiences? More importantly, what if the students who were not encouraged to be college bound could see a fuller range of possibilities?

To answer these questions, we'd have to fast-forward. You may not have heard the term *skills wallet* yet, but a new age is now dawning: the "skills-first" age. And, I will argue, it is already beginning to challenge our college degree culture.

And it's hard to see clearly at dawn, so let's pretend it's 2035; we need ten more years to bring this promise fully to life. A young can-can dancer in 2035 would not need to stand at the precipice of high school graduation and ask herself, "College or bust?" The skills-age learner or earner will be able to organize experiences, certifications, and links to artifacts or portfolios (that validate the skills) in her wallet. Unlike the airplane boarding passes and concert tickets that go in an Apple wallet on your iPhone in the mid-2020s, these wallets will be fully interactive. Every skill you gain, likely starting in high school—on the soccer field, in the theater, at after-school jobs—will be digitally documented. But there might also be skills validation for challenging life circumstances—say, resilience born from homelessness or having to care for your siblings.

The wallet has become a person's living résumé that shape-shifts like an AI-fueled Hollywood agent, positioning you based on the questions you ask. It coaches you about skills you need for different roles, and where and how to build those skills. It "takes meetings" with recruiters by sending a version of your skills profile customized to get you placed on the short list. We've moved beyond the "skills keyword" era, where automated hiring systems could only read the phrases you've known to put on your old-fashioned résumé. Now, it's the "skills intelligence" age. Students and workers are conditioned to think across the range of their abilities when considering career prospects, without the systemic barriers of access to traditional higher education. And they know where to turn to validate all their skills, including the "durable" ones employers ask for most, such as communication, teamwork, and critical thinking. (From here on, I will refer to "soft skills" as *durable skills*, as the field is trying to move away from the old army term and rally around one descriptor.)[11]

If designed with rigor, trust, and antibias as key user requirements, a skills wallet could become your GPS navigator for trips up and down your career path. And it might also provide advice and contacts, if you don't have a college adviser, a degree, or family members to guide you to your best career options. In fact, there's already lots of talk about AI-powered career advisers these days. Your wallet and GPS shouldn't replace humans, but they can supplement them. If your "adviser" says you need more skills, you can step into simulated situations to test or demonstrate these abilities. Think *World of Warcraft* meets the TV show *The Office*—highly produced, gamified skill tests made possible by advances in and better access to virtual and augmented reality. You might rack up mastery scores on teamwork, on resilience, on critical thinking. Ways to improve or shift your skill scores appear on your phone. Meetups are also available if you want situational experience in a specific industry. When our skills can be earned from many venues and neatly organized, will we need traditional degrees?

TWO MOVEMENTS ACCELERATE CHANGE

OK, really? You probably raised your eyebrows once or twice during that imagined future narrative. Will these things be real in 2035 and available to the average job seeker? Just as importantly, will we trust virtual navigators? It might sound far-fetched and utopian. But two movements are speeding us in that direction, and recent developments in AI will be their "racetrack," as we'll hear later. The first movement is employer driven (or should be): it's called skills-first hiring. In late 2023, three of the largest employer groups came together to endorse this trend with a statement: "Adopting a skills mindset has the potential to transform the workplace. Companies can expand talent pools when they look beyond traditional four-year degrees, and workers can open more doors to meaningful careers when they are able to showcase their full skill sets."[12]

The second movement is more insidious, but rather sudden: the erosion of the reputation of the college degree. It has been building over the last decade, stoked by the student debt crisis, the steady price hikes of college tuition, technology-driven consumer behaviors, politics, institutional distrust, and even the COVID-19 pandemic.

The skills-first hiring movement will push us into the future. As employers hire more of their professional workforces without requiring degrees—and I believe they will eventually, out of necessity—the education landscape will change dramatically. The degree's bad rap could help us let go of the past. But might it unleash negative consequences, even as it levels the playing field for the half of Americans currently shut out? Could one movement hasten the demise of the other? Or vice versa? Let's unpack them both.

Movement 1: Skills, Not Schools

It is hard to believe that the skills-mapping work has already been under-way for over a decade.[13] It was around 2014 that a few dedicated techies started skunkworking the plumbing for a big idea: to create a giant digital skills map that could eventually replace college transcripts. Every skill you learned would map (or not) to job roles you might qualify for. A few large universities got into the act, mapping skills into a national genome—so-called competency frameworks—and then rich skill descriptors, so that they could be ready for the AI interfaces that could bring them to life ten years later.[14] It was also roughly the time when more colleges started to shift their courses from being defined by a list of six to eight "learning outcomes" to poten-tially many more skills competencies.[15] This might seem like a nuanced shift, but learning outcomes tend to be general and more scholarly descrip-tions of what students can expect to leave a course knowing. Competen-cies, on the other hand. are more likely to track what you can do. Employers like that.

For skills-based hiring to gain attention, we would have to convert most or all of learning to the language of skills. One of my mentors used to say, "95 percent of learning happens outside the classroom," which made this seem like a pipe dream. How would we capture all that random learning in ways that would be meaningful to employers?

The emerging activity was one of the reasons I started the nonprofit Ed-ucation Design Lab in 2013, to begin piloting this idea that we had to start unbundling higher education and naming the marketable skills that stu-dents were learning because employers and learners were getting fed up. In 2014 a Gallup survey made a splash saying that 96 percent of college chief academic officers strongly agreed that their graduates had the necessary skills and competencies to succeed in the workplace, yet only 10 percent of CEOs and 15 percent of all Americans agreed with them.[16] A small disconnect?

Other surveys documented the shifting reasons for attending college. After the Great Recession, students doubled down on listing financial security as the top thing they wanted from college, and the majors they selected reinforced the trend: computer science, business, engineering.[17] There were many debates during this period about how the liberal arts degree, particularly humanities majors, might actually be the best way to develop critical thinking skills. And employer surveys showed that employers believed critical thinking to be a top durable skill that would help workers rise in their careers. Yet I noted sadly, as an English and political science major, that the humanities majors started their slide toward obsolescence during this period.[18]

Part of our early thinking about skills at the Lab was to break college up into more skill-related pieces that prepared budget-conscious learners for entry-level roles in well under four years and could be stacked with more chunks of learning as the student began to earn a living. (More on this in chapter 4.) Many experiments were going on well beyond the Lab, but we had front-row seats across different pockets of innovation. Some of the early players included the larger universities that were less constrained by tradition and regulation: Western Governors University, Arizona State University, and Southern New Hampshire University, as well as the Competency-Based Education Network (CBEN) and many others.

The breakthrough year for skills-first hiring was 2020. That's when big-name employers and states really got into the game. Why? It's when panic briefly came to a head over two loosely related issues. The first issue was the COVID-19 pandemic, which triggered the biggest talent shake-up since the Great Depression, resulting in layoffs and unemployment followed by massive talent shortages. Finding workers had already been a well-publicized concern across skilled trades and new tech fields, but COVID-19 brought the nation—some would say the world—to its knees as we all learned how unfilled jobs can complicate our lives. We scavenged for over-the-counter medications, electronics, and meat when truck drivers and factory and dockworkers became scarce. And those of us lucky enough to have remote jobs ached for our friends and loved ones, many of whom dangerously manned the front lines of the early pandemic or were laid off or quit.

This was the moment that skills as the currency for hiring came into sharper focus for me. We were working with the Federal Reserve Banks of Cleveland and Philadelphia, which released their research on "skills adjacencies." I was moved to publish a piece titled "Has the Fed Discovered a Cure for Displaced Workers?"[19] The theory was that if you lost your job as a waitress, you could calculate the skills of waitressing and search for new fields that have a high skills match, such as sales, urgent care facility management, or other customer-facing roles. The banks provided a search app to help people map their skills to other fields.[20]

The pandemic showed us how fragile the economy could be. It was a wake-up call to all employers and workers that we need a fully dynamic, sector-by-sector skills map. Several folks have been calling it a "skills genome."[21] A genome is a complete set of DNA, or genetic material, for an organism. A complete set of skills for all jobs and career progressions would be a game changer to help workers "see" their shortest paths to new job prospects and security because they may need to shift roles and careers many times in their lives. Skills agility would become the antidote to the economy's fragility.

So one catalyst for skills-first hiring that summer was the pandemic unemployment scare. The other was human tragedy at a very personal level: the murders of George Floyd and Breonna Taylor amid a series of other race-related police brutality incidents. Together, at a moment when our lives were on pandemic pause, they caused a national racial reckoning, a forced reflection period to take stock of systemic racism across our institutions. Among many other lines of inquiry—concerning everything from law enforcement to homelessness policies—hiring practices rightly came under the spotlight.

That moment crystallized what many employers saw as a moral imperative to think hard about how their hiring systems had excluded skilled candidates—candidates who did not have the piece of paper that in some ways only proved that you could make it through the gauntlet of college deadlines. Skills-first hiring could be a way to open the talent funnel to consider the 62 percent of adults who don't hold a bachelor's degree, who the nonprofit Opportunity@Work has dubbed STARS (Skilled Through Alternative Routes). That group estimated that thirty-seven million workers would qualify for higher-paying roles if they could break through "the paper ceiling" caused by the college diploma. A large percentage of those workers were minorities.[22] Screening for jobs by college degree excludes three out of four Black applicants and four out of five Latino applicants from occupations that require degrees, according to Opportunity@Work.[23]

Weeks after Floyd's death, fifty organizations came together for an unusual Summer of Design, curated by the funder Strada Education Network, to look at systemic barriers to the hiring process. It included big companies, foundations, nonprofits, and a few universities. I cochaired the Rapid Skilling Work Group. Our design question was, "How might we create more efficient ways for learners/consumers to understand the skills they need, acquire those skills, and signal them to employers?" Skills-first hiring was hailed across the sessions as a means to a better end.

As we dialed in virtually from the comfort and safety of our COVID-protected homes for a series of design sessions, there was significant guilt and a vague sense of panic that the US's best-in-class economy could be felled by a combination of workers saying, "Take this frontline job and shove it," and a hopeless mismatch of skills available and skills needed as workers embarked on an alarming reshuffle, which would, unbeknownst to us at the time, result in nearly fifty million workers quitting their jobs in 2021, and that same number again in 2022.[24] But that moment also brought the systemic plight of STARS—and, by association, the new majority learners I described in the introduction—to the virtual Summer of Design boardrooms. They upended the system, at least briefly. They got our attention.

Government Tries to Set an Example.   In the middle of the Summer of Design, Donald Trump made a bold move, no doubt to both ease the hiring woes of employers and boost his image with his base of voters during an election year. (Voters without a college degree had preferred him by 8 percentage points in the 2016 election.)[25] He signed Executive Order

13932 encouraging all federal agencies to remove degree requirements: "This order directs important, merit-based reforms that will replace degree-based hiring with skills- and competency-based hiring and will hold the civil service to a higher standard—ensuring that the individuals most capable of performing the roles and responsibilities required of a specific position are those hired for that position—that is more in line with the principles on which the merit system rests."[26]

Implementers from the Trump administration only had six months to follow through, but after Trump's 2020 defeat, they enjoyed pointing out that, according to them, this was the only one of Trump's many executive orders that the Biden administration kept in place.[27] In fact, Joe Biden's administration not only kept the order but bolstered it by 2022 to set aggressive timelines.[28]

In the meantime, the federal action started the snowball rolling down the hill. Red and blue state leaders saw this move as a rare bipartisan layup during the rest of the pandemic and into the 2024 election year. Maryland gets credit for being first, and twenty states have followed with executive orders—or, in many cases, legislative action—in record time.[29] What easier way for governors and politicians to signal support for employers struggling to find enough workers, and workers unable to afford college?

I spoke with one Maryland official who oversaw the implementation. He said Governor Larry Hogan looked at it and said, "There is no reason *not* to do this." The Department of Personnel started with three key areas—administrative roles, IT, and customer service—and, the official said, there really wasn't any pushback. Within six months, Maryland said the program was showing early signs of working as intended. The number of state employees hired without a four-year degree in that period was up 41 percent from the year before, while the number of all employees hired was up 14 percent.[30] Initially, skills-first hiring seemed to be hurtling toward reality.

Movement 2: Is College Worth It?

The second trend also emerged around 2013, although I hadn't really focused on how the two connected until writing this book. This more insidious movement was the chipping away of the reputation of the college degree, that stalwart success formula of the previous hundred years in America. Just as the college debt total crossed the trillion-dollar mark, surpassing credit card debt, the *Wall Street Journal* and University of Chicago research group NORC started tracking the value of higher education with their "Is College Worth It?" survey.[31] In 2013, they released the first version, asking Americans the question, "Is college worth the cost because people have a better chance to get a good job and earn more income over their lifetime?" That year, 40 percent of Americans said no, which was surprising enough and won a lot of headlines, but the *Wall Street Journal* and NORC repeated the survey in 2017 and 2023, and it just seemed that the college degree took a bigger beating each time. By 2023, a clear majority, 56 percent of respondents, did not believe college was worth the cost.

Opinion polls can be canaries in the coal mine, but enrollment trends are what continued to truly alarm colleges. The pandemic provided the worst scare, when enrollment dropped 8 percent in three years after already falling 10 percent over the previous decade. Community colleges had lost 37 percent of enrollment between 2011 and 2023, with a little uptick in the 2023–24 school year, but not enough to replace the lost millions.[32] And newer research showed that over half of new college grads were underemployed, only landing jobs that did not require a college degree.[33] Customers and alumni were not only lamenting the diminishing value of their investment; instead, they began and continue to vote with their feet.

Student debt also plays a key role. The debt crisis seemed to hit middle-class families the hardest, particularly at the most expensive private colleges. One president confided to a private college gathering I attended that a weird cultural horseshoe has emerged. Her student body consisted of lots of kids from wealthy families and a significant minority of low-income kids who qualified for "needs-blind" admission, but hardly any students in between whose families made, say, between $50,000 and $150,000 a year. The president described the scene: the lucky few from the lower income bracket survived on Pell Grants, scholarships, and work-study and stayed in the dorms over spring break, while their wealthy classmates flew to the Caribbean.

For the sizable middle class, families were having to make harder and harder choices as even the better state colleges became more expensive and the average cost overall of a four-year degree rose to $36,000 per year.[34] In her book *Indebted*, anthropologist Caitlin Zaloom uses a phrase that I believe is very apt, saying that as the cost of college rose, families had to engage in "social speculation," like playing the stock market with their savings to hope their child succeeded on the career front.[35] But with articles proclaiming headlines like "more than 1 million college students drop out of school each year," this futures market felt risky, creating stress and tension in the middle class that previous generations had not experienced.[36] During almost every interview with a high school parent or student that I conducted for this book, the concern about debt was an unprompted refrain and a reason to consider other options outside of college.

The drumbeat gets louder every year, and the pandemic continues to throw curveballs into the pipeline. I had not realized how lost learning time and absenteeism in K–12 schools might continue to harm college readiness and motivation for the traditional college route, but later in the book, high school administrators lament the pandemic's drag on college going. And confidence in degrees still wanes. In 2020, at the height of the pandemic, a Strada Education Network study found that a surprising 62 percent of Americans preferred shorter-term skills training and nondegree credentials to degree programs, and according to surveys, those preferences haven't really changed since then.[37]

ARE DEGREES LOSING GROUND?

Of course, colleges have a lot working in their favor. Public institutions have enjoyed huge capital investments, often thanks to state bond referenda, which means that they are significant real estate players and employers in their communities. The outstanding research at many universities drives innovation across industries and teaching hospitals. The branding power of the college sports machines has never been stronger. Loyal alumni networks are like a force field protecting some colleges. I remember ten years ago a private women's college in my state, Sweet Briar College, was sinking into enrollment purgatory and the alumni swooped in to save them from closure at the eleventh hour. A decade later, they are still operating in the red, with fewer than five hundred students, but hanging on, perhaps thanks to nostalgia.[38]

Despite the momentum from states passing laws and executive orders, when you interview individual employers, large and small, they tell you that, today, there are still many roles that require a bachelor's degree or higher. However—while estimates vary widely depending on who's doing the research—many indicators point in the direction of employers removing more degree requirements from job posts. The mega job board Indeed says degree-required jobs on its site are now below 20 percent, and LinkedIn says that while 70 percent of its jobs require a degree, that percentage is dropping rapidly.[39] But how quickly are we moving from intention to action?

A 2024 study by the Burning Glass Institute and Harvard Business School suggests that, overall, employers are not moving very quickly. They could only document that 3.6 percent of total newly de-degreed roles went to applicants without college degrees, but they found that many companies were setting up processes "in the direction of goodness" without hints of "virtue-washing," according to my interview with study coauthor Joseph Fuller of Harvard Business School.[40] This report, as well as others, cites impressive progress by "Skills-Based Hiring Leaders," including companies like IBM, one of the first large companies to rebrand 50 percent of its jobs as "new collar," back in 2019. IBM reports now that 20 percent of all professional roles are being filled by non–college grads.[41]

It doesn't take a college-educated rocket scientist to understand that résumés of college graduates today still fare better than those who try to climb the ladder on their own. I had firsthand experience comparing these when I removed the BA requirement from my search for an executive assistant at the Education Design Lab a few years back. I hired someone for this role roughly every eighteen months, as we used it as an entry point for an education designer in training. Around 2017, our small but growing organization decided we had better take a dose of our own medicine and assume a "skills, not schools" hiring stance.

But as the first round of non-BA résumés started coming in (and we received about two hundred of them for this one role), I was deflated. They told a clear story: "No one is helping me play the game." The skills keyword game, the frame-your-experience-succinctly game, even the spellcheck game. I decided to interview some of the candidates who had potential and found some amazing stories, of women who felt trapped in frontline retail jobs and single moms who demonstrated resilience. But I ended up hiring the class valedictorian at Gettysburg College, who majored in studio art and couldn't find a job in her field. She had significant visual design experience. So while I succeeded in opening up my job posting in support of the "skills, not schools" movement, even I choked in the end. (That incident was several years ago now, and I believe college-alternative programs are getting better, as we'll see in the book, at helping their students with skills prep and, importantly, packaging themselves for the professional job market.)

The Holdout Jobs

If you are a parent or a student considering college, bear in mind that some jobs will likely require the degree for decades. Not to sound cynical, but simply put, any supervisory roles to do with liability or safety will be the last holdouts. Until or unless we can replace the blunt instrument of the undergraduate degree with a similarly onerous certification process that stands up in court, requirements at the top of the medical field, the legal field, parts of cybersecurity, and parts of finance and engineering will remain in place. Of course, higher education and roles that lead to scientific research jobs will still require what's known as terminal degrees, PhDs, where your hiring portfolio is created out of your doctorate journey. Also, in the very field that prompted our first American university, Harvard, to train ministers, most denominations and religions still require a degree to lead a congregation or qualify for seminary.

The iron fist for many of these degree requirements is state licensing laws. "Occupational licensing" has spread to include jobs held by 30 percent of the US workforce, up from just 5 percent in the 1950s.[42] And recent research demonstrates that when a profession is licensed, the relative share of workers in the profession declines by 27 percent.[43] The practice now has a significant bearing on workers of all skill levels, and it extends far beyond the occupations of doctors, lawyers, nurses, and teachers.

Some licensed professions are known for their high-stakes entrance requirements. You actually can go to law school without an undergraduate degree, but only four states allow you to take the bar exam to practice law without law school. In all but one of those states, you have to have an undergraduate degree.[44] It's only in California that you don't need any degree to practice law, as long as you pass the bar and apprentice for a lawyer or judge, which is the way most became lawyers until the late 1700s.[45] Medical schools have no loopholes, which is probably a relief to most of us. Licensing boards require a college degree before med school. And nursing has five levels; the bottom two don't require a degree, but they all require a license.[46]

Accounting has upped the barriers to entry in recent years, with all fifty states adding the equivalent of a master's degree requirement. Leaders at the American Institute of Certified Public Accountants, the field's credentialing body, have described the rule as a "purposeful hurdle" intended to elevate the profession.[47] But has that upping of the education ante caused a shortage of certified public accountants? LinkedIn points to accounting as one of the professions with shortages that are shifting most quickly to drop degree requirements from job posts, suggesting employers are attempting to find work-arounds.[48]

In the K–12 teaching field, degrees are required in all fifty states. With the teacher shortages of the past decade, however, states have begun relaxing the rules, now allowing students to become student teachers earlier in their college journey. The more painful and prolonged the shortages in any of these fields, the more likely a softer requirement will start showing up on job posts, such as "degree or equivalent." One can predict a gradual softening of degree-related licenses for all but the top roles in the fields just described. But the rules have to be revised state by state, so it will be messy for learners to understand the changing landscape.

However, that leaves a very large number of well-paying roles in the "degree not necessary" category, including in medical and legal fields, but even more so in tech, cybersecurity, AI, business, arts management, hospitality management, manufacturing, real estate, construction, nonprofit management (in fact, any kind of project management), and creative services such as marketing, advertising, and digital design. I predict that talent shortages in these areas will cause employers to get more and more creative, as we'll see in chapter 3.

WALLET WORLD AND SKILLS VISIBILITY

While some employers are loosening requirements, a different set of players is building out what I call "wallet world." These players include a loose collection of states, colleges, and employer groups, supported by an emerging tech-enabled cottage industry. A host of entrepreneurs are helping schools and employers digitize learning and employment records in an attempt to reinvent the skills and hiring landscape. The hope is to digitally reimagine our one-size-fits-all journey from school to college to the job market to professional success. I summarize the value of this important work with one phrase: skills visibility. As I said in a 2022 paper on skills visibility, there are four key steps in the learner's journey from skills acquisition to landing in a career—"the learning journey, the transcript, the resume and the job posting"—and all of them are broken.[49]

It's early days, but companies like SmartResume, based in Little Rock, Arkansas, are figuring out how to connect the dots among the silos.[50] Is a piece of the wallet dream available today? A provider like SmartResume can help you prepare your résumé and verify your credentials in a digital format, so that your résumé will trigger interest because you were advised on the best keywords to use. And your résumé will automatically be fed to interested employers in the regions you specify. SmartResume provided an example on its YouTube channel, showing a worker named Pamela who enrolled in a short-term certificate course in medical insurance coding through the University of Arkansas.[51] She needed a new career. Partway through the course, her certificate instructors encouraged her to use Smart-Resume to create a step-by-step interactive résumé. The résumé app had information about her course, so it prompted her on how to describe her skills. Employers were also part of the partnership, so as she finished, the app matched her with employers who were looking for the skills in her course. Pamela says she got a job right away, and it was the easiest hiring process she'd ever been through.

Innovation hubs are springing up all over the country to link these sorts of wallet experiments. Upwards of fifty colleges, states, and broad consortia (as of publication) are testing components, often facilitated by big-name groups like the National Governors Association and the chamber of commerce and funded by Walmart.org, the Charles Koch Foundation, Strada Education Network, and Ascendium.[52] The Chamber of Commerce Foundation (the chamber is the largest employer network in the world) is testing a tool that will allow employers to validate skills and signal to their regions which skills are in demand.[53] The chamber has also been working for a decade from the ground up with groups of employers in different regions to "skillify" their job postings across industries.[54] These tools will only work when people can digitize their skills, and they'll need wallets if they want to automatically beam their skills to an employer.

Many of the boldest experiments are coming from surprising corners of the country. Alabama and North Dakota (as of this writing) are at the forefront testing the limits of wallet world. And you need an environment the size of a state or very large metropolitan area to test an end-to-end wallet. Alabama is calling its effort the Talent Triad, which gets at the three sets of stakeholders who have to be on board: learners and consumers, employers, and training providers. Alabama, like many states, has a workforce participation problem. This kind of initiative looks beyond trying to get more kids to college.[55] It begins to think about talent as infrastructure, like roads or bridges. And it considers how to utilize all potential workers, no matter age or degree.

When you look at what Alabama is building, you can see the future for all of us. It is attempting to build a statewide credential catalog that includes degrees, certificates, and licenses; an employer portal that helps hiring managers transition their job descriptions to the skills-based future and find applicants; and a career and college exploration tool that shows learners all of their options after high school and helps them arrange their verified credentials in their wallet to show off their skills to employers. The head of the state workforce council, Tim McCartney, explained at the launch event, "This system will finally accomplish what we have been talking about doing for decades—connecting talent to the economy using skills."[56] Essentially, while it is still early days, the design of the Talent Triad is meant to help solve a few of the issues I have mentioned in this chapter: the narrative problem (how does the state show students all the training pathways, not just college?); the skills mismatching problem (how can employers signal the skills needed?); and the worker visibility problem (how can workers show off what's in their wallet?).

North Dakota is believed to be the first state with a functioning wallet for all high school students. Already at this writing, high school seniors are using it to send their transcripts to colleges with their applications. But the system's architect, Tracy Korsmo, was able to show me how public colleges, like Bismarck State, are gearing up for the next version by publishing all the competencies they teach in their university as one universal, stackable skills map that correlates with national industry certifications, at least in fields where these exist, like cybersecurity.[57] This creates visibility, at least for technical skills, where competency can be measured: can you perform this coding exercise, do you have this industry certification, and so on. But most skills today don't fit neatly into a spreadsheet, because we don't know how to measure them. This is one of the biggest hurdles for colleges, training providers, and employers; we don't have a common language to describe the component parts of the burgeoning credential world. And we certainly don't want each region or state to make up their own. It would be a disaster in our connected, fluid world if each state created a wallet island.

The work of the nonprofit Credential Engine is to create a national and international catalog of all credentials and agree on data standards and common language. CEO Scott Cheney describes it as fundamental work across many states, and now international groups, that is happening more quickly than many expected. "For Apple Maps, Google Maps, and Waze to all work, they use agreed upon definitions of stop signs, four corner intersections, and speed limits. [Our standard] provides the same open data structures for education and training, skills, outcomes, quality indicators, and more. And as a result, we will be able to build GPS navigation tools for students, workers, and employers."[58]

READY OR NOT . . .

While you may still recognize the current college landscape in twenty to thirty years, you might be surprised by how few of your children or grandchildren are compelled by the traditional model when we get to the 2050 price tag. The alternative, a skills-first universe I've painted, is just gearing up to compete and will broaden its array of nondegree paths, which I will describe in coming chapters. Certainly, skills-first hiring, wallets, and the hope of a GPS career navigation system could all get derailed by trends ranging from massive unemployment to disenchantment with AI-powered self-actualization tools. But most folks I interviewed predict that the movements I've described in this chapter—skills-first hiring and softening of the market for college degrees—are here to stay.

A statewide skills wallet system will likely be a feature of most state school and college systems in the next five years. For those folks outside school, there are already small pilots happening in military services, prisons, and workplaces, as well as some started by plain old entrepreneurs racing to launch the killer consumer app.[59] It is less a question of whether programs and tools will exist to position you for roles in faster and less expensive ways, or whether wallets will be available to do all of the things described by 2035; instead, the real driver of how fast or fully our country moves to adopt these tools is whether the learners and workers who need them most will take advantage of and trust them. At the personal level, a high-functioning skills wallet can put the learner in the driver's seat for the first time, providing access to information about job demand and the translation power to decipher one's own potential in a rapidly changing world of work. Today, most of us are even confused by the names of the new job roles that pay well, let alone the skills we might build or parlay to thrive in those sectors. And AI, with all its privacy and quality red flags, can help solve for the most daunting of problems in career navigation: you don't know what (and whom) you don't know.

Perhaps the most important trend to convey here in this introductory and landscape chapter is that for learners and employers, patience has worn thin. The unprecedented skills shake-up of this decade has brought on a new calculus. If college is not easily accessible for students, or if the talent pipeline is not forming fast enough for employers, many are taking matters into their own hands. For both parties, the college degree is too expensive, too opaque, and too long. It is a risky proposition. But what are learners and employers doing instead? It's hard to say. The coming chapters try to answer that question.

2

The Rise and Fall of Bootcamps

I'm not here to steal your students. I am here to retrofit them after they graduate, so they are fit for the workplace.

—JAKE SCHWARTZ, FOUNDER OF BOOTCAMP GENERAL ASSEMBLY,
SPEAKING TO COLLEGE LEADERS

Hadoop, JavaScript, Ruby on Rails, MongoDB, data visualization, data cleaning, MATLAB, R, Python, SQL and NoSQL, AI and machine learning, Quantum, NLTK, spaCy, SEO, Scrum, Agile, UX/UI design . . .

This is the new language of "hard" skills. And don't feel bad if some of these are Greek to you. You are not alone. But these are the "starter skills" that can land you your first job if you are lucky enough to be in a technical field that knows how to make starter skills really clear to applicants. These days, LinkedIn advises that just having one of the keywords above on your résumé could send your application to the "ready to interview" pile.[1] But don't blink, because the hot keywords change quickly.

Historians and technologists tell us that this decade has brought and will bring the biggest, most sudden, and broadest shift in skills demand ever.[2] LinkedIn reports that specific skills on job postings changed by 25 percent between 2015 and 2022.[3] Think about that. And this was before it was estimated that 40 percent of all work hours could require new or different tasks and skills over the coming decade because of AI.[4] Employers have created and morphed new job roles in that short time, often adding new technical requirements or the ability to interface with increasingly complex systems. But it takes up to a decade for those needs to get translated into a pipeline of talent in the old-school cycle. And when the new pipeline of talent does finally come online, it isn't necessarily in the right geographic location.

LinkedIn has tried to hasten the feedback loop for learners and colleges in this remarkable period by providing a tool called the Economic Graph. GitHub, the organization that helps coders demonstrate their skills, is hosting the site.[5] If you look at any example, any industry, you'll see the top ten keywords representing the skills employers asked for in 2015, and next to it, how that list had changed by 2022.

Take manufacturing, one of the potentially highest-paid fields where degrees are arguably less important: seven out of ten of the top skills in 2022 were not among the top ten skills just seven years earlier. That's a rate of change of one top-ten skill per year. And given that this analysis happened before the introduction of ChatGPT and the proliferation of easy-to-use AI applications, skill watchers are expecting an even faster rate of change for the next decade. It is no exaggeration to call this period we are in the major skills shake-up of the modern age—some would argue, of any age.[6]

It is in this context that we turn to bootcamps, which are short, focused, often immersive skills-training programs. Whether you are an employer or a learner, bootcamps can fill the need for speed that has emerged from this gigantic skills shake-up. Today, however, bootcamps only represent a tiny fraction of the postsecondary learning market—so why focus on them?[7] Because the story of bootcamps showed us what was possible. They were bold. They were disruptive. They were the first major attempt to unbundle the degree, to offer learners a more direct training path to high-paid professional jobs, to offer new skills at the same pace that innovation requires them. Before bootcamps, when someone said, "Go back to school to get a good job," college and trade school were really the only options. And yet bootcamps haven't had the meteoric rise you might expect; in fact, they've now fallen out of fashion with investors. There is a lot to learn from their story.

THE RISE OF ALTERNATIVE CREDENTIALS

Bootcamps rose in popularity starting a decade ago alongside the "alternative credential" market. In fact, bootcamps were often a vehicle to earn a certificate or certification in a coding language or project management, for example. The word *alternative* has always had a negative connotation in the education field. At first, it meant less than a high school degree; in the past decade, we've carried the term over to higher ed and slapped it on all the exploding credential types and programs that are not part of a full-time degree track.

We now have more than one million credential types in the US alone.[8] Separately, a million college students enroll on campuses annually to earn certificates rather than degrees, and that number is up 15 percent since 2019.[9] But two-thirds of credential types are offered outside colleges, which may surprise people.[10] Off campus, we have bootcamps, apprenticeships, vocational training, and nonprofit programs like Year Up, City Year, and UnCollege. We have industry groups that issue certifications, and companies like Google that provide certificate programs for high-demand roles. Over the last decade, many millions more learners have flocked to alternatives outside the traditional college system in search of "job-ready" skills training that college either isn't offering or isn't marketing well enough.[11] And we don't yet have a lot of data to generalize and conclude that short-term credentials pay off, that they are worth the investment. We know that short-term credentials in certain fields like tech and construction—which tend to be male dominated—can yield higher earnings.[12] Interestingly, learners of color are more likely than their white counterparts to choose a short-term program, to take advantage of employer training offerings, and—according to at least one major survey—to rate these programs' quality and value higher than white students rate these programs.[13]

Colleges themselves have sharpened their offerings to include alternative credentials, as you'll hear in chapter 4. But they tend to fall under the heading of "noncredit" credentials and generally can't be paid for with student grants or loans. So if you are in college getting a noncredit credential, perhaps because you need a shorter path to a well-paying job in tech or health care, you might be treated like a second-class college citizen, like an outsider. No funding, little or no career advising, no academic counseling, because you are not at college to get a degree. You are alternative, you are "nontraditional." The colleges are starting to recognize these unintended consequences of a federal funding system set up to support traditional degree students. And finding ways to bring the "nons" into the fold.

It's sort of funny—in other fields, the word *alternative* has a largely positive connotation. The music industry provides a good example. In my view, Motown was the original alternative music scene. Black artists couldn't get contracts under mainstream labels, so in 1959 Berry Gordy provided an alternative brand with that R&B sound, blended vocals, and synchronized dance moves. It didn't take long for all of America to embrace the sound of Motown. Within ten years, Motown became part of the mainstream. And into this century, many of the bands that incubated in the hip underground of the alt scene eventually made the crossover, from the Talking Heads to Alanis Morissette, even My Chemical Romance. Plenty of others remained in the niche category, often by choice. I got to experience the music of the pioneers of the horror punk subgenre, the Misfits, to whose concerts I had the pleasure of escorting my own underage teen. I gathered these bands didn't want to sell out to mainstream acceptance. They wore "alternative" like a badge of honor that protected their antiestablishment reputations.

Here's the difference. Alternative music scenes are edgy and cool. An artist may only sell one hundred thousand records instead of a million in a subgenre music market like punk or heavy metal. But they don't have to win the approval of the mainstream to be successful. In the credential world, however, the person who earns an alternative credential is most often trying to gain acceptance by a mainstream employer. They are not trying to be edgy. Most employers, large or small, are establishment. They tend not to be risk takers in their hiring strategies. They might think it's cool or scrappy that someone learned how to code at a bootcamp, but there

THE RISE AND FALL OF BOOTCAMPS   37

are so many bootcamps of varying quality that it is often safer to hire some-one with a degree, unless the employer is desperate.[14] So while bootcamps and alt providers might want edgy marketing to stand out to alternative learners, they want to cross over to wide employer buy-in as soon as possible. In this chapter, you'll meet some of the alt entrepreneurs who wanted to be Motown and learn how the alternative label ultimately branded them. But what they learned—not to give away how the story ends—is that to be an alternative in the education market and still be successful, you need the traditional education establishment's warm embrace. You have to sell out.

GENERAL ASSEMBLY: FIRST MOVER

When I think of alternative education providers, I think of Jake Schwartz, the cofounder of General Assembly (GA). Full disclosure: GA is near and dear to me because my own daughter used one of its part-time virtual digital marketing bootcamps during the COVID-19 pandemic to break into the digital marketing field, without a college degree. But I will tell that story later. I met Jake almost a decade earlier, in 2012.

GA was a hip coworking space company, competing briefly with WeWork. The coworking business was really starting to boom in urban tech hubs around the country as the growing number of start-ups were hungry for a broader community and flexible office leases. That October, a bunch of us who were thinking about launching new models of higher education met in Midtown New York City at one of GA's slick offices, where jean-clad, organic-coffee-wired gig economy and start-up mavens gathered in clusters around whiteboards and computer screens. These were heady times for "uncollege" entrepreneurs. In the wake of the Great Recession, unbundling college was a big idea. It was also the moment that billionaire Peter Thiel (PayPal cofounder) told college students he would pay a few of them $100,000 if they would drop out and start businesses or nonprofits.

The next year, GA would pivot away from the coworking business, because it was earning far more money teaching classes in the office spaces it was trying to lease. Essentially, it had become a school for people to build the "skills of the future" that they didn't learn in college. It was a new idea.

Some well-known players were already in the field offering coding camps for kids, afterschool programs for teenagers, or tuition-free IT training for unemployed workers. But the notion that anyone could buy a short "stack" of training modules to build the skills of the future came alive at this moment. Why now?

The answer is always convergence. In this case, three trends in 2012 drove the rise of training programs outside of companies, outside of colleges, and outside of the job training centers for the unemployed. First, there was a flood of private investment capital suddenly fueling the bootcamp market. Second, massive open online courses (affectionately referred to as MOOCs) were popularized by Stanford University and gained international buzz. MOOCs demonstrated that any professor could unbundle a course from the college they taught at and offer it to the masses, a development that sent entrepreneurial minds tripping on the possibilities for democratizing higher education. Third, with the expansion of tech fields, there was excitement about how we could finally break into the black box that was the college degree and pull out some skills training that could get you hired now. These included several categories of IT, front-end web development, cybersecurity and software engineering, and the emergent fields of cloud computing and data analysis, as well as more creative skills like user and web design and digital or product marketing.

Jake offered a new package to the savvy skills climber—the training, mentors, and community that were not really available outside the rare investor-sponsored incubators for start-ups in New York and San Francisco. But as soon as he relaunched GA as a bootcamp—and these were heady days with lots of press hype—Jake realized he had a "moat" problem. Any competitor could get into the castle to offer alternative learning experiences and teach skills aimed at specific job roles. And because this was a time when employers were screaming for tech workers, "immediately," he recalled, "I had like 70 groups competing with me."[15]

Bootcamps cropped up all over the country, mostly in urban centers, as if everyone realized all at once that college wasn't getting the job done. To be fair, job descriptions for more technical roles were starting to look like they were in Greek. Colleges focused on their more theoretical role of preparing students, but how were graduates supposed to get from theory to practice?

This theme was being reinforced in my own house. My other child (not the GA bootcamp daughter) was a newly minted college graduate and back home living in their old room with a pit bull, having the career disconnect crisis that many of their friends were also having. They had a degree in the fast-changing field of neuroscience. One internship in a lab was enough to decide they didn't want to become a neuroscientist, which required a PhD. What broader jobs were they qualified for instead? None that they could find. They went to work in a bike shop, but not happily. Jake said he had had a similar experience going to Yale and then to Wharton Business School, two of the most elite schools in the country. He said he felt a low-grade rage toward Yale, which sent him off with the attitude that he had "arrived." But where, he wondered? He didn't feel employable.

After graduating from Wharton (which he felt should have been organized as a much shorter bootcamp, rather than the "stretched out, two year cash cow"), Jake knocked around in the start-up world. He felt like an outsider. He felt alternative. He built GA as a for-profit company, at a time when many for-profit universities were taking hits for pocketing their profits while students failed to get hired. His model at first was to fashion eight-week-to-six-month "immersives" in computer programming, data science, user experience and user interface design, and product design. These were intensive training programs, usually in person, that would take learners through a targeted skill-building, practice, and demonstration gauntlet. Those who made it through a six-month immersive would be "job ready" at a price tag of about $15,000. As Jake explained it, they might not be super comfortable with the skill yet, but they would speak the language and "be ready to occupy a seat, almost like an apprentice, an extra pair of hands," to begin adding value at a company and gaining the expertise they would need to progress. He felt the learner had visibility into what they were signing up for at GA. They could look at the syllabus up front and inspect the instructor's industry chops. And in the early years, GA reported what percentage of graduates were getting jobs.

I still laugh when I think about the time I invited Jake to speak to a group of university presidents and deans. These were innovators inside the traditional higher ed system who were designing with the Education Design Lab to test new ways to address the concerns of employers and families who were losing faith in the degree. Someone—it might have been me—threw the grenade into the conversation. "So, Jake, is General Assembly here to compete with colleges? Will you take market share away from them?" Mind you, the audience was in suits and Jake stood before them in jeans and sneakers, with a boyish haircut and impish smile. "No, no, you don't have to worry," he replied, with a wave to push away their troubles. "I'm not here to steal your students. I am here to retrofit them after they graduate, so they are fit for the workplace." Stunned silence. When I recalled this story for Jake recently, he laughed and confided that Larry Summers, then president of Harvard University, had coached him not to challenge higher ed directly. The issue was that in 2015, most college officials in the room had not thought about the "last-mile" problem of getting students from the degree to the job offer.

In many ways, GA's trajectory is the story of the rise and struggles of all bootcamps as an independent category for alternative credentials. Jake says he didn't need Summers to tell him not to compete directly with colleges, because he couldn't compete with them anyway to bring college-age students in the door. While GA was getting major buzz in the tech and start-up world, he felt the "market distortion" of having to compete with colleges when they could offer a fully financed product and he could not offer his learners a Pell Grant or a student loan backed by the government. He felt that, even though colleges were not publishing job placement rates, students were blindly showing up there expecting the kind of skills training that would land them their first job. "I felt like I was fighting City Hall," Jake said. "Those brands are so powerful. Not just elite colleges, even big state schools. I felt [tiny] next to, for example, the University of Florida."

COMPETING AND PARTNERING WITH COLLEGES

That realization forced bootcamps to sharpen their marketing. Clearly, the way to differentiate from the four-year degree or master's programs was to focus on speed and results, what bootcamps call "placement rates." "We'll get you hired in 3, 6, or 9 months." GA reported its placement rates at that time through 2021. They varied between 75 percent and 95 percent depending on the programs and the hiring environment that year.[16]

There are three types of learners who might look for bootcamp-style skills training: first-time skillers who are not going to college, upskillers who are in a job and hoping for a promotion or better job in the same field, and reskillers who need or want to change roles or professions entirely. The group that has $10,000–$20,000 to spend on skills training is usually that middle category, upskillers who currently have at least a middle-wage income. (Today, the average full-time cost across all tech bootcamps is roughly $13,000.)[17]

As they grew, bootcamp providers found that about 75 percent of their market remained people who were already in the workforce, not only because of the brand power of local colleges to maintain their hold on the younger student who might be vague on career plans but also because of the price point.[18] Most camps realized this and developed online and part-time, shorter offerings at lower price points—averaging from $3,500 to $5,000—but the placement outcomes were not as strong. Some groups offered scholarships or private loan programs; others used a new model called income sharing agreements where you paid after you finished, but those terms scared away many students.

The way to expand to a younger market was to partner with colleges. Jake didn't want to do that. He didn't want to take federal money and become subject to regulations, losing control of his brand. As the first national bootcamp of this era, GA had "first mover" status, and Jake hoped he could keep his model clean with private capital.

But newer bootcamps didn't have this sort of brand recognition. They saw partnering with colleges as a brilliant strategy. And it was the proverbial win-win. Colleges felt bootcamps could solve a few problems for them. They could provide additional revenue in a decade when traditional enrollment was dropping. They could mitigate the nagging reputation problem, the return-on-investment complaints that colleges weren't teaching skills that were immediately hireworthy. There was a third problem for colleges, which I came to understand while serving on the board of a public university. Colleges couldn't, in most cases, ask their own professors to run bootcamps, largely because tenured faculty—who had been through the seven-to-ten-year higher ed gauntlet to get their PhDs—weren't likely to have recent experience with the latest technologies and business practices.

So these college-bootcamp partnerships quietly proliferated. But most remained outside core academic programs. They were offered as a way to bring new learners in under the college roof, but the bootcamps mostly offered the same programming and price points they would typically offer on their own, outside the college context (in the "alternative" learning world). If you scroll through a consumer site like Course Report, which aggregates information on all bootcamps, it appears most colleges partnering with bootcamps are charging the same prices as independent bootcamps, often without offering college credit or government student aid.[19]

BIG BRANDS BRING CREDIBILITY

One way today's bootcamps are adding marketing pizzazz is by bringing well-known consumer brands into the mix to give them street cred with learners. One of my favorite examples is Sneaker Essentials. This cohort-based, virtual bootcamp is a three-way partnership between Fashion Institute of Technology, Complex Media brand, and the intermediary bootcamp provider Yellowbrick.[20] Rob Kingyens left Cornell University to run Yellowbrick because he saw it as a way to empower learners who wanted to break into the entertainment business he had wanted to enter. Until the past decade, to get trained by the best-known university educators in entertainment (e.g., New York University, Parsons, the Fashion Institute of Technology, or the University of Southern California), you had to pay $200,000 for a full private college degree. "Why should tech get all the boot camps?" Rob asked. A fair question.[21]

Rob doesn't oversell the sneaker bootcamp. He positions it as providing access, like a gym membership. For $1,000, students get access to one year of asynchronous classes, meetups, and projects. He says many sneakerheads have used it to fuel their passion for urban street design and culture, and to pick up skills. It has the feel of an artists' collaborative. Not everyone is going to get hired by Nike—but, for a self-starter, it can be a springboard.

Jon Cotton certainly believes that it helped his own career. Jon is a Bronx native who went upstate for community college, he says, to try to "stay out of trouble."[22] But he didn't finish; he "stopped out," which is the nonpejorative term colleges have developed for dropouts, in hope that they will come back. Jon went home to the city and started working at Foot Locker to try to learn the business. He clearly had DIY entrepreneurial skills: he built a rap name for himself locally and also started designing streetwear. He'd always loved sneakers. He had loved getting looks of approval when friends checked out his footwear ever since kindergarten.

But the distance from working in a sneaker store to designing the shoes they stock seemed big and vague. Jon signed up for the Sneaker Essential certificate program in 2019. The price point was very doable. And the schedule allowed him time for his other projects. He learned, for example, how to cultivate and retain fashion industry relationships for networking, how to design a compelling logo, and how to design a plan for a dream store. He told me over Zoom that his real breakthrough came in his final project. He designed a sneaker for the Nike Bespoke program that got picked up by blogs as if it had been released by Nike. And that has led to a collaboration with sneaker brand Saucony. Jon's becoming known for a vibrant "colorway," as they say in the business. Loud, bold colors and prints. "Everyone can't wear it and pull it off, but if you start putting yourself in a box, then people put you in a box too," Jon told an interviewer covering his launch.[23]

Yellowbrick forges collaborations with colleges and entertainment brands. It bought one training program it considered to be the brand leader in training animators for movies, Animation Mentor. Rob showed me a list of six recent feature films that he said employed a total of 150 graduates of Animation Mentor, films like *Frozen 2* and *Spiderman: Into the Spider-Verse.*[24] The website pitch doesn't mince words about college versus bootcamps: "Why spend 4 years and $120,000 on a university degree, when you can get a demo reel and professional animation skills in 18 months for

$15,000?"[25] Of course, the site has slick animation that make the point sharper, and it features alumni showing their work and talking about their jobs. The site also sports the logos of the biggest names in animated movies, from Disney to Pixar to DreamWorks.

Few people will make it as an animator or a sneaker designer. We often want our children to have a "backup." Sneaker Essentials is new and has served eight thousand sneakerheads in its "career discovery"–type program since 2019. Animation Mentor boasts fifteen thousand grads in the last decade. Rob says that while Yellowbrick doesn't use the term *bootcamp* in marketing its programs, it still employs the central practice of the model, which is to rely on instructors who actively work in the field. However, having the Fashion Institute of Technology brand and select pieces taught by professors creates a hybrid approach that gives students some level of old-school trust and new-school industry street cred. It's an interesting model that I encourage colleges to consider.

My overriding question about bootcamps, though, is, Why do most students only find these programs after college?

Like other bootcamps, the graduates and students at Animation Mentor and Sneaker Essentials have almost all come to the programs after college failed to help them launch.[26] They often don't know that their degrees may not set them up for success. Or maybe their degrees open certain doors, but the key that will open the final door is undisclosed until students finish the quest, like a "level-up" gem hidden in an animated video game. But without that knowledge, many students will continue to choose college first. After all, according to College Board research, only 20 percent of students have heard "a lot" about options after high school besides a four-year degree.[27]

COLLEGES BECOME WARY

The year 2021 appeared to be the high-water mark for collegiate partnerships when, according to investor research firm HolonIQ, two hundred colleges around the world partnered with bootcamp providers.[28] In 2023, the journalism outlet the Hechinger Report did a report on university-based bootcamps and found they were being delivered "with few, if any, quality controls or assurances in place to protect students. . . . The boot camp companies recruit students, develop curricula, and teach classes," while the college brings the brand to the table to provide legitimacy.[29]

It's funny: I work with colleges, and they don't really talk about the bootcamps they are partnering with. I asked Amy Heitzman, deputy CEO at UPCEA, the membership organization for the parts of universities that provide nondegree options, Where did bootcamps go?

"They [faculty] wouldn't call what they are doing a bootcamp because it is not a very academic phrase," Amy explained. "You're not going to hear that phrase in the Faculty Senate. What you might hear is 'industry-based credential' or 'doubling down' or 'stringing together three courses in a major and having those three courses equal a certificate.' Those are the kinds of things that most are innovating with. Not very many are innovating with bootcamps at this stage, in part because the outcomes have not been proven."[30]

Along with a lack of academic grounding, some colleges are wary of the lack of regulation around bootcamps. One president whose college got burned when their bootcamp partner folded told the Hechinger Report, "There is not yet a regulatory framework that provides boundaries for how colleges should do this."[31] Colleges have also struggled to recruit working adults for bootcamps, given their lack of well-developed consumer marketing capabilities. Perhaps the best bootcamp market that colleges could capture is their own alumni, but surprisingly, even though colleges know how to find their alumni (for fundraising), the idea of selling bootcamps for lifelong learning has never really caught on among colleges.

So far we've met bootcamp providers who are running for-profit businesses. Most of this market is for-profit, and increasingly, online.[32] These companies were fueled by investors' interest in "edtech" and "talent tech" throughout the last decade. Investors are still bullish on the market because they believe that the model that took hold in the US has driven higher demand around the globe, in countries where college is often inaccessible. As HolonIQ described in 2022, "Tech bootcamps re-skilled and up-skilled over 100,000 professionals globally in 2021, up from less than 20,000 in 2015. We expect this number to reach over 380,000 by 2025 representing over $3B of expenditure with significant upside as tech up-skilling models and modes overlap and converge."[33] But it's important to keep these global numbers in perspective—they pale in comparison to the traditional college market in the US. The number of students enrolling in college may have dropped by three million a year now compared with 2010.[34] Bootcamps are clearly not capturing very much of that displaced market, at the undergraduate level at least, but perhaps over the last decade they have caused budget shoppers to second-guess the value proposition of a fully loaded, full-price college degree?

You've met a few of the tech entrepreneurs trying to fill the skills gap left between today's fast-changing knowledge economy and the almost four-hundred-year-old college system my colonial ancestors experienced. But their investors have pushed them to think about scale. What's preventing them from serving a million learners a year? One of the key takeaways you may have noticed by now is that all these bootcamp players have struggled to scale because their customer base is limited to only part of the market: those who can pay out of pocket. The hiring platform Indeed recently conducted a national survey asking consumers how they are upskilling. Seven percent said they have used bootcamps. Of those who didn't, two-thirds said it was for financial reasons.[35] Dhawal Shah is a blogger and founder of the popular alternative credential review site Class Central.[36] He says that for bootcamps, 30–40 percent of the revenue from each customer goes toward marketing costs to get them in the door. And that doesn't improve much with scale. So, the argument goes, they have to charge what they charge, $10,000–$20,000 for a full-time camp. What if learners could tap into federal financial aid, as they do for even higher-cost college tuition, to fund bootcamps? How might the landscape change?

NONPROFIT BOOTCAMPS JOIN THE FRAY

As the bootcamp market grew in the last decade, there were many social (nonprofit) entrepreneurs watching the space. The excitement about how a targeted, job-role-focused model could help the populations who needed quicker and cheaper solutions than college could be felt in conference rooms around the country. But what to do about the price tag? And the need to provide wraparound services?

It never stops surprising me how many people I meet working on the skills gap problem who, like me, came from "the other side." The other side in this case is K–12 education reform. Many of us who were working in K–12 in the early 2000s had bought into the "college for all" movement. It seemed that the best way to break the cycle of poverty and mitigate "zip code destiny" was to make urban and rural schools better and ensure that everyone was brought up believing that college was possible.

Nitzan Pelman was one of the believers. She came up through that most fervent of teacher corps, Teach for America, to become executive director of a charter school in New York City. She believed that the most good she could do in the world was to offer a group of students the learning opportunities that she hadn't had herself in order to launch them into the college experience that had been her transport ticket.

After sixteen years working to prepare students for college readiness, Nitzan went to the other side. It was her first foray into the college side of students' lives. Her efforts in K–12 to position eighteen-year-olds for a success trajectory just weren't bearing enough fruit. You could get many of your students into college, but then you said goodbye, and the stories that came back to teachers and mentors like Nitzan were heartbreaking—former students failing out of their college classes, no emotional support, life or jobs got in the way, student debt and no degree. In Black communities, for example, only 40 percent of college attendees were finishing a degree.[37]

So Nitzan decided to switch horses, to work on the college problem rather than the college access problem. I still remember when she came to my office in 2014 with the idea for Re-Up, to find learners who had not finished college and make it easy for them to reenroll. It was a much-needed service. I encouraged her. She recalled recently, "It was only when I got to Re-Up did I realize, 'Oh my God, I've had a lot of blind faith that these organizations [colleges] are going to do their job for these people.' And they're not."[38] The colleges were sympathetic, but often students couldn't transfer their credits or had to spend money and lose time fighting the bureaucracy. And many gave up again.

After three years of trying to help people return to college to finish, she changed her mind about her life's work. She told me, "If I want to help people break the cycle of poverty, I should just help them get jobs." So she joined the alternative movement and founded Climb Hire, a nonprofit bootcamp provider.

Nitzan approached the bootcamp space differently. She wanted learners to have skin in the game, but as a nonprofit, she wanted to offer a "no money up front" program aimed at folks who were on the wrong side of the college divide and couldn't afford traditional bootcamps. She would lead with the wrap-around services, specifically the networking and hiring part of the "last-mile" training. She set up her first cohort in 2019 with a very focused offering to help people become Salesforce administrators. It was a doable skills lift in five months, and when she started just before COVID-19, the market was hungry for Salesforce administrators. She would recoup her costs on the back end, but only from those who ultimately landed better jobs. The rest of the budget would be covered by philanthropy.

Yrel is one of Climb Hire's success stories. He already had a degree in computer science but hadn't managed to launch professionally, he says, because he didn't have any experience and hadn't had time or contacts to land internships during college. Living in San Francisco, the first in his family to scale the ivory tower in the US, Yrel spent six years after college working retail at Burlington Coat Factory. He barely got raises past minimum wage for that entire period. In 2019, he saw a LinkedIn post about Climb Hire offering a program to train Salesforce administrators. "You only had to pay back the $7,200 if you got hired at a job making $45,000 or more," Yrel told me. "I was making $22,000. I thought it was sketchy."[39] But he decided he had nothing to lose, since the program only met in the evenings, six hours a week. He didn't have to quit his job.

Yrel and Nitzan learned that the most important thing is not instruction in the technicalities of Salesforce administration, which Nitzan learned to curate from various sources and Yrel could have found online. The special sauce for a nonprofit bootcamp is helping unnetworked people build their network, credibility, and confidence as job applicants. As the college leaders who met with Jake learned, it's all about the last mile (although likely with different emphases for a different demographic).

Nitzan found that the moment of racial reckoning after George Floyd's murder drove a lot of philanthropic and employer interest in her model. There was much discussion about structural hiring barriers that contributed to racism. People saw the appeal of bootcamps as professional shortcuts to college, but the private sector wasn't in the business of making them fully affordable. And an important barrier to get past was the professional career networking and hiring cabal that was mostly accessible to children of professionals and new entrants who managed to score a spot in an elite university. Could social networking be taught? Could networks be infiltrated?

Nitzan expanded Climb Hire into other job disciplines, such as customer service, cybersecurity, and digital marketing. She kept the demographic specifically focused on the folks she knew she could help. To become a Climber, you have to be between twenty-four and forty and make less than $30,000 per year. The job preparation had to be doable in five months, part time, and have the potential to launch Climbers into a career with at least a $20,000 salary lift. During the pandemic, Climb Hire was placing 80 percent of all graduates, but now, with a slowing job market for Salesforce administrators and tech in general, placement rates have slipped to 65 percent. So Nitzan has pivoted to include other learning tracks. Bootcamps have to be nimble. As I mentioned earlier, to be valued as a middleman between consumers and employers, bootcamps have to design new programs at the speed of change in a way that most colleges can't.

Porchea was another college "stop-out" student, like Jon Cotton, the sneaker designer. Porchea did come back to college, again and again. She should get a medal for her efforts to make the traditional education system work for her. But it didn't. Porchea attempted college four times in her hometown of Sacramento, California. She was in the foster care system up until she applied to college, and suddenly she was on her own. She took a bunch of courses, she tried cosmetology, she got twelve credits toward a human resources degree, and then six credits in welding, but "life got in the way." She says she became a "justice-involved" student and then a mom. "It really became hard when I was breast-feeding with my second kid," she told me on a Zoom call from her car, with her impressively sunny manner. "I realized I needed this piece of paper [the degree] but I didn't think I would ever get it. It was really hard."[40]

Porchea found Climb Hire through another nonprofit that recommended the program. "I thought it was a scam, they seemed so helpful," she recalled. Porchea chose the customer experience track and spent time with her mentor, organizing her LinkedIn profile so that she could have the right keywords on her résumé and give the most relevant responses in her interviews. She was offered side training in resilience and emotional intelligence to build the durable skills I mentioned in chapter 1. Climb Hire helped her translate those to résumé-worthy skills. "And it worked. I got 3 or 4 unsolicited job inquiries from employers. I was scared," she laughed. "I just took the first one that made a firm offer." It was a patient support associate job with a health-care start-up. She could work from home, which helped her manage the movements of her now three children.

After interviewing a few of Nitzan's graduates, again it struck me. Bootcampers either have a degree or have knocked around trying to get one. In all my research for this chapter, it's been hard to find students to profile who went to these programs instead of college, straight from high school or even within two to three years of high school. The comment Jake Schwartz made ten years ago has held true for the most part all this time: Bootcamps are not "instead of college." They "retrofit" you. Which makes sense with the skills landscape changing so quickly, and since an estimated 54 percent of grads over twenty-five don't work in their field of college study and need retrofitting.[41] The average bootcamp participant is between twenty-seven and forty-two,[42] a range that captures the market of folks who never attended college as well as the forty million Americans who tried college and found that it didn't work out.[43] But why can't bootcamps also be a toe in the water toward career training or college for folks fresh out of high school, rather than mainly serving the wizened twenty- or thirtysomething who has spent years looking to open the right door?

Ajuah Helton was charged with this question at the KIPP Foundation, one of the country's largest charter school networks, serving 120,000 K-12 students nationally. Her job was to lead KIPP Forward, the strategy for what happens to KIPPsters after high school. We'll hear about the changing "college for all" landscape and how high school college counselors are grappling with this shift in later chapters. But Ajuah's insights about bootcamps are useful here. "Boot camps haven't figured out 18 to 24 year olds," she says. For this reason, she didn't feel comfortable setting up partnerships with any of the growing number of local and national players directly. "It's the wrap around services they [the eighteen-to-twenty-four-year-old students] need, like counseling for how to put your resume together or how to ace a job interview, how to show up as a job-ready adult," Ajuah explained.[44] Her view, after researching, was that most of the tech bootcamps can do well by that B-average high school student from a low- or middle-income family who didn't get the college scholarships and so can't afford to go, but who also has no problem showing up and getting work done. The other issue is that bootcamps are job or field specific, so students have to know what they want to do—a tall order for many eighteen-year-olds.

WHAT CAN WE LEARN FROM BOOTCAMPS?

I started this chapter with Jake's story about founding the US's first national private bootcamp. What happened to him and General Assembly? Did he become Motown? After a few years of fighting off competitors, no. GA didn't go mainstream. As they say in the start-up world, the company pivoted. GA couldn't scale to compete with the trusted brand names and financial aid offered by colleges as a direct-to-consumer business, even though colleges haven't been able to scale these programs either. GA also couldn't compete with the DIY movement; much of the skills training of Jake's bootcamps was soon being offered by online marketplaces like Coursera for a small fee or, better yet, on YouTube for free. So, many independent bootcamps like GA have shifted their focus to the other customer in this equation: employers. And the US bootcamp market is plugging along, growing slightly by some accounts, but key investors have become wary.[45] As Matt Greenfield, founder of venture capital firm ReThink Education, told me, "We believe employers should be paying for upskilling."[46] Bootcamps became "solution providers" for employers, with a customized set of services to solve their huge unfilled job gaps. That's how Jake eventually sold his company for a sweet amount of money to the world's largest staffing company, Adecco. Today, GA still touts itself as the largest tech bootcamp but, as an Adecco brand, now the focus is on helping companies solve hiring and employee retention problems. They have even introduced apprenticeships, which we'll learn about in the next chapter. And Jake has moved on to a new start-up, to solve an easier societal problem: health care.[47]

I hope to end each chapter from here on out by teeing up what we in the human-centered design world call "design criteria." If we believe we need new national higher education models and financing mechanisms, and if we believe the bootcamp model presented in this chapter is not positioned for success or scale, what must be true to change those beliefs? Or how might the best attributes of bootcamps, from the learner and employer perspective, be carried over into new models of higher education? Models that are accessible to and understood by the 60 percent of US adults who don't have a bachelor's degree?[48]

Design Criteria from Bootcamps

What we learned from bootcamps is that the commercial version works better for the upskiller who is already in the workforce. For bootcamps to be effective for younger or less affluent learners, more support needs to be in place. These observations underpin the design criteria for how to take the best of bootcamps and build it into future designs for our education system.

Design Criteria from Bootcamps

1. Learners should be able to unbundle learning, to acquire focused skills taught by industry experts without having to enroll in a degree program.
2. Wrap-around services (coaching, durable skills training) are essential add-ons to technical skill training.
3. Education providers must design instruction and skill-building offerings at the pace of workplace innovation.

Students really respond to two features of bootcamps: first, they allow learners to pick and choose short-term, "hot" skills training piecemeal, without having to enroll in a degree program; and second, some of them provide "last-mile" wrap-around services (coaching, durable skills training, résumé prep) that most colleges don't offer at the industry-specific level. What employers like about bootcamps is that they move quickly enough to create training programs closer to the pace of industry innovation and talent needs.

What keeps more people from signing up? In a nutshell, accountability, price, and awareness. From a societal perspective, I believe the most important lesson that bootcamps have taught us is that career preparation curricula have to move at the speed of innovation or only be a few years behind rather than a decade slower. Bootcamps taught colleges that they were not solving the last-mile problem or providing key starter skills that could help learners get a foot in the career employment door. That requires hiring some professors who have come directly from the field recently, not a decade ago. It requires the approval times for new curricula to move more quickly than the academic year. It requires marketing capabilities that compete in a modern world to reach learners and earners in their moments of skill discomfort. As we'll see in chapter 4, it requires colleges to build out their employer engagement teams.

BE A DOUBLE THREAT

The skills gap could account for $11.5 trillion globally in lost revenue by 2028, according to the World Economic Forum.[49] Statistics like this call on us to train people faster or use more targeted approaches. But the call to action is muddy. The skills gaps, we hear, are in technical fields and medical care, the trades. Yet the World Economic Forum has another study that shows the top ten in-demand skills deemed to be "on the rise" globally, and only one "hard" or technical skill made the 2023 list: "AI and big data."[50] Technical literacy makes the list, which means workers need to understand the technologies at a basic level and how to employ them to get work done. But the rest of the skills are durable skills, with "creative thinking" taking the top spot.

To address the muddiness of the fast-changing landscape, I coach students to use higher education to become a "double threat." (I borrow that term from my days in musical theater, where the height of employability is to be a "triple threat." You send a video verifying your skill level to qualify for auditions of your singing, acting, and dancing skills. If you can demonstrate all three, you are a shoo-in at least to be in the chorus of a professional show.) To be a double threat outside the theater world is sufficient. I tell students to build some verifiable "starter hard skills," maybe with industry certifications, but also to find ways to demonstrate "starter durable skills" in creative thinking, analytical thinking, collaboration, communication, curiosity, resilience, or motivation. This demonstrates to an employer that the applicant can be useful from the get-go and also has the beginnings of a "range of motion," the ability to adapt as skills change.

Bootcamps and colleges need to teach durable skills the same way a coding camp approaches computer language or data security certification. But it's hard to isolate and teach the subcompetencies of creative problem solving (something I am attempting in my teaching at George Mason University). Perhaps bootcamps have missed their moment, in part, because they failed to recognize or honor the interdependency of skills. Matt Sigelman of the Burning Glass Institute, one of the country's leading observers of the skills-first hiring movement, puts it another way: "Here's the thing to bear in mind. Skills are like pack animals, they travel together. And you have to look for co-occurrence. It's not enough to say, 'Okay, well, there's a lot of jobs that need machine learning. I'm gonna go take this Coursera course on machine learning, and I'm going to be a hot tamale in the job market.' The reality is that when you look at those jobs that ask for machine learning, they ask for other things, too."[51]

Today's bootcamp market may be anemic, but these providers helped bring many short-term credentials to prominence. Very few microcredentials have broken through the noise to be generally recognized by the public and employers, but they light the way for designing the future. In my interviews across the industry, I asked each learner, bootcamp provider, and employer, Which ones (that entry-level talent can aspire to) are instant calling cards to get hired? Sadly, not very many come up outside of traditional trades, and maybe only two—project management professional and Scrum (another project management method)—suggest a combination of technical and durable skills. It's worth being aware of the ones that, as of this book's publication, have become known broadly in hiring and bootcamp circles, bearing in mind that even these ebb and flow in hiring demand:

TECH
- certified information systems security professional (CISSP)
- certified cloud security professional (CCSP)
- certified data professional (CDP)
- Cisco certified network professional (CCNP)
- certified ethical hacker (CEH)
- AWS certified solutions architect
- Microsoft Azure associate

PROJECT MANAGEMENT
- project management professional (PMP)
- certified Scrum master (CSM)

HEALTH CARE
- certified medical assistant
- limited medical radiologic assistant
- licensed practical or vocational nurse
- emergency medical technician

Bootcamps aren't going away. They will still be around to offer these programs in many flavors—nonprofit, for-profit, full-time cohort, night classes online. But some of the action for delivering these early micro-credentials has moved to community colleges and do-it-yourself programs online. My hope is that third parties, focused on skills and with close ties to employers, will still be engaged to deliver and design these skill-building opportunities. My take is that the funding model was and is the biggest reason bootcamps have not disrupted the higher education market in the way that, say, Uber and Lyft have disrupted the taxi market. In the process of this decade-long experiment, we learned so much through bootcamps about how to shift to a skills-based approach to career preparation. We're able to see the gaps, the challenges, and the victories in the form of Yrel, Jon and Porchea. Every college should feel compelled to take on some aspect of the bootcamp model.

In this chapter, I have specifically stayed away from describing alternative credentials as trade school. They have become so much more, but the word isn't out. When I tell people I am writing a book titled *Who Needs College Anymore?*, most say, "Oh, I know someone who went to trade school. He's making good money." Trade school is the noncollege route that comes to mind because it's been a tried-and-true alternative since the dawn of our republic. We don't need to work so hard to burn those pathways—electrician, carpenter, HVAC repair, commercial truck driver, and so on—into a new narrative because they are already there (although the fields worry about their aging workforces). Learners and their anxious families, as well as colleges, need to understand that there is much more to this story, that the lines between white-collar and formerly blue-collar jobs are blurring. The hard skills of today—cloud technology, mechatronics, computer networking, clean energy, radiation technology, and cybersecurity, to name a few—when coupled with durable skills, can be leveraged toward high-trajectory careers without a college degree. Or if they can't easily today, the walls are coming down, as we'll see in the next chapter.

Part II

The Silos

3

Employers

Do They Need Colleges?

*In a five-year period of time, I've seen all businesses step back
and say, "I'm not sure I want all these college graduates.
I don't want all their baggage coming with them."*

—LOVEY HAMMEL, STAFFING COMPANY CEO

This chapter raises the question, What is the purpose of college? In the days of my ancestor John Wise (the colonial Harvard grad), he needed to learn directly and in person from his professors to be trained as a minister. There was no other way. The first printing press in America had recently been set up at Harvard, but book access and ownership were dreams of the future for Wise. The library was nascent, and there were no professional associations or certification programs or YouTube channels. Most colonial professionals either apprenticed or winged it. Only a tiny few took the college step. Remember, in 1673, there was one college in the colonies, and Wise's class had four students.

Are we now headed full circle, this time with targeted tools at our disposal and millions of businesses to offer training ground for the majority of learners who are locked out of college or undertrained for jobs of the future? Will we get to the point where the rich will send their kids to traditional college—kind of like what used to be known as "finishing school"—and everyone else will go straight to a stepladder work path, maybe picking up degree equivalency along the way?

I've been thinking about whether many colleges will get left behind since 2017, when I ran a design session for the Lumina Foundation called "Good Future, Bad Future." We were trying to understand the potential of this new concept of skills-based hiring, and I was cochairing a working group for Connecting Credentials.[1] Most of the participants were from higher education, and we asked them to sketch out best-case and worst-case scenarios looking forward ten years. The worst-case scenario that gripped the group was that employers might eventually give up on looking to colleges for talent because colleges weren't delivering job-ready workers, or at least not fast enough. They might cut out the middleman in their quest to hire people who met specific skill needs. In that scenario, who would take on the job of more broadly forming minds and future citizens of the world? Presumably no one. This alarmed all of us.

That session was almost a decade ago, but then and now employers would say they have no grand plan to cut out colleges. However, as they watch the shrinking number of people coming out of colleges, as they observe the nonspecific preparation for many degrees, as they get caught up in the conflicting narratives of college's value versus necessity, many employers believe they have to take action to secure their talent pipelines.[2] Particularly those, as we'll hear in this chapter, who are in sectors that are highly technical, less sexy, new, or desperate.

These sectors need workers, and colleges are not delivering enough "loyalist" employees, or folks who come to stay. The addition of a "grow your own" training strategy is motivated by a combination of factors that are making it harder for certain industries: aging demographics, social media's promotion of quick ways to get rich, insufficient interest in tech and engineering among large swaths of the population, and the growing inclination, particularly of men, to build their learning path by teaching themselves.[3] As one tech employer said to me, "How do we recruit the young men living in their parents' basement learning on YouTube?"[4] The "grow your own" strategy is about at least identifying, if not capturing, young workers who can be tested, perhaps while still in high school, in hope that they form an early, if not lasting, attachment.

This chapter will look at the different ways that employers are mining professional talent beyond the college campus. It will examine early adopters of the direct-to-employment approach after high school, both students and employers. It will look at "lock-in" methods, which include apprenticeships that recruit high school learners. It will profile students who use alternative currency to the college degree, such as industry certifications, to break into professional roles in tech. And it will explain what I saw as a universal trend among the twenty-five employers, large and small, whom I interviewed: hiring managers are looking for candidates with experience, and they want to help students cross the "experience chasm."

A decade ago, when the tech skills gap first gained attention, a phrase took hold in the workforce community: "Talent is the new oil."[5] It means that a job-ready candidate was becoming a scarce and precious commodity. Just as geophysicists have moved from the divining rod to sophisticated seismic surveys to find oil, employers have moved from the passive college fair to keyword skill algorithms and now to whole-résumé digestion via AI and what we might call "fishing upstream." The only barrier to bypassing colleges in order to fill their skill gaps is the chaos of the talent marketplace. Employers need someone or some way to organize training and to find partners, but it doesn't have to be a college. As a hiring manager friend at Goldman Sachs told me ten years ago, the degree and the résumé have always been "blunt instrument[s], but we don't have anything else." He complained that he often regretted making hires based on the blue-chip colleges the graduates attended or their 4.0+ GPAs. "I needed relationship managers." He found very little correlation between those traditional hiring metrics and success on the job.

IS EXPERIENCE THE NEW DEGREE SILVER BULLET?

Lovey Hammel is a corporate talent expert in northern Virginia, a region that has more college-degreed adults than almost any in the country.[6] She has run an employment solutions company for four decades to fill talent gaps for big and small companies in many sectors, from financial services to IT, cybersecurity, and manufacturing. She's pro-college; in fact, I met her when we both served on the board of George Mason University, Virginia's largest public university. But Lovey describes the endeavor of sending everyone to college these days as "counterproductive." "In a five-year period of time," she says, "I've seen all businesses step back and say, 'I'm not sure I want all these college graduates. I don't want all their baggage coming with them. I'm just looking for workers that I can train into my industry. I need a certain amount of college graduates so don't get me wrong, but I need to be looking at this more holistically.'"[7] The baggage, according to Lovey, is that entry-level employees don't know what they want to do and, as a result, they have no loyalty. Recruits just out of college, she says, are naturally going to move around until they find the right fit, so more employers today are reluctant to spend money to train junior employees (particularly after the Great Resignation, when one hundred million workers quit their jobs between 2021 and 2022).[8] She said they would rather send successful employees back to school for training or to obtain a degree than require the initial degree to get into their field. She added that it's become a better long-term investment for both employee and employer.

For every employer I interviewed for this book, from the largest tech companies to smaller and medium-size businesses in cities or rural America, the most important résumé signal today for candidates to get hired is not where they went to college, or even whether they went to college, but their experience relevant to the role they'll be asked to perform. And experts anticipate that this will become even more of a trend if AI begins to eliminate more entry-level jobs.[9] Obviously, this creates a chicken-and-egg problem for someone new to the workforce. How do you get an entry-level job on your career track when many entry-level job descriptions ask for two to five years of experience?[10] What can stand in for experience?

Cutting Out the Middleman

Patrick is a young software engineer whose path helps us tell the story of one growing trend: industry certifications can be a shortcut to the professional workforce, without experience or a degree, at least in tighter hiring markets. Patrick was headed to community college in 2018, but he got happily intercepted as he graduated from high school. His high school was in northern Virginia, one of the country's top pressure-cooker environments for teenagers. As I just mentioned, the Washington, DC, metro area is ranked in the top three for education level of adults in the country.[11] That translates to a lot of degreed parents with high expectations for their children. And it translated to a lot of Patrick's friends taking SAT prep courses and stressing about college applications. "There was a ton of pressure coming down from the [school] administration on you," Patrick told me. "It's not even a question whether you are going to college . . . like, you're going to college."[12]

Patrick was up front and almost apologetic about why he bucked this trend: "I will make it very clear that I was not good academically. I did not get good grades. I didn't try in school, because I didn't care." But Patrick was lucky that his school was Chantilly High School—coincidentally, next door to my own high school, where decades earlier, I would argue, there wasn't such pressure to go to college. Back then, my high school housed the regional hub for "vocational-tech" classes in cosmetology, carpentry, and auto shop, into which many students disappeared, never to return to college prep classes. Now, Patrick's school is my county's vocational training hub, but the offerings have been modernized to include computer and engineering classes, for which you can receive college credit, earning this hub the impressive name Governor's STEM Academy. And according to Patrick, lots of students dabbled across college prep and the expanded vocational world.

Patrick's buddy told him about a class in computer networking. He said he was lucky to get a slot as it was very popular, and from there he took four classes that were specifically set up to prep students for technical certifications, as well as college credit, through Chantilly's dual enrollment program. (Dual enrollment means students take college courses while still in high school, and as we will hear later, it is the fastest-growing offering at community colleges nationwide.) Patrick earned the A+ and Network+ certifications, which are offered through the IT field's leading certifying body, the Computing Technology Industry Association. He also earned an entry-level networking certification issued by Cisco, a multinational digital communications technology conglomerate. Patrick didn't know it at the time, but these are among the top eight industry certifications requested by IT employers.[13]

While he did end up applying to one "reach" college (he didn't get in), Patrick assumed he would end up at the local community college. So he put his résumé on the job platform Indeed to try to get some summer work in the meantime. An Amazon Web Services (AWS) recruiter got in touch pretty quickly, attracted by the certifications. As Patrick tells the story, "They said, 'Hey, we've got datacenter operations positions that we think you'd be good for. If you're interested.' And I was like, hell yeah, I'm interested. I want to work for Amazon." What started as a contract job turned full time quickly, and Patrick was making $63,000 with benefits within five months, at eighteen years old. And several months after that, Patrick felt he had the experience to look around and land a more interesting job as an entry-level systems engineer.

He was lucky to find CACI Products, today a five-hundred-person subsidiary of the technology giant CACI. CACI Products builds drones, custom data centers, and data solutions for military and civilian clients. Patrick didn't know this, but over 30 percent of CACI Products professionals do not have college degrees. The culture is that way in part because 40 percent of employees come from the military, and many of those have specialized skills but no degree. Patrick had no military connection, but he benefited from a skills-first recruiting culture. CACI brings folks in to test their skills before a four-person hiring team, where Patrick apparently nailed it. He learned in the phone screening call that the job required a "beast of a software program" that helps manage the life cycle of virtual machines, a program called Foreman, which he did not know. "And so in between the phone screen and the interview," Patrick explained, "I went through and, like, stood up a little home lab at my house to sort of get that little bit of starter knowledge. . . . So I'm not coming in completely blind to this interview." Once he was on board, CACI Products told him, "As soon as you said you installed it at home, we were like, 'Oh, yeah, he's got the job,'" even though he'd never used the program before. He had enough experience to get to the interview, and then he hacked his way into the role.

Throughout his first two years of working with a significantly older crowd, teenage Patrick felt little pangs of FOMO (fear of missing out) when his buddies at college would come home and try to convince him to join them in their learning and partying experience. He tried community college at night that first year and got credits toward an associate's degree in cybersecurity.

But now, three years later, as he's making a six-figure salary with knowledge of many software programs under his belt, he muses, "I probably wouldn't even put the degree on my resume at this point, even if I did finish it. It's not as relevant as all my experience."

So Patrick had arrived. His is the story of someone who managed to get across what experts call the biggest hurdle for people who don't get a degree, or anyone, really: "the experience chasm." And he used industry certifications to do it.

Certifications: Entry Ticket or Stepping Stone?

So let's learn more about industry certifications. How do they work beyond Patrick's case?

There are two important caveats. One, they work best in a strong economy and region where employers can't access enough talent solely by relying on experienced candidates. Second, sadly, entry-level industry certifications only exist for certain parts of certain industries. Employers request industry certifications on job postings most frequently for IT, cybersecurity, and some medical fields. But there are also important certifications in fields such as project management, financial planning, human resources, food handling, and Adobe and Microsoft Office suites.[14] For the most part, these industry certifications are not courses—they are basically tests, often proctored by a third party, where you have to show your mastery of the process, product, or tool in an old-fashioned, time-based, stress-producing exam. If you fail, no certification. But you can buy a test guide on Amazon and try again. As one company's certification lead explained, "It verifies that you are a minimally qualified candidate, this is the line in the sand. And if you pass the certification, we are giving you a stamp for being able to do the job role."[15] Given all the noise in the market, certifications can be a powerful signal.

I spoke with the certification leads at AWS, Google, and Microsoft to understand what role certifications play in hiring. These three companies dominate the list of top tech certifications requested by employers every year, as companies move their operations to the cloud.

Liberty Munson is a Microsoft psychometrician who has been designing and evaluating the company's certifications for seventeen years. Like those at the other companies, she describes the purpose of certifications as driving adoption of the company's products across the IT industry.[16] But they also perform an important role for hiring and promotion at Microsoft and companies that use its cloud certifications. It found that new hires with IT certifications get up to speed in their roles on average a month faster than hires without certifications, and they see more promotions over their careers.[17] The most popular entry-level certifications are Azure administration associate and Azure developer associate.

Jennifer Riccuiti manages certification programs at AWS. Her own story influences her views on the importance of a college degree versus experience. She got a degree in computer science twenty years ago, but she felt back then that, because she was a woman and didn't have any experience, the degree only got her in the door with a role as the secretary for a group of engineers. She swallowed her pride and took the female-oriented support role to get the experience. Her gamble worked out. A year later she was off and running on her computer science career.[18]

She uses the story to emphasize the importance of experience, still critical in all fields, but now used as a targeted hiring tool for some roles. Twenty years ago, we didn't have many established certifications outside of unionized trade roles and some medical and heavily regulated fields. And this is an important distinction, because only now can certifications become stepping stones, or experience "hacks." But certifications are only relevant in the fields where they are widely recognized across an industry and widely publicized to learners via bootcamps, websites, or colleges. And certifications cost, on average, between a few hundred and a few thousand dollars, so access is an issue for most who are not working already, or whose school or employer is not funding the exam or exam prep.

Most industries have not been "certificationized." Only an estimated 6 percent of US adults hold an industry certification.[19] As I described earlier, about 30 percent of jobs require a license, meaning that a government body requires the passing of an exam as a prerequisite for employment. And then you've probably heard the term *certificate*, which is commonly used to describe a broader credential you might earn for passing some noncredit courses. Some are completion certificates that you can use to verify that you finished a skill-related experience, such as an internship or apprenticeship.[20] (We'll learn more about certificates in the next chapter, as colleges are using them to get into the short-term credential game.) It is difficult to get a handle on the relative popularity of certifications, licenses, and certificates. Companies like the ones I spoke to don't tend to share the numbers for competitive reasons.

It is also difficult to get a handle on how effective certifications versus other credentials can be. Most of the studies lump all short-term programs together. We do see that college graduates get a bigger earnings boost when they earn an extra credential.[21] And experts agree that industry-recognized certifications are more consistently high quality than other nondegree credentials. Since they are "based on legally-defensible, industry- or profession-wide job task analyses that are updated regularly, a credential seeker can be assured that the assessed competencies in the certification represent current skills of the occupation."[22] Interestingly, one recent study suggests that people who earn credentials outside of a degree have more confidence about their job prospects than college graduates.[23]

APPRENTICESHIPS

Credentials endorsed by employers are one approach, but wouldn't it be even better to be learning those endorsed skills in the actual workplace, since employers value experience most of all? As Ryan Craig's recent book,

Apprentice Nation, points out, if you were going to design higher education from scratch, apprenticeship would be at the center.[24] It provides an equitable stepladder from school to work, a blended launchpad for learning while earning. If it's true that seven out of ten people land their jobs through connections or internships, helping students make connections and gain experience while in school is a no-brainer.[25] And it can help solve the unfortunate elitist reality that only students who have the luxury of time to take low-paid and unpaid internships get career-related job experience while in school. Those who have to work at Chick-fil-A or Starbucks to help pay for school or support their family have to wait till they graduate, and then they have an experience gap problem and no connections. This is no small proportion of learners: almost 75 percent of students work part time and 40 percent work full time during college, and hardly ever in career-preparatory roles.[26] And research shows that getting a low-paying first job can depress your earnings for the rest of your career.[27]

There are currently over 640,000 civilian apprentices in the US registered with the Department of Labor—a number that grew in the last decade but has stagnated despite significant pushes from Republican and Democratic administrations recently.[28] In no way is the movement currently poised to service the four million students currently in college or, if students started earlier, as many apprenticeships do, the over seven million juniors and seniors in public high school.[29] Most registered apprenticeships are in the trades, with residential construction leading the way. In fact, there are many trade fields where apprenticeship is the only way in the door, according to the Department of Labor, including some surprising ones like piano tuner.[30] In many cases, the journey is as long as getting a college degree, three to five years, although your salary increases along the way. A traditional instruction component is required (144 hours per year, which can count toward a college degree), and many apprentices have to fund that part, even while they are paid for the on-the-job training.[31]

As we'll see, new employers are braving the complicated bureaucracy and getting on the bandwagon, well beyond the trades. While there are outliers, the new apprenticeship enthusiasts seem to fit into three industry categories, all of which are facing talent gaps or a fear of coming talent shortages: not-so-sexy industries, emerging sectors, and already desperate industries.

Not-So-Sexy Industries

How do you convince a shrinking pool of college grads in the age of TikTok to become insurance underwriters? This was the dilemma that got Pinnacol's CEO, Phil Kalin, interested in apprenticeships in 2015. The State of Colorado was forming CareerWise, the first nonprofit to bring the success of the youth apprenticeship model from Switzerland to the US. Pinnacol's 650 employees handle workers' compensation policies for fifty-three thousand Colorado businesses, but Phil was concerned about his aging workforce, one-third of which was set to retire in the coming decade.[32] He went on a field trip with other business leaders to learn about the Swiss program and came back a convert. Swiss educators and researchers have created a kind of policy tourism boom by attracting apprenticeship designers from around the world. Switzerland's Vocational and Professional Education and Training system is renowned for enrolling two-thirds of all Swiss teens, upon finishing their equivalent of high school, in apprenticeships well beyond the trades.[33] Some American high schools and Swiss-modeled local intermediaries, like CareerWise in Colorado, are trying to adapt this high school or post–high school apprenticeship option and also advocating for the "permeability" of the Swiss system, which allows students to change their minds and move more easily between a college track and a direct-to-employment path.[34]

Colorado has the same problem as every other US state—a very leaky, high-stakes education pipeline—but it does a better job than most states of openly tracking the alarming statistics to make it really clear where they lose young people. For every hundred Coloradans who start ninth grade, only forty-two will get to college. Thirty-two return after the first year of college, and only twenty-five of them will graduate from college within six years (figure 3.1).

Pinnacol thought, Why compete for the one in four college graduates when risk management and insurance is ranked around two hundredth in popularity of majors for college students?[35] The company saw opportunity

Figure 3.1 The leaky education pipeline

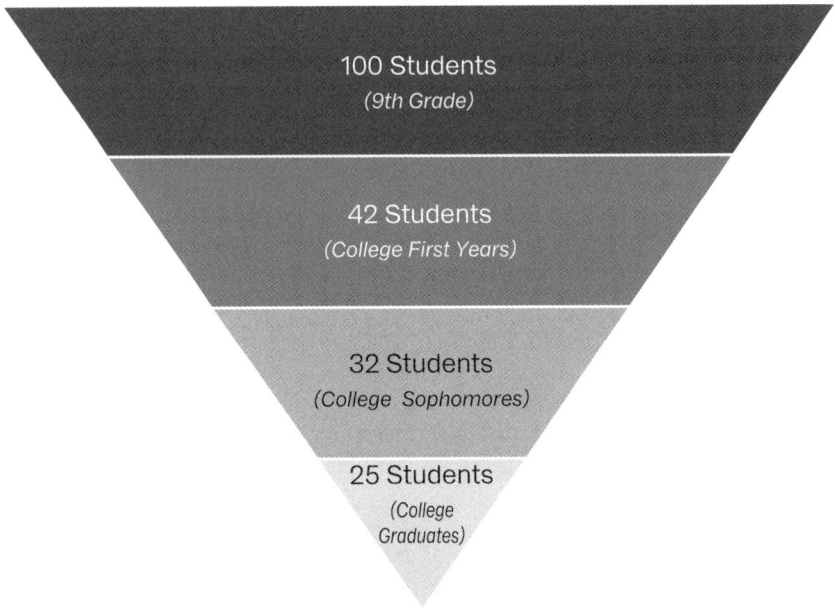

100 Students
(9th Grade)

42 Students
(College First Years)

32 Students
(College Sophomores)

25 Students
(College Graduates)

Source: Compiled by Pinnacol, using data from the Colorado Department of Higher Education, BestColleges, and College Factual.

in the seventy-five students out of every hundred who leak out of the education pipeline before college graduation, and it decided to target its apprenticeship program directly at high schools.

Today, Pinnacol has nine apprenticeship programs registered with the Department of Labor, four of which are in business operations, underwriting, claims, and human resources. On the tech side, there are choices in cybersecurity, user experience design, data science, and software development. Twenty-three apprentices have started, and nineteen have been all the way through the three-year program. Pinnacol's is what's known as a youth apprenticeship program. The students begin as juniors in high school. They start out working sixteen hours a week at $18.29 per hour, Colorado's minimum wage, and increase their salary and hours over time. The third year includes time and tuition support to take college classes. After high school graduation, some apprentices have opted to go straight to the work-force in other roles; some go on to college. But they leave having crossed the job experience chasm. Thirty percent of the apprentices finish that third year and get hired by Pinnacol. (Throughout the Denver area, 57 percent of apprentices who finish get job offers from their companies.)[36]

I interviewed one Pinnacol apprentice, Naarai, who made it all the way through and has already been promoted to a role as an underwriter at age twenty-one. She apprenticed as a business development representative, which meant she worked relationships on behalf of the company and wrote up contracts. Now, she manages two thousand workers' comp business accounts. "I knew that going to college, I wouldn't gain the experi-ence of actual work," Naarai said. And because she had not figured out career plans, she didn't know what to study in college. "Over time I went from wanting to be a judge to a ballerina to a doctor." Her third year of apprenticeship allowed time for college courses, and she took some at first, but like Patrick at AWS, Naarai kept getting promotions at work. At first, her own parents were split over her choice. She and her siblings were the first in their family to have the opportunity to go to college, and her mom was pushing college hard. In fact, Naarai laughs now as she recalls when she first brought her parents to see her workplace: "Mom thought it was sketchy that the company was hiring high school students."[37]

One sister chose college, but Naarai and her brother, who apprenticed at a Denver bank, felt they didn't need it, at least not now. In fact, they re-cently purchased a house together.

"I don't need it [college] at this point, but I do have it as a personal goal. And Pinnacol will help me pay tuition," Naarai said. "Debt is very scary to me. I think that's my biggest fear is being old and having a lot of debt. Work-ing at Pinnacol offers me a lot of benefits that mean I'm set. A lot of my peers in my age group are not."

For a registered apprenticeship, the US Department of Labor authorizes the employer's training plan, making sure that it includes a significant ed-ucation component, on-the-job training, and a fair wage. Julie Wilmes runs the apprenticeship program at Pinnacol. She believes it takes buy-in from the senior team and dedicated resources to pull this sort of program off, particularly to go the registered apprenticeship route with the required structures, approvals, paid education component, and reporting rules. "So at first, it was a little squirrely," Julie reflected. "Now, six years later, it's much more solidified and the registered apprenticeship model gives us a blueprint of what we need to teach, what we need to train, and what we need to aspire to with our apprentices and it also gives our apprentices that guarantee that they're going to get a high-quality experience."[38]

Emerging Industries

We just learned about an established industry that has trouble getting a shrinking workforce excited about insurance. Apprentices like Naarai prove out the model: catch them early, build loyalty. At the other end of the spectrum are brand-new fields that have a different problem.

Clean energy is an interesting case study for apprenticeships. Lots of students are passionate about saving the earth and working on climate change. The US has pledged to get to net-zero greenhouse gas emissions by 2050 and has increased clean energy jobs in every state (adding 114,000 jobs, for example, in 2022).[39] That translates to a sudden uptick in need for electric vehicle workers; geothermal, solar, and wind plant operators; and energy efficiency retrofitters. So when Richard Lawrence at the Interstate Renewable Energy Council is asked the question, Who's going to build and maintain the electric vehicle charging stations around the country so that we'll all be comfortable taking an electric vehicle on a road trip? he's thinking that apprenticeship is a great pipeline model. And many of the big federal investments in clean energy are offering big tax incentives to employers to hire apprentices as a way to build the field quickly.[40]

Electrician Brian Rhodes-Devey is in his mid-thirties and never expected to be comfortably off financially even though he earned a college degree on a track scholarship at the University of Texas, Austin. Brian says he walked away from a $50,000 starting salary (plus commission) in telecom sales a year out of college. "When I worked at my desk job, I saw a lot of people making money and I realized that, like, if this is what having money requires, I'm just super not interested," he said. Brian then tried his hand at organic farming. He lived in an old school bus and he went on several gig jobs, but eventually he felt called to the stability of a trade role. "I've now been with ReVision Energy for five years. This is the most adult thing I've ever done."[41]

While an electrician's apprenticeship is four years long (as long as a bachelor's degree), Brian and company executive Vaughan Woodruff explained that ReVision has one of the first "in-house" registered apprenticeships in the country, at what is called a "distributed energy installation company." That allows paid apprentice electricians to move from free classroom training to jobsite seamlessly. Vaughan, who has also been appointed by Maine's governor as the chair of the state workforce board, says it really helps with recruitment when apprentices don't have to go to school, often a long drive away, for five hours at the end of their workday. "I don't think we as a society recognize how significant a lift it is to get an electrical license in most states," Vaughan explained. "It's an incredible investment."[42] Brian, the apprentice, says this kind of learning feels better than college. "I just finished my fourth year of school. I'll be able to sit for my journeyman exam in the next month or so. And wow. It's really allowed me to learn, like learning how to do something, then, someone showing me how to do it. And I don't have to wonder about how I'm gonna get paid."

The call to work on the cutting edge of global warming also spoke to Brian, even though he spends some cold days outside in Maine. "Green-collar" worker, he says, is a moniker he wears proudly. He thought about it: "I wouldn't say that I am only at ReVision because of the benefits of the climate. I think that's certainly a big part of it for me. I was looking at a trade to where I could be kind of at the cutting edge of like, doing EV stuff [electric vehicle charger installation]. Yeah. I am at the absolute tip of the spear. That's fun." He added with a chuckle, "You know, it's like what it must have been like to install the first gas stations."

Richard, as senior director of workforce and employer engagement at the Interstate Renewable Energy Council, connected me to ReVision Energy, because they and Maine are at the cutting edge of making the onerous training schedule more streamlined to attract new folks. (Maine has the oldest population in the country.)[43] The state has initiated a "helper's license" which allows apprentices to help meet the outsize demand for work, under supervision. But demand from customers, Vaughan and Richard say, is ever changing; first it was wind energy, then solar, now electric vehicle chargers, batteries, and heat pumps. Richard has to work with existing construction unions to ensure that new roles are different enough from those of general electricians to justify a specific training track. It's difficult to map a consistent set of skills and the training required as a new field is emerging. It's the same problem colleges have moving at the speed of innovation to plan high-quality training. And the unions do become gatekeepers, partly because they want to ensure that their workers who spend years as apprentices will have job security in a stable field that doesn't change too quickly.

Richard says many smaller employers are going for what's colloquially called "small a" apprenticeships, which don't bother with government approval. They use many of the design elements but don't have the reporting and oversight requirements. "Everybody's always used 'on the job' learning to train their employees, but it hasn't been in a structured, formalized, standardized, consistent way," Richard says. "We joke and call that the 'school of bloody knuckles' because workers have learned through mistakes on the job, rather than through a managed training program." Richard also says it's much easier for nonconstruction industries like financial services and tech, two other areas where there is significant growth, to get new apprenticeships approved, because the established unions are not feeling territorial. But where the talent shortages are making national headlines year after year, even in unionized fields, he says, we are starting to see more apprenticeship innovation, including in manufacturing, health care, and even teaching.

Desperate Industries

Cybersecurity, AI, and data analytics get a lot of the buzz for being industries with sky-high job openings, but the teaching field is an excellent example of desperation forcing change. Fifty years ago, one-third of all college women majored in education (in part because that was one of the few fields open to women). Today, just over 4 percent of bachelor's degrees are in education, and only 6 percent of women are earning them.[44] Nobody expected teachers to be able to be trained by the apprentice route. Each state has a regulatory licensing process, and the teachers' unions had a tight hold on managing supply and tried-and-true student-teaching requirements as part of the teaching degree.

But COVID-19 was the tipping point. Our nation was already suffering from an acute shortage of teachers, particularly in rural communities and the southern US, but teacher vacancies at the start of the 2023 school year had risen 50 percent from the previous year. Teachers were burning out, with postpandemic quit rates projected to level out around 12 percent each year.[45] The reality in many schools is that dedicated people without licenses were running classrooms as long-term subs, because shortages were so deep, but they weren't being paid as teachers. The estimated total number of these underqualified folks operating as teachers or covering subjects they aren't certified to teach is 270,000 nationwide.[46]

Crystal Acosta always wanted to be a teacher; in fact, she burst into tears as she told me this over Zoom, but life got in the way. She dropped out of college and became a dental assistant in her small hometown of Morgan City, Louisiana, on the Atchafalaya River. It's oil country, north of New Orleans. When she became a single mom through divorce, and the sole breadwinner for her two boys, she took a job as a paraprofessional (teacher's aide) so she could be on her kids' schedule. Just as COVID-19 was starting, Crystal was invited into a unique program, a fast-track, paid, and fully job-embedded apprentice program to help school support staff gain the necessary credentials to become certified teachers. And not just through apprenticeship. They earn an apprenticeship *degree*.

This was the brainchild of nonprofit Reach University, which managed to gain regional accreditation to run degree-conferring teacher apprentice programs across the country. The model turns on the idea that workplace experience is "creditable"—worthy, that is, of academic credit. The result is a new pipeline of talent. It makes sense to grow your teachers from inside school buildings, when 85 percent of teachers teach within forty miles of where they grew up.[47] Crystal took the plunge (it's a three-to-four-year part-time commitment) with two friends, the head custodian and computer lab manager who also worked in her school.

What's affirming for Crystal is that she is now about to turn fifty and she is finally living her dream. At this point in her life, she hadn't thought it was possible to be a third-grade teacher at Julia B. Maitland Elementary School, the very school she attended as a child. "It's a perfect route for single moms," she told me, "because it allowed me to still work, which financially, I mean, I had to. There's no way around that."[48] Crystal says that for people like her, in small towns, a traditional university is thirty to forty-five minutes away, and it is difficult to get to class when you have a full-time job and kids. With the teaching credential, earned while she is working full time as a teacher's aide, she believes she will double her salary.

Like other licensed fields with shortages, such as nursing, electrician work, and clinical therapy, which we'll hear about later, the teacher licensing process is poised to be further streamlined. How many Crystals are there who are dedicated enough to manage a full-time job for three to four years to get that teaching degree? It's a hard role to outsource when you don't have enough teachers. When the rubber meets the road, will we fill up classrooms with extra children, which could cause more teachers to quit? Will we pay teachers more? Teachers make, on average, 25 percent less than similarly educated degree holders.[49] The apprenticeship model helps, just like it does at ReVision Energy in Maine. You can put someone on the job with a "limited license."[50] And that's what is happening in all these fields, as well as health care; it's sort of a triage approach.

In response to this need, Reach University recently founded the National Center for the Apprenticeship Degree to support peer institutions of higher education, government agencies, and employers in launching their own apprenticeship degrees in high-need fields and industries.[51]

WHY CAN'T WE DO THIS?

All the apprenticeship examples I just shared raise the question, Can these programs scale? Apprentices require supervision, and that can limit growth, even after the companies have laid down all the groundwork. As for certifications, once an industry has agreed on a way to test applicants to set the entry bar, scale is easy. But here, we have a breadth problem—certifications (plus licenses) only exist, by my back-of-the-envelope calculation, for 25–30 percent of roles.[52] How do we create certifications across more industries? Later we will ask this same question about durable skills. I have been asking the scale question in all of my interviews. What would it take for certifications and apprenticeships to scale? If it is not in the cards politically or practically, what can we learn for them to be taken forward to a national model of college reform?

Can Apprenticeships Scale?

Let's start with apprenticeships. As I stated earlier in this chapter, apprenticeships have the most potential for scale, if we can solve the supervision problem, the mapping of the learning journey, and the question of who pays. We have seen apprenticeships become large-scale models in a few other Western countries with corporate incentives and union-type infrastructures to manage the processes, at no cost or low cost for young people. Most of our experience with employer incentives for training is largely centered on tuition reimbursement for traditional college classes. Most workers don't tap into it, meaning that hundreds of millions of dollars the government offers to fund the programs are unused.[53] Apprenticeship and certification experts have their eyes on that funding, but Congress has been unwilling to open up those programs to be used flexibly.[54]

If you compared funding for apprenticeships and college, you would assume our policy makers don't value apprenticeship as a viable path to meaningful careers. But we are on a journey from an education-first system to a skills-first system. And it's moving faster than most expected.

The Department of Labor's Apprenticeship Office was only set up in 2015 with $30 million to distribute as grants. And while that grant funding was up dramatically to $285 million in 2023, direct annual funding of apprenticeships works out to hundreds of dollars per apprentice.[55] That is a tiny fraction of the $240 billion the federal government spends each year directly subsidizing students in the traditional college system. So the per-student support for college students averages about $16,000 per full-time student equivalent, if you include average state support. You can see the whopping investment discrepancy between apprenticeships and college.[56]

Rebecca Agostino is a great person to ask about whether apprenticeships can scale in the US. She is the vice president of learning for Multiverse, which was founded by the son of the UK's former prime minister Tony Blair to help scale apprenticeships there. Other Western countries watched with interest when Britain began charging large corporations a 0.5 percent annual levy on their payroll to fund apprenticeships for all employers in 2017, which will increase the government funding pool to 2.7 billion pounds annually by 2025.[57] (Compare that number with the $285 million national funding commitment in the US when our country is five times larger.)[58] While the apprenticeship tax is controversial with employers, Rebecca believes in the importance of government funding blended with the support of third parties, intermediaries tasked with taking the friction out of the process for students and making apprenticeships turnkey for employers. There are 1,200 intermediaries now in the UK, and they are funded for each apprentice they train.[59]

Multiverse brought two types of apprenticeships in data analytics to the US but found different expectations. "The funding both normalizes and funds longer programs in the UK," Rebecca says. "We can do longer and broader programs there. . . . With government funding comes patience for results. . . . In the UK everyone says, 'Oh, you're an apprentice, you'll be learning for a year.' In the US, everyone says, 'I don't really know what an apprentice is, but I'd like you to know these skills by tomorrow.'"

A big infusion of federal funds for apprenticeships is not expected in the US anytime soon, although California has announced a program that provides expanded state funding and, according to the Urban Institute, two-thirds of states provide some incentives to employers. And the state programs are growing.[60] Just as this book headed toward publication, President Joe Biden authorized another $200 million to be used to incentivize use of apprenticeships in big federal contracts and backed it up with an executive order.[61]

Hire, Train, Deploy

Ryan Craig isn't waiting for the government. He is putting his money behind the private sector to scale apprenticeships. Through his venture capital firm,

Achieve Partners, Ryan used to fund tuition-based models, mainly boot-camps. But he developed a view over time that bootcamps were not pro-ducing the outcomes for learners that made for good business. "They were solving the skills gap, but they were not solving the experience gap for con-sumers," and, he says, "that's just getting wider and wider."[62] Ryan has landed on apprenticeship as the only model that solves both the skills gap and the experience gap. He has helped to fund an industry group, Apprentice-America, to spread the word and best practices and advocate for funding.

He calls his model Hire, Train, Deploy. This approach accepts the belief that corporate America has no patience, at least not without low-hassle gov-ernment funding. So we'll need specific companies to take on the risk of training workers in high-demand fields. This would become their business—not quite bootcamps, more like training and staffing agencies, but the train-ees are on the payroll of the training companies, not paying tuition.

His best example of Hire, Train, Deploy is a Virginia-based company, Revature, which calls itself "the world's leading tech talent enablement company."[63] Revature says it has churned out two hundred thousand trained computer science workers since it took on this new focus in 2013. When it started with the model, it only hired college graduates into the program. Revature would offer training to college students, hire the suc-cessful ones at graduation, provide some "last-mile" training, and contract them out to companies, at higher rates, much like a staffing agency, with market-competitive salaries. The newly minted workers have to sign a two-year contract and be willing to be deployed anywhere in the US. They face financial penalties if they leave early. But in return, they get across the experience chasm.

The model was interesting to me from the beginning, but in researching this book, I learned that Revature has now gone all in on recruiting workers without college degrees. That made it much more intriguing. So I connected with CEO Ashwin Bharath. Like others in technical fields, Revature turned to nondegreed workers because it could not meet demand. The number of computer science grads in the US is growing, but not fast enough.[64] So how could Revature turn to the high school students, community college grads or stop-outs, or workers from other fields to offer them a chance to level up to the requirements of what the Department of Labor calls Zone 4 jobs, occupations that need considerable preparation?[65]

Revature created a free, shortcut training program, which is not for the fainthearted, as it takes about the equivalent of two college semesters to complete, but it's fully flexible and largely online. The idea resonated with the largely male DIY crowd I mentioned earlier. Ashwin told me that two hundred thousand aspirants started this course in 2022. He didn't disclose how many stuck with it, but he says that of the people who finished, he hired 27 percent of them to work alongside the college grads that Revature had been hiring.[66] And he was pleased to report that these noncollege learners slightly outperform their college grad colleagues in the placement tests Revature gives before assigning them all out to work as contractors. Why? He believes Revature has trained them in one year specifically on the skills employers are asking for, while the four-year college training is more theoretical. It's an interesting data point as we rethink how long the college degree should take.

For their employees who didn't attend college or stopped out, Ashwin says Revature solves more than the experience or opportunity gap. "For me to solve the opportunity gap, I need to solve the belief gap. A lot of these people don't think they can be programmers. And a lot of the companies don't believe they can be programmers. . . . They need external catalysts like Revature to enable them. . . . A very small percentage of people are self-enablers."

Can this work in other industries, where apprentices are essentially hired by a training company that takes on the financial risk and the patience factor that most companies don't have time for? Through his venture capital firm, Ryan Craig is also funding Hire, Train, Deploy companies in other sectors, including health care, Salesforce, and human resources.[67]

Major companies like Accenture, Aon Insurance, and IBM have made public commitments to increase the use of apprenticeships, using "big A" and "small a" approaches. And many more small and medium-size companies are using pieces of the construct with a low-investment approach and gradual pay scale to "try as they buy." I am seeing the best adoption when a regional intermediary like CareerWise in Colorado or CityWorks in Washington, DC, takes on the painstaking work of designing with each employer and recruiting each learner. And the Biden administration's new 2024 executive order calls on federal agencies to step up their apprenticeship programs, so those will be interesting to watch.[68]

What About Certifications? Can They Scale Beyond Tech?

There are more than seven thousand separate industry certifications, according to Credential Engine, the nonprofit we met in chapter 1 that is trying to organize all credential types into a digital Dewey Decimal System.[69] As one cloud certification lead at a large tech company described to me on background, "A computer science degree is not going to show you how to work within Cloud. But if you're using the learning paths, the certificates, the certain certifications, we have all of that mapped out for you."[70]

Megacompanies that drive the cloud industry or other industry groups can be excellent organizers and promoters of certifications. The IT group Computing Technology Industry Association, construction's National Center for Construction Education and Research, and the Manufacturing Institute are good examples. Perhaps the most well-developed frameworks come from the government's national standards agency, which worked with industry and academia to create NICE (the National Initiative for Cybersecurity Education). NICE has named seven job categories and fifty-plus roles, spelling out the skills for each one.[71] The site is used by governments, employers, and educators to coordinate training and certifications. NICE is unique among industries, likely because the certified talent shortages are so acute, creating a forcing mechanism toward collaboration. Employers work together to address the almost four million unfilled cybersecurity jobs globally, an estimated 75 percent of all the current roles in the field, which are affecting security and operations.[72]

Even where shortages are not so acute, Liberty Munson, the certification lead from Microsoft, believes we can map more job roles into meaningful industry-recognized certifications, but she says it is hard, hard work.

> There are so many jobs where there's no organizing body in charge of the field, like there is for many medical positions. A lot of jobs in tech fall

under [no organizing body]. So, in trying to make recommendations and look at policy levers, it becomes more challenging. But there's a lot of value in leveraging certification as an alternate path to degree programs for applicants and employees to demonstrate that they have specific skills. . . . I do think that there has to be a better blending of learning and assessment to inform certification. That breaks a lot of rules around what makes something a certification, so we need to figure out what that right balance is.[73]

Groups ranging from the Education Design Lab to Walmart to the Opportunity Skills Network to the Educational Testing Service to Harvard's Skills Lab to MIT are working to design assessments that stand in for the experience gap and the degree gap and attempting to determine the means to validate broader skills than coding or cloud computing, in order to bring more opportunity and confidence to nondegreed learners who seek job roles that don't have certifications currently. They are also attempting to create the skills genome that will power the GPS of talent navigation for learners and employers. Today, we don't have enough data points to define the journeys.

There is also new hesitancy since the Supreme Court's 2023 affirmative action ruling that race can no longer be used as a "plus factor" in college admissions to ensure a diverse student body.[74] The concern is that the court's reversal of this law will have a ripple-and-chill effect in the workplace, and that to withstand bias lawsuits, newer efforts to hire or promote workers based on skills will need the kind of documentation that the tried-and-true degree seems to enjoy de facto.[75] The employer mood after this decision highlights the need to design clear-cut certifications that can be agreed on by most or all of a sector's employers.

WHAT CAN WE LEARN FROM EMPLOYERS WHO ARE BYPASSING COLLEGES?

As this decade proceeds into the next one, desperate employers will rely more on expanding types of certifications to find entry-level employees like

Patrick at AWS. The talent scarcity that is here in some fields, such as IT, health care, and manufacturing, will become more acute. And that will drive change. Lovey Hammel, the staffing executive, tells me that what drives these not-inexpensive work-around strategies for her employer clients is already the bogeyman of 2025–26. That's when the enrollment "cliff" begins to rear its ugly head, a diminished applicant pool based just on declining US birth rates, which is expected to depress the number of applicants for colleges and jobs.

Byron Auguste is using this fear to try to drive collective action. Byron is founder of Opportunity@Work, the group I described in chapter 1 that is trying to build a movement to recognize seventy million–plus STARS (people Skilled Through Alternative Routes).[76] I remember sitting in his office as we were both starting our nonprofits over a decade ago. He told me then he wanted to take a systems architecture approach to rethinking talent and rewire the education-to-work system that he saw as structurally biased to exclude marginalized communities. He is working with groups of employers to harness data that visualize the talent shortfalls before us. He describes his pitch: "In tight talent industries, it won't work to poach. We help them see where the pools of STARS talent that they're overlooking are. . . . It's half the skilled workforce. . . . If you don't have a STARS talent strategy, you don't have a talent strategy. And secondly, we are running out of recruits and need to change the entry rules."[77]

It seems every few weeks another study comes out showing that employers are removing degree requirements from their job postings. But we have learned that a solid majority will continue to do things the way they have done until it stops working.[78] Clay Lord, from the Society of Human Resource Management (SHRM) Foundation, is charged with helping HR departments see why and how to change. "What we're trying to do at SHRM is to create the conditions where employers can get there before it's a crisis," he said. "The Foundation has identified obstacles that keep employers from adopting [skills-first hiring]. The first is that the ROI [return on investment] isn't clear on why they should change. The second is that the [technology] systems are difficult and not trustworthy and third is that they can't guarantee the quality of their hiring decisions if they do change."[79]

In this chapter, we have learned from the early adopters that the waves of a massive sea change in the skills and hiring ocean are headed toward us. Most importantly, we have learned what works for the early adopters, providing lessons that could be useful for all players. In design thinking, we look at the needs of "extreme users" to find designs that will benefit all users. The typewriter was designed for a blind person who needed a way to feel the letters she was writing. The telephone was designed by Alexander Graham Bell as he worked with deaf students to help them hear the vibration of voices.[80] In this chapter, there are two sets of extreme users: needy employers and alternative learners, who, together, are finding what works to move their industries and their lives forward. Employers from new sectors, old-school industries, and pockets of desperation are the extreme users on one side of the hiring equation, and nondegreed entry-level job applicants are the extreme users on the other side. Both need a solution to bridge not only the skills gap but also the experience gap at a time when LinkedIn reports that one-third of entry-level jobs require three years' experience.[81]

In my research and interviews with employers, employer groups, and intermediaries, the tools that rose to the top were industry-recognized certifications and apprenticeships. Bootcamps taught valuable lessons and worked for those who are looking for promotions or job switching. But for most employers looking for entry-level workers, apprenticeships and certifications were the best proxies for job readiness. And a seasoned apprentice, in particular, demonstrates both the maturity that Lovey's employers were looking for and the verification that you could apply your skills in the context of a specific job role. Additionally, in an apprenticeship, a learner has a chance to demonstrate those "pack animal" skills. Remember, Matt Sigelman from the Burning Glass Institute explains that skills tend to travel together. An employer wants someone who can code, perhaps, but who can also collaborate with colleagues, or assess when to flag an issue for their supervisor. It's really only on the job, or perhaps in simulated versions of a job, that you can demonstrate both the starter hard skills and the durable skills that will make a broader range of employers comfortable with non-degree hiring and promotion.

Design Criteria for Employers

What are the design criteria to take forward as we look toward a new paradigm for a national education model?

Design Criteria for Employers

1. Certifications must be industry recognized.
2. Certifications must be universally understood by learners and employers.
3. Apprenticeships must provide an authentic workplace that contributes to career growth.
4. Learners need to be paid.
5. Employers need to be incentivized, if not paid.
6. Apprentices, particularly those in high school, need clear exit ramps or opportunities to explore more than one job role.
7. Apprenticeships need to provide community, with coworkers, but even better with a cohort model for learners.

For certifications, I would call out two design criteria that seem to make them powerful stepping stones. First, certifications must truly be "industry recognized." I would argue that that means having no fewer than five significant regional or national employers sign off on mastery requirements for the group of competencies that make up a skill, and adding up the skills needed to be eligible for a particular role. And second, certifications need to exist across all fields—a heavy lift, no doubt. Other sectors talk about NICE's cybersecurity skills model, but few have acted across their industries.

And what about apprenticeships? If we can't make apprenticeships available to all who want them, what design criteria could be incorporated into a new higher education model? There is a lot to say here.

First, learners need an authentic workplace experience, complete with the good and the bad of workplace culture, the networks, solving the "belief gap" that they can belong there. And it needs to legitimately be seen as experience when it later shows up on a candidate's résumé.

Second, learners need to be paid or have their work qualify as part of credit-bearing high school or college. And they should be able to tap into financial aid for the classroom element of their apprenticeships.

Third, employers need to be incentivized, if not paid. We have to at least make it easy for employers to sign up for apprentices. A hard part is figuring out how to fund and design the 144 instruction hours, which in other countries is free to the learner. Another hard part is learning how to utilize a worker who is coming and going between school and work. Intermediaries like Multiverse or CareerWise, or even staffing companies like Revature, are critical to making at least the process turnkey.

Fourth, the best apprenticeships have an aspect of career exploration, with exit ramps for learners who find this field isn't for them. Pinnacol, the insurance company, for example, encourages college classes and allows apprentices to try out different departments.

Finally, we must design for a community of belonging. I found a certain wistfulness in my interviews with "direct-to-employment" young people that saddened me. They definitely felt that there was at least a social price to pay for skipping out on college. They formed a work family, but their colleagues were older. A college-like community is one of the most treasured lifelong assets that learners report missing out on when they opt out of college.

The siren's call of "direct to employment," debt-free, is capturing the imagination of many young people.[82] I can feel it in the high schools and community colleges I visit. Even in the university class I teach on higher ed redesign, the frustration is evident. But there is a long distance to travel to make the necessary models and tools that might work in, for example, Switzerland viable in a country the size of the US. Alternatives today face several issues: the wheels are not greased, the narrative is outdated, the pathways are not normalized, the funding is spotty, and the fear that bad actors lurk keeps Congress from allowing the funding to follow students to their new frontiers.

All that said, we can see the future from here. And the future, as we'll see in the next chapter, is a blended model, the blending of training and education, except in the most elite research colleges. In all but the tightest of job markets, experience, we have seen, trumps other forms of preparation. But most colleges stop short of providing experience. Can employers be incentivized or compensated for their role as educators working alongside colleges? Will colleges be willing to adapt and converge? What would it look like to open up some of the $240 billion that the federal government reserves annually for the traditional college student, or some of the $460 billion spent on public high schoolers, to support the new models, which many learners and their future employers seem to be searching for?[83]

4

Colleges

Can They Adapt?

We recognized that employers weren't willing or able to wait four years or six years for us to pump out a new crop of baccalaureate educated or master's educated students.

—LYDIA RILEY, UNIVERSITY OF TEXAS SYSTEM

It is often lamented that we spend way too much time talking about elite colleges that hardly anyone can attend. I did the math. I estimate that seventy-five thousand hardworking and lucky students land a coveted spot at an "exclusive" university each year. All in, only 2 percent of college students sit in an elite seat. (I define *exclusive* or *elite* as a private or public institution that turns away at least 80 percent of applicants.)[1] It is important to exclude these colleges from the discussion we are about to have in this chapter. Why? The "top" seventy-five colleges are not likely to change, except around the margins. They don't need to. In most cases, their application rates have never been higher, despite increased attacks from the political Right alleging that colleges have become too insular or too liberal, or antisemitic, what one conservative columnist calls "the Great Awokening."[2]

Angel Pérez, CEO of the National Association for College Admission Counseling, calls it ironic that the colleges not under attack are the ones struggling for students.[3] The reasons the elite schools become more popular each year have to do with dropping SAT and ACT requirements, the accessibility of the "Common App" portal, and, I would argue, the increasing consumer trend that assigns value to brands—the more expensive, the more they matter.[4] Historically Black colleges and universities (HBCUs) also deserve a mention here. Many of their application rates have also soared in the past few years. As Fisk University president Agenia Clark told listeners at a recent innovation conference I attended, her students are drawn by the HBCU's 155-year-old tradition. "They are coming for the culture," she said, "so my job is to protect it."[5]

This chapter addresses the other 5,740 colleges in the US, where, for the most part, flagging enrollment is a big concern.[6] And this is where the vast, vast majority of learners go to school. Besides elite colleges, Angel explained in an interview, "everyone else is really struggling, whether they're public or not. And so, a big piece, I think that admission officers across the country probably want to get on board with is, 'Is there a different way of thinking of college?' . . . But, that hurts their financial bottom line, right?"[7]

A different way to think of college? As we've seen in previous chapters, these institutions certainly feel the pressure of the "experience is the new degree" mantra from employers, politicians, and even consumers. There are so many headwinds pushing colleges to be more responsive to early career preparation and to act quickly, which creates a sort of frenzy of well-meaning ideation and piloting but, at the same time, a "waiting-for-data" mind-set that feels both prudent and risky. These colleges have watched 1,100 other institutions close their doors or merge since higher education's heyday around 2010.[8] These institutions see the statistics that lower-income as well as Black and brown learners have shockingly worse odds of getting through the gauntlet of higher education.[9] And they also know that opportunities to gain career experience during college are much more readily available to wealthier students who don't have to work at Chick-fil-A to pay the bills.[10]

Most states have been pulling back their funding for public colleges for more than a decade.[11] With higher ed becoming more highly politicized regarding race, political protests, alleged elitism, and diversity, equity, and inclusion, the appetite in some Republican state legislatures to fund colleges is dropping further.[12] Most tangibly, as I mentioned in the last chapter, the enrollment cliff will create an even bigger fight for the dwindling number of college-age students.[13] Surveys show that Gen Z is most distrustful about higher education, but for colleges, the drop in adult student enrollment since COVID-19 is an even greater concern.[14] This adds up to the perfect storm of an existential crisis for the nonelite majority of colleges, particularly small, private ones. (I would argue all these factors have caused nonelite colleges to put the brakes on tuition increases in the past few years, to stop adding fuel to the headline fire of "soaring" admissions costs.)[15]

But can the average college keep the ship afloat over the coming decade? In this and the final chapter, I will make the case that some of them can—if they alter their mind-sets about what it means to deliver "college." The further they are from being elite, the less entrenched their faculty, and the less powerful their alumni, the easier it is to listen to what parents, students, employers, and, yes, politicians are asking for. There are many experiments, from pay-as-you-go pricing innovations to "nudging" and engagement strategies to keep students in school, but in this chapter I will focus on the efforts to address the "last-mile problem"—that is, why so many graduates have such a hard time getting hired in their fields and why some employers are looking elsewhere. This, alongside the price of tuition, is giving the value of college its bad rap. If colleges could solve the last-mile problem, they would suddenly have a repeatable service to offer every time their alumni shifted careers.

FIVE MODELS ON THE PATH TO "EXPERIENCE FIRST" COLLEGE

We heard in the previous chapter that what employers want most is to hire people with experience, as relevant to the role as possible. If this holds true, colleges should deliver graduates with experience. Would this save the traditional degree and reduce the cost? As I considered this ah-ha, I tried to imagine colleges completely pivoting their model to "experience first." Huh.

A future state where college and preparatory work are woven together to get the best of both worlds. That seems impossible for most traditional colleges because they would be offering a different product from the one they offer today and, frankly, one they are not even authorized to shift to, given the current confines of financial aid and accreditation—not to mention the different skills their own workforce would require.

With an experience-first model, what would college even look like? Colleges might not be in the business of teaching in classrooms; they would be in the business of teaching on the job or teaching in the context of the job, as apprentice supervisors do. Is that what students, parents, and returning adults want out of college? They certainly signal that increasingly in surveys before and after they experience higher education.[16] If consumers can acquire knowledge on their phones, should colleges provide a different take on knowledge by offering skills mastery and validation services related to careers? Many workforce advocates and intermediaries are using the term *skills first* to frame the shift that needs to happen. But I would argue that only a few colleges are set up to live in that world.

This chapter will profile five colleges that show us where innovation is headed for all nonelite institutions and that illustrate the philosophical and practical challenges of getting from here to there. In researching this book, I found that colleges are testing five distinct models in their journey from traditional lecture-

> **Models That Build Toward Experience-First College**
>
> 1. Making skills visible
> 2. Validating "job-ready" skills
> 3. Experience sampling
> 4. Micro-pathways
> 5. Embracing the weave

based learning to what the Education Design Lab calls "the weave." They are based on the strengths that each of these colleges can bring to bear, not to mention what the faculty will bear at their institutions.

The journey often begins when a college tries to define the "job-ready" skills that already live in the courses it offers. I will call this model *making skills visible*: naming them in the syllabus and talking about them with students, a lot. A second innovation that could build on the first is to offer students meaningful credentials to *validate those job-related skills* with a micro-credential other than the degree, ideally one certified by industry. A third model is to provide opportunities for students to gain a career-enhancing experience related to a skill or a chosen career, *experience sampling*. A fourth, more dramatic innovation is to say, OK, our learners care less about the degree than the job preparation, so let's focus on *micro-pathways*, skills preparation for specific roles, and de-emphasize the degree at the outset, when that seems to be getting in the way of completion. A fifth model is to *embrace the weave* and provide career-enhancing jobs through the degree, to make college the prep, reflect, prep, reflect container in which students start their careers. It's important to note here that different models work for different types of colleges, which serve different types and volumes of learners and have to answer to different types of traditions, faculty, and alumni.

Model 1: Making Skills Visible

Western Governors University (WGU) wouldn't describe itself as an experience-first college. It is the youngest and the largest institution profiled in this chapter, born with the digital age. In 1997, nineteen governors got together and pressed Congress and philanthropists to help jump-start a private, nonprofit distance-learning college to serve their growing western states. They wanted to help their far-flung constituents use this new thing called the internet to earn a college degree in high-demand fields. WGU was the first "competency-based" college to be certified, meaning you didn't have to attend a class, even online. You move through online course material and then take assessments along the way to demonstrate mastery. The tuition model is kind of like a Golden Corral all-you-can-eat buffet. You have course instructors who can help you if you get stuck and a program mentor who is your coach throughout your degree. The faster you complete, the less you pay.

Today, some six hundred colleges are developing competency-based education programs, but WGU has been the first of these colleges to develop a comprehensive list of fifteen thousand "rich skill descriptors" across 175 clusters of jobs that track from WGU's four colleges: health care, teaching, business, and IT.[17] Each descriptor in the massive library shows faculty and students what skills an employer would expect, down to a detailed level. It's an entirely different language from the "learning outcomes" that most professors share on the syllabus to give students a road map of what they will master in a class. I would say, as someone who is grappling with this in my own teaching, that it's hard to move from theory to action or from distant context to direct context. This disconnect has been causing employers and students everywhere to challenge the relevance and value of the college degree.

Kacey Thorne, who has the awesome title at WGU of senior director of skills architecture, explains how it works even for required general education courses that might seem tangential to your chosen career field. "So let's take an English course," she explained. "You're going to be learning about 20th century literature. It's still a valuable way to teach skills, but we just need to transition how we're talking to students about it. Skills first, through a content lens."[18] So, for instance, in the business school, a mentor will help you see your required English literature course in the context of your expressed career interest in, say, human resources. Anyone can skim through the open collections to see eight job families and skills collections in HR. And the mentor "will work with the students each term to set SMART (Specific, Measurable, Achievable, Relevant, and Time-Bound) goals around specific skills that they want to develop," Kacey explained. WGU calls it the SkillED Profile, or, more generically, a skills profile. This mapping at WGU is already digitized to live in students' achievement or skills wallet that I described in chapter 1. WGU's president, Scott Pulsipher, is excited to be able to capture the work world's increasingly granular view of skills. He believes it gives students more clarity and confidence about what jobs to apply for. He added, "And that has to happen, because guess what? Individuals are acquiring skills in all sorts of different dynamics. And if they're not able to surface those, to the employers in the workforce, it gets increasingly hard for them to actually identify that I'm the talent that you need for this or that role."[19]

WGU is perhaps the gold standard for making work skills visible while in college, but the university is now starting pilots to provide its younger students with hands-on work experience, beyond required teaching and health-care practicums. As an online university that has swelled, as of publication, to 175,000 students, experience provision has not felt like an option with the scale required. Besides, the classic WGU student was a working adult, often doing a degree to get a better role in a field where they already work. I found it intriguing that, during the pandemic, interest in WGU soared among younger, first-time college goers. But even now, postpandemic, that interest in a skills-first, all-you-can-eat model continues to grow among young adults.

For very large colleges, online or otherwise, providing career experience is difficult. WGU has worked with other large institutions, such as Arizona State University and Southern New Hampshire University, to form a nonprofit called the Open Skills Network in order to bring attention to these skills libraries and foster adoption. The hope is that a Wikipedia-style network can form between colleges and employer groups, and that AI will help keep them up to date. As of mid-2024, this is the closest version I can find to the skills genome I expressed hope for in chapter 1, the master map that shows us what skills we need for what jobs. Who will have the awesome task of updating and improving this? Currently, the federal Department of Labor runs the closest cousin, O*NET, which catalogs jobs, but not really skills.[20] Pulsipher says employers hold the key to making this work.

Clearly, any college that wants to become an experience-first college needs to connect what it is selling (learning outcomes) to what employers are buying (skills). Mapping those connections and making them visible to both parties is the first step to a functioning visible career GPS.

Model 2: Validating Job Skills on Top of the Degree

The second innovation on the path to "experience first" is to validate skills. It's one thing to tell students, "These are the skills you are learning," but it's quite another to help them acquire an industry-recognized credential, much as Patrick did in the last chapter. The University of Texas (UT) System jumped into the game in 2022 with a big play, in clear Texas style, which is understandable since the system is made up of eight large public colleges serving two hundred and fifty thousand students that range in flavor from the flagship in Austin to UT Rio Grande Valley. These are the more selective public colleges in the state, and they have typically been more traditional. The community college system had already been experimenting with micro-credentials since 2018, particularly Alamo District in San Antonio.[21] The Texas legislature passed HB 8 in 2023 as a "pay for performance" approach where community colleges would be funded for graduating not just degreed students but also those who finish certificates and other "credentials of value."[22] That's one step in the direction toward normalizing a skills-first approach.

But in the more prestigious four-year universities, it was COVID-19's extreme talent shake-up that moved leadership to action, as employers were crying for help, particularly in fields such as cybersecurity and health care. As the pandemic disrupted talent pipelines, "we really started thinking about credentialing," said Lydia Riley, who codirected a systemwide task force. "We recognized that employers weren't willing or able to wait four years or six years for us to pump out a new crop of baccalaureate educated or master's educated students. They needed some quick assistance to fill all these high-quality jobs."[23] And while the employment shake-up has settled somewhat since, the sentiments from employers are still coming through loud and clear. But the challenge became how to retrofit skills and experience into a system that was built for classroom-based teaching.

Lydia says the UT task force was moved by research demonstrating that learners who supplemented their bachelor's degrees by also earning a non-degree certificate report that their degrees became more valuable.[24] Rather than partner with certificate providers in different industries, UT found one-stop shopping by running a pilot using the platform Coursera, which bundles some 7,000 courses and certificates from well-known companies, as well as other colleges. UT's goal became to offer 30,000 undergraduates a certificate alongside their degree by 2025. Roughly 6,500 students had been through the pilot by early 2024, taking certificates from Google, IBM, Microsoft and other providers.

Sofia Cavenaile earned the Google Project Management certificate as a junior in 2023 at UT San Antonio. She had just landed a part-time job as a legal assistant and she believes the certificate has helped her perform organizational tasks better. But she admits she only signed up for the certificate because her humanities professor offered a whole letter grade of extra credit to anyone who completed it. She said about thirty folks signed up, but three months later, she was told she was one of only two who finished it. "Yeah, it was just like a lot of work. It was, I would honestly say, an additional course I was adding to my course load," Sofia said. I signed up myself to see the course load and skills firsthand, and I was surprised that Google recommends spending twenty hours a week if you want to finish in three months. Sofia added a refrain that I often hear from my own students: "I don't want to bash my own generation, but I just think right now, it seems like a lot of college students that I know . . . that it's hard to get people to do more than just the bare minimum right now. . . . So I think that this would extend to a micro-credential, where if you're not offering money or a job or credit, it's going to be hard to get people to finish them."[25]

What I have seen in my own research and focus groups over the years is that college students don't know what they need until after they get into the hiring game, after they graduate. This presents a design challenge for colleges. Students rely on their professors and advisers to prepare them for work. One student at UT Austin, Brody Feldberg, was incented to take the Data Analytics certificate because his brother works at Apple and convinced him that Google certificates could really help him get hired. So Feldberg made time by reducing his courseload in his final semester of his senior year and, yes, he felt the certificate and his comfort level talking about the related skills made a difference when he hit the job market with his more theory-based economics degree. "I think it definitely gave me a leg up in interviews, for sure, because I leveraged it to the best of my ability. . . . I always say that my degree gave me the problem-solving ability and the certificate gave me the technical ability to solve any problem."[26]

Two barriers stand in the way before we will see the micro-credential floodgates open: time and cost to students, who already have steep time commitments and tuition bills, and a lack of faculty buy-in to include certificates inside a college major.

If you or I wanted to earn a micro-credential on Coursera, we would pay forty-nine dollars per month for a membership in 2024. UT is committed to covering those costs for its students and hopes to raise more money from the Texas legislature if these early pilots show positive outcomes for filling talent gaps, or at least higher alumni satisfaction with degree value. Early satisfaction surveys at UT show positive results.

But the second barrier is tougher to break through. Many faculty might well be resistant to building their classes around what is essentially corporate training. The faculty buy-in challenge is difficult and has kept many, many colleges from moving forward. The recent UT grad, Feldberg, who now uses his data analytics tools on the job as a cost analyst for an engineering consultancy, recommends baking the certificates into specific classes. In fact, he is retaking the Data Analytics certificate in his part-time MBA program at UT Austin where the professor is weaving the Google modules directly into his classes. He believes it's easier to absorb the material this way, compared to a learn-on-your-own extra credit approach.

Faculty have told me time and again in every type of institution that the effort to integrate these real-world and contextual learning opportunities into their courses adds too much to their workload given the efficacy data that are currently available; plus, there isn't enough time in the schedule to fit additional modules directly into the class schedule. (I can attest to this myself as an adjunct professor.) UT solved for this by starting the initiative with faculty, introducing cash stipends to two hundred teaching and instructional design staff to become certified to manage the microcredentialing process for their students. And that seems important, because if you go on Coursera's website, there are 1,600-plus certificates mixed in with thousands of courses. If we are asking faculty in these cases to move from being a "sage on the stage" to a "guide on the side," they still have to understand the outside curriculum and the context, as well as the hiring power of each certificate.

An Aside on Naming Conventions.   This is the moment to stop and clarify a few terms that are confusing students, faculty, employers, and just about everyone else as they navigate this fast-changing world of microcredentials. In this chapter, I am describing certificate programs, which are distinct from the industry certifications featured in the last chapter.

Those are often a gateway to employment without a degree because they are exams, much like occupational licenses, but without the government getting involved. Certification involves meeting specific industry standards, with exams proctored by a standards body, an industry association, or a company that provides the technology for which learners are being certified.

Certificates are usually positioned more as an introduction and overview to a field, although some can prepare you for certification exams. They work well for students or career switchers exploring whether they want to pursue, say, IT support, cybersecurity, or data analytics. But it's very confusing, because many certificates tout job readiness as the goal and use marketing language like "get certified." I believe the nomenclature and truth in advertising will improve in short order as buyers and sellers better understand the differences, but in the meantime, a general warning to readers: many providers and employers in this field use the terms *certification* and *certificates* interchangeably, and it becomes particularly confusing when we all use the same nickname for both types of micro-credentials: *certs*. If a learner wants to use the certificate to get hired, it is smart to also look for industry certifications for the two or three most critical skills inside the course—for example, for project management, consider getting Scrum certified or get the Project Management Institute's project management professional certification.[27]

Google is the best way to look at how certificates have become important in job training or career exploration. Grow with Google is the company's economic opportunity initiative, designed to help consumers grow their skills, businesses, and careers. When Grow with Google launched the Google Career Certificates program in 2018, they quickly became a dominant upskilling offering. Google was struggling to fill entry-level IT roles, so it put together a pilot to see whether young workers at Year Up, a national job training program, would learn enough in three months with a structured online program to be hire ready. The answer was yes, and the Google Career Certificates program was born.

Fast-forward to today and there are over 250,000 certificate graduates in the US (and over 600,000 globally).[28] Google reports that most of that growth has occurred just in the past few years.[29] Colleges of all types and nonprofits are now building them into their own programs, even high schools. As of early 2024, the UT System collaboration is Grow with Google's biggest yet with a college. The certificates, if the student passes the more than one hundred assessments along the way, are recommended by the American Council on Education for up to fifteen college credits, which is the equivalent of five college courses. And part of Grow with Google's "scale" plan is to partner with large and small colleges.

Certificate Fever?   Google claims that 75 percent of graduates report some kind of positive job outcome (e.g., new job, promotion, or raise) within six months of gaining the certificate.[30] Obviously, as more people have earned the certificates, the likelihood that they would get hired at Google, like the first Year Up cohort, has dropped dramatically. But what's been interesting to watch is how the Google brand cuts through the noise of the roughly five hundred thousand nondegree credentials out there.[31] The top three certificates from any provider on the Coursera site are Google certificates in cybersecurity, data analytics, and project management.[32] IBM and Meta also have popular offerings. All this suggests that, like the rest of the consumer product world, as well as politics and media, known brands sell better. It's the celebrity effect, which I predict will become a factor in certificate popularity among learners. In talking to students at UT who majored in subjects less correlated with tech brand expertise, such as government or biology, I discovered they were struggling more to figure out what lesser-known certificates would be a good fit for their job plans.

For me, this raises the question of what this landscape will look like in ten years. I predict certificates could become as popular as degrees (the early trends are heading that way). But it will only happen if more fields get "represented," as it were, by well-known proxy companies or celebrities. Will government or political science certificates be issued by famous politicians? Will celebrity scientists like Anthony Fauci or Neil deGrasse Tyson offer public health or astrophysics certificates? You could imagine Disney teaching hospitality management and customer experience, and Walmart teaching logistics and supply chain. I mentioned in chapter 2 that colleges like New York University are already experimenting with media brand partnerships for their Sneaker Essentials course and other arts-related majors.

As of publication, this pilot at UT does not offer experience—the Google certificates are fully asynchronous, online, and self-paced.[33] And when you look around the career advice websites that offer advice on the value of certificates, there are many warnings that these are not guaranteed to get you hired at Google or anywhere else.

It is early days. But Amy Heitzman from UPCEA, whom I mentioned in chapter 2, points to her members as a microcosm of innovation efforts. They represent what has long been called "Continuing Ed," the part of a college that is offering "other programs" besides degrees. Many colleges have been testing shorter-term credentials through these sandboxes because they sit outside the "for-credit," faculty-driven mothership of traditional colleges. She names three reasons colleges make the attempt to test micro-credentials: to increase revenue, to serve the elusive adult learners, and to make the degree more relevant to today's jobs.

Amy says innovations that start in continuing education departments could be adopted by the degree-granting part of the university, but it doesn't usually happen that way.

Model 3: Experience Sampling

Now to get to actual attempts by colleges to provide "experience" to their students. Jeff Holm, the vice provost of the University of North Dakota (UND), is an optimist. He sits inside the mothership of a flagship university (meaning the most prestigious public institution in the state), but he didn't go the micro-credential route. He chose to grab the experience bull by the horns. He wants UND to be the first public flagship university in any state that can say, "Every program that we offer, whether it be theater, cybersecurity, fine arts or philosophy or business, has a work-integrated component to its academics."[34] But how do you do that in northeast North Dakota with a sizable student body of fourteen thousand who need experience? UND is located in Grand Forks, just sixty miles south of Canada. Jeff knew he would need to import employers to provide enough opportunities to match the breadth of educational programs at a flagship like UND.

This is a model I'll call *experience sampling.* Over the past three years, Jeff has convinced maybe 5 percent of faculty to use an experience-matching platform called Riipen, and he's testing another service called Forage. These companies and others are trying to fill the need described in this chapter, not providing turnkey industry credentials but matchmaking students with the elusive turnkey industry experience that can be the magic on their résumé, through real-work projects or, when that fails, simulated ones.[35]

Riipen boasts thirty-five thousand employers in the US and Canada and caters to companies that want free help and are willing to utilize green talent to get it.[36] But most colleges have the rule that if you are earning credit for an "experience," you can't get paid. That means, at this stage, students might "sample" various professional experiences inside their traditional classes. Marketing adjunct professor Robert Warren has woven twenty-seven small and medium employer projects into his classes. For example, his students are helping beauty product and real estate companies research and test marketing plans with, he says, eye-opening results for the learners. "The one that sticks out in my mind was one student who said 'I never thought I'd be working with a Canadian entrepreneur living in Baltimore, selling fresh herbs to restaurants in Philadelphia.' . . . The East coast is much more aggressive, so that was a shocker for him." Warren grades the students on their employer deliverables, which he breaks down into five assignments, but the students present to and interact with their work partners. "You have to set it up in a way that you can grade it. But you also have to make sure that there's some academic component to it, because we're not trade schools," Robert says. "I am not turning out somebody who can write a marketing plan because there's no future in that. But what I am turning out is somebody who's going to be a future manager, who should know what to look for when writing a plan." (His view is that the rise of AI requires professors to train students to a higher level these days.)[37]

Jeff, the vice provost, says it's been relatively easy to sell "work integration" to the early adopters on the faculty like Robert in all eight UND colleges (except the graduate schools, which feel they can provide their own opportunities and practicums). Three thousand undergrads have engaged in work experiences in fields such as aviation, nutrition, political science, and chemical engineering. But Jeff doesn't know how much further any college can get without a mandate from the top. "You have to deal with a whole department, a whole program's faculty, and that's been really difficult. Right? Well, I'll say it's been impossible. I really have not been able to move the needle on that yet." Robert (the marketing instructor) believes that the more research-based the university, the harder it is to rally faculty around something that feels very different from their primary incentive structure: doing research to get tenure. And conversely, the fewer dollars that are coming from prestigious research grants and the more that are coming from a shrinking number of students, the more interest there is in meeting learners where they are. Wiley, a textbook company in the education space, surveyed students on this topic. It found that 80 percent of students say it's important or very important for schools to offer real company-led projects, but only 30 percent of instructors nationally say they offer these opportunities.[38]

Model 4: Micro-pathways

After my first five years working on college redesign models, I became convinced that community colleges are the place to start, for one reason: leaders of community colleges faced more of an existential crisis than four-year universities as their enrollment numbers fell harder over the past decade, so they were open to new ideas. Community college enrollment has fallen 37 percent since 2010, by nearly 2.6 million.[39] And the data were telling colleges that more students wanted career-focused, shorter-term programs.[40] While four-year universities have an average attrition rate of 25 percent after the first year, at two-year colleges, it's almost twice that bad, which suggests the old degree model is not meeting enough of them where they are.[41] If anything can save these colleges, numbers show that it is probably shorter-term certificates, which are gaining in popularity at many community colleges.[42] (The other fast-growing offering at community colleges is dual enrollment, when high school students take college classes.)[43]

Abigail, a nineteen-year-old from Tucson, Arizona, was one among the missing millions. She told her adviser that she always felt like she "struggled with school, even though she never struggled."[44] After high school, she tried a few classes at Pima, the local community college in Tucson, but things didn't work out. Pima's traditional mission had been to help students get their associate of arts degree and hopefully transfer to the flagship public University of Arizona, in the same city. Nationally, only 13 percent of financial aid recipients who start community college get all the way through the four-year degree.[45] Pima's statistics track with the national averages. To Abigail's credit, when community college didn't work out for her, she saw something else on Pima's website that caught her eye: Fast Track, a certificate to become an emergency medical technician.

Abigail was struck by the twelve-week length of this new program and that the $1,500 in tuition would be covered by workforce grants at the college. After she completed the program and passed her National Registry of Emergency Medical Technicians certification exam, it took Abigail only a couple of months to secure a position with a local emergency medical services agency. According to her program mentor, Abigail is now considering the next step on the stepladder of micro-pathways, the higher-paying paramedic and firefighter program and certification. And while her initial certification program doesn't earn her college credit now, it will count for 9.5 credits if and when she enters the college's paramedic or nursing degree program.

Ian Roark, the senior vice president of workforce training at Pima, says he was surprised when the website first went up introducing six micro-pathways ranging from health-care technology to automotive technology. The college wasn't ready to handle the demand and learned that it needed to move to monthly rolling start times, which is not typical for colleges. "When we did our first marketing campaign, in the first month, we had 1,000 people reach out. We've never seen a response like that to any other new program," he recalls.[46] Ian has been most pleased that the majority of graduates so far, 114 as of publication, are stop-outs, people who are coming back to Pima a second time, to try a new and shorter approach to community college. Another 100 enrollees came from a city partnership with a local homeless shelter.

Nationally, the nonprofit Education Design Lab is working with seventy community colleges and state community college systems to implement the micro-pathway, stepladder approach across more than one hundred job roles so far. The new programs are called micro-pathways because they are shorter than a two-year degree, fully focused on preparing learners for a particular high-demand role, but providing visibility and credit toward a degree pathway if the learner wants it later on. These roles account for about 30 percent of job openings nationally, and designing the credential programs with employers is meant to solve the issue that, in many cases, regional employer demand doesn't match what is being taught or offered.[47]

The micro-pathways are required to include "design criteria" aimed at standardizing quality and return on investment for learners.[48] The criteria range from length of program (a year or less), to industry endorsement of the skills taught, to meaningful job demand at family-sustaining salaries for graduates, and—one that might surprise—to training on soft or durable skills, which regional employers are called on to recommend. Most of the three hundred large and small employer partners have chosen a "critical thinking" credential to add to the pathway. "Collaboration" is the second most popular. For Abigail's EMT certification, the employers chose "intercultural competency."

Where do micro-pathways fit on the "experience-first" continuum? To be honest, most colleges in the first cohort didn't start out in 2020 thinking about building experience into the pathways—instead, they were responding to the freefall in degree applicants and strong interest in certificates.[49] But as the micro-pathway model evolves, work-based experience has become a goal because employers are asking for it, and so are learners. "These work-based learning experiences provide a safety net for community college learners," says Lisa Larson, senior vice president of the Education Design Lab. "They give learners an opportunity to work with an employer in a way that's less risky than going out and looking for that first job."[50] Colleges are creating micro-pathways with on-the-job training for roles ranging from construction management in Seattle to health-care administration in Montana. Lisa says that Toyota is weaving students into the workflow, building a work schedule around their school schedule, to train next-generation auto mechanics in Idaho. All of these paths are being or will be offered as paid work-and-learn experiences at the community college and on-site at the company. This is not so far off from the fully integrated model I said was near impossible at the beginning of this chapter, but the numbers so far are very small.

What the colleges don't have yet, as these pilots and programs start up in different variations around the country, is clear data on how well the pathways set learners up for a professional career trajectory. This is why I am still unwilling to state that there are surefire pathways to professional success outside the degree. Not that college is surefire either. As we will see in the next chapter, the debt-versus-degree trade-off has paid off less and less over time for all groups of college goers.[51] But do these micro-pathways set learners up for lifelong learning, for a stepladder approach to building agile career paths with work-ready milestones? We don't know yet. Remember, these are mostly "noncredit" learners. Their journeys were not tracked. Now, with all the interest from consumers and employers, the data infrastructure is being put in place.

As this book is being written, Congress is considering landmark legislation that would extend federal financial aid to noncredit micro-pathways like these, if they show hiring results and economic gains for students. While Pima has figured out how to cobble together workforce grants to fund short-termers like Abigail, it's not typical that colleges can find grants to fund their noncredit students, and it's not typical that employers are stepping up. The out-of-pocket cost is certainly suppressing enrollment for short-term programs, according to my conversations with several community colleges.[52] And congressional action could change that dramatically.

Model 5: The Weave at Scale

If you don't believe that students and their parents are turning up the dial to demand experience-first education, consider Northeastern University in Boston. In the past four years, application rates have risen almost 50 percent, to ninety-six thousand by 2023, making the once upstart the most highly sought-after private college in the country.[53] Northeastern has lately become one of those elite schools offering a handful of slots to the lucky seventy-five thousand students I mentioned earlier. Its acceptance rate, 5.6 percent in 2023 at the flagship campus, now rivals those at some of the schools in the Ivy League.[54] It is quite a Cinderella story for a college that was started by the YMCA at the end of the nineteenth century to offer Greek working immigrants flexible, low-cost classes. "And that's all because of co-op," says Connie Yowell, until recently senior vice chancellor for educational innovation at Northeastern and now head of special projects.[55] This college's co-op program is the envy of higher education.

Northeastern students usually do two years of traditional class work, including a co-op prep class where they learn how to interview, how to get their résumés together, and how to work in a professional setting. Then, one of the university's 250 co-op coordinators (no, that's not a typo) helps them get a real job for six months. They leave the university, they stop paying tuition while they are working, and then they come back. Which, for some, means a slightly longer road to graduation. I myself was drawn in by the buzz even back in 2012 when I took my daughter to Northeastern on a college tour. I was amazed at the hundreds of parents and high schoolers from all over the world who packed the auditorium on a spring weekday morning, eyes popping as the job placements where our kids might work during college flashed on the presentation screen . . . Coca-Cola, ABC-TV, the White House. Wow.

Jonathan Mejia, a recent grad, believes his smooth school-to-career transition was made possible by the co-op program. As a first-generation college student, he had wanted to study journalism since high school, but until he did really well his first year at Salem State University, he didn't feel confident applying to top schools. He felt lucky to be able to transfer into Northeastern on a full-ride scholarship, tuition plus room and board, but he only realized how lucky when he stepped through the doors of CNBC global headquarters outside New York City for his co-op job. "I think it was the moment I was able to secure the dream, to get in," Jonathan recalled. "As you know, it's so hard to get into the TV industry, but they say once you're in, anything can happen."[56] (I can attest to this myself, as someone who spent thirteen years in TV news. Experience has always been more important than a degree in that field.)

Most students do two six-month co-ops and they are paid at least fifteen dollars an hour, but many, in engineering, for example, are paid much more. The university also tries to help with housing. Connie says, "Anecdotally, what our students will tell you is that the value of the first co-op often is to learn what they don't want to do. The value of the second is to start building skills towards a career."

Focused on journalism from the outset, Jonathan only needed one co-op experience to launch his career. After he learned how to be useful in the CNBC newsroom and then took a class/internship that summer traveling abroad to report, by the end of his junior year, he had a paid job writing for WHDH, a Boston TV station. When he graduated in 2019, he had enough experience to be hired as an on-air reporter at the CBS station in El Paso, Texas. When we interviewed, he was negotiating to move to a much bigger market, Houston, and I later learned that he got the job!

In every semester, ten thousand of the thirty thousand undergrads and grad students pause their tuition payments, accept jobs, and are out working in their co-op placements. The current strategic plan, titled Experience Unleashed, could be a blueprint for other colleges to consider. However, Connie acknowledges that managing this at scale is a "massive, massive undertaking." Part of the unleashing is coordinating all these students coming and going. Only a college or university that has set up the infrastructure, faculty, and student support systems, plus the alumni network, from the start can make this work. "The thing that is so hard about experiential learning is that it requires that you [the college] go out in the world to have an impact," Connie explains. "You can only do that with partners. And universities are horrible at partnering and partnerships." I wouldn't discourage schools from trying, and lots of colleges are building up their employer engagement capacity, but it requires some dedicated resources and leadership focus.[57] Northeastern's website touts that 97 percent of students are employed or in grad school within nine months of graduation.[58]

But every one of them has traversed the experience chasm, and not with a job at Chick-fil-A.

CAN MORE COLLEGES DELIVER EXPERIENCE?

What are the lessons that come out of this chapter as we meet some colleges that are skillifying the degree and a few that are solving the catch-22 of getting students hired without experience? First, two caveats. For one, let me admit that some of the colleges I profile are not like the others. Northeastern is an outlier that forged its "experience-first" model one hundred years ago, at its inception. When we see a "radical model," chances are it was built in at the inception of that institution or department, or it was instituted under a suburban governance structure (outside the credit-bearing part of the college). Northeastern and WGU are two radical models. The other colleges profiled demonstrate the milestones and challenges of the journey as traditional colleges try to adapt to the changing consumer and employer markets they serve.

The other important caveat is that all colleges are not created equal, so this evolution will have many flavors. The country's technical colleges and most community colleges have no aversion to the T-word (*trades*) or the V-word (*vocations*). Many of the degrees in these colleges have always been designed to prepare learners for roles such as auto mechanics and HVAC repair technicians, construction workers, and forklift operators. Four-year colleges, from state comprehensives to land grant universities to prestigious research institutions, have traditionally seen themselves as preparing learners to be corporate managers, researchers, doctors, nurses, lawyers, IT specialists, entrepreneurs, educators, and policy makers, to name some major fields.

But what is interesting is that technology is blurring the lines of all these professions, in a good way. The continuum from advanced auto mechanic roles to roles in the semiconductor industry is making it hard to tell which is a trade role and which is "white collar." Is an electrician "blue collar" and an electrician managing conversion of the electric grid to get the country ready for electric cars "green collar"? IBM is calling some 50 percent of its jobs "new collar," and the only distinction is that they are professional roles that no longer require a college degree. But in this chapter, I have tried to convey that most traditional four-year colleges have yet to fully embrace the blurred continuum. And they are leaving a lot of job preparation opportunities on the table in their fear of being labeled trade schools. They are willing to name the skills they are teaching and to provide job experiences, up to a point, but they see it as a slippery slope. The more elite the college, the less likely you are to see the word *training* in the mission statement or strategic plan. Fair enough.

Design Criteria from Colleges

As I have asked in previous chapters, what lessons and "design criteria" can we take forward for a new national model? These colleges bring into living color many of the elements that demonstrate what is possible today in the current higher education system, so they are important to consider as we throw pennies (or NFTs) into the wishing well. And the pushback we see in today's colleges represents valid concerns that we should not let the pendulum swing too far from preparing scholars to preparing workers. I will pull all these ideas together in the last chapter, as we explore a blueprint for the next national education model, but here I will summarize one core user need identified through each of the five models we just explored.

Design Criteria from Experience-First College Pilots

1. Job-ready skills should be mapped into every course.
2. Students need an incentive to finish time-consuming micro-credentials.
3. "Real-world" experience should be mapped into classes.
4. Inexpensive, stackable micro-pathways should be an alternative to college or a path back for stop-outs.
5. Ideally, degree students should be provided two work experiences, one to explore and one to get their foot in the door.

I use the term *experience first* in this chapter, knowing full well that most colleges can't get to the full weave between classroom learning and on-the-job learning. But each of the case studies in this chapter demonstrates how colleges are trying to bridge the last mile between school and hiring.

1. WGU shows us how job-ready skills should be mapped into every college course, with a coach to help you figure out how to translate learning outcomes into skills and gather important industry context.[59]
2. UT shows us that students need an incentive to finish mostly online and time-consuming micro-credentials, such as having certificates count as credit toward their majors.
3. UND tries to map "real-world" experience into classes to provide résumé-enhancing "starter skills."
4. Pima Community College has reengineered its certificates into inexpensive, stackable micro-pathways, designed with employers, to give college stop-outs a shorter-term model to come back to.
5. Northeastern University provides degree students with two work experiences, one to explore and one to get their foot in the door. And they don't have to pay tuition while they are "experiencing" with employers.

The Harvard Project on Workforce has researched interventions that colleges have considered to help students achieve career outcomes, and the most widespread, researched, and successful practice currently is internships.[60] I don't feature internships in the book because they are well understood and widely offered. The debate about internships is access: the more exclusive and smaller the school, the better the chance its students can land a meaningful, paid internship. For example, 40 percent and 50 percent, respectively, of Black and Latino college students attend community colleges, which have few resources to source career-enhancing work experiences that pay students enough to quit their day jobs.[61] As this book was going to press, the Mellon Foundation announced a large program to fund paid internships for humanities majors at five public universities, although not community colleges.[62]

In this chapter I have tried to capture how colleges are responding to pressure to change their job preparation model. The two iron gates holding back more than incremental change are the inside stronghold of faculty and the outside stronghold of the accrediting bodies, which determine whether colleges get or keep their access to government funding for tuition. Together, these hold much innovation in check, until the outside pressure becomes so strong that concessions have to be made. I believe we are at that point now, which is why bipartisan funding bills are before Congress to broaden the definition of a "college student," or at least how much time they spend in the classroom. In the not-too-distant future, I believe more learners who are on nondegree career prep tracks will be eligible for federal financial aid. This is a huge shift in thinking. And already, several states have moved to a "pay for performance" model, forcing colleges to change. Laws like the one I mentioned in Texas and at least fourteen other states have begun rewarding colleges that get their graduates to meaningful work, and if this means redefining or shortening the degree, or thinking about how to build experience into college, that's now acceptable.[63]

5

High Schools

Is "College for All" Dead?

We are very, very good at supporting our highest academic
students. . . . We're not able to do that for students who
are choosing professional pathways.

—ANALISE GONZALEZ, DENVER SCHOOL OF SCIENCE
AND TECHNOLOGY

If you're wondering who is on the front lines of the battle to save the college dream, it is just about everyone involved in high school education in
America—teenagers, parents, teachers, administrators, and the unsung
warriors, counselors. On one hand, it's their job to sell college. But in many
quarters it's getting harder. At one high school I visited, a fiercely devoted
college prep school, two students told me their teachers were recommending that they think twice before attending college because they (the teachers) were still paying off loans. High schools now see significantly fewer
students opting to attend college after graduation compared with twenty
years ago.[1] But what alternative paths can counselors be recommending
without being accused of "tracking"? Tracking is the now maligned practice in which K–12 schools decide who is college material and who is not,

sealing kids' fates with the classes they place students in or the postsecondary paths they don't push them toward.[2]

Tracking is often as subtle as determining, without consulting a student's family, whether the student will be placed in Algebra 1 in eighth grade versus ninth grade. The former would give a student time to get all the way through Calculus by senior year, an important signal to competitive colleges. More dramatic forms of tracking include sending students to career and technical education (CTE) programs, often as early as ninth grade. Those are programs that help a high school student prepare for a noncollege track, for roles in aviation, auto mechanics, what used to include the "trades" but now, as we'll see, cover much more.

Anthony Carnevale, founder of Georgetown University's Center on Education and the Workforce, says the end of tracking and beginning of "college for all" was a reaction to the landmark 1983 *A Nation at Risk* report, in which the Reagan administration's Department of Education laid out a depressing picture of the country's education future readiness. Tony explained, "So, suddenly, if you're a governor or mayor, and you were a good soldier, you went in and did the right thing and built a 'college for all' system, with testing, the whole thing. And then suddenly you're graduating classes from high school and half the kids had nowhere to go. . . . We built a 'college for all' system and much to the detriment of a lot of less advantaged people in America."[3]

ARE WE STILL TRACKING?

"College for all" gained traction throughout the 1990s and was at full steam when I joined the public charter school movement in the 2000s.[4] So I was surprised when I recently began conducting interviews for this book, a decade after leaving the charter school world in 2012. I can say from my meetings with counselors, teachers, students, and researchers that the messaging about college is changing on the front lines. Now, stigmas about trade jobs and preferences for college are getting scrambled. More students are asking to be tracked if it means sidestepping college debt or an uncertain financial gamble toward a better life. More CTE paths require the same math and English proficiency as the college prep requirements. (One mom told me her son's CTE track had more rigorous requirements than the college prep diploma.) As I said in the last chapter, the lines between trade and professional roles are blurring. Yesterday's stigma is today's high-demand, potentially high-salary, profession. But do families know this?

Around the US, that is the conundrum. As high schools get better at evaluating the paths their alumni have taken, they are recognizing that a "college or bust" strategy isn't working for an alarming proportion of the student body. We'll meet some of those schools momentarily, but what pathways should be recommended instead? That's the dilemma several counselors and school administrators painted for me. The options are unclear, underfunded, unproven, and mostly noncredit, meaning financial aid hasn't covered them.[5] And most of them don't offer what sociologist Caitlin Zaloom describes in her book *Indebted* as "open futures."[6] Or what national workforce nonprofit Jobs for the Future advocates for in various reports: "no dead ends."[7] Or what Swiss researchers explaining their own system call "permeability."[8]

ON THE FRONT LINES IN DENVER

I interviewed a high school senior named Daniel who sticks with me, because he was extremely articulate about his choices on one level.[9] His friends had briefed him about the pros and cons of trade school versus college, but he didn't know much about what it would take to get to his dream job.

"I'd like to do an apprenticeship because I think I know how the trade life works," Daniel said. "You can go to a trade school for, like, a year to get your certificate. Then you could be without a job for the next three years because you have zero experience. So that's the problem with trade schools is that trade schools don't give you experience."[10]

We met on the low couches in the student lounge at the Cedar campus of the Denver School of Science and Technology (DSST), where the walls were covered with pennants from the colleges the teachers had attended.

It's part of the "visual culture" to normalize college going for DSST's 7,200 students. DSST allowed me to look under the hood and meet counselors and students who are grappling with a changing world that feels like it is challenging their mission. The administrators had chosen some students to speak to me who were on the fence about college, even though this campus had the highest college enrollment rate of all Denver public schools in 2023.[11] Daniel was more than on the fence. He told me, "Even if I had the money, right, if I had all the money in the world, I still wouldn't do it. Because I just don't feel like it's worth the time, I wouldn't want to put one year or two years of my life into something and then halfway through realize that I don't want to do it."

It's November, showtime for college applications. Daniel feels the anxiety that I heard from all the seniors I interviewed. In his case, his mom worked hard to get him into lottery-based DSST because she wanted him to have the college dream she could not secure for herself, as her own mom became ill in Mexico and she had to drop out of college there. "I feel like she really gets on me about college because she lost, like, almost everything that she wanted to do," Daniel wistfully explained. "Because she wasn't focused on college and everything that happened to her, like losing her opportunity to be a nurse and to become a doctor. Like it wasn't her fault. But, I don't think she believes that."

Despite his mom's pressure and the school's expectations, Daniel is not currently planning to go to college, because, like many of the young men I interviewed in different states, he dislikes the academic setting and can't imagine four more years of it. Many of them told me, "I want to work with my hands" and start earning money now. Daniel disclosed that he'd like to maybe work with cars. In fact, he said he'd like to design cars one day.

But is a mechanical engineering role likely to be available to someone without a degree? It is not always clear to students that some "working with your hands" jobs have limited career trajectories. I described Daniel's situation to Paul Sinanian, head of apprenticeships at BMW, who sits three thousand miles away in Spartanburg, South Carolina. He's hungry for well-schooled folks like Daniel. He said an apprenticeship would be a viable track these days. You can rise through different roles to work on car design without a degree at BMW.[12] But since Denver doesn't have car manufacturing apprenticeships, what options does a student there realistically have? To date, apprenticeship searches and placements have been a local affair, unlike the college sweepstakes that take many families on road trips around the country in pursuit of a best-fit future.

Analise Gonzalez is now head of postsecondary success for all five of DSST's high schools. But she started by overseeing the college-going mission at one school that opened in 2019. She recalled, "It was very much like a four year 'college or bust' kind of mindset. And so I honestly did feel a lot of pressure with our founding class to reach for your 100%, as many kids as possible, a 'do whatever it takes' kind of mentality [to get them to college]."[13]

Like a lot of the college prep public charter schools that proliferated in the 2000s, DSST focused hard on data, tracking what happens to its students after high school. DSST has data to be proud of, when compared against the national averages. The vast majority of the students are Hispanic, and a strong percentage come from lower-income families. Eighty percent sign up for college, and 71 percent actually showed up in the fall of 2022, at mostly four-year universities, more than double the national average for Hispanic students.[14] But sadly, almost a third of those students end up leaving college without graduating.

As the data have become clearer, the school has shifted strategies. "It's not that we're swinging back all the way to the other side," Analise explained, "but we're trying to see the nuances behind the data a little bit. And also reflect on what unintentional harm we may be doing to students, by pigeon-holing them into a particular choice." Recently, she and her team have been charged with building out a more individualized advising practice that still remains true to the school's mission to prepare everyone for college success.

To see the dilemma faced by schools and counselors now, it's useful to step into "senior seminar." This is a weekly class focused on getting all the kids into college, devoting a bigger block of the precious schedule to advising than most schools around the country. By the day I attended in November, the students had already submitted at least one college application. It's required. And now they were given class time and counseling to research scholarships. I was given permission to walk around and chat with students. While most were confidently working with each other and seemed upbeat, a few looked uneasy about the assignment. I stopped at Cristofer's desk.

"So, what are you thinking about college?" I half whispered.

"It's too risky," he half whispered back.

"Why?"

"It's not what I know. It's not what my people do."

"What do they do?"

"Construction, trades."

DSST and some of the other charter networks were not conceived to help students like Daniel and Cristofer find a noncollege path. Many have built brands around "no excuses," pushing all of their students toward the dream of college, often setting up shop in urban or rural districts where the competing traditional public schools had lower college-going rates. They were born from a mission view that all students could get to the college dream with the right support. (A caveat here: Many traditional public [noncharter] schools also provide rigorous curricula and strong college access supports. I acknowledge that the charter school movement has become controversial in that its schools compete with traditional neighborhood schools for funding and don't always deliver better results.) Public charter schools serve roughly 8 percent of the K–12 population, and a strong proportion of these are low-income students and students of color.[15] Many of the charter schools were founded in the early 2000s, on the heels of landmark education legislation No Child Left Behind, around the time that candidate George W. Bush popularized the phrase "the soft bigotry of low expectations."[16]

As Analise explained, "We are very, very good at supporting our highest academic students. So last year, we had 11 Quest Bridge scholars across the network, we had three Gates scholars.[17] So I would say we are supporting students who are choosing the most selective schools, we're really able to counsel students on a nuanced level. We're not able to do that for students who are choosing professional pathways."

Professional pathways. DSST is very thoughtful about language. As its administrators have thought about how to destigmatize the term *trade school*, they've chosen to use the phrase *professional pathway*, which encompasses trades and other nondegree trajectories that could lead to family-sustaining wages. It means that you are leaving high school for a more immediate and focused path to a profession. The word *professional* itself connotes a career with upward prospects rather than just a job.

Analise doesn't feel like DSST is tracking. Every student leaves DSST with a college acceptance letter in hand and at least one AP class under their belt. But even here, at a school that parents specifically apply to because they want their kids to attend college, the rising tide of questioning the degree sends some strong waves onto the beach.

Showing Students All Their Options

In 2023, DSST partnered with a new service called Willow Education that is beginning to expand to other charter schools in Denver and elsewhere.[18] Willow is creating an online pathway recommendation tool that blends college options with trade and noncollege programs. This is a major departure for college-focused high schools—that is, to combine the suggested list of options in an apples-to-apples format. The students take an interests quiz that suggests personality strengths such as "organization wizard" or "practical problem solver." Then it provides five choices in a personalized list of college and training options, which students can "heart" or reject. The recommendations are skewed to their college or noncollege aspirations, as well as their responses on affordability, completion rates for their demographic, and their high school GPA.

James Cryan, founder of Willow Education, is himself a charter school network founder and was fully on the "college for all" bandwagon. He has now embraced a new calling: creating a more holistic recommendation system, one that recognizes the blending of all the possible paths to family-sustaining careers. "It's kind of a false binary way to see the world, that the world is either college or not college, or college and professional programs," James says. "Half of students who graduate high school will never go to college. And, back of the envelope, of those who do, about half will graduate, and so really the current system of guiding people into college is only serving about a quarter of high school graduates every year."[19] So the recommendation engine uses the data you might have heard about—namely, that a college degree, if you graduate, could earn you an extra $1,200,000 over a lifetime (compared with the high school degree)—but it customizes those data to take into account the likelihood that someone both with your grades and in your demographic will graduate.[20] I was surprised by how many students were familiar with the term *return on investment* (ROI). The recommendation list includes the cost of programs in the ROI calculation, whether it's a degree or a certificate or trade school, so that families can judge the programs by the same metrics. And frankly, comparing the choices, the lifetime ROI looked better for some of the short-term programs.

All of the counselors I spoke to suggested that many of today's students are anxious about these choices, so "college dream" counseling has to take into account the anxiety and readiness factors. Perhaps they've always been anxious, but now the data overwhelmingly show that at least 40 percent of all students don't graduate, and for every two Black and Hispanic students who take the college step, nearly half end up back at the starting gate, or worse, if there is debt involved.[21] If they feel like they are being pushed or can't see themselves in college, James argues, "let's help them take a smaller, less expensive step. Let's show them options that keep doors open."

So, for example, Daniel's recommendation page showed two four-year college recommendations: aerospace engineering at the University of Colorado, Boulder, and finance management at Regis University. It also showed several shorter-term programs, including a car mechanic program and an HVAC apprenticeship. Each was curated based on Daniel's GPA and responses about distance from home and affordability.

I had been following Willow Ed's work for several months when College Board, the biggest and oldest player in college access, went public in 2023 with its own expanded "college" search tool, BigFuture. It had begun to include nontraditional pathways alongside college options for student-initiated searches. This was a big admission on the part of the one-hundred-year-old College Board—perhaps we have come to the point at which college can be redefined more broadly. Allison Danielson was leading the BigFuture development at the time. "So much of the data had indicated that [college] was the right thing to unlock economic mobility for people to really get more people into the middle class," she said. "But I think, you know, after a couple decades of seeing the results where you have a lot of people who still don't start at a four year institution. And for those who start, what you're seeing is that many of them don't complete, right?"[22]

Nearly 90 percent of all high school students interact with the College Board, through tests like the PSAT and SAT, which these days are offered free to everyone during the school day. As of early 2024, fifteen million users had searched for a "pathway" choice in the expanded search engine. And the board is currently working to broaden the choices even further to include programs like Year Up and apprenticeships. "College choices are career choices," Allison explained. "Everybody is out there trying to get to a good career and build a successful life. And so, if we start to see college as a pathway and not a destination, and then you see it alongside other viable pathways, I think it becomes a lot more obvious how you lean in and try to solve this problem. But if you try to define people as 'college kids' or 'career kids,' you kind of go back into that old paradigm, that's where we get into trouble."

The federal government, after years of work, has stepped up the transparency requirements for all colleges, short-term programs, and other pathways. Starting in 2026, all players will be required to report how affordable loan payments will be and whether programs are successful at delivering a meaningful earnings bump for graduates.[23] This information will find its way, for sure, into the growing number of holistic recommendation engines, helping parents, students, and counselors pick out what the field has begun calling "credentials of meaning." That's a broader, more inclusive term for pathways after high school.

To Go or Not to Go: It's All About GPA

I was drawn to college prep charter schools for part of this research because they are outliers in their focus on college prep and they share their data even when things go south. They are what I defined in an earlier chapter as "extreme users" of the college dream construct. This is often why parents enroll their children: to access their services and to provide their children with acculturation toward a college path.[24] For many families, the charter school stands in for the connections, consultants, and private prep classes that wealthier families can afford.[25] So there is a lot to learn from these schools about the college-going trends at the front lines.

I was quite surprised how willing the nation's largest charter school network, KIPP, was to share how the college-going climate at its forty public high schools around the country has changed. Tessa Kratz at KIPP NYC says that in her school, interestingly, money is not the main obstacle for their two thousand high school students.[26] It's GPA. Ninety percent of students come from low-income families, so they qualify for federal Pell Grants plus a New York State version of the Pell Grant (the Tuition Assistance Program), which fully cover their college costs in the City University of New York system. And if they have the top GPAs to get into an expensive, elite college, those tend to be "meet full need" grants, so their families won't have to pay out of pocket.

It's a "nothing to lose" situation if you have the grades. Yet KIPP NYC's college enrollment numbers are down, from a very impressive 92 percent in 2019 to 78 percent for 2023. A big reason for the drop, Tessa says, was an intentional shift in strategy to counsel students with GPAs below 2.0 toward CTE pathways.[27] Even before the pandemic, only 20 percent of their alumni with a high school GPA below 2.0 were graduating from community colleges.[28] GPAs took a big hit during the pandemic. And, she says GPA performance affects desire to go to college. "If they have a 2.0 GPA, they haven't shown an academic identity or feel confident in their abilities. There's a real risk, then, of pushing a college-going option on them. We want to make sure that they're understanding what all their options are and feel really confident about whatever option they're choosing and connected to it," Tessa says. She expects a COVID-19 ripple effect to continue for several years, with this being one more pressure point steering students away from college.

Nationwide, KIPP has 275 preK–12 schools. As Ajuah Helton, vice president of KIPP Forward at the KIPP Foundation, mused, "This is a very,

very interesting time." She was up front about how they've had to change up the mission at the national office. Before the pandemic, KIPP's national office was supporting their regions with a "multiple pathways" approach, meaning kids who didn't want to go to college would be advised about other options. But by 2023, alarmed by the pandemic's corrosive effect on academic performance around the country, they retreated from that strategy to double or triple down on the front end: making sure students were academically college ready. Says Ajuah, "We are a school, we need to get school right. The number one goal: 100% college readiness for true choice. It's not true choice if you're not eligible for your state college system, right?"[29]

So even as more students linger at the college doorway, KIPP National sees its role contracting. Now the goal is making sure students are college ready.

KIPP NYC has bucked the trend among KIPP's thirty regions. Its administrators felt compelled to try to do both: double down on academics and double down on supporting the growing numbers of students who are not college bound. It's one of a few KIPP regions nationwide to provide advising after graduation to those students who are not on a college track. KIPP NYC has joined forces with another charter school network, Achievement First, to create the Postsecondary Success Collaborative, which provides six years of support services to all of its alumni, and recently expanded the offering to KIPP New Jersey and KIPP Philadelphia, which are seeing the same trends away from college and are hungry to do more than watch students slip away.

THE NEW CTE

Remember Patrick from chapter 3, when we explored employers who intercepted high school students on their way to college?

For this chapter on the front lines of the college dream, I thought it would be useful to go back to Patrick's public high school, now seven years after he graduated, to get a look at what I figured, even back then, was a modern approach to CTE at a suburban high school. I was particularly curious because his high school has now replaced my own as Fairfax County,

Virginia's CTE hub.[30] Would it be different from how my high school, W. T. Woodson, treated CTE in the 1970s? The only career training I could see at my two-thousand-student high school was for carpentry, auto repair, and cosmetology. And to me, it quite literally seemed like the movie *Grease*, in which John Travolta and his friends feel like outsiders in their vocational classes, being snubbed by the college-bound kids in their letter sweaters. It seemed like the VoTech kids got tapped on the shoulder in tenth grade and stepped across a threshold to a different world. I would only see my former girlfriends when they took parking lot smoking breaks in their pink beauty school smocks.[31] (Yes, smoking was allowed on campus in the 1970s.) What had piqued my interest in Patrick's story, decades later, was that he didn't have to choose between a vocational track and a college track as students did when I went to high school in the same district. He could dabble. And not get tracked.

Since Patrick graduated from Chantilly High School in 2018 and took his IT classes and certifications at the STEM Academy, the countywide vocational center has seen a surge in interest. While Fairfax County is among the top five richest counties in America, it is also very diverse demographically.[32] A third of the students are from low-income families.[33] Administrator Scott Settar cites the pandemic (again) as one reason that more students are trying to get away from their traditional classrooms. During COVID-19, he says, "they missed the opportunity to connect with other people and missed the opportunity to problem solve together. They missed the opportunity to have hands on a machine or to use a tool to fix a problem. They didn't have that opportunity to do this sitting at home on a computer. We've always been near capacity here in our classes, but after COVID our numbers have increased astronomically, really."[34]

More students are signing up, and more employers are knocking on the door to hire students before they get to college rather than waiting to find them on job boards. Settar describes visits from the local hospital system, home builders, tech companies, and government defense contractors. In the case of one defense contractor, Scott says they are trying to intercept students and help them get required security clearances before they "make mistakes" in college that could render them ineligible. Another company told me that one-third of its applicants wash out when it comes to drug test-ing. Marijuana use is legal in Virginia, but not under federal law. It's be-come a big hiring obstacle.

Scott offered to provide me a tour of the campus, which is attached to the traditional high school. Instead of pennants commemorating sports victories in basketball or football (or the college pennants from teachers' alma maters), this campus's entrance boasts skills pennants, in both tradi-tional trade skills and some crossover skills. The academy has won national SkillsUSA championships in customer service and barbering, for example, and a state championship in technical math and veterinary assisting. Here, the visual culture promotes building competencies, and afterschool clubs in cybersecurity and robotics draw students to compete in skills challenges.

As we stepped into classrooms, up and down two long hallways, I was impressed to see "hands on" come to life. The medical assisting class was working on Hal, a life-size computerized patient whose symptoms can be controlled remotely by the teacher. These students, mostly girls, were work-ing toward their CPR and then their medical assistant certifications. In one of the classes that Patrick had taken, students—all boys—were learn-ing computer wiring, working toward their Cisco networking certification. Another class was fully outfitted with a computer-aided design system, 3-D printer, and robotic arm for students to learn how to program automation tasks.

What's different about the new CTE? If I had to boil it down to one phrase, I would say *blended and permeable learning*. In my day, when the CTE program felt like a fork in the road of life, whether you were "tracked" or not, you made a career choice by age fifteen or sixteen. It was hard to turn back. And the choices were limited at that.

HOW TO REWIRE HIGH SCHOOL AND THE NARRATIVE

It's useful at this point to step into a community where technology is really blurring the lines between trades and professional roles for some of the best jobs in town.

As I mentioned earlier, Paul Sinanian is head of apprenticeships at BMW's only US auto plant in Spartanburg, South Carolina, where a luxury car comes off the mostly automated line every seventy-three seconds. When he came on the job in 2019, it was a struggle to find highly technical workers. They had an apprenticeship program, but it wasn't producing enough pipeline. And now, with an electric battery plant coming online in 2026, he's felt the pressure to double down to build new mind-sets across the board. "So, what we're doing this year is we are going into fourth grade. We're going into middle schools. We're going into high schools. We are actually hosting a teacher and guidance counselor camp on site to teach them about what manufacturing is," Paul explained. "That it's clean. It's not a dingy textile mill." (South Carolina was home to 14 percent of all textile workers in the US until the industry waned in the 1990s.)[35]

BMW has a unique offer in Spartanburg and nearby Greenville: a free two-year apprenticeship that includes hybrid classroom training and a free associate of arts degree at one of the nearby South Carolina technical colleges. "The parents don't support it as much because they don't understand the idea of a two-year technical degree versus a four-year degree," Paul said. "They don't understand the benefits and potential for a lucrative career. And the students don't get engaged as much because their parents don't push it." Paul continued, "Plus guidance counselors and teachers have a difficult time understanding it too, so our focus this year is to try to bring the education for those three key people, the guidance counselor, the parents and the teachers." It's almost like Paul has to rewire the thinking and mind-set of the whole community in a manufacturing town with companies like BMW, Michelin, and Lockheed Martin that hasn't caught up with the new narrative.

Larry Miller serves at one of the technical colleges, Greenville Tech, as vice president of learning and workforce. He sees things a little differently. School districts have been rewired to support dual enrollment programs. That's where students can take college courses while still in high school, and millions have begun doing so around the country in the past few years.

Greenville Tech has recently made its dual enrollment program free for all students, boosting enrollment by 40 percent. The college is just beginning to build student interest in using some of those college credits for technical certification. But here's where the silos slow things down. Larry describes how the "five buses" problem makes it hard to deliver a job-ready student by the end of high school.[36] Learners have to be shipped around between their home high schools, five county career centers, and the college campus, back again, and to workplaces if they have an apprenticeship. And matching dual-enrolled students with companies is a "boutique" enterprise; companies take between ten and twenty students, and each one has special needs. Neither high schools nor employers are wired yet to prepare young people for the kind of technical training high-end manufacturers need, when they need it.[37] Blended learning, what we call the weave, isn't easy, academically or logistically.

A good technical or community college system can be the market maker. Managing and staying current with different employers' skill needs is not for the fainthearted. Larry provides some color: "Just as a good example, [manufacturing] plant automation is getting such that the Internet of Things is creating cybersecurity threats on the shop floor. I've got demand now [from employers] to also cross train my Mechatronics [robotics] students and other students in how to harden the shop floor from the threat of cyber-attack, as such attacks are on the rise. So how do we do that within the credit hour limitations of a certificate or degree program?"[38] Larry says he is working to break down the silos at his own college to cross-train robotics students with enough cyber and AI skills to protect and maximize plant operations. In South Carolina, increasingly, the technical college is being asked to prepare the high school grad for technical work readiness or apprenticeship, since most students are choosing to go either directly to work after high school or to a four-year college.

It's important to stress how rare these visible pathways are for students, their parents, and school counselors. Paul is given space to make the sale. He works for a German company, and Germany is a country that embraced apprenticeships early. And Larry at Greenville Tech has Apprenticeship Carolina behind him, a state-funded initiative based at his college system's office that recruits employers across the state. I interviewed these players because their programs are exemplary, and the rewiring is underway.

But there are so few Paul Sinanians and Larry Millers who are able to lean into their regions to break down the silos and change the narrative. Until and unless the US rewires the silos, how will the smaller companies, towns, and schools get the word out that professional roles come in many flavors and that they are not Industrial Revolution–era factories anymore? The jobs that await are not necessarily trade jobs, even though some are on the shop floor. And what are the alternatives to being tracked into closed futures, if you don't want to pursue a degree right away? Daniel in Denver would really benefit from this knowledge. Remember, he dreamed of being a car designer, but the trade programs in his area were more geared toward car mechanics. Where is the information that could start him on an open-ended path?

To see how far this blended model of CTE might go, several experts in the field, including Jobs for the Future, pointed me toward the work of New York City, the nation's largest public school system, which is moving quickly to navigate a blended model "at scale." In less than three years, New York City has launched a new initiative called FutureReadyNYC, which really begins to blend school and the workplace for everyone from the very beginning of high school and is now in over 15 percent of the city's high schools.

Sixty-seven high schools were chosen the first year (2022–23) to be FutureReadyNYC schools, which increased to a total of one hundred for 2023–24. Each now offers at least one pathway like data science or other roles in tech, education, health care, and business.[39] The pathways blend in certifications and, taking it one step further than Chantilly, they require work-based learning, which means all students spend time in a workplace, applying what they've learned in class. Granted, this is a relatively easy task in New York City, with its myriad employers and affordable subway transportation.

New York City Public Schools, DSST, KIPP, the Governor's STEM Academy in Virginia, South Carolina's technical colleges—these are thoughtful players that the field has pointed me toward. There are many others, more in cities and suburban centers than in rural areas, given the lack of resources and large employers in the latter. The high schools

I profile are interesting in that they are trying to have it both ways in these confusing times: For one, the bigger schools with more resources strive to "not track" by offering a weave approach with traditional and technical offerings starting in ninth grade. And second, they all—large and small—consider it part of their job to evaluate and present all options to their graduating seniors, with data but without judgment. They are trying to elevate the term *professional pathways* to sit alongside *college pathways*.

In his work at a number of organizations, researcher Alex Cortez has reached a realization: "The only way out of tracking is to focus on the individual," he told me. "To find each person's version of happiness."[40] At his latest post at Bellwether Education Advisors, Alex has built a model for next-generation postsecondary advising that is predicated on the maxim "Choice is power."[41]

Yet a third insight hit me as I compiled research. Every single male new majority learner I interviewed for this and previous chapters wanted "hands-on" learning. Whether they are headed for college or trade school, or anywhere in between, hands-on, career-focused learning gives desk-weary learners some validation that they are employable, or that they can pass different kinds of tests, whether they like academics or not. Might more hands-on learning save any student who would otherwise lose their "academic identity"? Chronic absenteeism in K–12 schools nationwide has remained high after COVID-19, prompting the White House to call for schools to take action.[42] Are high school students voting with their feet, and do hands-on classes make a difference? Research suggests that the answer is yes. High school graduation rates and college readiness levels are much higher for students who enroll in CTE programs.[43]

DESIGN CRITERIA FROM HIGH SCHOOLS

The last chapter of this book will outline design criteria for a new national higher education model, but part of that model has to take into account high school and what we have learned about "user needs" that are causing students to make certain choices and foreclose others. Do we need a senior year of high school? Should it become a career exploration year, with opportunities to breach the experience chasm for those who want to start their next chapter early? Many students are doing it anyway, on their own. One-fifth of all community college enrollment is now made up of high school students.[44]

I'll make recommendations in the last chapter, but I will capture two categories of user needs here.

Design Criteria from High Schools

1. Hands-on learning keeps students engaged.
2. Dual enrollment courses from colleges should be structured to offer career sampling and industry certifications.
3. CTE in high school should be blended with college prep, at least for those who want both.
4. Students need a holistic presentation of all of their high-quality post–high school options.

The clearest design criterion is perhaps the sharpest lesson across all the chapters, brought home by the pandemic: we have to make high school more hands on if we want to sell college as four more years (or any more years) of academia. That might sound simplistic, but it becomes an important design principle when you consider that Gen Z, and frankly all of us, can hear the giant sucking sound of our dissipating attention spans.[45] As I will discuss in the next chapter, men are opting out at alarming rates, claiming that seated academic learning is not for them.[46] But for practical careers, several workforce trade experts told me that men are perfectly willing to weave classroom time with on-the-job training. As we heard electrician apprentice Brian Rhodes-Devey explain cheerfully, he was fine with significant class time as long as it was broken up by on-the-job training.

Second, we need to pry loose some flexibility in the high school schedule for learners to explore careers and to gain certifications that—even if they are college bound—can boost their hourly take-home pay by

25–50 percent, maybe for that part-time job to pay for college, or to get on a stepladder to higher earnings.[47] Perhaps the quietest game changer of the past few years has been the creative use by high schools and colleges of dual enrollment funding, but the use of it is not well connected to learners' career preparation, at least not yet. Research here is limited.

And finally, it was good to see in my research for this chapter just how many groups are now focused on curating quality alternatives to college, and with notable support—or at least without judgment. It is a positive sign that learner-focused groups are finally organizing the data points to build our holistic career GPS. Students need a holistic presentation of not just possible professions, or possible education or training pathways, but how far those pathways might take them and where they tend to dead-end. It is very early days, but groups are coming together to curate higher-quality options to share with students like Daniel and their counselors on the front lines. We haven't had those tools in the past, but it's a new day. And the federal visibility requirements coming soon will make our vision clearer. When empowered by full visibility to unlock the power of choice, schools are less likely to be accused of tracking.

There is an urgency to this work that can't be overstated. As I will describe in the next, penultimate chapter, we can't tear down the leading narrative for the ticket to the American Dream without providing another solid backup. We must build the infrastructure, the GPS, to provide visibility into multiple pathways that start early and don't end in cul-de-sacs. When you listen to the voices of leaders in the counseling world, you hear frustration but also a conviction that they aren't ready to throw the college dream overboard, not until a twenty-first-century noncollege American Dream is ready for prime time.

For example, Analise Gonzalez at DSST shares, "It's really tricky. It's a tricky thing to balance. Because many times it is white people in power, saying '*Those* kids can go to trade or vocational' while they're not sending their kids. They would never choose that for their own children."

Similarly, Ajuah Helton from the KIPP Foundation asks, "Why should our students aspire differently than the wealthiest white kids in America? And so as long as that's the premise, and until we start to see kids who would have gone to Yale, but instead are doing certificate programs, that's when I think that the zeitgeist might somewhat return to what we had been cultivating over the last few years of many pathways." (Ajuah is referring to KIPP's shift to, and then away from, a "multiple pathways" advising approach with its graduating students.)

Angel, CEO of the National Association for College Admission Counseling, voices the same concerns. "What really bothers me is that there are very highly educated, for example, news professionals as well as politicians who are out there saying you don't need to go to college, but they would never say that to their own children. And that is what really, really drives me nuts."[48]

And as we consider how to work out a new narrative—how to grow new, less risky models for higher education, evaluate them, and sell them to families—we have college-ready students like Daniel in Denver who are feeling the effects of the vacuum. "I look at my college application," he says, "and I think to myself, like what am I doing? You know, because I feel so far out of the loop, like everyone is here, and I'm all the way over there. And I feel like I'm looking at everyone. And I'm thinking to myself, is what I'm doing actually the right choice? Like, am I making the right choice? And I start getting in my head too much, because then I start second guessing everything."

6

Learners

Who Still Needs *College?*

I hear a lot of, like, "college isn't for everyone." . . . But I also hear a lot of "if you don't go to college, then you're . . . basically like, nothing."

—SEBASTAIN, HIGH SCHOOL JUNIOR

All the chapters up till now have set the stage for the real question: Who *does* need college anymore? The "who" includes a kaleidoscope of learners in different circumstances, and for each, the answer may be different. The "anymore" reflects that we are at a huge inflection point. Each year brings more examples of states and employers removing degree requirements, more stories about six-figure-salaried college bypassers. AI brings new visibility into who has skills and who needs skills. A GPS-style skills mapping system is on the horizon while, meanwhile, we're all bracing for historic shortages of skilled talent, as well as the potential erasure of some entry-level jobs that artificial intelligence may replace. Data from the past about wage gains from college may not predict the future. How should we guide the next generation?

I will argue in this chapter that we have reached the cusp of an era when the glass is half full and half empty at the same time. It's half full because a degree is no longer a required pathway for professional-level economic success. It's half empty because the institution of college has been devalued. Or has it? It has certainly been labeled as not worth serious debt for some types of financially constrained learners, or not worth the risk given their GPAs or academic preparation. But which types? How do we break that down? Who should go? Who can afford to skip college, and who should regroup for a couple of years and reconsider? In this chapter we will explore, for example, why young women and Black and Hispanic learners feel more need to attend college than white men.[1]

A 2024 survey of high school parents and counselors suggests families are hungry to understand micro-credentials as a pathway instead of college, but they don't have enough information.[2]

Design thinking helps us consider the "who" question. In this chapter, I present typologies of learners who do and don't need college today. We call these *personas*. They help us demonstrate that college is necessary for some groups, while others can more easily bypass it if they want to or have to. I have interviewed researchers and learners to build this set of personas, and they are also a reflection of my own twenty years of meeting families and learners at the biggest decision point of their lives. I then pressure test these archetypes against outcomes research. But the first challenge is to cut through all the hype surrounding the role of college on both sides. When you have two competing narratives about college, you end up in a message vacuum. And, as I will lay out in this chapter, the vacuum and the dynamics that create it harm new majority learners the most.

TODAY'S MESSAGE VACUUM

Here, we come to the central challenge that led me to write this book. It's a fixable challenge, unlike some of the doomsday issues we are handing off to the next generations. I mentioned that we now have two competing narratives at the national level that seep into every community, every high school, and every unemployment office. The messages and price tags that families hear are driving them away from college, but the solutions for what they might do instead are underfunded, underdeveloped, underevaluated, and, in short, undermining the "college for all" drive of yesteryear.

The competing narratives can be summed up as follows:

Narrative 1: College isn't worth it, and it's become unaffordable or too risky.[3]
Narrative 2: 72% of "good jobs" jobs require college.[4]

How did we get here? Anthony Carnevale believes it's a holdover from the "college for all" decades, and maybe even earlier. He's the founder of the Center on Education and the Workforce at Georgetown University. Tony told me it's remarkable how "training has a horrible history in American public policy."[5] *Training* is the term he uses to summarize alternative learning pathways, from Franklin D. Roosevelt's Depression-era Civilian Conservation Corps to modern-day programs like Job Corps. As founder of the academic center that publishes the go-to data on why college *is* worth it, he says the Census and other data behind his studies make clear that college graduates in the past have been better off to the tune, on average, of $1.2 million over their working lifetimes compared with high-school-only grads.[6] *If* they graduate, and that's a big if, they make on average 75 percent more than their high-school-only counterparts over time.

Yet, over the last decade, we have seriously diluted the message that college is the ticket to prosperity for those who want to upgrade their family standing or economic foothold. We have done so with actions and words, data about who is *not* graduating, out of guilt about debt, swings in the economy, and, to hear Tony tell the tale, raw politics: "The answer from my point of view, having spent a lot of my life doing political work, is that the Democrats need the blue wall. Republicans have got to hold on to the white working class. . . . So the President [Biden] runs around saying there are $160,000 a year jobs coming for people with high school degrees. That is correct, but it's less than 1/10 of 1% of high school [only] graduates."

So both parties are vying for the noncollege graduate.[7] That accounts for some of the messaging. But the retreat from "college for all" includes the systemic step back from a government commitment to college as, at least, a partial entitlement. In the 1970s, for example, states covered 75 percent of the cost of tuition at their public colleges; by 2015 that percentage was down to 23 percent.[8] The news media have heavily covered the surveys and research, where headlines become caveats and warning labels that the "college = American Dream" bargain has become a crapshoot.[9] And the negativity appears on many fronts, whether it's CEOs railing against the preparation of graduates when they hire them, or stories about the college stop-outs who are racking up extra debt because they can't make their loan payments.[10] We have built an archive of woe that exposes the dark side of the college gauntlet.

As just one example, the Federal Reserve Bank of St. Louis published a study in 2019 suggesting that Black and brown college graduates in their forties may have earned more, but they are no better off, if you measure by family wealth, than their nongraduate counterparts.[11] So , instead of a clear national message, we dilute the sunny optimism of the American Dream, leaving the nonwealthy public scratching its collective head in confusion: To go or not to go?

And now, on the other side of the equation, we are bombarded with messages about the changing "future of work." Media and research messages warn us that degrees are becoming increasingly important because of the complexity of work that humans will do. First, automation was the bogeyman. Now it's AI. AI reportedly could erase the need for entry-level career roles from assistants to researchers to accountants to architects . . . to Hollywood writers.[12] The degree is the best antidote to becoming irrelevant, as marketing professor Robert Warren told us in chapter 4. But Ryan Craig told us in the employer chapter, chapter 3, that experience is a better career inoculation to an AI-enabled world of work. It can help you leapfrog past entry level to the jobs that will still exist. Yikes. If you attend a college that hasn't figured out how to help you gain experience, would it be smarter to look for an alternative? Which is it?

I asked Jim Shelton, a longtime college access entrepreneur and social impact investor, "How well are we doing updating the 'college for all' narrative for the public?"[13] He shook his head and said, "It's terrible, terrible.

There are all these other pathways now into careers that have both longevity and that can transition to other opportunities, as industries come and go . . . but most kids still don't even know they exist. . . . We just haven't built a discipline around exposure."[14]

In this chapter I will attempt to offer advice to the growing number of confused consumers and the practitioners who serve them. I will categorize, in broad strokes, learners who still do need college at this juncture and those who could feel reasonably comfortable skipping over the degree gauntlet. Or at least they might defer it to a slightly later stage of life, maybe until we can redesign college models to address their needs of affordability, flexibility, length, and relevance. A few words of warning about my methodology: these personas are meant to form a composite sketch of categories of consumers. There will be some overlap and some smaller subgroups that you might feel are left out.

WHO DOES *NOT* NEED COLLEGE?

Let me start with four groups or personas that I believe can, in today's dynamic career preparation world, give the college degree a pass. Perhaps I should add the caveat that this applies in a decent to tight labor market.

> The four groups who may not *need* college are:
> - The connected career switcher
> - The motivated do-it-yourselfer
> - The prepackaged-career starter
> - The undecided, maybe later

I want to reiterate that everyone could benefit from college. That's not the debate here. The central question in my book is, Have we evolved to the point where certain groups can hack their way to the same economic gain, or professional success, by skipping it? Or at least deferring to test the waters of the real world?

The Connected Career Switcher

The eighteen-year-old who started a job without college and several years later wants to be in a better role or different industry is, I would argue, perhaps the clearest candidate for a shorter training path than a two- or four-year degree—given one important caveat, which is why I added the adjective "connected": if they have a well-connected network to guide them and, when needed, funding to cover shorter program tuition. Non-college programs are rarely government funded or subsidized.

I will start very close to home. I would put my own daughter in this first category because she did not attend college and our family has no regrets. Our daughter, Amelia, started her ballet career twelve years ago, in 2013. Like most professional ballet dancers, she went straight to apprenticeship from high school. At the time, we all assumed that she'd have to get her degree when she retired from ballet.[15] But now, a decade later, the landscape has changed dramatically in our view and hers. The further she got away from her high school friends who chose college—and all of them did—the less it mattered to her. She told me in a FaceTime interview, "I had been led to believe that college is this Lego block that you need to build the rest of your life. The longer I was out of that mold, I looked around and said, 'That's not true at all.'"[16] And while I am sure I influenced her earlier belief in "college or bust," after high school she got no hand-wringing from her parents, because I was watching the unbundling of skilling programs during that time frame and began to see training programs she could use as shortcuts when needed.

When her whole ballet company was laid off during the height of the pandemic, she did a part-time online bootcamp at General Assembly to build some digital marketing skills and a starter portfolio. (We, her parents, split the cost with her, which was $3,700.) And now, back in her pointe shoes, she has managed to work side gigs in digital marketing ever since, while dancing. As she thinks about her next career in marketing, I certainly tell her she doesn't need college because she has already crossed the experience chasm. And the more-senior roles in business that marketing might lead her to, for the most part, look to experience rather than degrees these days. However, if she had career aspirations in a licensed field, like registered nursing or clinical therapy or law, I would be giving her different advice. She would have to check the

Table 6.1   Examples of careers that do not require a degree (in gray highlight)

Health Care	Tech	Business	Adv. Manufacturing	Education
Health-care aide	Help desk tech	Digital marketer	Quality control inspector	Teacher's aide
Paramedic	Network support specialist	Sales	Mechatronics engineering technician	Pre-school teacher
Medical biller	Network administrator	Quality assurance specialist	Stationary engineer	College admissions officer
PT assistant	Data scientist	Call center manager	Fabricator	School librarian
Medical technician	Database administrator	HR specialist	Machinist	Guidance counselor
Dental hygienist	Cloud engineer	Business analyst	Mechanical engineer	K–12 teacher
Registered nurse	Database administrator	Project manager	Power plant operator	College professor
Physical therapist	Cybersecurity analyst	Risk manager	Electrical engineer	School/college administrator
Nurse practitioner	Software developer	Entrepreneur	Robotics engineer	
Physician associate				
Doctor				

Source: Roles are organized by salary level within each industry from lowest to highest paid based on average starting salary. Data primarily from the US Bureau of Labor Statistics' *Occupational Outlook Handbook*, as well as Indeed.

degree box, and perhaps go to graduate school, which is a tough journey to start in your thirties.

One trick in this category, and others for that matter, is to know where the degree requirements still exist. With my research assistant, I've pieced together a chart with available data from five growing sectors (table 6.1). The good news for learners is that the rules are relaxing over time.

And when degree requirements are relaxed, the types of learners who benefit, in this category, are self-starters and self-funders. Perhaps you need a little help gaining credentials and a portfolio in a new field, and building the ever-important network, but you can take it from there. So I should certainly emphasize and acknowledge that learners who come from a position of family wealth and family connections have the easiest time switching careers without a degree.

The Motivated Do-It-Yourselfer

Why are men opting out of college? Many researchers have picked up on this aspect of the college slide over the last decade, where men are creating the drag on enrollment, producing a now 40–60 percent split between men and women at four-year colleges.[17] Significantly fewer young men are starting college right after high school, according to enrollment data.[18]

There is another trend that might hold part of the answer: education hacking. By 2019, 42 percent of employed Americans said that, when they needed more education, they turned to the internet and taught themselves.[19] My theory here is that the kinds of jobs where self-teaching can actually translate to a better job mostly fall into male-dominated fields: tech, business, entrepreneurship, and other roles that don't require hands-on practice with equipment or required classroom hours.[20] Remember all the young men I interviewed in previous chapters who said they didn't want to sit in a classroom?

Is it a coincidence that the biggest group of people skipping and dropping out of college are males?[21] I don't think so. One Pew Research Center survey shows that more men than women who choose against college straight out say they didn't need it, or that they just didn't want to go.[22]

I learned pretty quickly that the place to find education do-it-yourselfers is on Reddit, the wildly popular social media site where you can get advice on anything. A "Redditor" posts a question or situation, and upwards of 1,000 members respond with comments that other members vote up or down, often within minutes. On a subreddit called "Career Guidance," boasting 2.7 million members, my research assistant found an engaging alternative pathway careerist named Robert Gessler, who was cheerfully dispensing advice to his fellow man. I say "fellow man" because posters on this subreddit—and one called "Skills You Can Learn off YouTube"— appeared to be overwhelmingly male.[23]

Robert consented to a Zoom call from Kansas City, during which I found a perfect archetype of a learner who hacked his way to economic prosperity via YouTube and, at a later stage, a short bootcamp. Robert started working at his local Discount Tire store during high school. "I hated high school," he said. "I loved learning, but I couldn't sit still."[24] His plan to enlist in the military like his father was thwarted by childhood asthma, and so he worked his way from slinging tires to call center sales. From there he studied sales techniques and soft skills by Googling, and he landed a fairly lucrative sales job as a freight broker. "Since I could communicate well during the interviews for those roles, I don't think the interviewers particularly cared about my education status, even though the position was advertised to require a 4 year degree," Robert said.

Then, while Robert was working as a freight broker, an engineer mentor friend told him that his company might have openings on the tech side of the house if he could learn some computer languages. Robert's manner projects confidence, without arrogance. "So I started looking up some YouTube videos on, you know, low level coding stuff, you know, entry level to Python or JavaScript," he explained. "I was like, I can totally learn this. This is just a language. It's not that hard."

At this point, Robert decided to add in a fourteen-week online bootcamp course at DevCode Camp because his father had some spare credits from his veteran benefits. One coding credential later, in the summer of 2022, just as the tech hiring frenzy was slowing down, Robert landed a job as an associate software developer at $72,000. "I like to think that I could have gotten the job without the bootcamp. The biggest reason I opted for the bootcamp instead of going the fully self-taught route for this job is that I could focus 100% of my time on education and get my living expenses paid for. It seemed the most efficient way to tackle the situation." He was twenty-two years old. And now, he's tickled to be training the college interns, engineering students, who are his age.

Robert is typical of the stories you hear about self-taught upskillers. I would argue that the type of learner who can hack their way to the same economic gain as a college grad needs to be, above all, a self-starter who, again, has the family connections or innate social skills to find at least a small network to advise them. Robert's parents couldn't advise him, but he found a sales mentoring group on his own. Without teachers or college advising services, you have to know what and how to learn and how to position yourself for employment. What certifications do you need? What self-initiated projects could stand in for actual experience?

And Robert is paying it forward, now helping other do-it-yourselfers. Interestingly, Reddit provides an unfiltered place to do that. Robert finds himself advising tech wannabes on which platforms to use for their hiring portfolios and encouraging them to teach themselves. When I described all this to a tech employer friend, his immediate reaction was, "How do we capture this talent market that's out there, teaching themselves, and maybe or maybe not learning the skills that will get them hired?" How do employers tap the growing DIY market that is getting by on the duct tape version of career training, like the software lab Patrick set up in his house to prepare for a job interview or the crowd-sourcing and free videos Robert used to get his first few professional jobs?

The Prepackaged-Career Starter

This is where apprenticeships come in. A high school student can get a very clear picture of their path if they choose what I call a prepackaged career. You get on a track to become an electrician or a carpenter, to name the two most popular unionized tracks, and your path is prescribed. It might take two years or four years, but your starter job helps you build skills (and confidence) while you are being paid. Other prepackaged roles that may not be unionized, but where training is tailored to lead to employment readiness, include certified medical assistants, emergency medical technicians, massage therapists, and police or corrections officers. These fields do not require a degree but do require licenses or certifications, and the license prep process has long been built into the classroom. Many career starters like the security and structure of this approach, even if it means giving up the possibilities of exploring the life of the mind and many career choices. As we heard in chapter 3 on employers, mind-sets are expanding as to what professional roles can be included in the prepackaged career category. Hungry employers in finance, tech, cybersecurity, many aspects of health care, advanced manufacturing, and even consulting are all joining the apprenticeship game to burn an easier path to their doors.

We met Brian Rhodes-Devey in chapter 3. He was the electrician working to build out the nation's electric battery grid. Even though he finished his college degree and then worked a lot of gig jobs and tried organic farming, when he wanted to start a family, the certainty of a prepackaged training-to-career path and a known salary scale were suddenly appealing: "When I started thinking about it, I'm like, man, that actually sounds kind of nice. To get onto a track where someone tells me what to do. And then I know how to do that. And like I can then, like, go somewhere with that."[25] While Brian had to get an old-fashioned, union-stamped electrician's license, his is a new profession.

Harvard researcher and associate professor Peter Blair studies, among other topics, how licensing can play an analogous role to education. He told me, "Licensure is a kind of human capital, you know, and it's also kind of a job market signal that puts it on par, in my view, with degrees. So we ought to think about licensure reform as a part of a broader strategy with reforming the way that we think about our credentialing system."[26] His research shows that, as with degrees, the expense involved with obtaining training and licensure in many fields becomes a barrier, as do the requirements in many states barring the formerly incarcerated.

If we agree that apprenticeships provide a less risky path than an open-ended degree, shouldn't there be more of them? Registered apprenticeships, with their built-in paid training regime, provide a turnkey and sometimes the only path to lucrative licensed roles. As of publication, however, apprenticeships are held by 0.4 percent of US workers, and most of those are white men.[27] But this is an area to watch—there is a huge market opportunity for more career paths to be visibly prepackaged and offered by colleges or intermediary entrepreneurs as micro-pathways.

Can we hasten the expansion of prepackaged careers to higher-paying roles in more fields? College students today seem more anxious about that last mile of getting hired. We see more fields, including teaching and nursing, adding more turnkey school- and work-based learning combo packages to entice workers into these fields, where extreme shortages are expected to get worse. Those packages at first might include degree requirements, but as we have seen in other fields, necessity will become the mother of invention.

The Undecided, Maybe Later

Several of the students we have met in this book tried college and pretty quickly stopped out. Porchea from chapter 2 tried college four times. Each time, she tested out a new career idea. Each time she left, it seems she felt it was harder to go back. Luis, a high school senior I met in Denver, from a lower-income family, seemed wracked with concern about getting himself financially situated before considering college even though he is interested in mechanical engineering.[28] He was concerned about taking money out of the family coffers. He explained, "I imagine in my head or something, I would be totally upset if I took the money from them [my parents] and I didn't even pursue or do what I intended. Uh, yeah, so I'm on the fence," he said.[29] Porchea and Luis are both examples of learners who could benefit from waiting on college, or from selecting a high-touch alternative that specializes in career sampling. We'll meet some of these alternatives in the last chapter. Porchea and Luis were undecided about their career plans, and sadly they did not have the family resources to spend time trying on different options at a pricey four-year university.

A few years ago, I helped lead a design challenge with four community colleges from around the country and the four main universities they fed students into. We were all motivated to begin the Seamless Transfer Pathways Design Challenge because of the tragic statistics. Of the students beginning community college, only 13 percent manage to go on to obtain a four-year degree.[30] At our first big gathering, we had asked each college team to bring the best data they could muster so we could all piece together the mystery of who was succeeding and who was not. We looked at majors, we looked at race and income, we looked at how many credits they were earning toward a major. We saw many interesting trend lines, but one stood out to me as a surprise: "undecided" students were dropping out, ones who had not picked a degree focus, some before they got an associate of arts degree, but even more when they got to the four-year college and hadn't chosen or had changed their major.

The problem is, for folks using financial aid—and that's a majority of students today—the clock is ticking. There are only so many credits you can take outside your major. And several states have excess credit rules, requiring students to be financially penalized if they take too long to graduate.[31] Perhaps as damaging is that switching majors can add extra years to get to the finish line, causing some to give up or run out of federal grant money. The National Association of Colleges and Employers quotes one study that says only 20 percent of students who spend half of their college career undecided ever finish.[32]

So an important category of learner who should think twice about college or at least an expensive option is the undecided student. This learner may "need" college, but their chances of succeeding are compromised. Undecideds, when finances are a concern, should choose carefully.

I have a twenty-five-year-old relative, Joe, who has tried community college twice. The irony is that you may want to "try out" college by going to an inexpensive community college, but your odds are much better if you enroll in a more expensive four-year college, where retention and graduation rates are higher. Joe was taking classes at Northern Virginia Community College and living with his parents. He was undecided about his career and major but went with entrepreneurship. It seemed general enough. Then, in a work-based class project, he was placed with a healing arts practitioner and decided he wanted that career. He didn't need college to become a healing arts practitioner. So he left.

The point is, I don't discourage anyone in their twenties from trying college if they can do it affordably for themselves and their families. But community college graduation outcomes are better for those who have a plan—a career track in medical technician roles, or construction management, or advanced manufacturing, or plans to transfer to a four-year college to pursue engineering or nursing or teaching. For career wanderers, community college can be an affordable way to test specific career waters or try different courses, as Joe did, establishing low-risk data points for life planning. You can always come back to college, but it is best to do so with a career plan. That's what emergency medical technician Abigail from Pima Community College did, as we saw in chapter 4.

Connected career switchers, motivated do-it-yourselfers, prepackaged-career starters, and undecided, maybe laters: these are the four personas that I believe capture the broadest and most common reasons why learners might succeed without college, or might mitigate one of the biggest financial risks—no career direction. These categories do not include the students who feel they cannot enroll in college for many other reasons, such as health, neurodivergent needs, an economic or family requirement to provide care or earnings, incarceration, military service, or even political or religious beliefs. However, these categories do capture the patterns that shed light on where the opportunities lie. How do flexible learning providers and employers reach out to career switchers, do-it-yourselfers, apprentices, and the undecided? Human-centered design teaches us how to design new versions of college to meet their needs.

WHO DOES STILL NEED COLLEGE?

This is a trickier set of personas to neatly organize. On one level, you would think most parents would still advocate college for their children, even if they can't afford it. Who wouldn't want their offspring to have a potentially transformative experience, explore careers, make lifelong friends, and take advantage of college as the training wheels for adulthood? I daresay most readers of this book would. If we can scrape the dollars together between savings and loans and navigate the Free Application for Federal Student Aid form, we likely buy into the notion that our eighteen-year-olds need four to six years to grow up, find themselves, and learn to think critically and get along with others. And we've learned, with the advent of neuroimaging over the last twenty years, that the adolescent brain isn't fully mature until age twenty-five, giving many of us parents a new reason to still treat our college-age students as children.[33]

Interestingly, in two studies in 2021 and 2022, only Asian parents overwhelmingly said that college is extremely or very important for their children's success.[34] White parents were least likely to say so. That made sense given the concentration of generational wealth and networks and college-going norms among white families.[35] But I was surprised that fewer than a third of white parents cared very strongly about college for their off-spring, as long as they were happy in their careers.[36]

The diminishing parental hopes for college make sense when the average price tag including room and board for the average four-year degree has become $145,000, and top private college tuition is inching toward $100,000 a year. College has become a luxury good, overriding all those "nice to haves" I just listed.[37] Particularly when it's a gamble as to whether your child will have a transformative experience in college. It's a gamble as to whether your child will even finish, increasing the possibility of negative financial returns and crippling debt.

So, just as I did earlier in considering who can potentially skip over college, here I will look at the other side of the cost-benefit ledger and offer four categories of learners or families where the need for college has persisted or where the economic or social gains a college degree can deliver for these groups can't likely be matched by today's underdeveloped alternatives.

Who does still need college?
▪ Class transporters
▪ Legitimacy label seekers
▪ Degree and license workers
▪ Longing-to-belongers

Class Transporters

Class is a tricky thing to talk about. In the US, unlike in some other countries, class is largely associated with income; it's only when you achieve a certain income, for example, that you are said to be middle class.[38] Often stereotypes are tacked onto income regarding education, housing status, job status, or race, resulting in discrimination or snobbery. But for the purposes of discussing who needs college, this group includes the children of anyone who has ever said, "I don't want my child to have to work as hard as I did to make ends meet." It also includes any young person who sees college as a lifeline to escape poverty, abuse, or just dead-end employment.

Many class transporter families are refugees, immigrants, former Rust and Steel Belt or coal country workers, families descended from slaves from the US South, Native Americans, frontline workers, and disabled veterans. With one college degree in the family, it has typically only taken a single generation for many of these families to leave poverty or the low-income working class behind.[39] Again, this is with an important caveat: they have to finish their degree. My immigrant family in the 1600s is the example that opened the book. More recently, we can provide countless American Dream success stories, well-known folks who give some credit to their college degree. Folks like Oprah Winfrey, daughter of a single teenage mom; Supreme Court Justice Sonia Sotomayor, whose parents moved to New York from Puerto Rico and encouraged her to go to college; or Paul LeBlanc, just-retired president of Southern New Hampshire University and first-generation student. In fact, three modern presidents of the US were first in their family to attend college: Gerald Ford, Jimmy Carter, and Bill Clinton.[40]

The research of Raj Chetty and his team made a big splash in 2017 when they showed how certain "midtier" public universities were shining as "engines of upward mobility," including many of the affordable campuses of the City University of New York, California, and Texas systems, credited with catapulting graduates and their families from the lowest income bracket to the middle class or higher.[41] This is the profile of many of the students and parents I have interviewed over the years. And it always strikes me how, without prompting, the students often reference their mother as the beacon, the drill sergeant, the believer that college is the ticket. Mothers like Daniella Ceballos, who saw college as her family's engine to a better life.

Daniella grew up as a migrant laborer in Porterville, California. Her own parents are Mexican; between them, they had an eleventh-grade education. They had twelve children, creating their own family workforce. The younger ones still live at the Woodville Farm Labor Camp, picking peaches, walnuts, and grapes, depending on the season. Daniella stayed in school through high school, not typical in her family, despite getting pregnant her senior year. She never considered college, and no one, certainly not her school, was pushing her. "I think a very typical Latino thing to do is, once you're out of high school, your next thing is to get married and have kids and then be at home. Wife. And I was very much on that trajectory," Daniella said. "I graduated in June. I got married in August and went from there."[42]

But a few years later, gang violence racked their rural community. One night when bullets loudly whizzed past their four-year-old son, Daniella said, "we went inside and my husband just looked at me and said, 'We need something different.' And I was like, 'You're right.'"

They had recently seen a TV airing of the documentary *Waiting for "Superman,"* which tells the story of how some traditional public schools tracked lower-income students like Daniella toward noncollege paths, while, the film argues, public charter schools were attempting a full college-prep promise to all students who earned a place by lottery.[43] Daniella told me, with some anger in her voice, that she was "tracked." "We watched that movie and we were like, how do we find a charter school?"

With no charter schools in their area, they made what felt like a crazy decision to move to Denver, where many public charters were starting up. All for their children's education. Daniella had a brother there, but they had not lined up jobs. Looking back, she says, "Honestly, it was the best decision I ever made."

Fast-forward twelve years. Her two kids are now at the Denver School of Science and Technology, the prestigious charter high school I profiled in the last chapter. Her daughter, Malyah, was a freshman when I interviewed them. Her son, Sebastain, a junior, despite the AP classes and the required college applications, is falling under the spell of the male line in his family: hardworking, self-sufficient. When his parents separated recently, he wanted to drop out of high school.

Daniella lamented, "So, we're very Mexican. When his dad and I split up, Sebastain said, 'I see you struggling, I see you working really hard. Let me just not go to school and I'll work and I'll provide.' So much machismo, his manly way of coming in and saying, like, let me, let me go and do this."

But he is also conflicted. As soon as I began talking to Sebastain, he laid out the confusing messages he's hearing as a junior at a top high school.

"I hear a lot of, like, college isn't for everyone. So you could do a trade school or community college or something like that. But I also hear a lot of if you don't go to college, then you're not going to be much. I feel like, as important as it is, it's not everyone's thing. But if you don't go then you're basically like, nothing."

His sister, Malyah, is on board for college. In her case, she is persuaded by her mom's stories. Plus, she likes school. Daniella told her kids in front of me, on a Zoom call, that she's had to work "tooth and nail" to provide for them without a degree, and that their lives could be easier. She appealed to them: "You've seen the struggle of me having to like, stay here at work and it's 6 P.M. and, like, prove myself time and time again to actually get where I am and not even make equivalent to a person that went to college because they have a degree backing."

Daniella is seeking economic security for the next generation of her family. That's the key to the class transporter group. Like many immigrants or first-generation Americans, she felt it was too late for her. She believed that her K–12 education had failed her and that she couldn't get as far as she might want. I was struck by her lack of confidence in, for example, her skills in writing grammatically correct emails, even though she has risen to the level of an assistant principal for administration in the school where she works.

Sebastain and Malyah also help illustrate a growing trend among Latino students: Latino men are turning away from college, while their sisters are the ones propping up the increases that we see in overall Latino college participation. In 2011, 42 percent of Latino men were in college, but that number fell to 33 percent in 2022.[44]

Will they both secure spots in the middle class? Having met them and Daniella, I am optimistic and so is she, actually, because she has made herself a savvy expert to guide her kids. Sebastain, though only a junior, has been accepted into a welding program, and he's willing to consider community college to get the basics down for the business he hopes to start. Perhaps we can say it was Daniella who needed college to transport herself to the middle class. In many ways, she got there on her own. But life has been hard, and now more so since she became a single mom. She believes college would have eased the path.[45]

Legitimacy Label Seekers

The second category of learners who, in my view and based on research, do still need college includes anyone who feels society and employers won't take them seriously without a higher degree, whether or not their families are currently economically secure. College and grad school can be tickets to legitimacy and perhaps insurance to mitigate against various forms of discrimination or stereotyping.[46] Or even to help mitigate one's own self-doubt. But the surveys and research are mixed. Some surveys suggest that Black parents, for example, highly value a college degree as a means to economic prosperity, more so than white parents, and studies have shown that for Black men who finish four-year degrees, at least, the degree can be an economic equalizer.[47]

But another study finds that white workers with a college degree have median wages that are 23 percent higher than college-educated Black workers, partly because Black college students often gravitate toward majors in fields that involve lower salaries, such as public service, social work, and administration.[48] One of the coauthors of that study, Peter Blair, agreed that this kind of research confuses the college degree narrative for Black learners. He asked me, "Do we say, let's give up all hope and stop going to college because college is not going to be the panacea, and give into cynicism, or do we say, even in the face of this data, no, college is really what we need to be pushing for?"[49]

We know that Black men, like most other male groups, are pulling back from enrolling in college, while Black women are holding fairly steady.[50] For many, Peter's question creates a belief that they need more education, more insurance to be taken seriously, more certainty to get the salary and promotions they deserve.[51] Twice as many Black students who go to graduate school have student debt, compared with white students. And half of them report that their debt is higher than their net worth.[52] Could we say that Black learners go out on a limb to get more educated? Women do so more than men, according to enrollment numbers.

I interviewed Penny Mickey Smith, a senior adviser on workforce development for the Heartland Fund, which supports rural America. It was the week after Harvard's first Black female president, Claudine Gay, resigned under pressure from lawmakers and donors. "Claudine is just a poster child for another example of how Black women kind of feel and can't always express," Penny said. "It's like we always feel like we have to be twice as good." Like many Black women, Penny wanted all the education she could get. "It's almost like this fear-based over-achievement for black women," she explained. "Either our integrity or our ability is always going to be challenged. All in all, it feels like we are more susceptible to being set up to fail."[53]

Penny's dad achieved a middle-class life for his family without a college degree in the 1980s. "My parents were first generation high school graduates," Penny said. "They had not known anyone in their family that even had a high school diploma." Penny was the first and only among her siblings to make it through college, at Fisk University, the in-demand HBCU (historically Black college and university) in Nashville I mentioned earlier, which is trying to protect its culture.

Penny's father was recently celebrated at a retirement ceremony for being the first Black utilities lineman in the state of Kentucky.[54] "And so their dream for the three of us, myself and two siblings, was that we would be the first to have a college degree," Penny explained, "but they really didn't know how to point us there in terms of like college selection, and understanding the importance of how to position yourself, from GPA, standardized testing, to even apply to certain types of colleges that were maybe more selective. So that whole conversation about selective colleges never happened in our home. It was college, that was it."

Penny got there. After Fisk she got her doctor of education degree at Vanderbilt, but she always felt like she was overcoming odds. "In my Kentucky high school, Blacks didn't go to college," she told me. After an impressive career in university administration, today Penny has her own social venture, a popcorn company that exclusively trains and hires victims of abuse.

And now she finds herself guiding her own son on a career and technical education (CTE) path. Geoffrey is a junior in South Haven, Mississippi, who is on the autism spectrum and has trouble landing good grades in some subjects.[55] "I thought that it would be a good idea for him to explore if [CTE] was something he was interested in," Penny said. "Because our motto is education and a quality job. It's both." They weren't exactly "tracked" into the CTE program, but Penny does wonder whether the honors students were getting the same flyers her son did.

Geoffrey had to apply to the not-college route, the CTE program in his high school. There were limited slots countywide. Geoffrey signed up for logistics and supply chain because Walmart hires from the program and he was excited that it involved learning to fly drones. But being a school-to-work expert herself, Penny second-guesses their choices. Frankly, there aren't many. What kind of legitimacy would Geoffrey need to establish himself as a Black man in the South and as a neurodivergent learner? The validation markers other than college are still fuzzy. Is a degree the best route for him? Probably, if he can succeed. But skill building and experience through an apprenticeship are becoming more readily available. Penny is an education expert, but this is new territory for her to navigate.

I was surprised by a statistic that a 2024 study from the Center on Education and the Workforce highlighted: "Women need at least one more degree than men to have equivalent earnings. Unless these earnings gaps close between men and women with the same level of education, women will continue to have strong incentives to seek more education than their male counterparts."[56]

I certainly don't want to compare the ease of my own white journey, without racial discrimination, to those of my Black and brown counterparts. But writing this chapter got me thinking about the idea of "legitimacy" and my own reasons to pursue my bachelor's and then my master's degree. I too wanted a legitimacy label; I had a desire to be taken seriously in what was, in the 1970s, a man's world. I didn't know any woman in the "professional" working world besides my schoolteachers. When I was in high school, I remember my college-educated mother being excited when she landed a job selling furniture at Bloomingdale's, to escape the monotony of her typing job with my dad. It was watching the fictional *Mary Tyler Moore Show* in the 1970s (the main character was a TV newsroom producer) that gave me the idea that I could blend my performing experience with book learning to become a TV newscaster, the most exciting world that I could glimpse from my suburban tract housing development. TV anchorwomen Barbara Walters and Jane Pauley became my role models. They seemed to be taken seriously.

When I got my first TV job after college in the South, at the CBS affiliate in Durham, North Carolina, it was hard to be taken seriously, degree or not. If you've seen the Will Farrell movie *Anchorman*, set in the 1970s, you'll know what I mean. I have to say that my male colleagues were much more supportive than the misogynistic news cowboys satirized in the film. But when I went into the field to conduct interviews with my long blond tresses and twenty-one-year-old jitters, I had imposter syndrome, maybe only partly brought on by the politicians, cops, and businessmen who called me "darlin'," or the state head of the Ku Klux Klan who offered to marry me during a taped interview.[57] I decided the antidote was a master's degree from Harvard—that would show them.

It's fascinating today to think about which groups still need a legitimacy label, a leg up to get onto a level playing field, if that's even possible. The mantra now is that skills matter more than a degree. That can be true—up to a point, and depending on so many variables. For those who feel they need the insurance of legitimacy, college is still necessary. Whether they actually need it or believe they need it, it leads to the same decision: to find the money, or to go into debt, to get that degree.

Degree and License Workers

The third category or persona that still needs college is deceptively simple but ever changing. Basically, anyone who wants a job that requires a degree needs to go to college. It can be hard to track who falls into this category because, as I laid out in chapter 1, between 2017 and 2021, the number of all jobs that require a degree fell from 51 percent to an estimated 44 percent, according to the Burning Glass Institute.[58] But the holdouts are largely what you would expect: The key fields where degrees themselves, or licenses that require degrees, are required as of 2024 include many medical fields (doctors, physician associates, registered nurses, physical therapists, clinical therapists, etc.). Other degree-only professions in most states include lawyer, certified public accountant, university professor, schoolteacher, researcher, economist, and data scientist. Some fields within engineering are holdouts, but tech-focused fields including software engineering and cybersecurity are starting to open up for a simple reason: desperate employers. Experts like Anthony Carnevale, Matt Sigelman from the Burning Glass Institute, and Byron Auguste from Opportunity@Work told me these shortages are only expected to increase the shift away from degree requirements. However, surveys of employers also warn that a majority may take up to a decade to shift behavior.[59] So this category of learners who "need college" will continue to shrink, but how fast depends on the economy and talent shortages.

An example of the rethinking of necessary degrees comes from Colorado, where a coalition of employers, colleges, and the state licensing board in behavioral health is creating shorter-term pathways to deal with the worker shortage. I spoke with Jenn Dale, dean of academic success at Community College of Aurora. She is coleading an effort to examine what micro-pathways could be created for mental health job roles. "We had seen this extremely elevated need for behavioral health services and support and an extreme lack of available, highly trained individuals to serve that need," Jen said. "So higher ed doesn't want to respond to a community and industry need by saying yes, in eight years, we will have lots of Licensed Professional Counselors and Licensed Clinical Social Workers trained up for you."[60]

Eight years—that's how long it takes to get through university training for these roles. And even after that long road, the jobs don't pay that well. "Poverty is a very real situation that a majority of our students deal with," Jen explained, "and how do we support students in learning a field, a skill, getting into an industry that provides a living wage and more?" The roles they are creating have titles like behavioral health assistant, peer support specialist, and client/patient navigator. These will be entry-level jobs that fill a gap for the community while allowing learners to earn a living while they build further skills. It's a practical stepladder approach for an industry that had been asking for all types of workers to have at least a master's degree.

Longing-to-Belongers

Most of us are familiar with Abraham Maslow's hierarchy of needs, which lists in rank order the five needs that help humans survive and thrive.[61] Number three on the list is love and belonging. What I've gleaned from all of the young people who bypassed college is that many experienced that FOMO feeling, fear of missing out. If they were part of a high school community where most friends went on to college, they were suddenly "otherized," left out, when they didn't. Charter high schools often refer to the transition from high school as "removing the scaffolding" and the support systems. Community college experts refer to the nexus of belonging, agency, and ability to grow as the success factors for student engagement and persistence.[62]

So one of the reasons *not* to skip college is if a ready-made community feels important to you. A student's growth, or the structure of deadlines, teaching feedback, or peer accountability may well feel essential to get through the job preparation gauntlet. And then, many people simply consider themselves social creatures, even extroverts, who draw energy from a ready-made community. I certainly picked up on this theme from following Reddit postings for a year. One redditor posted on the "Career Guidance" subreddit that they regret not going to college right now, and a host of responses ensued, some egging the author on to get started, others saying that college is only for the rich and could be a very lonely experience.[63]

Interestingly, students in college don't rank community as one of the very top values of their college experience.[64] But whether they recognize it or not, data on student experience suggest that it is critical to helping them graduate and meet their career goals.[65] I mentioned my relative Joe earlier in this chapter; he left community college after trying it a second time. I explained one reason he left: through the community he met there, he discovered a passion, healing arts, and it didn't require a degree. But I saved his other reason for this section. He was told that most of the courses for his entrepreneurship major were only offered online, even though he had a car and lived nearby. That news came as a buzzkill from his point of view. As someone who had tried online courses in college, he found that most of the students were "phoning it in," so the interactions and even the way multiple choice tests were administered online felt perfunctory and boring. He decided that completing a whole degree that way would be depressingly disengaging.

The sad truth is that the less expensive the college, the fewer resources are provided to create community and mentorship for students.[66] Students who do pick a community college route are less likely than four-year college goers to engage with other students or clubs outside class, as are any students working more than thirty hours a week.[67] So learners need to be careful how they choose a college experience if community is a big part of why they are going.

Class transporters, legitimacy label seekers, degree and license workers, and longing-to-belongers: four groups who, I argue, still need college as a pathway to professional success or, in the case of the belongers, to engage with a community. In generating these personas, and the previous four who might bypass the degree, I have left out many subgroups that I am sure folks will call me to task for, ranging from learners in the creative arts to potential professional athletes, to veterans (if you have access to the GI Bill, use it, by all means), to those with disabilities or neurodivergent learning styles. And let's not forget a group that will be increasingly important as talent shortages become more acute: degree importers. That is to say, immigrants who have college degrees from other countries that don't qualify them for degree-required jobs here. Nearly half of immigrants who come to the US hold at least a bachelor's degree.[68] I met several of these learners in bootcamps. These doctors, lawyers, engineers, and businesspeople can't believe they might have to complete a second degree, and they do whatever they can to gain shortcut degree status with certificates and certifications.

THE INTANGIBLE BENEFITS OF COLLEGE

What should we take forward from this penultimate chapter to our final discussion on a new model for how to rewire the national education network and system? I think the central message is this: hurry up with the new narrative. And build the infrastructure that treats all paths to good jobs equally. How fast can we get to a blended stepladder system that allows for visibility and recognizes that college needs to be designed for new majority learners, which I defined in the book's introduction as the 60+ percent who have struggled to or not even tried to earn a bachelor's degree?

The tragic irony is that most people in my "need college" categories can't afford or access the colleges best set up to help them. The time, the money, or the selection process stands in the way. So they are the ones pushed to make the financial gamble. And when they choose the least expensive options, those are the options with the poorest outcomes.[69] Why should their futures be so speculative?

The groups that can more easily afford to skip college, that can hack the work-arounds, already have some advantages. Here, I was struck by how the deck stacks in favor of males, particularly white males. They can risk skipping college for three reasons: the prepackaged careers and existing apprenticeships cater to their strengths (often literally their physical strength); in the tech sector, which for many reasons men gravitate toward, it is easier to self-teach than in female-dominated roles in health care, for example; and pay differentials lead women to feel they need an extra degree to get to the same salary level.[70]

I would argue that the do-it-yourselfers, who learn skills on their own, outside a college community or a prepackaged apprenticeship, give quite a bit up. While you can find community in these targeted, often online pathways, your chances of building lasting relationships with professors, other students, and advisers seem lower. This is another reason that if a learner can find the dollars or test a low-cost college option, it is hard for me to argue against college, even as more skills are made certifiable. I benefited so much from the community that surrounded my college and grad school experiences. They later provided what I would call the "unforeseeable career bumps" that really only emerge when a well-connected network takes you there. Let's illustrate with my story for a minute.

Remember, I was a rookie TV reporter in North Carolina, earning $12,000 a year, covering anything ranging from the latest KKK rally to

"Fireman Helps Cat out of Tree." I sensed that I needed a credibility boost in order to become a foreign correspondent, my dream in the early 1980s.

Harvard seemed the ticket, a master's in public administration. My father said he wouldn't help me pay when I got the acceptance letter. He called it "stupid" for anyone to give up a good job for more school. I was trying to get to the "network," as we called it in the business, to get picked up by one of the three national broadcast networks. I used loans and my savings to go, and it worked, and I certainly think the Harvard degree helped me stand out, as it wasn't a typical route in the 1980s. It took a few years, but by 1988, I was the youngest news correspondent at ABC News.

One of my memories there was the day I met Peter Jennings, the legendary urbane and fabulous ABC News anchorman, who famously had a chip on his shoulder for never completing college. (He didn't need the legitimacy label, but underneath his James Bond looks, he clearly harbored a little self-doubt.) He made sure to put me in my place. When introduced to me, he teased me loudly, so the entire Manhattan evening news crew could hear. "It's our Haaavard girl! Kathleen, what did you learn at Haaavard?" And later, whenever he was editing my scripts, like during the early days of the Persian Gulf War, he quizzed my knowledge of the facts on the ground—in one case, under a tense deadline, my knowledge of the Republican Guard in Iraq—to prove that he knew more than me. He always did.

I achieved my career goal, but the "unforeseeable career bump" came a few years later for me. And if I hadn't been in the Harvard community it wouldn't have happened. I got a call from one of my mentors from the Kennedy School of Government. Would I consider joining the Clinton administration as the first female spokesperson for the Pentagon? He happened to be putting the team together for the new defense secretary, Les Aspin.

These "unforeseeable career bumps" are the adjacent opportunities, jumps, leapfrogs, and possibilities that you never contemplated when you signed up for college, or grad school, or didn't. Hacking your way to your perceived goal can work, now more than ever, but are you shortening the string of possibilities, which I largely attribute to the network more than the label that college provides? But again, if you have to work a full-time or part-time job to pay for college—which a majority of today's students do—the available time to build or take advantage of the network a college community might offer is extremely limited. If networking could become a central component of an "experience first" college . . . well, we'll get to that in the last chapter.

DESIGN CRITERIA FROM LEARNERS

As I interviewed twenty researchers and learners for this chapter, I began to form the view that we have to redesign college to meet the needs of all eight of these groups—the ones who could skip college but could benefit from it; the ones who could get away with not going; the ones who need it but can't afford the time or money or the gamble, given their risk profile, or don't have access to a college network community.

So let's summarize what these personas show us about user needs for redesigning college.

Design Criteria from Learners

1. We need affordable, no-debt pathways.
2. Advising should be available for career switchers, do-it-yourselfers, and class transporters.
3. Prepackage more career paths.
4. Programs should emphasize belonging and career exploration.
5. Create more legitimacy labels, not just the degree.

Some of these needs are present across categories, whether the learner is college-bound or not. First, affordability stands in the way for so many would-be students. Studies show that this is the major reason learners hold back from college or alternative programs. Second, we need more systematic funding and methods to help career switchers, do-it-yourselfers, and class transporters or legitimacy label seekers who don't have connections to make training choices and find their way into jobs with meaningful career trajectories. Third, we know we can prepackage more careers through apprenticeship or even certifications to create turnkey paths to professional careers. Fourth, can we look to the last year(s) of high school to build in career exploration and post-high school programs that provide a bridge year of scaffolding and coaching? Lastly, we can create more legitimacy labels beyond the degree. Licensing and certifications show us the way.

So can I answer the question now? The one that pushed me to write this book? Would I tell a relative, a friend, or a mentee that they don't need college anymore? When I started the Education Design Lab in 2013, I would have said no, despite all the "uncollege" start-ups and bootcamps that began to flower in that period. Today (and it seems like another lifetime) I can say confidently, "It depends." It depends largely on four things that perhaps summarize the personas described in this chapter: a learner's bankroll, desired profession, network, and self-motivation. The bankroll is, sadly, the most important piece. If a learner is just starting out, and they have the money, of course, they should go to college. And one of the best trends in college reform at the moment is the focus on tracking return on investment (ROI). It pays to encourage learners to do their research, using sites like the federal government's College Scorecard, now that ROI data are available by college.[71]

It's not quite the case that the more expensive the college, the more students mitigate their risk. There are a surprising number of value options, mostly public colleges that demonstrate good outcomes with low-income students, as economic mobility research has demonstrated.[72] Students can try to qualify for federal Pell Grants and carefully select the best ROI school they can afford with those grants. Everyone in between should see where they best fit among my personas. And I will issue one warning: my model will break down in bad economic times. We've had a hiring slowdown since 2022 in some of the fields that were among the hottest nondegree tickets, such as tech. Bootcamps and do-it-yourselfers are suffering. If a learner is going to switch careers, or try a training hack on their own, they should keep an eye on the "hot careers" reports from groups like the LinkedIn *Talent Blog* and the Burning Glass Institute, or even the US Department of Labor's Bright Outlook occupations tool.[73]

How do we redesign college without attempting to build a unicorn? How do we recognize that Congress and many state legislatures are not in the mood to spend more to entitle students? And that elite colleges will continue to remain in the spotlight the way exclusive fashion brands dominate the runway even though most of us can't afford the clothes? Fashion is aspirational. College is aspirational. We are aspirational. But we can fix this. We can fix the narrative and we can build a school-to-work system that supports the personas who, today, are left to gamble.

Part III

Convergence

7

The Great College Reset

There is no hurt until the very end. That's true in every disruption story.

—MICHAEL HORN, CLAYTON CHRISTENSEN INSTITUTE

Imagine a time in the not-too-distant future when the four-year college degree is obtained by a smaller and smaller percentage of the population, like the buggy whip as we entered the early automobile age. Only the horse-drawn-carriage stalwarts remained loyal, until that method of transportation just became impractical on busy roads. Antiquated. Maybe even dangerous. What's so special about four years and 120 credits, anyway? In fact, a few universities are already being allowed to experiment with three years and fewer credits.[1] Many graduate school degrees have been shortened to salvage enrollment.[2] And a million students now come to college to earn certificates instead of degrees.[3] Online platforms like Coursera serve hundreds of millions more learners.[4] Amazon may not be far behind in entering the learner shopping market and changing the nature of college.

Can the four-year degree be saved? Not for most learners, I would argue. Once less expensive alternative pathways become clearer and surer, a full-on degree will seem impractical for new majority learners. And new

165

majority learners are, by definition, most learners. The four-year degree has been the market signal we've led with for almost four hundred years in this country. But why does the degree have to be the only product that colleges sell? And why can't the American Dream be achieved by other college products, other constructs of career preparation or adultification? I hope to lay out a case in this final chapter that college must be redefined, broadened, and reset to reclaim broad support across economic classes, races, political parties, and rural-versus-urban divides. The degree may be in trouble, but college can be saved.

When I think about disruption in a market, the teachings of academic and business expert Clayton Christensen often come to mind. I had the chance to be in a room where he explained disruption theory to a private group of elite college presidents around 2014. It went over like a lead balloon. This couldn't possibly apply to them. Michael Horn, cofounder of the Clayton Christensen Institute, writes and teaches about disruption cycles. Like his mentor, who is sadly no longer with us, Michael uses the example of how the steel companies gradually ceded parts of the value chain to "mini-mills" until those value players came after them and beat them out on price and volume.

Michael explains that disruption can take many years—four decades in the case of steel. "In fact, while it's playing out, the leading players feel better and better and better about the world, because it's interesting," Michael says. "There's no hurt until the very end. And that's true in every disruption story. It's like, slowly, slowly, slowly it feels good. It feels good. It feels good. Everyone thinks you're crazy. And then it's all at once and it all collapses."[5] Many folks debate whether this sort of collapse could happen in higher education, a regulated industry and a public good that, perhaps, like banks, wouldn't be allowed to fail. But would the age-old products be allowed to morph into different shapes and sizes?

Paul LeBlanc was the longtime president of Southern New Hampshire University, and he grew his institution to become the nation's largest university. "The higher ed sector, like healthcare, is not a market driven reality," Paul told me. "They are regulated industries. And to the extent that federal financial aid dollars are the lifeblood of the industry, it's going to be very hard for non-traditional providers to get in on that trough. Right? Because it both hinders innovation in many ways. And it also buffers the incumbents from the disruptive newcomers."[6]

Ted Mitchell runs the largest association of colleges in the US, the American Council on Education (ACE), and believes that even schools in trouble will stand by their model unless disruption forces their hand. "Modern America has a definition of college that is immutable," he says. "And even in these moments of sort of crisis and 'let's throw everything up in the air' and everything is fair game, we still come back to an incredibly narrow view of what college is, whether we love it or hate it. And I don't think that that is going to change."[7]

Ted is talking about universities where degree granting is their main business. But what if degrees become the buggy whip? Or if short-term credentials become the mini steel mills? Is the funding model the main thing holding the dam in place, as Paul LeBlanc suggests? Both Ted and Paul would agree that, around the edges, the Great College Reset has begun, and both have been inside innovators helping to urge parts of it along.[8] So why can't we all lean in? I believe it will happen in some form, whether we lean in or not. Groups like the US Chamber of Commerce Foundation are prototyping new "talent finance" models; one is similar to a health-care flexible spending account, funded by federal tax credits and managed through your employer.[9] My hope is that we can design a new ecosystem so that consumers, particularly new majority learners, can still buy affordable tickets to the American Dream, without playing the lottery.

REDEFINING COLLEGE

At the Education Design Lab, and in the college classes I teach, I have approached the awesome task before us as a "design thinking sprint." As I tell my students, or the colleges that have partnered with the Lab over the years, a human-centered design sprint is a short, disciplined set of brainstorming sessions. It's a useful way to break down any systemic problem and reimagine solutions from the point of view of the most important stakeholder: the end user.

First, we frame a design question that is aspirational enough to push divergent thinking and actionable enough to feel like we can reach grounded ideas for solutions. Our design question for this book has been, How might we redesign or redefine "college" to meet the needs of all learners? I put college in quotes because I believe that college needs to morph into an umbrella for a variety of more specific market signals, such as durable skill and hard skill certificates, apprenticeship experiences, community-building cohorts, career navigation weekends, and even a "credit for prior learning" test you buy online to prove that your two years as a navy logistics coordinator qualifies you to do the same work in the private sector, without a degree. And with a college reset, these pathways and experiences need not take a linear form.

In chapter 1, I described the traditional four-year degree as an elevator. We can have "college for all" if we think about college as a stepladder instead: you take a step to build skills, go out and earn money against it, then tackle the next education step, or wait, if life gets in the way. Either way, you build earnings power in shorter chunks and gravitate toward a flexible goal, and you can pivot to a new ladder if your taste or the market changes, throughout your working life.

What we saw in previous chapters is that degrees will always be available for wealthier, younger students who are not in a hurry to earn a living. With this new college reset, we can also set up a new construct with multiple college products, offered by more providers, that, when proven out, can take learners to the same destinations as the degree, maybe further in some cases. But learners need to be able to see their possible futures from the ground before they start up a ladder.

TEN DESIGN PRINCIPLES

A design sprint allows us to prototype and move quickly. And we need to act with urgency. In each previous chapter, I've been keeping track of the "unmet needs" that underpin a human-centered design process, as I draw from what bootcamps, employers, colleges, high schools, and learners themselves have shown us. And now is the time to convert those needs into design principles or criteria; in other words, "what must be true" to create guardrails for a model that restores belief in the value of college and expands access to anyone who chooses it. When you add them up, you can see why we have a crisis, why learners are voting with their feet to manage work-arounds or going without the education their parents could more easily access. Without dragging the reader through a one-for-one conversion chart, I have synthesized the design principles mostly for learners, but also for employers, because both are end users in the two-sided marketplace.

One aside: colleges and other learning and training providers don't get to have needs in this design challenge, even though they have a lot of skin in the game. Facilitating successful graduates into successful careers is their livelihood. But human-centered design is not about satisfying facilitators or builders of solutions. Colleges and other education providers are the curators, the coaches, the evaluators. Of course, the business models have to work for them to provide services, or else we'll all be moving to automated, DIY education.

So here are Ten Design Principles to provide guardrails for the Great College Reset.

Some of these design features are relatively straightforward or already practiced in limited form, such as creating affordable but meaningful options to the degree or in-person community opportunities. Others sound like logical innovations, but regulation and tuition funding, or a lack of data and defined standards, create barriers. A few feel like outlier stretch goals because they require too many of the school-to-employment silos to line up their incentives and priorities. So here's another take on my design principles list, this time grouped by viability, based on what I see happening (or not) not just at colleges but across the postsecondary and training ecosystem that many siloed players are beginning to build (table 7.1).

These are achievable design criteria. We don't have to cram all of these qualities into one unicorn model or organization. In fact, one of the things I see happening is that some players are beginning to go broad, while some are going deep to specialize. As a philanthropist, I have funded some start-up prototypes that featured one or two of these design criteria.[10] And we don't have to cram them all into the traditional college years. Many

Ten Design Principles

Design Principles to Meet the Needs of Learners

1. Quality learning programs must be affordable.
2. Learning must be visibly connected to career goals and offered in a flexible, stepladder approach.
3. Learning institutions must be permeable, with portable credits, so that learners can move between providers and institution types.
4. Relevant, paid work-based experiences must be offered, or simulated versions that learners and employers value.
5. Learning must include durable skills alongside technical skills; both should be taught and certified in the context of the learner's industry of choice.
6. Education providers must build career exploration and industry-specific career advising into the learning path.
7. For younger adults, providers must offer in-person encounters and cohort opportunities, to engage learners beyond their own bubbles, to provide community, and to help them imagine possibilities.

Design Principles to Meet the Needs of Employers

8. Education providers must design instruction and skill-building offerings at the pace of workplace innovation.
9. Government and the ecosystem must figure out how employers can be paid, or at least incentivized, to train students in the workplace.
10. Industry groups should be incentivized to name the skills necessary for job progression across their sector, not just the highly technical roles. They should create certifications for all job roles.

Table 7.1   Ten design principles to keep college relevant

	Design Criteria	STARTING TO HAPPEN	NEEDS TO HAPPEN	COULD THIS EVER HAPPEN?
For Learners	Affordable, quality programs	✓		
	Community or cohorts	✓		
	Built-in career advising	✓		
	Visible connection to careers, stepladder	✓		
	Paid work experiences		✓	
	Certification of technical and durable skills			✓
	Permeable, portable institutions			✓
For Employers	Instruction moving at the speed of industry	✓		
	Employers paid or incentivized to train learners in the workplace		✓	
	Employer groups name skills to make career progressions visible			✓

observers and silo busters believe twelfth grade, senior year of high school, should figure prominently in college redesign efforts. And the term *sixty-year degree* has also inspired many colleges to think about how to provide upskilling services on the backside of college, throughout a learner's life.

THE NEW COLLEGE MARKETPLACE: THREE FRONT DOORS

The Great College Reset has begun with two distinct provider types emerging alongside traditional colleges to challenge the existing degree model. Positioned on either side of the typical college model, these providers are what I would call bookends, driving much of the innovation and pushing "business as usual" colleges to adapt. Together, these three players represent three front doors. Over time, learners will decide which to walk through based on the design criteria that matter to them most.

First, we already see the rise of some national online universities and companies beginning to play the role of consumer aggregator or college marketplace, an education version of Home Depot, or even Amazon, for the post–high school education consumer. This group of providers includes, for example, college course websites like for-profit Coursera, but also online colleges that serve a national population (and have run Super Bowl ads) like Southern New Hampshire University.[11] Many of these players deliver on the affordability design principle with "all you can eat" pricing, and some are making strides to offer the flexible stepladder approach and easy transfer of credits from either job experience or coursework at different colleges.

At the other end of the market, we see hyperlocal players that offer low-cost or no-cost learning and coaching experiences. These players include local mom-and-pop nonprofits and some high-touch community colleges or national players like Year Up, Per Scholas, and Merit America that run local skill-up programs around the country. These entrepreneurs, mostly nonprofits, tend to fundraise through philanthropy or receive public funding to keep learner costs to a minimum, so they score well on affordability—in fact, on all seven of my design criteria aimed at learners—but many of these programs are only open to a small group of low- or moderate-income students. Community colleges are obviously low-cost programs with open admission for all, but the funding model makes it tough for them to deliver the high-touch features, such as work experiences and coaching.

I predict that, within a decade, both of these outlier education types—hyperlocal and national platforms—either will be considered a "college" pathway outright or will fill the void for the nondegreed majority, with less stigma as we come to understand that these paths can lead to many of the futures that have been reserved for degree holders. I would argue they should all be referred to as "college," as we build a more inclusive language for multiple pathways. College should be defined as any post–high school path that sets a learner up for a family-sustaining wage and opens their eyes to their own possibilities. Programs will hopefully also provide a baseline of durable skills and professional readiness. Let's explore these two rising market segments in turn, as well as "business as usual" colleges, sandwiched in the middle, that may or may not be rising to the challenge to compete for a dwindling number of students.

National Platform Players

Despite the hangover America is still feeling about forced online education from the pandemic, it stands to reason that more and more education services will at least be packaged via platforms, even if some of the activities are hybrid or a homework simulation from your dorm-room laptop on campus. Today, half the US college market is getting part of its education online. A quarter is getting it fully online.[12]

When I worked at AOL in the mid- to late 1990s, at the dawn of the consumer digital era, we quickly developed a mantra when we saw how humans behaved on this new internet thing: "Portals are king." *Portal* was the word back then for "platform," or efforts to aggregate as much content as possible under one roof, to increase "eyeballs" and, thus, ad revenue. People flocked to places where lots of content was aggregated. The height of the mantra was in 1997, the year Jeff Bezos started Amazon. When I began helping colleges disrupt themselves nearly twenty years later, I watched the national platform players with interest.

Started by two Stanford professors, Coursera has been the noncollege player to watch so far, as the for-profit company morphed from aggregating populist-style massive open online courses to curating the best individual college courses, to offering corporate certifications, and now to delivering college degrees with university partners. LinkedIn also offers upskilling, although it's not as lucrative for it as its corporate talent hiring service.[13] But perhaps Amazon is actually best positioned to show us the future.[14]

Amazon currently manages an internal, more bespoke version of Coursera's marketplace, but only for its more than seven hundred thousand frontline employees. Amazon Career Choice provides free career coaching, prepaid college tuition (the federal tuition assistance program through employers allows up to $5,250 per employee per year), industry certifications for in-demand careers, and foundational skills like English language proficiency. At Amazon, the job-plus-education stepladder is becoming increasingly popular, with sixty thousand US workers signing up in 2022 alone when college tuition benefits and language programs were announced.[15]

"We're committed to empowering our employees by providing them access to the education and training they need to grow their careers, whether that's with us or elsewhere," said Tammy Thieman, global director of Amazon Career Choice, providing a quote for the book by email.[16] She added, "We have intentionally created a network of third-party educators and employers committed to providing excellent education, job placement resources, and continuous improvements to the experience." With two hundred thousand participants globally, Amazon's program likely represents the largest working model of the stepladder approach outside the US military.[17]

In talking to Amazon about how it brokers these programs directly between employers and learning providers, I could imagine just how useful it is to have an employer in the mix mapping skill-building pathways with other employers, particularly when the broker has the clout of Amazon. Amazon officials declined to opine on how well positioned they are to enter the education market and curate these employment paths for all consumers, not just their employees, but you could argue that most of the pieces are in place.

I believe that whether a learner is looking for a way to fit college around work or to stepladder to the next career role, some 50 percent or more of the edu-training market will come through front doors like Coursera, or companies like Amazon offering upskilling for their employees. These will be online marketplaces. Some colleges won't have the marketing budgets to compete at the front door, but their offerings can be inside. The biggest colleges, like Southern New Hampshire University, know how to partner with employers and can stand on their own as national platforms. Southern New Hampshire, for example, edged out competitor Western Governors

University as the number one largest single university as of this writing, with 250,000 students. But there are an array of colleges that know how to compete for students nationally. Most of them got into the online game early. They include, for example, Arizona State University and for-profit universities such as University of Phoenix, Strayer/Capella, and Grand Canyon. In-person enrollment has declined over the years, but these colleges see a bright future for online education.

Phil Regier, who has built a lot of the innovative models at Arizona State University, explained that the online degree market is growing by a million students a year. He believes their market collectively is all the forty million students and growing who dropped out of traditional college a first time.[18] "These people are stuck," he explained. "They probably have debt from their original college experience or experiences, right? They probably have life circumstances that make them non-traditional. They may be caring for others, they almost certainly are working full or part time. They may have mortgages. They have the full catastrophe of experiences that happen to humans, and yet they don't have a college degree."[19]

Convenience is critical for this part of the market. These learners are looking for a stripped-down version of the college experience, maybe just the piece of paper, when a career track requires a degree. They are certainly willing to give up the classroom, the community, maybe even the football team. We can expect more of the features we see on shopping sites, like the useful embedded user reviews and "Editors' Picks." Maybe even Black Friday sales? Maybe not. All kinds of products will be offered, from full degrees and upskilling classes to assessments to job simulations to Match.com -like services for apprenticeships. But education marketplaces are branching out to meet the lifelong learning and training needs of consumers. Scott Pulsipher, president of Western Governors University, who was an Amazon executive in his earlier days, told me it's getting easier as we enter the era when we can name every skill. "And when all that happens, it now becomes more 'first and next,'" he explained, "like what skills do I need for my first [job] opportunity, and my next opportunity, or the opportunity after that? And so college is not just a one and done model. No, I'm going to always be weaving together my educational pathway with my work opportunities. And that's a pretty beautiful thing, which means there's going to be an explosion of players."[20]

It Takes a Village

At the other end of the new college market, we need to take care of the folks who would otherwise fall between the cracks, learners who would like convenience and value that the DIY, online marketplaces offer, but who also might need structure, community, career exploration, connections, and, maybe most of all, a way to build confidence. They either don't see themselves in college or can't afford the time or money. And they may not access the national platforms, because it doesn't feel personal enough, or they don't know where to start.

This is where a human-centered version of college is beginning to take shape on the ground. In the hyperlocal space, the players include coaching and mentorship nonprofits, technical and durable skill providers, and internship and apprenticeship connectors, as well as some community and technical colleges that have found enough funding to embrace these roles. These innovators have bet that close-to-home brands and trust-based services speak to the part of the market that isn't packing up the SUV and "going away to college" but still craves and deserves a transformational experience. Maybe not at eighteen, maybe at twenty-five or even forty. This is where a lot of innovation is happening. And, if you recall the point about extreme users, the models we innovate for and with them may end up appealing to everyone.

In Denver, for example, the Denver School of Science and Technology (DSST) charter high school team is feeling somewhat optimistic. Not because their numbers of college enrollees will improve, but because the definition of college and postsecondary is expanding, and the bust part of "college or bust" is taking shape in a way that doesn't keep them up at night. It's specifically the bubbling up of new organizations, mostly nonprofits, to serve the non–college bound with a different model. I don't want to say "new" model, because many of these service organizations have been growing in major cities and through a few rural consortia for years, but their growth in numbers and connection between the K–12 system and the collegiate system, as well as the focus on high-demand, high-potential careers, is new.[21] In Denver, not only does DSST now use services like Willow Education that are helping to curate quality alternatives to the college degree, but the options themselves are proliferating and the groups are talking to each other.

ActivateWork calls itself a "little i" intermediary, training Denver-area learners for the latest hot tech roles and coordinating apprenticeship opportunities. But it has also won a state contract to be the "big I" Intermediary for the regional Tech Talent Partnership. In that role, it herds employers, colleges, alternative providers, and high schools. It functions, so to speak, as mayor of the tech talent pipeline "village." Kathryn Harris runs ActivateWork and explains the problem they are trying to solve. "It gets overwhelming for employers that want to be a part of that solution. There's so many different groups coming after them. They get their pet ones. And we never get to a place where we're thinking holistically about how to build pathways that we can scale to the jobs and skills that they most need."[22]

The village, which includes twenty large and smaller companies, including Bank of America and Western Union, has agreed on five high-need job roles: cybersecurity analyst, cyber governance, risk compliance, data analyst, and software developer. Kathryn says many of these roles will pay entry-level workers, after the twelve-month apprenticeship, $100,000–$110,000. At time of publication, she said she was brokering a deal to have the apprenticeship count for forty-five college credits, three short of an associate of arts degree. Either way, this is college through another door.

But let's say another student coming out of high school isn't interested in tech, or any profession. Realistically, the village is full of learners of all ages who would love the exploratory hand-holding that some traditional colleges offer. Jason Janz is a former Baptist minister and cofounder of CrossPurpose, a nonprofit that also serves the alt-college learner in Denver. His mantra is, "There is no significant change without a significant relationship." CrossPurpose holds weekly community dinners and describes its students as "neighbors." It comes across like a church community without the church part. Jason likes the quote popularized by radio host Steve Harvey, "The dream is free; the hustle is sold separately." He tells his neighbors, "If you'll hustle, we'll sweat, not more than you sweat, but we'll sweat by bringing the capital to bear and we'll bring coaching. And you'll put in the sweat to do the hard work of learning a skill."[23]

CrossPurpose has served about one thousand neighbors in the Denver area over the last decade with a promise of zero cost. What isn't covered by state or financial aid is funded by philanthropy. He believes college has been oversold, leaving many without a viable path. "What they need is a coach, a parental style coach," to help them choose from ten career tracks and get through the technical skills training. "There are not enough navigators," said Jason. "There's a lot of scholarship programs here but no one helps navigate with a capital N, bold, underline **Navigate**. Like, he or she has a parental ownership of that citizen, all the way to wealth building." Jason added proudly, on Zoom from his car, "What I'm trying to build out is the Ritz Carlton of services for the poor to get them to their generational wealth building."

The fascinating trend that crept up on me is that many of these nontraditional education providers are not actually providing the education. They are contracting it out to better-established third parties. I don't judge them for it; they are specializing to focus on the parts of college in the digital age that still benefit from in-person hand-holding and trust building. The technical skill building has become a commodity product that they can buy from someone else and deliver online. CrossPurpose focuses on the Cs: community, coaching, and capital (both social capital and financing for the training). It is a model most big colleges cannot match.

ActivateWork was thrilled to be selected as the first independent partner for national bootcamp Per Scholas. Per Scholas operates nonprofit, no-cost tech bootcamps in twenty-three US cities for low-income learners and has been lauded by funders as one of the few with consistently positive placement outcomes.[24] Now, it is attempting what appears to be a franchise model of sorts. Per Scholas provides four days a week of bootcamp training online for the fifteen-week program, and ActivateWork provides the cohort community and coaching and organizes twelve-month apprenticeships or job placement.

One concern I always hear is, How do these organizations scale? That's why many are partnering with colleges. Most of the players I have spoken to in local markets are serving fewer than three hundred learners in a year. CrossPurpose is not aiming for scale, says Jason. He hopes to get to a point where he can serve one thousand neighbors well each year with twenty different career tracks and then get other groups around the country "to copy the crap out of it." What hit me over the course of researching this book is that maybe the village players don't have to scale. It started to feel like another industry I have watched over the years, where small is beautiful: the craft beer market.

Remember I described the alternative credential movement in chapter 2 and how, in many industries, alternative is cool? Craft beer has managed to stay trendy since it was introduced in the 1970s as an antidote to the samey flavors of Budweiser or Pabst Blue Ribbon. And we began to take pride in our local breweries like they were sports teams. I root for Old Dominion and Port City in northern Virginia. Craft beer really exploded in the 1990s. Today the hyperlocal microbrewery market has captured 25 percent of the market share of the beer industry.[25] But except for a handful of pan-local brands, it's hundreds or thousands of labels you've never heard of.

Jobs for the Future (JFF), a workforce intermediary, has done a landscape analysis of nondegree credentials and reports that 25 percent of the market is made up of local intermediaries, many of them quite new.[26] Huh. That's the same size as the craft beer market, which, according to Wall Street analyst research reports, is healthy.[27]

"Business as Usual" Schools

The good news for traditional colleges is that while degree demand might be shrinking, college could be described as expanding. I predict that the "addressable market" for a more broadly defined view of college will include workforce training (currently sponsored by government) and corporate training (provided on the job or paid for by employers using federal tax write-offs) more so than it does today. I believe the colleges we think of today, with the football teams and leafy campuses, will account for a shrinking share of this broader market, but a smaller share of a bigger market can be a lifeboat. Best-selling author Jeff Selingo, who writes about college, told me that college institutions will have to cope when they are no longer the "unit of measure." They have to learn to serve a learner-centric ecosystem. "The university is now going to be a medium, a conduit, one of many, just like non-university learning partners, to help the learner direct their own learning throughout a lifetime," Jeff explains.[28]

The two bookends, hyperlocal providers and national platforms, are positioned for agility and thus drive much of the innovation. But colleges are figuring out, as Jeff says, that "skills are now the coin of the realm." Or to take this one step further, as I predict, if colleges could provide experience as part of a degree, they would compete better with other, shorter offerings. Enrollment numbers show that community colleges leaning into career preparation and partnerships are surviving better than those that aren't.[29] I believe that private and public-sector institutions vying for students in a regulated industry is the healthiest model for higher education. So I am rooting for existing colleges to remain in the game, but they have to adapt, with or without the two iron gates I mentioned earlier that hold back innovation (the inside stronghold of faculty and the outside stronghold of the accreditors).

Ted Mitchell from ACE and I riffed about what innovations colleges might consider in the future. His organization is helping them offer college credit for work experience, in the military and other fields.[30] And looking further out, Ted suggested that some colleges could team up, beyond the mergers we already see as the market contracts. "I think there will always be a place in the world for residential education centers. But whether those residential education centers are places that offer one brand, so, is it a Coca Cola bar? Or does it offer a combination of Starbucks and Coca Cola and Jack Daniels and more?"

"Could employers form the mall," I asked, "rather than colleges?"

Ted responded, "They could be either on the demand side or the supply side."

It would be very human centered for competitive companies to create a training campus together to provide teaching and on-the-job experiences for students. I haven't seen any examples yet, but desperation drives interesting behavior. On the education provider side, however, Ted's scenario is beginning to unfold. Not on many traditional campuses yet, where sharing students among colleges still feels like a zero-sum game. But it's happening in the new college village. The village education providers are not just dating; some of them have moved in together to organize one front door.

CONVERGENCE

As we near the end of our story, I wanted to provide a taste of what I predict will be the biggest trend among the three broader college markets I describe. And that is convergence, where all three will start to come together in different permutations, using trusted nonprofits, community colleges, or prestigious degree or high-traffic consumer brands as the front doors to capture customers. Talent for Tomorrow is an early example, a new kind of school that suggests how local trusted brands can come together.

Talent for Tomorrow houses five influential providers that offer college and noncollege tracks under the same roof. They share a literal front door on the fifth floor of an office building a few blocks from the Capitol in Washington, DC. The services range from high school mentoring to

---

Five groups form a new "college" offering for youth:

- Spark the Journey—high school mentoring
- Genesys Works—high school apprenticeships
- Year Up—post–high school direct-to-employment coaching, training, and internships
- Per Scholas—post–high school tech training
- New Futures—post–high school coaching and scholarships for college pathways

direct-to-employment training to internship and college placement to scholarships, all aimed at the low- to moderate-income learner. Each group specializes to save itself from being spread too thin, but they now band together to build a collective recruiting narrative, whether students want a degree or job training or both.

Year Up, the largest provider in the partnership, has been building a national brand for twenty-five years as a college alternative for low-income students in twenty-two locations around the country. Year Up provides a diverse talent pipeline to more than 250 employers (Bank of America and JPMorganChase are its biggest nationally) and has added a staffing agency called YUPRO. Traditional college is not usually part of this formula. The training part lasts from three to six months, five days a week, virtual and in person. Then everyone gets placed in a six- to twelve-month internship.

At the Talent for Tomorrow headquarters, I got the chance to interview three older students, in their mid- to late twenties, who are now in their internships. Anne had been to community college and found this a more direct route to professional employment. The other two bounced around for seven or eight years after high school until someone suggested Year Up. Ayanna wishes she had known about Year Up in high school. Her family could only afford to send their first daughter to college. She was the second.

She told me, "I was definitely open to, you know, other routes, other than college."[31]

I asked, "Were they clear to you, the other routes?"

She replied, "They were not clear, they definitely weren't. Because I feel like I just ended up working for a while." Now, ten years later, interning in IT at Danaher, a medical diagnostic firm, she feels Year Up has given her the same boost out of frontline service jobs that college might have. "They teach you, they give you the skills, they give you the experience, and then they also give you an internship, and that internship could potentially turn into the career that you want."

Should Year Up be included in a new definition of college? When I asked all the students this, they nodded vigorously. Ayanna said, "So literally, like, it's just a fast track. For me. I feel like if I were 18, and somebody told me about this program, I would have signed up for this immediately. Instead of college. Yeah. And then it's free. So I'm not losing any money at all." Her fellow student, twenty-six-year-old Daisean, a dad, made a motion of a rocket ship taking off. He added, "When I saw that it was actually possible to gain a corporate position, with just a high school diploma, and certifications. That's what opened my eyes to the fact that you don't have to take the traditional route."[32]

And Daisean believes he displays more confidence than the university interns he works beside at a mental health law firm helping with advocacy work because he's been trained specifically in project management and how to operate in a corporate setting.

"These are real big time organizations that nine times out of ten you need a college degree for, so me coming from an urban background, I'm coming from a working class family, poverty, but I'm surrounded by people that have the education and the family background." Fifty-two percent of Year Up grads get hired by their internship companies and 80 percent get a job, or sometimes education placements, within four months.[33] So it's not a slam dunk. But these students were bullish on their prospects.

It feels painful to realize that so many of the "alternative" learners I meet have bounced around for years looking for education or training. Honestly, these three students were almost giddy at their good luck to get onto this "rocket ship" and achieve the legitimacy their job placements afforded them, without the bachelor's degree. Year Up would love to meet more of its learners earlier. It has actually colocated in fifteen different community colleges over the past several years to test that combined-front-door approach.

A learner's choice in the future will be which front door to enter for one of three types of experience: a localized experiential journey; a traditional degree, or shorter residential experience for other services—or, for those who value convenience; or a fully online shopping cart to provide pay-as-you-go education virtually. These should all qualify as "college" in our new education world order if they meet quality standards.

Unfortunately, it's much easier to put these alliances together in cities than in rural areas, but there are many groups building them in different scenarios.[34]

The Biggest Roadblocks

I have described my twin strategies of "fix and disrupt." A world where traditional colleges enhance existing products, create new ones, and use the bookends to distribute unbundled and bundled pieces of college does, in fact, already exist. But to really serve learners as the education world and the world around us both change, we need to solve some key challenges. They make some of my design principles harder to tackle. I will pick three of the toughest to execute that I have studied over time.

1. If experience is a big part of the new degree, how do we provide experience for all, whether learners choose a short-term certificate or a long-term degree, not to mention paid experiences? Can simulated experiences help meet the demand if there are not enough internships and apprenticeships to serve all students?
2. If more and more people skip the liberal arts degree to save time and money, in favor of technical "job-ready" skills training, how might we salvage the "learning how to learn" part of the degree? How do we save what is affectionately known as "gen ed"?
3. The stepladder approach calls on us to assess all kinds of learning, wherever it occurs. How might our funding models incentivize us to build out the skills genome map and "credentialize" everything on it?

Each of these needs a little more explanation.

Simulated Work Experiences.   New-style "colleges" like Year Up might be leading the way to show traditional colleges how to be "experience first," but even they are struggling to provide the signature paid internship at $525 a week for all students.[35] Year Up is now investigating the possibility of simulated work experiences when it can't place everybody in an actual workplace.

I spoke with executives at two providers that Year Up is piloting with to test employer reaction, Forage and MAXX Potential. And both explained that the demand for simulation is coming from several quarters: intermediaries like Year Up, companies looking for talent pipeline, colleges, and even DIY students roaming the internet. Rob Simms, from MAXX Potential, explains how they got their start scaling internships for a technical high school in Richmond, Virginia: "We basically took the students, we placed them in a fictitious power company called MAXX Energy. And they have a job, they have a job description, they're in a department, they might be in software development and analytics, security, support, and they have a manager . . . it's not their teacher. They're there to expect them to do work, meet deadlines, go into agile stand ups, and, and get things done."[36] Now MAXX Potential is running three dozen simulations at any given time, mostly for *Fortune* 500 companies. Rob took me on a tour and we met several students who were training to be IT help desk technicians. They were clustered in Zoom-like breakout rooms. In another room, we said hello to one of the "bosses," also a live participant, not a bot.

Forage is the other simulation provider working with Year Up. Jeff Holm, from the University of North Dakota, whom we met in chapter 4, was surprised to find his students on Forage. It claims to have drawn six million students who engage in online simulations to test out companies and career roles. More than one hundred companies, like Ford Motor Company and KPMG, have paid for the creation of simulations. The companies focus on building awareness for tough-to-hire areas, and they use Forage as their agent in the digital marketplace.[37]

You can begin to see here how "experience first" could drive learners' choices as they weigh the options of going to college, following a micropathway, or going directly to work. College textbook giant Pearson Education recently announced a partnership with Forage, in a sense validating what students and employers were doing on their own. Could we also tap into work-study programs on campus or employers' tuition reimbursement plans to get to not just internships or work experiences for all but paid ones at that?[38]

How to Save "Gen Ed."   When I first explained the Education Design Lab's idea of micro-pathways to college administrators and pressed the point that we would be asking community colleges to include durable or soft skill credential requirements, I remember one observer remarked, "Thank God, you are going to save Gen Ed." Like everyone else, he was watching with alarm as general education courses were being extracted from curricula in favor of technical, shorter-term certificates. Cost-conscious students looking for a good job did not see the point of a required course in world civilizations. The great unbundling of education over the last decade has allowed them to pick the fast road to employment. But many, many educators are left wringing their hands about what will happen to a society that shuts down its humanities and social science departments. My stepladder approach doesn't really leave a natural step for "learning how to learn." Does it have to be force-fed? Critical thinking is the skill most requested by employers when we ask them to recommend durable skill credentials to include in a micro-pathway.

When I have these discussions, politics and civic engagement always come up. In my top ten design criteria for the Great College Reset, I include two that are really meant to drive this point home, in hope that unbundling will not give way to "just-in-time training" for all. First, shorter versions of college, nondegree options, must build in broader training than technical skills; both should be taught and certified in the context of the learner's industry of choice. Second, for younger adults particularly, providers must offer affordable in-person encounters and cohort opportunities, to engage learners beyond their own bubbles, help them find community, and expose them to networks that will provide "unforeseeable career bumps."

Critical thinking skills can be honed through the college degree, but if fewer people are signing up for the long-form version of college, we need other models to push us to carefully gather and assess information, to build our own fake news filters, to serve as that training ground for tolerance born of shared experience, forced collaboration, and resilience to get through any gauntlet. Thirty years ago, there was a push to provide non-military options for service, either before or after college or instead of it: AmeriCorps, City Year, Teach for America, Job Corps. But these are not as popular as they were in previous decades.[39] The ones run by government have been especially criticized for inefficiencies or poor results. There is no clamoring in our age of self-isolation or "bowling alone" to push young people to pick one of these experiences, or any other.[40]

I am a fan of the small movement that is looking at either reimagining the last year of high school or adding a year 13 that replaces the gen ed aspect of college and focuses on community or career exploration. Many communities are surprised by how many high school students are signing up for dual enrollment, getting college credits while in high school, to the point where one out of every five community college students today is a high schooler.[41] What is this telling us? Could high school end earlier? Could we blend late high school and early college? A few cities and states, such as Maryland, are looking at radical restructuring.[42] Can colleges serve this function, less expensively, without requiring degrees? Are the popularity of dual credit (high schoolers taking college courses) and the success of small-scale youth apprenticeships showing us the way?

Building the Stepladder.   I have talked about how to scale the experience part of college, how to think about saving general education, but perhaps the hardest challenge is reimagining college as a stepladder in a visible, certifiable way. I was hoping to get through the book without using the technical term *assessment*. But right now there are too few rungs on the ladder where all players agree on the skills required, let alone how to assess those skills. And students are learning much of what they do need on the job outside school, while some skills may come from innate abilities, or a spark of potential. This challenge holds the keys to the kingdom if we want to "save" college. Our journey to assess learning beyond the classroom is in its infancy. Ted Mitchell from ACE worries about this too. "It's tricky," he says, "to think about a policy that actually supports the learning instead of exposure."

To whom do I pay my tuition dollars if I am learning across the ecosystem, in a bootcamp training, on the job, from a simulation, through coaching from Year Up or on campus, perhaps all in the same year? In previous sections, I have stated that employers need to help build a skills map or genome. The need for assessment across parts of an expanding ecosystem means we have to map and track skills mastery, but also make a judgment as to where the student learns it, so the provider or the employer can be paid. It's a challenge that cries out for a harbormaster or quarterback in the ecosystem, which I believe colleges should resolve to become.

I have written that community colleges are particularly well suited to become the trusted talent brokers in their regional job markets. But they have to get better at the broker part. It's hard partly because of yesteryear's funding model that mostly incentivizes colleges to issue degrees. In a new world, they could be the master contractors, sharing their tuition funding with other groups that provide and assess skill building, employers, and nonprofits. If the colleges are going to continue to be the ones the government will trust to disburse financial aid, then they hold the keys to the new ecosystem of providers working together effectively.

In 2023, the nation's largest college accreditor made a bold move, announcing it would begin to evaluate nondegree credential providers to help colleges partner better. This is a big deal, representing a recognition that "college" is changing. The Higher Learning Commission and other accreditors determine which colleges are authorized to grant degrees and access federal financial aid. President Barbara Gellman-Danley told me the decision to begin, in effect, giving seals of approval to quality alternative providers was heavily covered by the media and received positively by the field. "We've gotten absolutely no pushback." She told me colleges need better information and that without transparency of the proliferating nontraditional providers, there have been "good alliances" and "some disastrous partnerships. We just want to help colleges make the right partnerships."[43]

I and others have been urging community colleges to get ready for "short-term Pell," which is the latest version of federal funding reform before Congress and would fund lower-income students to earn nondegree credentials. As we go to press for this book, it hasn't passed, but as I mentioned earlier, short-term Pell would help redefine college more broadly than a degree and allocate tuition funding to programs as short as seven weeks if they can build evidence of solid job employment results. Some of those programs might be alternative providers that traditional colleges can bring into the fold and hold accountable.[44]

. . . and Finally, the GPS Navigator

I asked you in chapter 1 to imagine a future world with a skills wallet connected to GPS. I think about some of the learners we met throughout this book: Porchea, who aged out of the foster system at age eighteen and tried community college four times; Yrel, who, after getting a degree, ended up as a retail clerk; Patrick, who earned valuable IT certifications in high school; Crystal, who broke down in tears when she told me she was finally going to get to be a teacher at age fifty. How might the Great College Reset have helped them? How will it continue to help them no matter their age, as well as the high school students now facing the "college for all" music?

My hope is that the ecosystem players—philanthropists, states and other government entities, and yes, the Googles, Amazons, and LinkedIns—invest in the mapping. That industry-sector groups and nonprofit intermediaries invest in certifying jobs and evaluating quality programs. And that colleges, village players, and national platforms invest in high-quality, affordable "experience-first" options, making their front doors accessible and visible. This is soon becoming a world where every learner must be their own agent, because we'll be picking and choosing smaller units of learning throughout our lives.

As Paul LeBlanc says, "We'll still have people wanting associates and bachelors and masters degrees and so on. I do think there'll be lots of other credentials that matter. It's kind of early in that movement, and it's kind of a mess, but I think that will clarify, that will clear, and I think the bigger shift will be much more fluidity."[45] In fact, Paul has left his college presidency to pursue AI learning solutions aimed at helping learners thrive in a self-driving education world.[46]

So I will ask you now to imagine, as I did in chapter 1, that it is 2035. Our design sprint is complete. We have prototyped new models to center the criteria for learners, we have partnered across the three front doors from which learners will choose education products across their working lives. And, perhaps most importantly, the map will be ready and the destinations will be both crowd-sourced and vetted by accreditors and government for quality control.

First of all, pull out your phone and scroll to your skills wallet app. Enter a destination—let's say, "good jobs with benefits in Denver."

The search takes you through choices by sector. Daniel, from DSST, for example, might enter "car designer."

Then you ask the map feature in your wallet app for a route to become a car designer. The app has access to your skills—in fact, it has inferred multiple skills that you hadn't thought of related to your part-time jobs, lived experiences, and your AP classes at a top-rated school.

So the app visualizes multiple paths to get to car designer, using the step-ladder method I described earlier, to build earnings power in short bursts, presenting a pay-as-you-go model with a series of micro-pathways. Learn, earn, learn, and earn. The learner has access to a menu of routes, including four-year colleges, of course, but also including recommendations for classes, certificates, and apprenticeships for each stage to get to car designer. Some employer destinations might require the full degree journey or licensing exams, immersive online experiences, simulations, or in-person adventures, like skill-building and community camps. The app would synthesize these requirements to make recommendations and provide feedback for consumers, as well as for accreditors who could determine whether employer demand or placement rates add up to a return on investment that justifies federal financial aid.

The final piece of the wallet is the two-way communication with employers. If you opt in to be "visible," they can find you. You might be thinking that many of these components of career navigation exist already. But today these disparate pieces only serve the intrepid or the lucky. Like health care, higher education, as a regulated field, is more organized to protect learners from bad actors than to serve them seamlessly and affordably.

AI IS THE RACETRACK

One of the best places to go for advice on how the learning market and the hiring market might conspire to deemphasize the college degree is Workday, the company that processes job openings for roughly 25 percent of US employers; it is a service provider for half of all *Fortune* 500 companies.[47]

I spoke to two senior leaders there who believe that AI is already helping job applicants expand their hirability to a broader range of jobs than the ones they thought they were qualified for. But how far are we from my GPS, available to all, that not only suggests destinations but then fills in possible routes? Chandler Morse is vice president for public policy at Workday. He tells me, "AI is like the race track. And now we're all realizing that we need cars to go on the track. So AI is sort of the pull factor."[48] Pulling what? Race car drivers, sponsors, and teams, to get on the track. Workday and several other providers already have talent tracking systems that help employers build their own internal skills genome. "Who have I got? What else are they good at? What would it take to move them, to upskill them to this new role where I have gaps?" In the internal business world of upskilling, the AI benefits we can see today mostly help incumbent workers and their larger companies.

But Chandler believes, as of 2024–2025, we are only a few years away from having examples of at least state versions of a more public talent GPS.

"I think we're a couple years out from having some really good examples that we can use to say, look, this is doable," he explains. "We can actually take a lot of the guesswork out of career planning and really provide it to people who need it the most."

And Chandler's colleague at Workday, Aashna Kircher, general manager of talent products, believes that early-career workers will benefit most because AI will help them and their prospective employers discern skills to draw helpful inferences, building a new language of what she calls "skills intelligence." In this language, there are two As: agility and adjacency. She explains, "In the context of skills intelligence, for example, we understand that one skill also could mean these other 10 related skills and maybe an adjacency over here. So even though they've applied to this job, they might be a better fit for this job . . . even though those skills don't match perfectly to the resume."[49] AI-driven skills intelligence could go a long way to helping us assess those skills that will help learners and workers move up their stepladders or over to a new one.

But this racetrack is perilous if we don't pave it with care. And time is short. As I get close to publication, yet another national survey has come out. Thirty-five percent of folks surveyed who are enrolled in college said they have considered dropping out in the last six months for reasons of stress and cost.[50] While enrollment numbers rallied a bit in the spring semester of 2024, college access groups are predicting another potential decline in the fall because of a "botched rollout" of the new federal government tool to apply for financial aid.[51] It will be a travesty if we have to watch the further contraction of the higher ed system that has been the envy of the world over the past hundred years, because we priced so many Americans out of the market and remained too rigid to continually address what entrepreneurs call "product market fit."

It's not too late. I have always been both wildly hopeful and practical in approaching systems change. I am optimistic in large part because the top thing that disrupted our field, technology, can also help save it, along with smarter funding and a resolve to move to a mind-set that college is an ecosystem, not a piece of paper. The ten design principles I drew from in writing this book, that provide guardrails for "what must be true," can be implemented across the three-headed evolution of college that I describe. Affordability sits at the top of the list. As we go to press, two more states, Maine and Minnesota, have just turned around their public college enrollment woes by significantly increasing state funding for free college.[52] Longtime observer and journalist Paul Fain says, "They're showing that if you take the bull by the horns, and don't pretend [enrollment decline] is not happening, maybe a different approach to college can work and ameliorate some of the collapse."[53]

We are also making progress to show that the learner journey is accessible, connected, portable, relevant, and visible. The blind handoffs from high school to college or training to career are becoming less blind, more integrated, with skills wallets on the horizon. The experiments of the last decade, since those early bootcamps, have heightened our awareness and changed the mind-sets of many. But we are poised to do much more.

Remember, I said I subscribe to the "fix and disrupt" school of innovation.

For the "fix" part of our challenge, I believe we are ready to rearrange and rethink tuition funding sources and employer incentives. We are poised to translate learning to skills in order to help learners connect them to career possibilities. And we are beginning to recognize that chances to gain experience should be an entitlement, alongside tuition.

For the "disrupt" part of our challenge, we need to fund the stepladder approach to learning, which will attract new players into the market. They can be managed for quality control if we build the data infrastructure now.

If nothing else, I hope this book can push us to come to terms with the collective damage of our unintended ambivalence. Today we should be clear-eyed about naming how bad the situation has become. Not the degree itself, which hasn't changed very much, but how the public does or doesn't interact with it. The years-long quests learners must embark on, as well as the noise of competing narratives, are stressing out our young people about their futures. Across this whole, expanded college continuum, we should stop using the words *alternative* and *non-* to describe other possible paths. By 2035, I am hoping those terms won't be relevant to describe any pathway to prosperity. I imagine that a holistic, no-judgment narrative will overtake the current one and that we will also make room in the schedule from middle or high school to expose learners to fast-evolving career choices.

What would my relative John Wise say? He's the one who, from across the centuries, was perhaps calling me to get involved in higher education reform. If he was a very early American "college access" success story in 1673, the son of an indentured servant who graduated from Harvard, what would he make of today's challenge? He was someone who later spoke out against the Salem witch trials and backed the controversial polio vaccine in his day, who foreshadowed the language of the Declaration of Independence by writing about equality and stating that "the end of all good government is to cultivate humanity and promote the happiness of all." He seemed to pick a lot of fights for a minister—he was apparently a champion wrestler.[54] Would he label our current situation insidious injustice, crying foul that today's American Dream caretakers are talking out of both sides of their mouths? "The college degree is essential—or is it?" "It is attainable—by whom?" Would he name the broken system that dampens belief in and access to the degree while not providing visible alternatives? We may not think of him, a colonial white male, as a new majority learner, but as a low-income, first-generation college student, in his day, he was. I'd like to believe that John Wise would want to reimagine and modernize college and the degree as the centuries unfolded, so that other new majority learners might have clearer choices.

Start a Conversation

Discussion Guides for Employers, High Schools, Colleges, Intermediaries, and Families

As I wrote this book, I was amazed at how just sharing the title, *Who Needs College Anymore?*, sparked a discussion wherever I went. There are so many perspectives, stories, victories, failures, worries, suggestions, and debates. I decided it might be helpful to recommend discussion guides for some of the key stakeholders, as well as families, who want to extend the conversation into their communities as we try to clarify the role of college or redefine it.

These guides can be downloaded, along with other resources, at the book's website: whoneedscollegeanymore.org.

I. DISCUSSION GUIDE FOR EMPLOYERS

1. How problematic is it for your company or organization if fewer job applicants have college degrees?
2. Would you consider removing two-year or four-year degree requirements from some job postings? Which categories? What would

be required, what practices would need to change, for nondegree applicants to actually be hired in those roles?

3. Can your job applicants and employees see what skills are required for entry-level roles and for advancement at your organization? Is it written down by role in a way that can be shared with them?

4. How important is "experience" when you are hiring for entry-level roles? Is it more important than a degree? How closely does the experience need to relate to the role?

5. Have you considered creating apprenticeships? What would it take to make them viable at your organization?

6. For what roles would you consider hiring students directly from high school? Has that view changed over time? Are you worried about talent shortages in the future?

7. Do you believe that industry certifications are a useful tool to validate job readiness? What percentage of your organization's roles have certifications that would help you in the hiring process?

8. How could your organization contribute to creating more industry certifications, across all job roles, that would provide better hiring signals to candidates?

9. How easy has it been to partner with colleges or high schools to create a greater talent pipeline for hard-to-fill roles? Do you have recommendations for them?

10. How could we clarify the "narrative" about who needs college anymore? What could your organization do to make the need (or not) clearer to young people, parents, and workers?

II. DISCUSSION GUIDE FOR HIGH SCHOOLS

1. How do you decide which students to guide toward college and which not? How do you get your information about quality professional pathway programs (those that take students directly into career-track jobs)? Do you like the term *professional pathways*? What language should we use to describe them?

2. Have your policies or practices on college advising changed over the years? What brought about that change?

3. Are you seeing students (and their parents) express more concern about college than, say, a decade ago? If so, what pressures have caused their concerns?

4. Are there unintended consequences to helping or pushing all students to become "college ready"? Are you able to learn how many of your students complete college and how much debt they take on?

5. Do you wish you could build in more career exploration experiences for students? What year during K–12 should this begin? What are the obstacles?

6. Should the last year of high school be restructured? What stands in the way in your community?

7. Dual enrollment has gained surprising popularity; one in five enrollees now in community college is a high schooler. What's working about the program at your school? How could dual enrollment in your district or state be better structured to prepare students directly for careers or shorten their degree path, depending on their choices?

8. How well does your school or district partner with colleges? With employers? With professional pathway programs?

9. When you consider the personas described in chapter 6, some types of learners that do and don't need college, where do you agree or disagree?
   Can afford to skip or delay college:
   • connected career switcher
   • motivated do-it-yourselfer
   • prepackaged-career starter
   • undecided, maybe later
   Needs the imprimatur or experiences only college can provide:
   • class transporter
   • legitimacy label seeker
   • degree or license worker
   • longing-to-belonger

10. Could your school help shape the narrative that there are multiple strong paths to a good life, not just college? Or do you support a different national narrative?

III. DISCUSSION GUIDE FOR COLLEGES

1. Are you worried about declining enrollment trends at your institution? Have those trends become a catalyst for change?

2. If your enrollment is steady or growing, how do you see your unique value proposition for students as the world changes around you?

3. Do you see it as your role to provide career-related work experience to your students before they graduate? If so, how hard is it to do that? What additional capacity needs to exist?

4. If you can't provide students with career-related job experience, how are you helping them demonstrate skills as they apply for entry-level roles? Could you include an apprenticeship inside the structure of your degree programs? If not, why not? What about industry certifications?

5. Do you provide students with a "skills profile," as described in the section about Western Governors University in chapter 4? Do you like this idea? Could it become part of a student's digital transcript? Are other work experience ideas, including "experience sampling" and micro-pathways, viable in your context?

6. How does your college or university treat "nondegree" offerings? Are there unintended consequences? Are students pursuing them treated differently from degree-track learners? Could you imagine merging these two parts of your institution?

7. How did you react to the eight personas in chapter 6, which describes four types of today's learners who may be able to skip college and four who very much need it?

   Can afford to skip or delay college:
   - connected career switcher
   - motivated do-it-yourselfer

- prepackaged career starter
- undecided, maybe later

Needs the imprimatur or experiences only college can provide:

- class transporter
- legitimacy label seeker
- degree or license worker
- longing-to-belonger

8. What would change at your institution if "short-term Pell" passes into law, making federal financial aid available for training programs as short as eight weeks?

9. The following statement from chapter 7 could apply to universities as well as community colleges. What is your reaction?

I have written that community colleges are particularly well suited to become the trusted talent brokers in their regional job markets. But they have to get better at the broker part. It's hard partly because of yesteryear's funding model that mostly incentivizes colleges to issue degrees. In a new world, they could be the master contractors, sharing their tuition funding with other groups that provide and assess skill building, employers, and nonprofits. If the colleges are going to continue to be the ones the government will trust to disburse financial aid, then they hold the keys to the new ecosystem of providers working together effectively.

10. What is your reaction to these lines from the closing chapter?

A learner's choice in the future will be which front door to enter for one of three types of experience: a localized experiential journey; a traditional degree, or shorter residential experience for other services; or, for those who value convenience, a fully online shopping cart to provide pay-as-you-go education virtually. These should all qualify as "college" in our new education world order if they meet quality standards.

IV. DISCUSSION GUIDE FOR INTERMEDIARIES, STATE AND LOCAL AGENCIES, AND NONPROFITS THAT SERVE THE SCHOOL-TO-WORK TALENT PIPELINE

1. Would your organization support or oppose a redefinition of college more broadly to include shorter-term pathways, such as certificate programs, apprenticeships, or programs like Year Up?

2. Could your organization become a "college" itself under a broader definition, potentially with other players?

3. How would you describe your organization's value proposition or distinct role with respect to either hastening the design of a college reset or, alternatively, doubling down on the existing higher education models?

4. How do you react to the following statement from chapter 7? Where does your organization fit in? Are these the right "jobs to be done"?

    My hope is that the ecosystem players—philanthropy, states and other government entities, and yes, the Googles, Amazons, and LinkedIns—invest in the mapping. That industry-sector groups and nonprofit intermediaries invest in certifying jobs and evaluating quality programs. And that colleges, village players, and national platforms invest in high-quality, affordable "experience-first" options, making their front doors accessible and visible. This is soon becoming a world where every learner must be their own agent, because we'll be picking and choosing smaller units of learning throughout our lives.

5. Do you agree with the book's premise that two counternarratives have created a harmful vacuum in which college is both unaffordable and also essential for a "good job"? What role might your organization play in clarifying the narrative?

6. How did you react to the eight personas in chapter 6, which describes four types of today's learners who may be able to skip college and four who very much need it?

Can afford to skip or delay college:
- connected career switcher
- motivated do-it-yourselfer
- prepackaged career starter
- undecided, maybe later

Needs the imprimatur or experiences only college can provide:
- class transporter
- legitimacy label seeker
- degree or license worker
- longing-to-belonger

7. If you serve learners directly, how would they want to define college? How much do they care about "the piece of paper" versus the skills? Are you seeing particular trends over time?

8. Will intermediaries become more important in the future of postsecondary education and career prep to connect the dots among the players, as learners seek skills and experience from more sources? How can you help avoid competing for resources and confusing the landscape with repetitive offerings or conflicting agendas? What would be the most important initiative to come together on?

9. As we all seek learning in smaller chunks, from a multitude of providers, career advising and navigation become more complicated. Who should deliver and fund career navigation? Will AI help make it better or cause us to automate it?

10. Do you like the notion of "skills wallets"? Do you think the ecosystem can work together to make these widely available by 2030 or 2035? Who should take the lead to make sure wallets are open and transferable and that the data are owned by learners?

V. DISCUSSION GUIDE FOR LEARNERS AND THEIR PARENTS

1. How do you react to the book's central point that we have two conflicting narratives about college that together send conflicting

messages that are holding some families back and creating stress for students? One narrative is that college is unaffordable and "not worth it." The other is that college is essential for a "good job." Has one of the two narratives swayed you toward or away from college?

2. Does it seem too risky *not* to go to college? Or do you feel the opposite? If you are advising your child, how have things changed since you went to high school?

3. Do you think "trade schools" carry a stigma? Is that changing in your community? Are professional pathways other than trade school available to you or your children?

4. Do you think there is too much pressure in the K–12 education system to push children to go to college, or even an elite college? What changes would you like to see?

5. Do you feel like you were "tracked" in school, meaning that you were guided toward college-prep or other noncollege courses to prepare you directly for work after high school? Did you initiate your track? Or is everyone at your school taking the same kind of classes?

6. How did you react to the eight personas in chapter 6, which describe four types of today's learners who may be able to skip college and four who very much need it? Do you (or your children) fit into any of these categories? And do you agree that you or they do or don't need college to be successful?

   Can afford to skip or delay college:
   - connected career switcher
   - motivated do-it-yourselfer
   - prepackaged career starter
   - undecided, maybe later

   Needs the imprimatur or experiences only college can provide:
   - class transporter
   - legitimacy label seeker
   - degree or license worker
   - longing-to-belonger

7. Do you have enough information to make informed decisions for yourself or with your teenagers about possible paths after high school? What sources do you use to do your research or make decisions?

8. Would you look to your local community college to find shorter-term career certificates? Or a local four-year college? Are you aware of ways to find apprenticeship programs in your area?

9. Employers in chapter 3 talked about the importance of industry certifications, which are available particularly in some tech, cyber-security, and medical fields. Would you want to earn those in high school? Do you know if high schools in your area offer them?

10. Should high school be redesigned to include career exploration or possibly youth apprenticeships? What could be removed from the high school schedule, in your view, to make room for it?

Notes

Introduction

1. Overall, college enrollment has decreased roughly 10% since the high-water mark of 2010. Community college enrollment has shrunk by 37%, although it made a slight rebound in the 2023–24 academic year. See Melanie Hanson, "College Enrollment & Student Demographic Statistics," Educational Data Initiative, January 10, 2024, https://educationdata.org/college-enrollment-statistics.

2. Of US adults, 38% hold a bachelor's degree. Another 10.5% hold an associate's degree. Katherine Schaeffer, "10 Key Facts About US Colleges," Pew Research Trust, April 12, 2022, https://www.pewresearch.org/short-reads/2022/04/12/10-facts-about-todays-college-graduates/.

3. While the number of people choosing college is dropping, the actual completion rate, for those who do enroll, has mostly been increasing. "Fast Facts: Educational Attainment," National Center for Education Statistics, https://nces.ed.gov/fastfacts/display.asp?id=27. But even at this high-water mark of completion, we've never seen numbers of bachelor's and associate degree holders higher than half of US adults. Schaeffer, "10 Key Facts."

4. *2024 Human Progress Report* (Princeton, NJ: ETS and Harris Poll, April 2024), 8, https://www.ets.org/human-progress-report.html.

5. The website CollegeVine uses an AI recommendation engine to help you meet colleges and get accepted: https://www.collegevine.com/.

6. Black college enrollment increased between 2000 and 2010 by 8 percentage points, and Latino participation by 10 percentage points. See Bill Hussar et al., "College Enrollment Rates," in *The Condition of Education 2020* (Washington, DC: National Center for Educational Statistics, May 2020), https://nces.ed.gov/programs/coe/pdf/coe_cpb.pdf.

7. Emma D. Cohen et al., *High School Longitudinal Study of 2009 (HSLS:09): A First Look at the 2021 Postsecondary Enrollment, Completion, and Financial Aid Outcomes of Fall 2009 Ninth-Graders* (Washington, DC: National Center for Education Statistics, April 2024), https://nces.ed.gov/pubs2024/2024022.pdf.

8. This report shows that "only about half of bachelor's degree graduates secure employment in a college-level job within a year of graduation": Burning Glass Institute and Strada Institute for the Future of Work, *Talent Disrupted: College Graduates, Underemployment,*

and the Way Forward (Indianapolis, IN: Strada Education Foundation, January 2024), https://stradaeducation.org/report/talent-disrupted/. A 2022 survey reports that one in three bachelor's degree grads say they believe their degree was not worth the cost: Nichole Torpey-Saboe, *Value Beyond the Degree: Alumni Perspectives on How College Experiences Improve Their Lives* (Indianapolis, IN: Strada Education Foundation, November 16, 2022), https://stradaeducation.org/report/pv-release-nov-16-2022/.

9. Melanie Hanson, "Student Loan Debt by Race," Education Data Initiative, December 2023, https://educationdata.org/student-loan-debt-by-race; Liam Knox, "Black, Hispanic Students More Likely to Drop Out," *Inside Higher Ed*, February 28, 2024, https://www.insidehighered.com/news/quick-takes/2024/02/28/black-hispanic-students-greatest-risk-dropping-out.

10. "Who Are New Majority Learners?," Education Design Lab, https://eddesignlab.org/newmajoritylearners/.

11. Cohen et al., *High School Longitudinal Study*.

12. *The Demographic Outlook: 2023 to 2053* (Washington, DC: Congressional Budget Office, January 2023), https://www.cbo.gov/publication/58612.

13. Govind Bhutada, "The Rising Cost of College in the US," Visual Capitalist, February 3, 2021, https://www.visualcapitalist.com/rising-cost-of-college-in-u-s/.

Chapter 1

1. Douglas Belkin, "Americans Are Losing Faith in College Education, WSJ-NORC Poll Finds," *Wall Street Journal*, March 31, 2023, https://www.wsj.com/articles/americans-are-losing-faith-in-college-education-wsj-norc-poll-finds-3a836ce1?mod=hp_lead_pos6.

2. George Allan Cook, *John Wise: Early American Democrat* (New York: Octagon Books, 1966).

3. Clinton Rossiter, *Seedtime of the Republic: The Origin of the American Tradition of Political Liberty* (New York: Harcourt, Brace, and World, 1953); Calvin Coolidge, "The Inspiration of the Declaration of Independence: Speech Given at Philadelphia, July 5, 1926," *City Journal*, July 4, 2021, https://www.city-journal.org/article/the-inspiration-of-the-declaration-of-independence.

4. Kenyn Careton, a minister who studies John Wise, made me aware of the inscription when he described to me tours he has given to church groups in Harvard Yard.

5. Rossiter, *Seedtime of the Republic*; Cook, *John Wise*; "The Rev. John Wise of Ipswich," Ipswich Historical Society, https://historicipswich.net/2022/11/15/john-wise/.

6. "Rev. John Wise of Ipswich." While John Wise's life and progeny are well recorded, I could find little record of his ten siblings.

7. "Highest Educational Attainment Levels Since 1940," US Census Bureau, last modified October 8, 2021, https://www.census.gov/library/visualizations/2017/comm/cb17-51_educational_attainment.html.

8. Alfred D. Chandler, *The Visible Hand: The Managerial Revolution in American Business* (New York: Belknap Press of Harvard University Press, 1977).

9. Jeffrey J. Selingo, "Is College Worth the Cost? Many Recent Graduates Don't Think So," *Washington Post*, September 30, 2015, https://www.washingtonpost.com/news/grade-point/wp/2015/09/30/is-college-worth-the-cost-many-recent-graduates-dont-think-so/.

10. "Soft Skills," Wikipedia, last edited June 28, 2014, https://en.wikipedia.org/wiki/Soft_skills.

11. Durable skills are also referred to as *twenty-first-century skills*, *power skills*, and *mobility skills*. They include critical thinking, collaboration, communication, creative problem solving, resilience, empathy, and initiative. See "Durable Skills in Action," America Succeeds, https://durableskills.org/. The Education Design Lab breaks down these skills into subcompetencies. See "The Lab's Durable Skills Micro-credentials," Education Design Lab, https://eddesignlab.org/microcredentialing/microcredentials/.

12. "Scaling Up Skills-Based Employment Practices for American Businesses," US Chamber of Commerce, October 6, 2023, https://www.uschamber.com/workforce/scaling-up -skills-based-employment-practices-for-american-businesses.

13. Early players included (among many others) Western Governors University, which pioneered work on Rich Skill Descriptors; Arizona State University; companies such as IBM and SalesForce; and organizations such as the Competency-Based Education Network, Concentric Sky, and slightly later, Credential Engine and the Open Skills Network.

14. "Skills Library," Western Governors University, https://www.wgu.edu/lp/general/wgu /skills-library.html.

15. T. R. Nodine, "How Did We Get Here? A Brief History of Competency-Based Higher Education in the United States," *Journal of Competency-Based Education* 1, no. 1 (April 2016): 5–11.

16. Brandon Busteed, "Higher Education's Work Preparation Paradox," Gallup, February 25, 2014, https://news.gallup.com/opinion/gallup/173249/higher-education-work -preparation-paradox.aspx.

17. Jeffrey Selingo, "College Students Say They Want a Degree for a Job. Are They Getting What They Want?," *Washington Post*, September 1, 2018, https://www.washingtonpost .com/news/grade-point/wp/2018/09/01/college-students-say-they-want-a-degree-for-a -job-are-they-getting-what-they-want/.

18. Jill Barshay, "Proof Points: The Number of College Graduates in the Humanities Drops for the Eighth Consecutive Year," Hechinger Report, November 22, 2021, https:// hechingerreport.org/proof-points-the-number-of-college-graduates-in-the-humanities -drops-for-the-eighth-consecutive-year/.

19. Kathleen deLaski, "Has the Fed Discovered a Cure for Displaced Workers?," RealClear Policy, July 21, 2020, https://www.realclearpolicy.com/articles/2020/07/21/has_the_fed _discovered_a_cure_for_displaced_workers_499544.html.

20. "Occupational Mobility Explorer," Federal Reserve Bank of Philadelphia, https://www .philadelphiafed.org/surveys-and-data/community-development-data/occupational -mobility-explorer.

21. See "The Skills Genome Project," Charrette, https://www.charrette.us/skills-genome.

22. Steve Lohr, "Up to 30 Million in U.S. Have the Skills to Earn 70% More, Researchers Say," *New York Times*, December 3, 2020, https://www.nytimes.com/2020/12/03 /technology/work-skills-upward-mobility.html.

23. "Skills-Based Hiring," Opportunity@Work, https://opportunityatwork.org/key-topics /skills-based-hiring/.

24. Greg Lacurci, "2022 Was the 'Real Year of the Great Resignation,' Says Economist," CNBC, last modified February 1, 2023, https://www.cnbc.com/2023/02/01/why-2022 -was-the-real-year-of-the-great-resignation.html.

25. Those without a college degree backed Trump 52%–44%. This is by far the widest gap in support among college graduates and non–college graduates in exit polls dating back to 1980. See Alec Tyson and Shiva Maniam, "Behind Trump's Victory: Divisions by Race, Gender, Education," Pew Research Center, November 9, 2016, https://www.pewresearch.org/short-reads/2016/11/09/behind-trumps-victory-divisions-by-race-gender-education/.
26. "Modernizing and Reforming the Assessment and Hiring of Federal Job Candidates," Federal Register, July 1, 2020, https://www.federalregister.gov/documents/2020/07/01/2020-14337/modernizing-and-reforming-the-assessment-and-hiring-of-federal-job-candidates.
27. Michael Brickman, who managed implementation of the executive order during 2020 from the Department of Education, in discussion with the author, July 2023.
28. "OPM Releases Skills-Based Hiring Guidance," press release, US Office of Personnel Management, May 19, 2022, https://www.opm.gov/news/releases/2022/05/release-opm-releases-skills-based-hiring-guidance/.
29. States with executive orders or new laws in place include, as of April 2024, Alaska, Colorado, Maryland, New Jersey, North Carolina, Ohio, Pennsylvania, South Dakota, Utah, Virginia, Connecticut, Florida, Arizona, Georgia, Minnesota, Massachusetts, Tennessee, Michigan, California, and Missouri.
30. Zaid Jilani, "Maryland Opened Up Jobs to People Without Four-Year Degrees," NewsNation, December 1, 2022, https://www.newsnationnow.com/solutions/maryland-opened-up-jobs-to-people-without-four-year-degrees/; Joe Farren (former chief strategy officer, Maryland Department of Labor), in discussion with the author, July 2023.
31. Mark Kantrowitz, "Student Loan Debt Exceeds One Trillion Dollars," interview by Melissa Block, National Public Radio, April 24, 2012, https://www.npr.org/2012/04/24/151305380/student-loan-debt-exceeds-one-trillion-dollars; Belkin, "Americans Are Losing Faith."
32. Bryan Mena, "Community College Enrollment Is Down. Here's What Will Happen to Workers and the US Economy If It Doesn't Come Back," CNN, January 7, 2024, https://www.cnn.com/2024/01/06/business/community-college-enrollment-economy/index.html.
33. Andrew Hanson et al., "Talent Disrupted: College Graduates, Underemployment, and the Way Forward," Burning Glass Institute, February 22, 2024, https://www.burningglassinstitute.org/research/underemployment.
34. "Average Total Cost of Attendance for First Time, Full Time Undergraduate Students in Degree-Granting Postsecondary Institutions, by Control and Level of Institution, Living Arrangement, and Component of Student Costs: Selected Years, 2010–11 Through 2021–2022," National Center for Education Statistics, November 2022, https://nces.ed.gov/programs/digest/d22/tables/dt22_330.40.asp.
35. Caitlin Zaloom, *Indebted: How Families Make College Work at Any Cost* (Princeton, NJ: Princeton University Press, 2019).
36. Jessica Bryant, "College Dropout Rate in the U.S.," BestColleges, January 25, 2024, https://www.bestcolleges.com/research/college-dropout-rate/.
37. "Public Viewpoint: What's Driving Americans' Interest in Short-Term and Virtual Skills Training Options?," Strada Center for Education, August 26, 2020, https://stradaeducation.org/report/certified-value/; *Success, Redefined: How Nondegree*

Pathways Empower Youth to Chart Their Own Course to Confidence, Employability, and Financial Freedom (Boston, MA: American Student Assistance and JFF, October 2023), https://www.jff.org/idea/success-redefined/.

38. "Sweet Briar College: Facts and Figures, as Reported in IPEDS 2022–23 Surveys," Office of Institutional Effectiveness, Sweet Briar College, April 5, 2023, https://www.sbc.edu/live/files/1816-sbc-facts-figures-2022-23.

39. Cory Stahle, "Educational Requirements Are Gradually Disappearing from Job Postings," Indeed Hiring Lab, February 27, 2024, https://www.hiringlab.org/2024/02/27/educational-requirements-job-postings/; Greg Lewis, "Fewer Job Posts Now Require Degrees. How Has That Changed Hiring?," *LinkedIn Talent Blog*, August 29, 2023, https://www.linkedin.com/business/talent/blog/talent-acquisition/fewer-jobs-require-degrees-impact-on-hiring.

40. Matt Sigelman, Joseph Fuller, and Alex Martin, *The Long Road from Pronouncements to Practice* (Burning Glass Institute, February 2024), 5, https://static1.squarespace.com/static/6197797102be715f55c0e0a1/t/65cc355c4935cb001349a4cd/1707881822922/Skills-Based+Hiring+02122024+vF.pdf; Joseph Fuller (Harvard Business School professor of management practice in general management and codirector of the school's project Managing the Future of Work), in discussion with the author, March 2024.

41. Paul Fain, "The Job: IBM on Skills-First," Work Shift, September 28, 2023, https://workshift.opencampusmedia.org/the-job-ibm-on-skills-first/.

42. Brad Hershbein, David Boddy, and Melissa S. Kearney, "Nearly 30 Percent of Workers in the U.S. Need a License to Perform Their Job: It Is Time to Examine Occupational Licensing Practices," Brookings Institution, January 27, 2015, https://www.brookings.edu/articles/nearly-30-percent-of-workers-in-the-u-s-need-a-license-to-perform-their-job-it-is-time-to-examine-occupational-licensing-practices/.

43. Peter Q. Blair, "New Frontiers in Occupational Licensing Research," *Reporter*, April 5, 2022, https://www.nber.org/reporter/2022number1/new-frontiers-occupational-licensing-research.

44. David Merson, "Can You Take the Bar Exam Without Going to Law School?," Juris Education, February 28, 2024, https://www.juriseducation.com/blog/can-you-take-the-bar-exam-without-going-to-law-school.

45. Susan Katcher, "Legal Training in the United States: A Brief History," *Wisconsin International Law Journal* 335 (2006): 339–41, https://wilj.law.wisc.edu/wp-content/uploads/sites/1270/2012/02/katcher.pdf; Mark T. Flahive, "The Origins of the American Law School," *American Bar Association Journal* 64, no. 12 (1978): 1868–71, http://www.jstor.org/stable/20745514.

46. Sarah Jividen, "Levels of Nursing and Ranks Explained," Nurse.org, February 25, 2024, https://nurse.org/education/nursing-hierarchy-guide/.

47. Lindsay Ellis, "Accountants Have to Go to College for Five Years. Some Are Rethinking That," *Wall Street Journal*, March 6, 2023, https://www.wsj.com/articles/accountants-have-to-go-to-college-for-five-years-minnesota-is-rethinking-that-cfd056b0.

48. Lewis, "Fewer Job Posts."

49. "Skills Visibility: Why and How a Skills-Based Economy Can Be More Equitable," Education Design Lab, March 2022, https://eddesignlab.org/resources/skills-visibility/.

50. Other companies include Greenlight Credentials and Learning Economy.

51. SmartResume, "Career Change Success Story: How I Got Hired Using SmartResume—Pamela's Job Seeker Story," YouTube video, 2:56, July 20, 2023, https://www.youtube.com/watch?v=EciJyY_W2qI&t=7s.
52. "Learning and Employment Record Use Cases," National Governors Association, https://www.nga.org/ler/; "Advancing a Skills-Based Ecosystem," SkillsFWD, https://www.skillsfwd.org/about; "New, Interactive LER Ecosystem Map Outlines Roles for Educators and Employers to Use Skills-Based Systems," US Chamber of Commerce Foundation, September 18, 2023, https://www.uschamberfoundation.org/workforce/new-interactive-ler-ecosystem-map.
53. Jason Tyszko (Chamber of Commerce Foundation), in discussion with the author, November 2023. The tool is called JobSide and will provide employers crowdsourced skills for specific roles. Full rollout is expected in late 2024.
54. This initiative is called JEDx (Jobs and Education Data Exchange), "a roadmap for a public-private data collaborative" to "improve the collection and use of standards-based jobs and employment data for public and private applications." "Jobs and Employment Data Exchange (JEDx)," US Chamber of Commerce Foundation, https://www.uschamberfoundation.org/solutions/workforce-development-and-training/jedx.
55. Mike Cason, "Alabama's Low Labor Participation Rate Increases Slightly," *Alabama Reporter*, December 22, 2023, https://www.al.com/news/2023/12/alabamas-low-labor-force-participation-rate-increases-slightly.html
56. Jacob Holmes, "Alabama Talent Triad Officially Launches," *Alabama Reporter*, December 20, 2023, https://www.alreporter.com/2023/12/20/alabama-talent-triad-officially-launches-receives-1-4-million-grant/.
57. Tracy Korsmo (Statewide Longitudinal Data System program manager at the North Dakota Information Technology Office), in discussion with the author, September 2023. The NICE Cybersecurity Workforce Framework is the foundation for increasing the size and capability of the US cybersecurity workforce. See "Information Technology Laboratory / Applied Cybersecurity Division," NIST, https://www.nist.gov/itl/applied-cybersecurity/nice.
58. Scott Cheney (CEO, Credential Engine), in discussion with the author, April 2024. The Credential Engine standard is known as Credential Transparency Description Language (CTDL). Full disclosure: I sit on the board of Credential Engine.
59. Experience You is a US Chamber of Commerce Foundation project that is housing many experiments with learning and employment records and wallets. See Taylor Hansen, "Experience You: Accelerating the Future of Work," US Chamber of Commerce Foundation, January 30, 2023, https://www.uschamberfoundation.org/workforce/experience-you-accelerating-future-work.

Chapter 2

1. Bruce M. Anderson, "Why It's Important to List Skills on Your LinkedIn Profile," *LinkedIn Talent Blog*, April 4, 2024, https://www.linkedin.com/business/talent/blog/talent-acquisition/skills-on-linkedin-profile.
2. Max Roser, "This Timeline Charts the Fast Pace of Tech Transformation Across Centuries," World Economic Forum, February 27, 2023, https://www.weforum.org/agenda/2023/02/this-timeline-charts-the-fast-pace-of-tech-transformation-across-centuries/.

3. *Skills First: Reimagining the Labor Market and Breaking Down Barriers* (Sunnyvale, CA: LinkedIn Economic Graph, 2023).

4. Ian Shine and Kate Whiting, "These Are the Jobs Most Likely to Be Lost—and Created—Because of AI," World Economic Forum, May 4, 2023, https://www.weforum.org/agenda/2023/05/jobs-lost-created-ai-gpt/.

5. "Future of Skills," LinkedIn Economic Graph, https://linkedin.github.io/future-of-skills/#explore.

6. Roser, "This Timeline."

7. Marc Juberg, Jemma Mercer, and Valentina Bravo, *State of the Bootcamp Market Report 2023* (San Francisco, CA: Career Karma, 2023), https://careerkarma.com/blog/bootcamp-market-report-2023/.

8. Credential Engine, *Counting U.S. Secondary and Postsecondary Credentials Report* (Washington, DC: Credential Engine, 2022), https://credentialengine.org/resources/counting-u-s-secondary-and-postsecondary-credentials-report/.

9. "Current Term Enrollment Estimates: Fall 2023," National Student Clearinghouse Research Center, January 24, 2024, https://nscresearchcenter.org/current-term-enrollment-estimates/?hilite=enrollment.

10. Credential Engine, *Counting U.S. Secondary.*

11. The US Department of Education and the National Student Clearinghouse track enrollment of college-based certificate programs. It's very difficult to aggregate the issuances from private groups and learning platforms such as Coursera, edX, professional associations, and badge issuers like Credly.

12. *Certified Value: When Do Adults Without Degrees Benefit from Earning Certificates and Certifications?* (Indianapolis, IN: Strada Education Network, 2019), https://stradaeducation.org/report/certified-value/.

13. "Number of Awards Conferred by Title IV Institutions, by Race/Ethnicity, Level of Award, and Gender: United States, 2021–22," IPEDS Data Explorer, National Center for Education Statistics, https://nces.ed.gov/ipeds/search/viewtable?tableId=35949&returnUrl=%2Fsearch. According to the Strada Education Network, "Black Americans rated the quality and value of nondegree credentials the highest among racial groups, while white Americans rated them the lowest. For example, 71 percent of Black Americans with a nondegree credential said their education helped them achieve their goals, compared to only 46 percent of white Americans." "Examining the Value of Non-degree Credentials," press release, Strada Education Network, July 28, 2021, https://cci.stradaeducation.org/pv-release-july-28-2021/. *The American Upskilling Study* (Washington, DC: Gallup and Amazon Research, 2021), https://www.gallup.com/file/analytics/354647/amazon-upskilling-report.pdf, describes the take-up rate for various demographic groups of employer-offered and independent training.

14. Bootcamps are not accredited in the same way colleges are. It is up to the consumer to research outcomes and other quality metrics. Sravya Tadepalli, "For-Profit Coding Bootcamps Prey on BIPOC Workers," Prism, August 12, 2022, https://prismreports.org/2022/08/12/for-profit-coding-boot-camps-prey-bipoc/.

15. Jake Schwartz (founder, General Assembly), in discussion with the author, September 2023. All quotations are taken from this discussion.

16. *2022 Student Outcomes Report* (New York: General Assembly, 2022), https://ga-public-downloads.s3.amazonaws.com/General-Assembly-Outcomes-Report-Latest.pdf.

17. Marc Juberg and Jemma Mercer, "State of the Bootcamp Market Report: 2023 Statistics and Share Analysis," Career Karma, June 14, 2023, https://careerkarma.com/blog/state -of-the-bootcamp-market-2023/.

18. Ilana Hamilton, "2024 Coding Bootcamp Statistics and Fast Facts," *Forbes*, March 18, 2024, https://www.forbes.com/advisor/education/bootcamps/coding-bootcamp -statistics/.

19. Jim Fong, chief research officer at UPCEA, the association that supports the offices at colleges that usually oversee bootcamps, agreed that when universities bring bootcamp partners onto campus, they usually charge roughly the same as the bootcamps charge independently, and he said that student aid is not usually available for these noncredit programs. Information provided by Jim Fong in discussion with the author, October 2023.

20. Complex Media is a multiplatform media and entertainment "youth culture" company with six million subscribers that was purchased by BuzzFeed in 2021.

21. Rob Kingyens (CEO, Yellowbrick), in discussion with the author, October 2023.

22. Jon Cotton, a.k.a. JaeTips (fashion designer), in discussion with the author, October 2023.

23. Mike DeStefano, "Jae Tips on His First Sneaker Collab: 'I Want to Break People's Necks,'" *Complex*, May 25, 2023, https://www.complex.com/sneakers/a/mike-destefano/jae-tips -saucony-grid-azura-2000-interview.

24. Animation Mentor tracks graduates working in feature films through IMDb credits but doesn't track placement rates overall.

25. "Why Choose Animation Mentor," Animation Mentor, https://www.animationmentor .com/why-animation-mentor/.

26. Based on Rob Kingyens (CEO, Yellowbrick), in discussion with the author, October 2023. But nationally, bootcamps report that a majority of their attendees already have a college degree, though not in the current technical fields that the students want to enter. Artur Meyster and Marc Juberg, "Online Coding Bootcamp Outcomes and Graduation Rates," Career Karma, May 17, 2023, https://careerkarma.com/blog/online-coding -bootcamps-rates-and-outcomes/.

27. Morning Consult and College Board, *Non-college Pathways* (Morning Consult, September 2022), https://research.collegeboard.org/media/pdf/Student%20Attitudes %20Towards%20Postsecondary%20Pathways_BigFuture%20Careers.pdf.

28. "Accelerated Digital Skills and the 'Bootcamp Boom,'" HolonIQ, February 28, 2022, https://www.holoniq.com/notes/accelerated-digital-skills-and-the-bootcamp-boom.

29. Olivia Sanchez, "When Universities Slap Their Names on For-Profit Coding Boot Camps," Hechinger Report, March 20, 2023, https://hechingerreport.org/when -universities-slap-their-names-on-for-profit-coding-boot-camps/.

30. Amy Heitzman (deputy CEO, UPCEA), in discussion with the author, November 2023.

31. Sanchez, "When Universities Slap."

32. Juberg and Mercer, "State of the Bootcamp Market Report."

33. "Accelerated Digital Skills and the 'Bootcamp Boom,'" HolonIQ, February 28, 2022, https://www.holoniq.com/notes/accelerated-digital-skills-and-the-bootcamp-boom.

34. Lyss Welding, "College Enrollment Statistics in the U.S.," BestColleges, February 7, 2024, https://www.bestcolleges.com/research/college-enrollment-statistics/ (based on National Center for Education Statistics data).

35. Indeed Skills-Based Hiring Survey, March 2023, provided by company representative.

36. Dhawal Shah (founder, Class Central), in discussion with the author, December 2023.
37. Emma D. Cohen et al., *High School Longitudinal Study of 2009 (HSLS:09): A First Look at the 2021 Postsecondary Enrollment, Completion, and Financial Aid Outcomes of Fall 2009 Ninth-Graders* (Washington, DC: National Center for Education Statistics, 2024), https://nces.ed.gov/pubs2024/2024022.pdf.
38. Nitzan Pelman (founder, Climb Hire), in discussion with the author, September 2023.
39. Yrel (Climb Hire bootcamp graduate), in discussion with the author, September 2023.
40. Porchea (graduate of Climb Hire) in discussion with the author, September 2023.
41. "1 in 7 College Grads Earn Less Than the Poverty Threshold," Intelligent, April 4, 2022, https://www.intelligent.com/1-in-7-college-grads-earn-less-than-the-poverty-threshold/.
42. Hamilton, "2024 Coding Bootcamp Statistics."
43. *Some College, No Credential* (Washington, DC: National Student Clearinghouse Research Center, 2023), https://nscresearchcenter.org/some-college-no-credential/.
44. Ajuah Helton (then vice president, KIPP Forward), in discussion with the author, August 2023.
45. Juberg, Mercer, and Bravo, *Bootcamp Market Report 2023.*
46. Matt Greenfield (long-time bootcamp investor), in discussion with the author at the ASU-GSV Conference, San Diego, April 2024.
47. Jake Schwartz founded Brave Health in 2017.
48. "10 Key Facts About US Colleges," Pew Research Trust, April 12, 2022, https://www.pewresearch.org/short-reads/2022/04/12/10-facts-about-todays-college-graduates/.
49. "Skills Accelerators," World Economic Forum, https://initiatives.weforum.org/accelerators-network/skills.
50. Victoria Masterson, "Future of Jobs 2023: These Are the Most In-Demand Skills Now—and Beyond," World Economic Forum, May 1, 2023, https://www.weforum.org/agenda/2023/05/future-of-jobs-2023-skills/. The top ten skills "on the rise" for 2023 are, in order, creative thinking, analytical thinking, technical literacy, curiosity and lifelong learning, resiliency/flexibility/agility, systems thinking, AI and big data, motivation and self-awareness, talent management, and service orientation and customer service.
51. Matt Sigelman (president, Burning Glass Institute), in discussion with the author, September 2023.

Chapter 3

1. "Connecting Credentials: A Beta Credentials Framework," Lumina Foundation, June 11, 2015, https://www.luminafoundation.org/resource/connecting-credentials/.
2. The trends are somewhat confusing. While graduation rates are improving, college enrollment rates are dropping. The year 2025 will begin to see a decline in college-age students, resulting from declining birth rates after the Great Recession. Kevin Carey has analyzed regional trends and predicts that northeastern, midwestern, and mid-Atlantic colleges will see up to 15% drops in college-age students to attract or compete for. And degree programs are suffering the most. Kevin Carey, "The Incredible Shrinking Future of College," *Vox*, November 21, 2022, https://www.vox.com/the-highlight/23428166/college-enrollment-population-education-crash.
3. Jon Marcus, "The Pandemic Is Speeding Up the Mass Disappearance of Men from College," Hechinger Report, January 19, 2021, https://hechingerreport.org/the-pandemic-is-speeding-up-the-mass-disappearance-of-men-from-college/.

4. Tech employer who hires significant number of nondegreed professionals, in discussion with the author, April 2024.

5. Jim Russell, "Talent Is the New Oil: OPEC of Tech," *Pacific Standard*, June 14, 2017, https://psmag.com/social-justice/talent-new-oil-opec-tech-77319.

6. "Educational Attainment Overall," Northern Virginia Regional Commission: NOVA Region Dashboard, https://www.novaregiondashboard.com/educational-attainment.

7. Lovey Hammel (CEO, Employment Enterprises), in discussion with the author, April 2024.

8. Jo Constantz, "Work Shift: What We've Learned from the Great Resignation," Bloomberg, June 6, 2023, https://www.bloomberg.com/news/newsletters/2023-06-06/is-the-great-resignation-over; "Quits: Total Nonfarm," Federal Reserve Economic Data, https://fred.stlouisfed.org/series/JTSQUL#.

9. Rachel Curry, "Recent Data Shows AI Job Losses Are Rising, but the Numbers Don't Tell the Full Story," CNBC, December 16, 2023, https://www.cnbc.com/2023/12/16/ai-job-losses-are-rising-but-the-numbers-dont-tell-the-full-story.html.

10. Steven Burns, "Why Entry-Level Jobs Now Demand 3–5 Years Experience," New Trader U, November 24, 2023, https://www.newtraderu.com/2023/11/24/why-entry-level-jobs-now-demand-3-5-years-experience/.

11. Tyler Arnold, "Study: DC-Arlington-Alexandria Is Third Most Educated Metro Area," *Chalkboard News*, July 24, 2019, https://www.thecentersquare.com/virginia/article_99c01f78-ae47-11e9-a1e6-4393d7cbd4e8.html.

12. Patrick (software engineer, CACI Products), in discussion with the author, October 2023.

13. "Top 8 IT Certifications in Demand Today," CIO, October 20, 2023, https://www.cio.com/article/193586/top-15-it-certifications-in-demand-today.html.

14. "10 In-Demand Career Certifications (and How to Achieve Them)," Indeed, last modified October 3, 2023, https://www.indeed.com/career-advice/career-development/certifications-in-demand.

15. A certification expert at a leading tech company who asked not to be identified, in discussion with the author, August 2023.

16. Liberty Munson (psychometrician, Microsoft Corporation), in discussion with the author, March 2024.

17. I was granted access to this survey, which was commissioned by and only made available to members of the IT Certification Council: *ITC Certifications Drive Improved Results for the Organization and the Employee* (Chicago: IT Certification Council, 2022).

18. Jennifer Riccuiti (principal product manager, AWS Cloud Institute), in discussion with the author, September 2023.

19. Michelle Van Noy, *Identifying High Quality Industry Certifications* (Newark, NJ: Rutgers Education and Employment Center, 2020), https://smlr.rutgers.edu/sites/default/files/Documents/Centers/EERC/identifying_high_quality_industry_certifications_issue_brief_110820_final.pdf.

20. "What Are Certifications and Certificates?," BigFuture, https://bigfuture.collegeboard.org/explore-careers/get-started/what-are-certifications-and-certificates.

21. Lindsey Reichlin Cruse et al., *The Non-degree Credential Quality Imperative* (National Skills Coalition, July 2023), https://nationalskillscoalition.org/wp-content/uploads/2023/07/The-NDCQ-Imperative-report_fnl2-1.pdf; "Examining the Value of Nondegree

Credentials," Strada Education, July 28, 2021, https://cci.stradaeducation.org/pv-release -july-28-2021/#.

22. Evelyn Ganzglass, *Certifications as Tools for Promoting Economic Mobility* (Ann Arbor: Corporation for a Skilled Workforce, March 2022), https://skilledwork.org/wp-content /uploads/2022/03/Certifications-As-Tools-For-Promoting-Economic-Mobility.pdf.

23. "(Not) Ready for the Workforce: Today's Graduates Face Stigma and Regret," Cengage Group, June 7, 2022, https://www.cengagegroup.com/news/press-releases/2022/cg-2022 -employability-survey/.

24. Ryan Craig, *Apprentice Nation: How the "Earn and Learn" Alternative to Higher Education Will Create a Stronger and Fairer America* (Dallas: BenBella Books, 2023).

25. Elsie Boskamp, "20+ Compelling Internship Statistics [2023]: Do Interns Get Paid?," Zippia, June 19, 2023, https://www.zippia.com/advice/internship-statistics/.

26. "College Student Employment," National Center for Education Statistics, last modified May 2022, https://nces.ed.gov/programs/coe/indicator/ssa/college-student-employment.

27. Kristen Bahler, "This Common First Job Mistake Can Cost You $10,000 a Year for Life," *Money*, May 23, 2018, https://money.com/first-job-underemployed-statistics/.

28. "Apprentices by State Dashboard," Apprenticeship USA, https://www.apprenticeship .gov/data-and-statistics/apprentices-by-state-dashboard. President Biden issued an executive order in March 2024 mandating that federal agencies step up apprenticeship programs. See "FACT SHEET: President Biden Signs Executive Order: Scaling and Expanding the Use of Registered Apprenticeships in Industries and the Federal Government and Promoting Labor-Management Forums," White House, March 6, 2024, https://www.whitehouse.gov/briefing-room/statements-releases/2024/03/06 /fact-sheet-president-biden-signs-executive-order-scaling-and-expanding-the-use-of -registered-apprenticeships-in-industries-and-the-federal-government-and-promoting -labor-management-forums/.

29. Based on NCES projections from 2022. See "Table 203.10: Enrollment in Public Elementary and Secondary Schools, by Level and Grade: Selected Years, Fall 1980 Through Fall 2031," National Center for Education Statistics, https://nces.ed.gov /programs/digest/d22/tables/dt22_203.10.asp.

30. "Data and Statistics," Apprenticeship USA, https://www.apprenticeship.gov/data-and -statistics. In fiscal year 2024 there are 641,044 active apprentices, which is 0.4% of the active workforce.

31. *Youth with Disabilities Entering the Workplace Through Apprenticeship: Understanding Apprenticeship Basics* (Washington, DC: US Department of Labor, n.d.), https://www .dol.gov/sites/dolgov/files/odep/categories/youth/apprenticeship/odep1.pdf.

32. Julie Wilmes (apprenticeship program manager, Pinnacol Insurance), in discussion with the author about the history of the company's apprenticeship program, November 2023.

33. Ricardo Franciolli, "Why Switzerland's Dual Track Education System Is Unique," SWI swissinfo.ch, January 27, 2020, https://www.swissinfo.ch/eng/business/school-and -work_why-switzerland-s-dual-track-education-system-is-unique/45512392.

34. Katherine Marie Caves et al., *A Ticket up and a Ticket Out: Promoting and Ensuring Permeability in Education System Reform*, CES Studies No. 32 (Zurich: ETH Zurich, February 2023), https://www.research-collection.ethz.ch/handle/20.500.11850/599202. This Swiss paper was graciously recommended to me by Brookings Institution researcher Annelies Goger.

35. "Bachelor's, Master's, and Doctor's Degrees Conferred by Postsecondary Institutions, by Sex of Student and Field of Study: 2019–20," National Center for Education Statistics, https://nces.ed.gov/programs/digest/d21/tables/dt21_318.30.asp.

36. Joseph Fuller, "The Options Multiplier: Decoding the CareerWise Youth Apprentice Journey," Project on Workforce, November 14, 2022, https://www.pw.hks.harvard.edu /post/careerwise.

37. Naarai (underwriter, Pinnacol Insurance), in discussion with the author, November 2023.

38. Julie Wilmes (apprenticeship program manager, Pinnacol Insurance), in discussion with the author, November 2023.

39. "DOE Report Finds Clean Energy Jobs Grew in Every State in 2022," US Department of Energy, June 28, 2023, https://www.energy.gov/articles/doe-report-finds-clean-energy -jobs-grew-every-state-2022. In 2022, the number of clean energy jobs increased in every state and grew 3.9% nationally (+114,000 jobs).

40. The Inflation Reduction Act provides 24% additional tax credits to companies that hire registered apprentices and meet prevailing wage requirements for federal projects. Richard Lawrence (senior director of workforce and employer engagement, Interstate Renewable Energy Council), in discussion with the author, January 2024.

41. Brian Rhodes-Devey (electrician, ReVision Energy), in discussion with the author, January 2024.

42. Vaughan Woodruff (former executive at ReVision Energy, chair of Maine's state workforce board), in discussion with the author, January 2024.

43. Richard Lawrence (senior director of workforce and employer engagement, Interstate Renewable Energy Council), in discussion with the author, January 2024.

44. Katherine Schaeffer, "A Dwindling Number of New U.S. College Graduates Have a Degree in Education," Pew Research Center, September 27, 2022, https://www .pewresearch.org/short-reads/2022/09/27/a-dwindling-number-of-new-u-s-college -graduates-have-a-degree-in-education/.

45. Anna Merod, "By the Numbers: Teacher Vacancies Jump by 51%," K–12Dive, August 30, 2023, https://www.k12dive.com/news/teacher-vacancies-rising-51-percent-research /692244/.

46. Tuan D. Nguyen, Chanh B. Lam, and Paul Bruno, "Is There a National Teacher Shortage? A Systematic Examination of Reports of Teacher Shortages in the United States" (EdWorkingPaper 22-631, Annenberg Institute at Brown University, August 2022), https://doi.org/10.26300/76eq-hj32.

47. Kavitha Cardoza, "To Fight Teacher Shortages, Schools Turn to Custodians, Bus Drivers and Aides," Hechinger Report, August 7, 2023, https://hechingerreport.org/to-fight -teacher-shortages-schools-turn-to-custodians-bus-drivers-and-aides/.

48. Crystal Acosta (teacher, Maitland Elementary School), in discussion with the author, December 2023.

49. Sylvia Allegretto, "Teacher Pay Penalty Still Looms Large," Economic Policy Institute, September 29, 2023, https://www.epi.org/publication/teacher-pay-in-2022/.

50. A limited license in these fields usually requires supervision or specifies types of work that can be performed.

51. Full disclosure: the deLaski Family Foundation has made a philanthropic grant to the National Center for the Apprenticeship Degree.

52. My loose estimate is based on interviews with certification experts and skills intermediaries, as well as the estimates that 30% of workers are in licensed roles, that there are seven thousand industry certifications, and that 6% of workers have industry certifications.

53. "Estimates of how many eligible workers use those supports vary, ranging from roughly 1 percent to 10 percent, and participation has always skewed toward white-collar workers. Employers can get a federal tax write-off up to $5250 per employee, but many set it up as a reimbursement plan, so employees have to front the cost." Levi Pulkkinen, "Millions upon Millions in Employer-Funded Education Benefits Go Unused," Hechinger Report, June 21, 2021, https://hechingerreport.org/millions-upon-millions-in-employer -funded-education-benefits-go-unused/; Jordan T. Krieger, "Employer Tuition Assistance: Current Approaches and the Application of the Implied Covenant of Good Faith and Fair Dealing," *Northwestern University Law Review* 117, no. 6 (2023): 1661–705, https://scholarly commons.law.northwestern.edu/nulr/vol117/iss6/5/.

54. Pulkkinen, "Millions upon Millions."

55. Craig, *Apprentice Nation*, 4.

56. Jennifer Ma and Matea Pender, *Trends in College Pricing and Student Aid 2023* (New York: College Board, 2023), https://research.collegeboard.org/media/pdf/Trends%20Report %202023%20Updated.pdf.

57. "How Are Apprenticeships Funded and What Is the Apprenticeship Levy?," *Education Hub* (blog), GOV.UK Department of Education, March 10, 2023, https://educationhub .blog.gov.uk/2023/03/10/how-are-apprenticeships-funded-and-what-is-the -apprenticeship-levy/.

58. Robert Lerman, "How the U.S. Is Barely Tapping the Potential of Apprenticeships," *Fast Company*, April 15, 2023, https://www.fastcompany.com/90873199/how-the-u-s-is -barely-tapping-the-potential-of-apprenticeships.

59. Rebecca Agostino (VP, learning operations, Multiverse), in discussion with the author, January 2024. The number of UK apprenticeships has dipped significantly in recent years, and researchers are struggling to understand how much of that is pandemic related. See "Apprenticeships: Bounceback Stalls and Disparities Persist," *FE Week*, May 29, 2024, https://feweek.co.uk/apprenticeships-bounce-back-stalls-and-disparities -persist/.

60. Shayne Spaulding and Stephanie Petrov, *State Incentives to Promote and Support Apprenticeship* (Washington, DC: Urban Institute and Mathematica, 2023), https://www .dol.gov/sites/dolgov/files/ETA/publications/ETAOP_2023_19_STATES_INCENTIVES _TO_PROMOTE_APPRENTICESHIPS.pdf; "Apprenticeship Innovation Funding," State of California Department of Industrial Relations, last modified November 2023, https://www.dir.ca.gov/DAS/Grants/Apprenticeship-Innovation-Funding.html.

61. "Executive Order on Scaling and Expanding the Use of Registered Apprenticeships in Industries and the Federal Government and Promoting Labor-Management Forums," White House, March 6, 2024, https://www.whitehouse.gov/briefing-room /presidential-actions/2024/03/06/executive-order-on-scaling-and-expanding-the-use-of -registered-apprenticeships-in-industries-and-the-federal-government-and-promoting -labor-management-forums/.

62. Ryan Craig (author, *Apprentice Nation*), in discussion with the author, October 2023.

63. "Revature Company Story," Revature, https://revature.com/our-story/.

64. "Bachelor's Degrees Conferred by Postsecondary Institutions, by Field of Study: Selected Academic Years, 1970–71 Through 2020–21," National Center for Education Statistics, https://nces.ed.gov/programs/digest/d22/tables/dt22_322.10.asp. The Bureau of Labor Statistics projects 23% growth through 2032. See "Computer and Information Research Scientists," US Bureau of Labor Statistics, https://www.bls.gov/ooh/computer-and-information-technology/computer-and-information-research-scientists.htm#tab-6.

65. I was interested that companies look to the Department of Labor's Five Zones of preparation to classify worker types. "O*Net Online Help," O*Net, https://www.onetonline.org/help/online/zones.

66. Ashwin Bharath (CEO, Revature), in discussion with the author, October 2023.

67. Bharath from Revature advises that the model can work in the following circumstances:
    1. Employers are desperate or at least concerned about their talent pipeline.
    2. The jobs are well paid enough that there is room for the training company to carve out a fee. (The apprentices don't have to pay for training, so someone has to.)
    3. The training company can't be in one region only; it has to be a national firm so the recruiting and placement footprint can be broad.

68. "FACT SHEET: President Biden Signs."

69. *Counting U.S. Postsecondary and Secondary Credentials* (Washington, DC: Credential Engine, 2022), 37.

70. A certification expert at a leading tech company who asked not to be identified, in discussion with the author, August 2023.

71. "National Initiative for Cybersecurity Education (NICE) Cybersecurity Workforce Framework," Cybersecurity and Infrastructure Security Agency, https://www.cisa.gov/national-initiative-cybersecurity-education-nice-cybersecurity-workforce-framework.

72. Michael Hill, "Cybersecurity Workforce Shortage Reaches 4 Million Despite Significant Recruitment Drive," CSO Online, October 23, 2023, https://www.csoonline.com/article/657598/cybersecurity-workforce-shortage-reaches-4-million-despite-significant-recruitment-drive.html.

73. Liberty Munson (psychometrician, Microsoft Corporation), in discussion with the author, March 2024.

74. Esther G. Lander and Amanda S. McGinn, "Impact of SCOTUS Affirmative Action Ruling on Employers," American Bar Association, September 6, 2023, https://www.americanbar.org/groups/labor_law/publications/labor_employment_law_news/issue-summer-2023/impact-of-scorus-affirmative-action-ruling-on-ers/.

75. Khorri Atkinson, "Affirmative Action Ruling Sets Up Clash over Workplace Diversity," Bloomberg Law, June 30, 2023, https://news.bloomberglaw.com/daily-labor-report/affirmative-action-ruling-sets-up-clash-over-workplace-diversity.

76. "STARs: Skilled Through Alternative Routes," Opportunity@Work, https://opportunityatwork.org/stars/.

77. Byron Auguste (founder and CEO, Opportunity@Work), in discussion with the author, October 2023.

78. Matt Sigelman, Joseph Fuller, and Alex Martin, *Skills-Based Hiring: The Long Road from Pronouncements to Practice* (Philadelphia: Burning Glass Institute and Harvard Business School Project on Managing the Future of Work, 2024), https://www.burningglassinstitute.org/research/skills-based-hiring-2024.

79. Clay Lord (director, foundation programs, SHRM), in discussion with the author, December 2023.

80. Jack Strachan, "Why Use Extreme Users?," UX Planet, October 19, 2017, https://uxplanet.org/why-use-extreme-users-345e97719e5.

81. George Anders, "Hiring's New Red Line: Why Newcomers Can't Land 35% of 'Entry-Level' Jobs," LinkedIn, August 18, 2021, https://www.linkedin.com/pulse/hirings-new-red-line-why-newcomers-cant-land-35-jobs-george-anders/.

82. Te-Ping Chen, "How Gen Z Is Becoming the Toolbelt Generation," *Wall Street Journal*, April 1, 2024, https://www.wsj.com/lifestyle/careers/gen-z-trades-jobs-plumbing-welding-a76b5e43.

83. Rick Wartzman, "'College for All' Has Failed America. Can the Education System Be Fixed?," *Fortune*, December 14, 2023, https://fortune.com/2023/12/14/college-for-all-bachelor-degree-income-inequality/.

Chapter 4

1. Christopher Rim, "Ivy League Colleges to Release Early Application Decisions This Week—but Don't Expect to See Their Acceptance Rates," *Forbes*, December 12, 2023, https://www.forbes.com/sites/christopherrim/2023/12/12/ivy-league-colleges-to-release-early-application-decisions-this-week-but-dont-expect-to-see-their-acceptance-rates/?sh=4acee0b340b3.html.

2. Russ Douthat, "Opinion: Harvard Couldn't Save Both Claudine Gay and Itself," *New York Times*, January 3, 2024, https://www.nytimes.com/2024/01/03/opinion/claudine-gay-harvard.html.

3. Angel Pérez (CEO, National Association for College Admission Counseling), in discussion with the author, January 2024. It should be said that some public colleges and systems, not all of which are elite by my definition, are under attack for, e.g., diversity, equity, and inclusion policies, teaching methods, and reading lists.

4. As my book neared publication, a few Ivy League schools were reintroducing SAT requirements. See Ayelet Sheffey, "Some Top Schools Are Bringing Back ACT and SAT Requirements—but Most Colleges Are Still Test-Optional. Here's What You Need to Know," *Business Insider*, April 3, 2024, https://www.businessinsider.com/do-colleges-require-standardized-testing-sat-admissions-what-it-means-2024-3.

5. "Challenges of Being a New President," ASU-GSV Summit, San Diego, California, April 15, 2024; Danielle McLean, "Some HBCUs Are Seeing Enrollment Surge," Higher Ed Dive, March 19, 2024, https://www.highereddive.com/news/hbcus-enrollment-surge-why/710494/.

6. "Fast Facts," National Center for Education Statistics, https://nces.ed.gov/fastfacts/display.asp?id=1122.

7. Angel Pérez (CEO, National Association for College Admission Counseling), in discussion with the author, January 2024.

8. Ben Unglesbee, "'We are not hospice.' The Race to Get Faster in Predicting College Closures," Higher Ed Dive, April 18, 2024, https://www.highereddive.com/news/predicting-college-closures-accreditor-HLC-conference-2024/713451/. According to the 2024 annual *Inside Higher Ed* college presidents survey, one in six presidents (16%) says that senior administrators at their institution have had serious internal discussions

within the last year about merging with another college or university. Among presidents already having serious merger conversations, two-thirds say their institutions should consider merging within the next five years. *2024 Survey of College and University Presidents* (Washington, DC: Inside Higher Ed, 2024), https://www.insidehighered.com /reports/2024/02/27/2024-survey-college-and-university-presidents.

9. Liam Knox, "Black, Hispanic Students More Likely to Drop Out," *Inside Higher Ed*, February 28, 2024, https://www.insidehighered.com/news/quick-takes/2024/02/28 /black-hispanic-students-greatest-risk-dropping-out.

10. Matthew T. Hora et al., *National Survey of College Internships 2021 Report* (Madison, WI: Center for Research on College-Workforce Transitions, University of Wisconsin–Madison, 2021), 3, https://ccwt.wisc.edu/wp-content/uploads/2022/04/CCWT_NSCI -2021-Report.pdf.

11. Mary E. Flannery, "State Funding for Higher Education Still Lagging," National Education Association, October 25, 2022, https://www.nea.org/nea-today/all-news -articles/state-funding-higher-education-still-lagging.

12. Scott Bauer, "Republican Leaders Say No More Money for University of Wisconsin or School Safety Office," Associated Press, June 27, 2023, https://apnews.com/article /wisconsin-budget-university-evers-republicans-veto -f0c216ee22e68150b0b88e2c783f43a5; Peter Hall, "Pa. House Democrats Renew Call for End to Blockade on State-Related University Aid," *Pennsylvania Capital Star*, September 26, 2023, https://penncapital-star.com/education/pa-house-democrats-renew-call -for-end-to-blockade-on-state-related-university-aid/.

13. Rachel Fishman, Sophie Nguyen, and Louisa Woodhouse, *Varying Degrees 2022: New America's Sixth Annual Survey on Higher Education* (New America, July 2022), https://d1y8sb8igg2f8e.cloudfront.net/documents/Varying_Degrees_2022_2022-07 -25_FINAL.pdf.

14. Gen Z comprises young people who are currently between the ages of twelve and twenty-seven. See Joshua Bay, "Gen Z's Declining Interest Persists Even Among Middle School Students," The 74, August 24, 2023, https://www.the74million.org/article/gen-zs -declining-college-interest-persists-even-among-middle-schoolers/. The enrollment numbers for 2023 show a slight recovery of adult enrollment, 1%, but only for students over thirty. See "The Nation's Community Colleges Falter as Enrollment Plunges," CBS News, April 3, 2023, https://www.cbsnews.com/news/community-college-enrollment -decline-higher-education/; "Current Term Enrollment Estimates: Fall 2023," National Student Clearinghouse Research Center, January 24, 2024, https://nscresearchcenter.org /current-term-enrollment-estimates/; Natalie Schwartz, "Fall 2023 Enrollment Trends in 5 Charts," Higher Ed Dive, October 30, 2023, https://www.highereddive.com/news /fall-2023-enrollment-trends-5-charts/697999/; and Rahul Choudaha, "Most Trusted Brands Report 2022: Universities," Morning Consult, https://pro.morningconsult.com /analyst-reports/most-trusted-brands-2022-universities. As the book was heading to press, the spring 2024 enrollment numbers came out, reporting an upturn, particularly for community colleges, but the growth was led by high school students enrolling in individual college courses. See Liam Knox, "Undergraduate Enrollment Picks Up Steam," *Inside Higher Ed*, May 22, 2024, https://www.insidehighered.com/news /admissions/traditional-age/2024/05/22/spring-enrollment-inches-second-straight-year.

15. Michael T. Nietzel, "Average College Tuition Increased Less Than Inflation for 2023–24," *Forbes*, November 2, 2023, https://www.forbes.com/sites/michaeltnietzel /2023/11/02/average-college-tuition-increased-less-than-inflation-for-2023-24/?sh =4b313232496f.

16. *2023 National Alumni Career Mobility Survey* (Washington, DC: Inside Higher Ed, 2023), https://www.insidehighered.com/news/quick-takes/2023/10/25/career-support -boosts-alumni-perception-college-value.

17. "Skills Library," Western Governors University, https://www.wgu.edu/lp/general/wgu /skills-library.html; Laura Aka, "The Growth of Competency-Based Education," Working Nation, October 19, 2022, https://workingnation.com/the-growth-of -competency-based-education/.

18. Kacey Thorne (senior director of skills architecture, Western Governors University), in discussion with the author, January 2024.

19. Scott Pulsipher (president, Western Governors University), in discussion with the author, April 2024.

20. O*NET OnLine, homepage, https://www.onetonline.org.

21. Luke Dowden (associate vice chancellor, Alamo District Colleges), in discussion with the author, November 2023.

22. Sneha Dey, "A New Way to Fund Texas Community Colleges Focuses on Student Success, Not Enrollment," *Texas Tribune*, January 2, 2024, https://www.texastribune.org /2024/01/02/texas-community-colleges-funding/.

23. Lydia Riley (codirector, Texas Credentials for the Future Initiative, University of Texas System), in discussion with the author, October 2023.

24. "New Report Finds Adults with Nondegree Credentials Rate Their Education Positively, Especially When Combined with College Degrees," Strada Education Foundation, July 28, 2021, https://stradaeducation.org/press-release/new-report-finds-adults-with -nondegree-credentials-rate-their-education-positively-especially-when-combined-with -college-degrees/.

25. Sofia Cavenaile (student at UT San Antonio), in discussion with the author, December 2023.

26. Brody Feldberg (alumni of UT Austin), in discussion with the author, August 2024.

27. "Professional Scrum Certifications," Scrum.org, https://www.scrum.org/professional -scrum-certifications; "Certifications: Project Management Professional," Project Management Institute, https://www.pmi.org/certifications/project-management-pmp.

28. Google internal data, January 2024, October 2023.

29. Background interview with Grow with Google spokesperson.

30. Of US Google certificate earners, 55% are learners of color. *Google Annual Diversity Report 2022* (Mountain View, CA: Google, 2022), https://static.googleusercontent.com /media/about.google/en//belonging/diversity-annual-report/2022/static/pdfs/google _2022_diversity_annual_report.pdf.

31. *Counting U.S. Postsecondary and Secondary Credentials* (Washington, DC: Credential Engine, December 2022), https://credentialengine.org/wp-content/uploads/2022/12 /CountingCredentials_2022-FINAL.pdf.

32. Rashmi Karan, "Top 10 Professional Certificates on Coursera," Shiksha Online, September 13, 2023, https://www.shiksha.com/online-courses/articles/top-coursera -certificates/.

33. The UT colleges are also piloting MayMesters for skill-building opportunities in fields where there are no certificates, such as biology.

34. Jeff Holm (vice provost, University of North Dakota), in discussion with the author, November 2023.

35. Other companies include Pluralsight, Virtual Internships, Parker-Dewey, and Maxx Potential.

36. Dave Savory (cofounder, Riipen), in discussion with the author, November 2023.

37. Robert Warren (lecturer, University of North Dakota), in discussion with the author, November 2023.

38. Brianna Hines, "The State of the Student Adjusting to the 'New Normal' . . . and All That Comes with It," Wiley, February 13, 2023, https://www.wiley.com/en-us/network /trending-stories/the-state-of-the-student-adjusting-to-the-new-normal-and-all-that -comes-with-it.

39. Jon Marcus, "The Reckoning Is Here," Hechinger Report, April 3, 2023, https:// hechingerreport.org/the-reckoning-is-here-more-than-a-third-of-community-college -students-have-vanished/.

40. Community colleges focused on vocational tracks are recovering some of the lost enrollment. In 2023–24, vocationally focused community college enrollment was up 16%. "Current Term Enrollment Estimates: Fall 2023."

41. Marcus, "Reckoning Is Here."

42. Certificate enrollment has increased by 15% since 2019 across college types. Community colleges with a high vocational focus increased enrollment by 16% in 2023, while other community colleges stabilized their year-over-year declines but remain 20% below their 2019 levels. Tabitha Whissemore, "Enrollment Growth Continues at Community Colleges," *Community College Daily*, January 24, 2024, https://www.ccdaily .com/2024/01/enrollment-growth-continues-at-community-colleges/; "Current Term Enrollment Estimates: Fall 2023."

43. Jill Barshay, "How Dual Enrollment Is Changing the Face of Community Colleges," FutureEd, August 23, 2023, https://www.future-ed.org/how-dual-enrollment-is -changing-the-face-of-community-colleges/.

44. Dionne Billick (director of lifelong learning, Pima Community College), in email communications with the author, December 2023.

45. Carolyn Thompson, "Few Community College Students Go on to Earn 4 Year Degrees. Some States Have Found Ways to Help," Associated Press, November 9, 2023, https:// apnews.com/article/community-college-credit-transfer-education-department -a020e6b501226504b569d49211e33905.

46. Ian Roark (senior vice president, workforce training, Pima Community College), in discussion with the author, November 2023.

47. Sara Weissman, "A Great Misalignment Between Credentials and Jobs," *Inside Higher Ed*, May 29, 2024, reporting on Jeff Strohl, Zachary Mabel, and Kathryn Peltier Campbell, *The Great Misalignment* (Washington, DC: Georgetown University Center on Education and Workforce, May 2024).

48. Micro-pathways are explained on the Education Design Lab's website: "Project: Community College Growth Fund," Education Design Lab, https://eddesignlab.org /project/growthenginefund/.

49. The first cohort included Pima, Ivy Tech Community College, Seattle Colleges, Austin Community College, Prince George's Community College, and four colleges in the city university system of New York, CUNY.

50. Lisa Larson (senior vice president, college transformation, Education Design Lab), in discussion with the author, December 2023.

51. Paul Tough, "Americans Are Losing Faith in the Value of College. Whose Fault Is That?," *New York Times*, September 5, 2023, https://www.nytimes.com/2023/09/05 /magazine/college-worth-price.html.

52. Pima and many of the partners of the Community College Growth Engine see falloff between signup and matriculation when learners see that financial aid does not cover noncredit micro-pathways.

53. Emily Spatz, "Northeastern Acceptance Rate Drops to 5.6% After Record Number of Applications," *Huntington News*, August 20, 2023, https://huntnewsnu.com/71869/campus /northeastern-acceptance-rate-drops-to-5-6-after-record-number-of-applications/.

54. Northeastern's acceptance rate at its flagship campus is in the range of the University of Pennsylvania and Brown, and not far behind Yale. Cornell led in Ivy League applications at sixty-nine thousand in 2023. Other Ivies saw applications in the fifty thousand range. "Overall College Admit Rates Class of 2023–Class of 2027," Top Tier Admissions, https://toptieradmissions.com/resources/2027-ivy-league-college -admission-statistics/.

55. Connie Yowell (senior adviser to the provost, Northeastern University), in discussion with the author, November 2023.

56. Jonathan Mejia (co-op participant, Northeastern University), in discussion with the author, December 2023.

57. The Education Design Lab provides this employer engagement tool for community colleges. "A Community College's Guide to Engaging Employers," Education Design Lab, https://eddesignlab.org/resources/a-community-colleges-guide-to-engaging -employers/.

58. Career outcomes are listed on the Northeastern University website, https:// careeroutcomes.northeastern.edu/.

59. My fall 2023 class at George Mason University ran a student survey. Of sixty-one respondents from across the honors college, 31% said the skills they need for their first job "are pretty clear to me."

60. David Deming et al., *Delivering on the Degree: The College-to-Jobs Playbook* (Cambridge, MA: Harvard Kennedy School, 2023). Full disclosure: I serve as an unpaid senior adviser to the Project on Workforce.

61. "Community College FAQs," Community College Research Center, https://ccrc.tc .columbia.edu/community-college-faqs.html; Hora et al., *National Survey*.

62. "Mellon Awards $25 Million for Paid Internships for Humanities Majors at Public Colleges and Universities," press release, Mellon Foundation, April 17, 2024, https:// www.mellon.org/news/mellon-foundation-awards-25-million-for-paid-internships-for -humanities-majors.

63. Erin Whinnery and Tom Keily, "Paying for College: The Latest Trends in Performance-Based Funding," Education Commission of the States, February 20, 2024, https://www .ecs.org/paying-for-college-the-latest-trends-in-performance-based-funding/.

Chapter 5

1. Joshua Bay, "Fall College Data Shows Big Gains—and Jarring Freshmen Declines," The 74, November 24, 2023, https://www.the74million.org/article/fall-college-data-shows -big-gains-and-jarring-freshmen-declines/.

2. The practice of tracking first became well known in education circles with the publication of Jeannie Oakes's *Keeping Track: How Schools Structure Inequality* (New Haven, CT: Yale University Press, 1985).

3. Anthony Carnevale (founder, Georgetown University Center on Education and the Workforce), in discussion with the author, February 2024.

4. Some of my own charter school activities included the following: I was involved in cofounding Building Hope, a charter school facilities fund, through the Sallie Mae Fund; I was a senior program officer at the Walton Family Foundation, which funded expansion of public charter schools nationally; and I served on the board of Thurgood Marshall Academy in Washington, DC, a high-performing charter school.

5. "Affordability for Non-degree Credentials," National Conference of State Legislatures, October 25, 2023, https://www.ncsl.org/labor-and-employment/affordability-for -nondegree-credentials.

6. Caitlin Zaloom, *Indebted: How Families Make College Work at Any Cost* (Princeton, NJ: Princeton University Press, 2019), 8.

7. "No Dead Ends: How Career and Technical Education Can Provide Today's Youth with Pathways to College and Career Success," Jobs for the Future, January 7, 2022, https:// www.jff.org/idea/no-dead-ends-how-career-and-technical-education-can-provide -todays-youth-with-pathways-to-college-and-career-success/.

8. Katherine Marie Caves et al., *A Ticket up and a Ticket Out: Promoting and Ensuring Permeability in Education System Reform*, CES Studies No. 32 (Zurich: ETH Zurich, February 2023), https://www.research-collection.ethz.ch/handle/20.500.11850/599202.

9. In this chapter, I use pseudonyms for the high school students to protect the privacy of minors.

10. "Daniel" (a high school senior at DSST in Denver), in discussion with the author, November 2023.

11. Date provided by DSST, March 2024. To view overall rankings of Denver high schools, see "Search Best High Schools," *U.S. News & World Report*, https://www.usnews.com /education/best-high-schools/search?state-urlname=colorado&district-id =112125&ranked=true.

12. Paul Sinanian (department manager, Talent Programs and Training, BMW), in discussion with the author, February 2024.

13. Analise Gonzalez (head of Postsecondary Success, DSST), in discussion with the author, November 2023.

14. Nationally, 33% of Latino students enroll in college. See "College Enrollment Rates," National Center for Education Statistics, May 2023, https://nces.ed.gov/programs/coe /indicator/cpb/college-enrollment-rate.

15. "Who Attends Charter Schools?," National Alliance for Public Charter Schools, December 19, 2023, https://data.publiccharters.org/digest/charter-school-data-digest /who-attends-charter-schools/.

16. "Text: George W. Bush's Speech to the NAACP," *Washington Post*, July 10, 2000, https://www.washingtonpost.com/wp-srv/onpolitics/elections/bushtext071000.htm.

17. QuestBridge Foundation and the Gates Foundation provide free college or last-dollar scholarships to select high school seniors who have shown high academic ability amid financial hardship. See "2,242 High School Seniors Are Awarded Full Scholarships to Top Colleges Through QuestBridge," press release, QuestBridge, December 1, 2023, https://www.questbridge.org/news-and-media/press-release-12-1-2023; and "The Gates Scholarship," Gates Scholarship, https://www.thegatesscholarship.org/scholarship.

18. Full disclosure: My family foundation, the deLaski Family Foundation, has made two philanthropic grants to Willow Education through its fiscal agents, the nonprofits America Succeeds and Colorado Succeeds, to support learning and development for holistic pathway recommendation research.

19. James Cryan (founder, Willow Education), in discussion with the author, January 2024.

20. Anthony P. Carnevale, Ban Cheah, and Emma Wenzinger, *The College Payoff: More Education Doesn't Always Mean More Earnings* (Washington, DC: Georgetown University Center on Education and the Workforce, 2021).

21. "IPEDs Data Explorer," National Center for Education Statistics, https://nces.ed.gov/ipeds/search/viewtable?tableId=12564&returnUrl=%2Fsearch.

22. Allison Danielson (former product lead, College Board Career Readiness), in discussion with the author, January 2024.

23. "Fact Sheet: Biden-Harris Administration Announces Landmark Regulations on Accountability, Transparency & Financial Value for Postsecondary Students," September 2023, https://www2.ed.gov/policy/highered/reg/hearulemaking/2021/gainful-employment-notice-of-final-review-factsheet.pdf.

24. Some national charter school networks that focus hard on college prep are Achievement First, KIPP, Mastery Charter Schools, BASIS Charter Schools, IDEA Charter Schools, and Success Academy. The Charter School Growth Network works with networks to improve academics and operations. See "About," Charter Grown Fund, https://chartergrowthfund.org/about/.

25. "Who Attends Charter Schools?"

26. Tessa Kratz (senior managing director of KIPP Forward, KIPP NYC), in discussion with the author, January 2024.

27. Kratz explains that in 2018 KIPP NYC hired its first CTE-focused counselor, and she attributed a 14-percentage-point drop in the college-going rate to that counseling, as well as to pandemic factors (between 2019 and 2023).

28. Outcomes data provided by Tessa Kratz, KIPP NYC.

29. Ajuah Helton (vice president, KIPP Forward, KIPP Foundation), in discussion with the author, August 2023.

30. From the history section of the website of Woodson High School: "A vocational wing housed a program drawing students from all over the county for classes in auto mechanics, cosmetology, carpentry, veterinary science, and electricity. The vocational programs were gradually phased out over the years and students interested in such classes now attend Chantilly Academy, a professional technical center located at Chantilly High School." "Woodson in the 1960s," Woodson High School, https://woodsonhs.fcps.edu/about/history/1960s.

31. In the 1978 movie *Grease*, John Travolta's character and his friends are CTE high school students who are made to feel "otherized." One song-and-dance number, "Beauty School Dropout," brings the students' anxiety to life.

32. "5 Wealthiest Counties in the U.S.," Insider Monkey, December 1, 2022, https://www.insidermonkey.com/blog/5-wealthiest-counties-in-the-us-1092190/4/.

33. Fairfax County is a district of 180,000 students, 60 percent of whom are nonwhite and 32 percent of whom are free and reduced lunch eligible. "FCPS Postsecondary Profile," Fairfax County Public Schools, https://www.fcps.edu/about-fcps/performance-and-accountability/fcps-postsecondary-profile.

34. Scott Settar (school principal, Chantilly Governor's STEM Academy), in discussion with the author, January 2024.

35. Robert Behre, "Knitting Together Greenville's Rich Textile Heritage: The True Fabric of an Upstate City," *Post and Courier* (Charleston, SC), March 28, 2014, https://www.postandcourier.com/archives/knitting-together-greenvilles-rich-textile-heritage-the-true-fabric-of-an-upstate-city/article_fe01496f-675c-53a5-bfed-0cd1a59d4ca5.html; "Southeast Region Employs the Most Textile Workers," U.S. Bureau of Labor Statistics, March 18, 1999, https://www.bls.gov/opub/ted/1999/mar/wk3/art04.htm.

36. Larry Miller (vice president of learning and workforce, Greenville Technical College), in discussion with the author, March 2023.

37. John Fink, Davis Jenkins, and Takeshi Yanagiura, *What Happens to Students Who Take Dual Enrollment Community College Courses in High School?* (New York: Community College Research Center, Columbia University, 2017), https://ccrc.tc.columbia.edu/publications/what-happens-community-college-dual-enrollment-students.html.

38. Miller, in discussion with the author, March 2023.

39. Representatives of New York City Public Schools' Office of Postsecondary Success, in discussion with the author, December 2023.

40. Alex Cortez (researcher, Bellwether Partners), in discussion with the author, August 2023.

41. Cortez's "choice is power" model has three components: information, navigation, and options. Alex Cortez et al., "An Investment, Not a Gamble: Creating More Equitable and Effective Postsecondary Pathways," Bellwether, April 2023, https://bellwether.org/publications/an-investment-not-a-gamble/?activeTab=4.

42. Laura Meckler and Hannah Natanson, "White House Urges Schools to Address Absenteeism amid Troubling Data," *Washington Post*, January 18, 2024, https://www.washingtonpost.com/education/2024/01/18/school-attendance-absenteeism-biden/.

43. The Department of Education reports that students who focus on CTE have higher earnings outcomes eight years after high school graduation. See "Bridging the Skills Gap: Career and Technical Education in High School," US Department of Education, September 2019, https://www2.ed.gov/datastory/cte/index.html.

44. "How Can Community Colleges Afford Dual Enrollment?," Community College Research Center, Columbia University, February 13, 2023, https://ccrc.tc.columbia.edu/easyblog/how-can-community-colleges-afford-dual-enrollment-discount.html; Gelsey Mehl, "Twenty Percent of Community College Students Are in High School. Now What?," New America, July 31, 2023, https://www.newamerica.org/education-policy/edcentral/dual-enrollment-growth/.

45. Suzanna Azmy et al., "Active Learning: Game-Changer to Short Attention Span in Gen Z" (paper presented at New Academia Learning Innovation, University of Technology Malaysia, Johor Bahru, Malaysia, 2022), https://www.researchgate.net/publication/366498656_ID-167_Active_learning_Game-changer_to_short_attention_span_in_Gen_Z.

46. Suzanne Blake, "Why So Many Young Men Are Abandoning College Degrees," *Newsweek*, December 27, 2023, https://www.newsweek.com/young-men-abandoning -college-degrees-gender-gap-1855825. According to Blake, in 2022, "39 percent of young men who completed high school [were] enrolled in college, down from 47 percent in 2011." Blake notes, "The reduced number of college students is largely led by men, with 1 million fewer young men in college today and just 0.2 million fewer young women compared to 2011."

47. For example, Indeed cites the average hourly wage for an EMT as $20.83, and for a certified medical assistant, $20.30. Payscale reports the average hourly rate for a desktop support technician as $22.89 per hour, https://www.indeed.com/career/emergency-medical -technician/salaries, https://www.indeed.com/career/emergency-medical-technician /salaries, https://www.payscale.com/research/US/Job=Desktop_Support_Technician /Hourly_Rate.

48. Angel Pérez (CEO, National Association for College Admission Counseling), in discussion with the author, January 2024.

Chapter 6

1. Tara Nicola, "Majority of Gen Z Consider College Education Important," Gallup News, September 14, 2023, https://news.gallup.com/opinion/gallup/509906/majority-gen -consider-college-education-important.aspx.

2. Kathryn Palmer, "Assessing Quality of Micro-credentials Is Difficult," *Inside Higher Ed*, February 6, 2024, https://www.insidehighered.com/news/tech-innovation/teaching -learning/2024/02/06/assessing-quality-microcredentials-difficult.

3. "The Growing Gap: Public Higher Education's Lack of Affordability for Pell Grant Recipients," National College Attainment Network, https://www.ncan.org/page/ Affordability; Megan Brenan, "Americans' Confidence in Higher Education Down Sharply," Gallup News, July 11, 2023, https://news.gallup.com/poll/508352/americans -confidence-higher-education-down-sharply.aspx; Josh Moody, "Inching Toward the $100,000 Sticker Price," *Inside Higher Ed*, April 3, 2024, https://www.insidehighered.com /news/business/revenue-strategies/2024/04/03/inching-toward-100000-sticker-price.

4. Anthony P. Carnevale et al., *Learning and Earning by Degrees* (Washington, DC: Georgetown University Center on Education and the Workforce, 2024), https://cew .georgetown.edu/wp-content/uploads/CEW-attainment-gains-full_report.pdf; *After Everything: Projections of Jobs, Education, and Training Requirements Through 2031* (Washington, DC: Georgetown University Center on Education and the Workforce, n.d.), https://cew.georgetown.edu/wp-content/uploads/Projections2031-ES.pdf.

5. Anthony Carnevale (founder, Georgetown University Center on Education and the Workforce), in discussion with the author, January 2024.

6. Anthony P. Carnevale, Stephen J. Rose, and Ban Cheah, *The College Payoff: Education, Occupations, Lifetime Earnings* (Washington, DC: Georgetown University Center on Education and the Workforce, n.d.), https://cew.georgetown.edu/wp-content/uploads /2014/11/collegepayoff-summary.pdf.

7. As I noted in chapter 1, President Donald Trump decisively won over the non-college-educated vote in 2016 and maintained it in 2020. Those without a college degree backed Trump 52%–44%. This is by far the widest gap in support among college graduates and

non–college graduates in exit polls dating back to 1980. Alec Tyson and Shiva Maniam, "Behind Trump's Victory: Divisions by Race, Gender, Education," Pew Research Center, November 9, 2016, https://www.pewresearch.org/short-reads/2016/11/09/behind-trumps-victory-divisions-by-race-gender-education/.

8. Danielle Douglas-Gabriel, "Students Now Pay More of Their Public University Tuition Than State Governments," *Washington Post*, January 5, 2015, https://www.washingtonpost.com/news/get-there/wp/2015/01/05/students-cover-more-of-their-public-university-tuition-now-than-state-governments/.

9. Paul Tough, "Americans Are Losing Faith in the Value of College. Whose Fault Is That?," *New York Times*, September 5, 2023, https://www.nytimes.com/2023/09/05/magazine/college-worth-price.html.

10. Jacob Lockwood and Douglas Webber, "Non-completion, Student Debt, and Financial Wellbeing: Evidence from the Survey of Household Economics and Decision-Making," US Federal Reserve, August 21, 2023, https://www.federalreserve.gov/econres/notes/feds-notes/non-completion-student-debt-and-financial-well-being-20230821.html.

11. William R. Emmons, Ana H. Kent, and Lowell R. Ricketts, "Is College Still Worth It? The New Calculus of Falling Returns," *Federal Reserve Bank of St. Louis Review* 101, no. 4 (2019): 297–329, https://files.stlouisfed.org/files/htdocs/publications/review/2019/10/15/is-college-still-worth-it-the-new-calculus-of-falling-returns.pdf.

12. Pranshu Verma and Gerrit De Vynck, "ChatGPT Took Their Jobs. Now They Walk Dogs and Fix Air Conditioners," *Washington Post*, June 2, 2023, https://www.washingtonpost.com/technology/2023/06/02/ai-taking-jobs/; "How AI Is Already Reshaping White-Collar Work," *Wall Street Journal*, July 6, 2023, https://www.wsj.com/video/series/wsj-explains/how-ai-is-already-reshaping-white-collar-work/839822A9-3A5F-4A5D-9390-E94EDF4A2336; Tom Carter, "Workers Are Worried About AI Taking Their Jobs. Artists Say It's Already Happening," *Business Insider*, October 1, 2023, https://www.businessinsider.com/ai-taking-jobs-fears-artists-say-already-happening-2023-10.

13. Jim Shelton is president of Blue Meridian Partners. He has been a senior player at the Gates Foundation, the Department of Education, and the Chan Zuckerberg Initiative.

14. Jim Shelton (president and chief investment and impact officer, Blue Meridian Partners), in discussion with the author, April 2024.

15. Dancers usually retire by thirty-five, or forty in a few instances. "FAQs: About the Artform," Kansas City Ballet, https://kcballet.org/faqs/?category=about-the-artform.

16. Amelia Grubb (bootcamp graduate), in discussion with the author, January 2024.

17. Richard Fry, "Fewer Young Men Are in College, Especially at 4 Year Schools," Pew Research Center, December 18, 2023, https://www.pewresearch.org/short-reads/2023/12/18/fewer-young-men-are-in-college-especially-at-4-year-schools/.

18. "Current Term Enrollment Estimates (CTEE) Expanded Edition: Fall 2023 Enrollment Overview," National Student Clearinghouse, published January 11, 2024, https://public.tableau.com/app/profile/researchcenter/viz/CTEEFall2023dashboard/CTEEFall2023.

19. *The Global Learner Survey* (London: Pearson, 2019), 22, https://www.pearson.com/en-au/media/2514267/pearson_global_learner_survey_2019.pdf. Based on eleven thousand survey takers globally. Rates of self-teaching were only higher in India and China.

20. Kathy Morris, "Male vs. Female Jobs: Jobs Dominated by One Gender," Zippia, January 26, 2023, https://www.zippia.com/advice/male-dominated-careers-female/.

21. Men across race groups have declined in their college attendance—but the drop from 2011 to 2022 is steepest for white men. Fry, "Fewer Young Men."

22. Kim Parker, "What's Behind the Growing Gap Between Men and Women in College Completion," Pew Research Center, November 8, 2021, https://www.pewresearch.org /short-reads/2021/11/08/whats-behind-the-growing-gap-between-men-and-women-in -college-completion/.

23. "Skills You Can Learn Off YouTube/Books If You Have No Degree/Experience," Reddit, https://www.reddit.com/r/jobs/comments/uk19q6/skills_you_can_learn_off_youtube books_if_you_have/.

24. Robert Gessler (self-taught learner and bootcamp graduate), in discussion with the author, November 2023.

25. Brian Rhodes-Devey (electrician, ReVision Energy), in discussion with the author, January 2024.

26. Peter Blair (associate professor, Harvard Graduate School of Education), in discussion with the author, December 2023.

27. "Data and Statistics," ApprenticeshipUSA, https://www.apprenticeship.gov/data-and -statistics. Active apprentices are 641,044 for fiscal year 2024, which is 0.4% of the total American workforce of roughly 167 million.

28. Luis is a pseudonym for this high school student, to protect his privacy as a minor.

29. Luis (student in senior seminar class), in conversation with the author at the Denver School of Science and Technology, Green Valley Ranch, Denver, CO, November 2023.

30. Carolyn Thompson, "Few Community College Students Go on to Earn 4 Year Degrees. Some States Have Found Ways to Help," Associated Press, November 9, 2023, https:// apnews.com/article/community-college-credit-transfer-education-department -a020e6b501226504b569d49211e33905.

31. "State-Adopted Credit Hour Policies Associated with Increases in Student Debt but Not Graduation Rates," American Educational Research Association, July 20, 2017, https://www.aera.net/Newsroom/News-Releases-and-Statements/State-Adopted-Credit -Hour-Policies-Associated-with-Increases-in-Student-Debt-but-Not-Graduation-Rates.

32. Joe DeGraaf and Becca Kleppinger, "Undeclared Students and the Career Decision," National Association of Colleges and Employers, May 15, 2022, https://www.naceweb.org /career-development/special-populations/undeclared-students-and-the-career-decision/. The authors are quoting from a 2016 study: Hongtoa Yue and Xuanning Fu, "Rethinking Graduation and Time to Degree: A Fresh Perspective," *Research in Higher Education* 58 (2017): 184–213, https://doi.org/10.1007/s11162-016-9420-4.

33. Sara B. Johnson, Robert W. Blum, and Jay N. Giedd, "Adolescent Maturity and the Brain: The Promise and Pitfalls of Neuroscience Research in Adolescent Health Policy," National Library of Medicine, June 27, 2010, https://www.ncbi.nlm.nih.gov/pmc/articles /PMC2892678/.

34. Jill Barshay, "Poll: Nearly Half of Parents Don't Want Their Kids to Go Straight to a Four-Year College," Hechinger Report, April 7, 2021, https://hechingerreport.org/poll -nearly-half-of-parents-dont-want-their-kids-to-go-to-a-four-year-college/; Rachel Minkin and Juliana Horowitz, "Race, Ethnicity, and Parenting," Pew Research Center, January 24, 2023, https://www.pewresearch.org/social-trends/2023/01/24/race-ethnicity -and-parenting/.

35. Aditya Aladangady, Andrew C. Chang, and Jacob Krimmel, "Greater Wealth, Greater Uncertainty: Changes in Racial Inequality in the Survey of Consumer Finances," FEDS Notes, October 18, 2023, https://www.federalreserve.gov/econres/notes/feds-notes /greater-wealth-greater-uncertainty-changes-in-racial-inequality-in-the-survey-of -consumer-finances-20231018.html.

36. Minkin and Horowitz, "Race, Ethnicity, and Parenting."

37. "Average Total Cost of Attendance for First-Time, Full-Time Undergraduate Students in Degree-Granting Postsecondary Institutions, by Control and Level of Institution, Living Arrangement, and Component of Student Costs: Selected Years, 2010–11 Through 2021–2022," National Center for Education Statistics, November 2022, https://nces.ed.gov/programs/digest/d22/tables/dt22_330.40.asp; Ron Lieber, "Some Colleges Will Soon Charge $100,000 a Year. How Did This Happen?," *New York Times*, April 5, 2024.

38. Jessica Walrack, "Why Is the Middle Class Shrinking?," *U.S. News & World Report*, March 29, 2024, https://money.usnews.com/money/personal-finance/family-finance /articles/where-do-i-fall-in-the-american-economic-class-system.

39. Andrew P. Kelly, "Does College Really Improve Social Mobility?," Brookings Institution, February 11, 2014, https://www.brookings.edu/articles/does-college-really-improve -social-mobility/.

40. Connie Matthiessen, "Celebrities Who Grew Up Poor and Went to College," Great-Schools.org, November 30, 2022, https://www.greatschools.org/gk/articles/famous -celebrities-first-to-college/.

41. Raj Chetty et al., "Mobility Report Cards: The Role of Colleges in Intergenerational Mobility," Equality of Opportunity, July 2017, 3, http://www.equality-of-opportunity .org/papers/coll_mrc_paper.pdf.

42. Daniella Ceballos and her two children, Malyah and Sebastain, in discussion with the author, December 2023.

43. "Waiting for 'Superman,'" Wikipedia, last edited July 12, 2024, https://en.wikipedia.org /wiki/Waiting_for_%22Superman%22.

44. Suzanne Blake, "Why So Many Young Men Are Abandoning College Degrees," *Newsweek*, December 27, 2023, https://www.newsweek.com/young-men-abandoning -college-degrees-gender-gap-1855825.

45. Raj Chetty et al., "Race and Economic Opportunity in the United States: An Intergenerational Perspective" (NBER Working Paper 24441, National Bureau of Economic Research, Cambridge, MA, March 2018), https://www.nber.org/papers/w24441. Looking over twenty-five years, economist Raj Chetty finds that Latinx, Asian, and white families are the groups that have really benefited from a gain in single generational wealth. His research suggests that Latinx families have managed to gain in wealth from one generation to the next. He doesn't link it to college specifically.

46. Kevin Lang and Michael Manove, "Education and Labor-Market Discrimination" (Working Paper 12257, National Bureau of Economic Research, Cambridge, MA, May 2006), https://www.nber.org/system/files/working_papers/w12257/w12257.pdf.

47. Barshay, "Poll"; Xiang Zhou and Guanghui Pan, "Higher Education and the Black-White Earnings Gap," *American Sociological Review* 88, no. 1 (2023): 154–88, https:// doi.org/10.1177/00031224221141887.

48. Steve Lohr, "Occupational Segregation Drives Persistent Inequality, Study Says," *New York Times*, September 4, 2023, https://www.nytimes.com/2023/09/04/business/black -workers-education-segregation.html.

49. Peter Blair (associate professor, Harvard Graduate School of Education), in discussion with the author, December 2023.

50. Black women enter college at higher rates than white, Hispanic, and Black men. For example, in 2020, Black women enrolled in college at a 40% rate, compared with 37% for white men, 31% for Black men, and 30% for Hispanic men. "College Enrollment Rates," National Center for Education Statistics, 2022, https://nces.ed.gov/programs/coe/pdf /2022/cpb_508.pdf.

51. Michelle Singletary is a *Washington Post* columnist who has long written an influential personal finance column. She tells her personal story and views about the importance of college for Black people. Michelle Singletary, "Stop Telling Black People They Could Close the Wealth Gap If They Valued Education More," *Washington Post*, September 25, 2020, https://www.washingtonpost.com/business/2020/09/25/black-parents-college -education/.

52. "Student Loan Debt by Race and Ethnicity," Education Data Initiative, https:// educationdata.org/student-loan-debt-by-race.

53. Penny Mickey Smith (senior adviser for economic and workforce development, Heartland Fund's Resource Rural Project), in discussion with the author, January 2024.

54. "Retiree Spotlight: Leon Smith—Changing the Song," LG&E and KU, April 18, 2023, https://lge-ku.com/newsroom/articles/2023/04/18/retiree-profile-leon-smith-changing -song.

55. Geoffrey is a pseudonym, used to protect this minor's identity.

56. Carnevale et al., *Learning and Earning.*

57. My interview subject was Glenn Miller, who would lock reporters and cameramen in their cars if they were not sufficiently Aryan in his view. "Frazier Glenn Miller," Southern Poverty Law Center, https://www.splcenter.org/fighting-hate/extremist-files /individual/frazier-glenn-miller.

58. Soren Kaplan, "How Important Is a College Degree Compared to Experience?," *Harvard Business Review*, February 3, 2023, https://hbr.org/2023/02/how-important-is-a-college -degree-compared-to-experience.

59. Theresa Agovino, "Skills-Based Hiring Is Gaining Ground," SHRM, March 21, 2024, https://www.shrm.org/topics-tools/news/all-things-work/skills-based-hiring-new -workplace-trend.

60. Jenn Dale (dean of academic success, Community College of Aurora), in discussion with the author, December 2023.

61. "Maslow's Hierarchy of Needs," Wikipedia, last edited July 6, 2024, https://en.wikipedia .org/wiki/Maslow's_hierarchy_of_needs.

62. *"Walk in My Shoes": An Actionable Learner Engagement Framework to Foster Growth, Belonging, and Agency* (Education Design Lab, November 2022), https://eddesignlab.org /wp-content/uploads/2022/11/EducationDesignLab_WalkinMyShoesLearnerEngageme ntFramework_November2022_SPREADS.pdf.

63. "I Regret Not Going to College Right Now," Reddit, 2023, https://www.reddit.com/r /college/comments/zrnkfb/i_regret_not_going_to_college_right_now/.

64. Elliot Felix and Amanda Lorenzo, "Student Experience Snapshot 2023: Eight Insights on What Students Value and How Well Colleges and Universities Are Meeting Their Needs," Brightspot, March 1, 2023, https://www.brightspotstrategy.com/whitepaper/student-experience-snapshot-2023/. A quarter of students put finding community or their identity among the top three values of their college experience.

65. Jodi Tandet, "What Factors Affect Student Retention?," Modern Campus, November 10, 2023, https://moderncampus.com/blog/factors-affecting-student-retention.html; Vincent Tinto, "Reflections: Rethinking Engagement and Student Persistence," *Student Success* 14, no. 2 (2023): 1–7, https://doi.org/10.5204/ssj.3016.

66. Ariel Ervin, "College Mentors Are Helpful: But Too Many Students Aren't Finding Them," Chronicle of Evidence-Based Monitoring, November 25, 2021, https://www.evidencebasedmentoring.org/savvy-students-get-the-guidance/.

67. Colleen Flaherty, "Survey: Inequities in Student Involvement," *Inside Higher Ed*, September 22, 2023, https://www.insidehighered.com/news/student-success/college-experience/2023/09/22/survey-barriers-college-students-campus.

68. Of immigrants who have arrived since 2010, 45.2% hold bachelor's degrees or higher. "Census Bureau Releases New Educational Attainment Data," press release, US Census Bureau, February 16, 2023, https://www.census.gov/newsroom/press-releases/2023/educational-attainment-data.html.

69. Jon Marcus, "The Reckoning Is Here," Hechinger Report, April 3, 2023, https://hechingerreport.org/the-reckoning-is-here-more-than-a-third-of-community-college-students-have-vanished/.

70. Carnevale et al., *Learning and Earning*.

71. "College Scorecard," US Department of Education, https://collegescorecard.ed.gov/search/?page=0&sort=threshold_earnings:desc.

72. Chetty et al., "Mobility Report Cards," 3.

73. "O*NET OnLine Help: Browse Bright Outlook Occupations," O*NET, US Department of Labor, https://www.onetonline.org/help/online/browse_bright.

Chapter 7

1. Josh Moody, "The First 3-Year Degree Programs Win Approval," *Inside Higher Ed*, September 1, 2023, https://www.insidehighered.com/news/business/academic-programs/2023/09/01/first-three-year-degree-programs-win-accreditor-approval.

2. Shannon Lee, "Fastest Online Master's Degrees for 2024," Online Master's Degrees, April 3, 2024, https://www.onlinemastersdegrees.org/features/fastest-online-masters-degrees/.

3. "Current Term Enrollment Estimates: Fall 2023," National Student Clearinghouse Research Center, January 24, 2024, https://nscresearchcenter.org/current-term-enrollment-estimates/.

4. Coursera's website reports 129 million registered users.

5. Michael Horn (co-founder, Clayton Christiansen Institute), in discussion with the author, March 2024.

6. Paul LeBlanc (former president, Southern New Hampshire University), in discussion with the author, February 2024.

7. Ted Mitchell (president, American Council on Education), in discussion with the author, January 2024.

8. Mitchell led one of the first efforts to help alternative credential providers partner with universities as deputy secretary at the Department of Education, and he has pioneered the granting of credit for alternative programs through his current organization, ACE. LeBlanc pioneered flexible online learning pathways and college completion programs.

9. This was one of the projects the US Chamber of Commerce Foundation workshopped at the 2024 ASU+GSV Innovation Summit. The broader initiative is explained here: "Talent Finance," US Chamber of Commerce Foundation, https://www.uschamberfoundation.org/solutions/workforce-development-and-training/talent-finance.

10. The deLaski Family Foundation has funded, for example, Enstitute, Degrees of Freedom, CityWorks, Climb Hire, Sitar Center for the Arts, the Community College Growth Engine Fund, Pima Community College/Catholic University, and the Catholic University of America–Tucson.

11. Some of Southern New Hampshire University's national ads are featured on its YouTube channel: Southern New Hampshire University, "SNHU Commercials," YouTube, https://www.youtube.com/playlist?list=PLgvtqIwqJjJtUZmFBer6b-BAOLwZWTuGl.

12. Lauren Coffey, "Students Distancing from Distance Learning," *Inside Higher Ed*, January 30, 2024, https://www.insidehighered.com/news/tech-innovation/teaching-learning/2024/01/30/online-college-enrollment-continues-post-pandemic.

13. "How Does LinkedIn Make Money?," Investopedia, December 18, 2022, https://www.investopedia.com/ask/answers/120214/how-does-linkedin-lnkd-make-money.asp.

14. Credit goes to Melanie Booth, executive director of Credential Lab at the Higher Learning Commission, for suggesting that I feature Amazon's Career Choice program.

15. "Amazon's Career Choice Program Saw Record Growth in 2022, Reaching over 110,000 Participants," Amazon, January 31, 2023, https://www.aboutamazon.com/news/workplace/amazons-career-choice-program-saw-record-growth-in-2022-reaching-over-110-000-participants.

16. Tammy Thieman (global director of Amazon Career Choice), in an email response to author's questions, April 2024.

17. "Thousands of Amazon Employees Are Landing Higher-Paying Jobs Through Career Choice. Here's How," Amazon, January 17, 2024, https://www.aboutamazon.com/news/workplace/amazon-career-choice-high-paying-jobs. Roughly two million Americans serve in the military. Free education benefits accrue after ninety days of military service. See Jim Absher, "Army Tuition Assistance," Military.com, October 31, 2022, https://www.military.com/education/money-for-school/army-tuition-assistance.html. Starbucks also has a well-known program. Twenty thousand Starbucks baristas have started or finished college through a free program with Arizona State University, according to my interview with the university's Phil Regier.

18. Sara Weissman, "The 'Some College, No Credential' Cohort Grows," *Inside Higher Ed*, April 25, 2023, https://www.insidehighered.com/news/students/retention/2023/04/25/some-college-no-credential-cohort-grows.

19. Phil Regier (university dean for educational initiatives and CEO, EdPlus, Arizona State University), in discussion with the author, February 2024.

20. Scott Pulsipher (president, Western Governors University), in discussion with the author, April 2024.

21. Notable groups to mention include Year Up, Merit America, Genesys Works, Per Scholas, and the Center on Rural Innovation.

22. Kathryn Harris (president and chief operating officer, ActivateWork), in discussion with the author, March 2024.

23. Jason Janz (CEO, CrossPurpose), in discussion with the author, March 2024.

24. Per Scholas's website touts 80% placement rates into tech jobs.

25. "National Beer Sales and Production Data," Brewers Association, https://www.brewersassociation.org/statistics-and-data/national-beer-stats/.

26. This was a private report that senior adviser Nate Anderson led for JFF in 2023, at the request of national nonprofit Stand Together.

27. "Craft Beer Market Size and Share Analysis 2024–2029," Mordor Intelligence, https://www.mordorintelligence.com/industry-reports/craft-beer-market.

28. Jeff Selingo (author, journalist), in discussion with the author, April 2024.

29. Joshua Bay, "Job Focused Community College Programs Grow—but Grim Transfer Trend Continues," The 74, March 5, 2024, https://www.the74million.org/article/job-focused-community-college-programs-grow-but-grim-transfer-trend-continues/; Sara Weissman, "Enrollments Rise after Pandemic-Related Declines," *Inside Higher Ed*, January 24, 2024, https://www.insidehighered.com/news/students/retention/2024/01/24/enrollment-rising-first-time-pandemic.

30. "Awarding Credit for Prior Learning," American Council on Education, https://www.acenet.edu/Programs-Services/Pages/Credit-Transcripts/Awarding-Credit-for-Prior-Learning.aspx.

31. Ayanna (intern at Year Up, Washington, DC, region), in discussion with the author, March 2024.

32. Daisean (intern at Year Up, Washington, DC, region), in discussion with the author, March 2024.

33. Based on national outcomes data provided by Year Up.

34. Groups helping rural alliances with shared "front door" experiences for learners include the Center for Rural Innovation, Education Design Lab's BRIDGES initiative, Colorado's Home Grown Initiative, and the work of many individual community colleges, such as Finger Lakes Community College in upstate New York and Patrick and Henry Community College in Martinsville, Virginia.

35. Year Up pays all interns $525 a week; the employer usually pays a significant part of that.

36. Rob Simms (chief technology officer and managing partner, MAXX Potential), in discussion with the author, March 2024.

37. Laura Mills (Forage company representative), in discussion with the author, February, 2024.

38. Maria Currasco, "Ending Unpaid Internships," *Inside Higher Ed*, April 11, 2022, https://www.insidehighered.com/news/2022/04/12/colleges-work-end-unpaid-internships.

39. *Evaluation of the National Civilian Community Corps (NCCC) Program* (Washington, DC: Office of Inspector General, Corporation for National and Community Service, December 5, 2016), https://www.oversight.gov/sites/default/files/oig-reports/17-05_nccc_evaluation.pdf; Annie Kim, "Out of School, Out of Work," *Washington Monthly*, April 4, 2021, https://washingtonmonthly.com/2021/04/04/out-of-school-out-of-work/.

40. Robert D. Putnam, *Bowling Alone: The Collapse and Revival of American Community* (New York: Simon and Schuster, 2000).

41. The Gates Foundation has funded twelve regions to explore new models: "About," Accelerate ED, https://www.accelerate-ed.org/about/; "Communities," Accelerate ED, https://www.accelerate-ed.org/communities/; Jill Barshay, "Proof Points: High Schoolers Account for Nearly 1 out of Every 5 Community College Students," Hechinger Report, July 24, 2023, https://hechingerreport.org/proof-points-high-schoolers-account-for-nearly-1-out-of-every-5-community-college-students/.

42. Maryland has recently initiated a new blueprint that codifies technical pathways and dual enrollment for college courses in late high school, alongside college prep. It also, interestingly, funds state grants to nonprofits that lead youth development, connecting the dots among employers, schools, and community groups. See "Blueprint Pillar 3: College and Career Readiness," Blueprint for Maryland's Future, https://blueprint.marylandpublicschools.org/ccr/.

43. Barbara Gellman-Danley (president, Higher Learning Commission), in discussion with the author, January 2024.

44. As of spring 2024, short-term Pell bills, which would fund programs as short as seven to fifteen weeks, had bipartisan support but had not advanced out of the House Education and the Workforce Committee. See Katherine Knott, "Bipartisan Progress on Pell Grant Expansion, but Hurdles Remain," Inside Higher Ed, December 12, 2023, https://www.insidehighered.com/news/government/student-aid-policy/2023/12/12/short-term-pell-bill-would-end-federal-loans-wealthy.

45. Paul LeBlanc (former president, Southern New Hampshire University), in discussion with the author, February 2024.

46. Paul Basken, "Online Pioneers Begin Urgent Pursuit of Value from AI," Inside Higher Ed, January 4, 2024, https://www.insidehighered.com/news/tech-innovation/artificial-intelligence/2024/01/04/online-pioneers-begin-urgent-pursuit-value.

47. "Workday Hiring and Talent Trends," Workday, https://forms.workday.com/en-us/reports/workday-hiring-and-talent-trends/form.html.

48. Chandler Morse (vice president for public policy, Workday), in discussion with the author, February 2024.

49. Aashna Kircher (general manager of talent products, Workday), in discussion with the author, February 2024.

50. Liam Knox, "Black, Hispanic Students More Likely to Drop Out," Inside Higher Ed, February 28, 2024, https://www.insidehighered.com/news/quick-takes/2024/02/28/black-hispanic-students-greatest-risk-dropping-out.

51. "Current Term Enrollment Estimates, Spring 2024," National Student Clearinghouse, May 2024, https://nscresearchcenter.org/current-term-enrollment-estimates/?gad_source=1&gclid=CjwKCAjwooq3BhB3EiwAYqYoEpxpVubbAHSZMIazYnb2fNJOv0aCmstKrvs43EXABr-eJlt6XDe3exoCZt4QAvD_BwE; Associated Press and Collin Binkley, "Experts Fear Catastrophic Declines Thanks to Botched FAFSA Rollout," WDBJ-TV, May 2, 2024, https://www.wdbj7.com/2024/05/02/experts-fear-catastrophic-college-declines-thanks-botched-fafsa-rollout/.

52. States are finding that community college "promise" programs and free community college can bolster enrollment—e.g., California, Tennessee, Maine, and Minnesota. See Liam Knox, "State Support Turns Minnesota's Enrollment Tide," Inside Higher Ed, March 27, 2024, https://www.insidehighered.com/news/government/state-policy/2024/03/27/enrollment-mn-colleges-after-historic-state-funding; Jessica Blake, "More Access

Means More Enrollment for Maine Community Colleges," *Inside Higher Ed*, January 18, 2024, https://www.insidehighered.com/news/institutions/community-colleges/2024/01 /18/more-access-means-more-enrollment-maine-community.

53. Paul Fain (journalist, Work Shift), in discussion with the author, April 2024.

54. "The Rev. John Wise of Ipswich," Historic Ipswich, https://historicipswich.net/2022/11 /15/john-wise/.

Acknowledgments

As I thought about writing my first book, the thing holding me back was "publisher shopping." It seemed impenetrable. So I must first thank Bob Schwartz, a longtime professor at Harvard's Graduate School of Education, who made it easy by suggesting I send a description to Harvard Education Press. I want to thank the whole publishing team there, particularly Molly Cerrone, my editor, for her insightful advice and always positive outlook and executive editor, Jess Fiorillo, for her belief in my concept. My two researchers also proved invaluable—Emily Demsetz, a master's student from the Harvard Graduate School of Education, and Afreen Ahmed, a master's student in public policy from the Kennedy School of Government. They provided informed, high-quality assistance during my year of writing and interviews, not to mention a much-needed community for thought partnership and bouncing ideas around. And thank you to Harvard's Project on Workforce, in particular Kerry McKittrick and Ali Epstein, for providing me with researchers and sharing ideas.

LAB COLLEAGUES

Speaking of thought partners, I owe much of my own learning on these issues to my colleagues at the Education Design Lab. Plus, as CEO of the Lab for ten years and now as board chair, I have had a front-row seat to see and assess the changes and innovations as players in the ecosystem respond to the great skills shake-up. The Lab has also afforded me the opportunity to meet hundreds of new majority learners, college leaders, and faculty on the cutting edge of innovation, as well as employers, intermediaries, and researchers. Thank you to the lab's leadership team for, first, being open to me telling my story and connecting me to the latest examples of how the system is changing. Particular thanks go to Naomi Boyer and Lisa Larson for connecting me to their work toward infusing skills into the current systems of higher education and hiring. And thank you to Leslie Daugherty, Kevin Stump, and Don Fraser for assistance with connections and perspective. I am particularly grateful to my successor, CEO Bill Hughes, for skillfully leading the team after my transition, and chief growth officer Larry Roth as they all take the Lab to greater impact and strength than I could have hoped for. I also want to thank the Lab's board of directors for their support of this endeavor, with particular insights about the landscape from Lou Pugliese, Rufus Glasper, and Kris Clerkin.

HIGH SCHOOLS

Also high on my list of thought partners and connectors was James Cryan, who is featured in chapter 5. As a former charter school network founder in Denver, James is now working on holistic solutions to recommend a full range of post–high school pathways to learners. James connected me with the folks at the Denver School of Science and Technology (DSST), several of the alternative providers in Denver, and mom Daniella Ceballos and her teenagers. Among the high school and K–12 leaders who were extremely helpful were Analise Gonzalez and the team at DSST. They graciously provided time and access, as well as their students, who gave me an unfiltered picture of their hopes and challenges. Other K–12 players who were very helpful include the KIPP Forward team, Ajuah Helton, and Tessa Kratz at KIPP NYC. I am also grateful to New York City Public Schools' Eliza Loehr and Scott Settar at Chantilly High School's Governor's STEM Academy, in northern Virginia. System-level leaders Angel Pérez, CEO of the National Association for College Admission Counseling; Nina Rees, who led the National Alliance for Public Charter Schools for many years; Mike Petrilli from the Thomas B. Fordham Institute; Katherine Bradley of CityBridge; and Eric Waldo at the DC College Access Program were instrumental in helping me understand how the college access movement has changed since I was more deeply involved from 2001 to 2012.

EMPLOYERS

On the employer side, I want to thank several connectors and experts for sharing how the hiring market is changing and where the degree does and doesn't solve for their talent needs. Kelley Fitzgerald, head of recruiting at CACI Products, was particularly helpful and led me to young software engineer Patrick, the high school grad who never got to college. The team from Workday, Donna Troeger, Chandler Morse, and Aashna Kircher, provided many insights, as did Lovey Hammel from Employment Enterprises, Carrie Engel from Indeed, Jake Hirsch Allen from LinkedIn, Julie Wilmes from Pinnacol, Paul Sinanian from BMW, David Leaser (formerly with IBM), Elise Tasooji from Grow with Google and Margot Baron from Google, Liberty Munson from Microsoft, Jennifer Ricciuti from AWS, Yuanxia Ding and Katherine Pokrass from Amazon, Vaughan Woodruff (formerly with ReVision Energy), Peyton May of BitSource, Kim Aftergood with Accenture, Ashwin Bharath with Revature, Clay Lord with the SHRM Foundation, and Jason Tyszko with the US Chamber of Commerce Foundation. Richard Lawrence from the Interstate Renewable Energy Council and Zach Boren and Annelies Goger from the Brookings Institution were instrumental in helping me understand how the registered apprenticeship world is taking shape. Also in the apprenticeship movement, Rebecca Agostino from Multiverse and Jenny Niles, who is building out apprenticeships in Washington, DC, through CityWorks, provided illuminating insights. And of course, Ryan Craig, who has become a passionate spokesperson on the need for apprenticeships, served as a thought partner and connector.

WORKERS AND LEARNERS

Early-stage worker interviews were critical to understanding whether alternative pathways are delivering for learners, so I am grateful to Nitzan

Pelman from Climb Hire for introducing me to several bootcamp graduates, and I want to acknowledge the workers I interviewed: bootcamp
grads Yrel, Porchea, Kavitha, and Jon Cotton from Sneaker Essentials, as
well as army veteran Ethan Wharton, who earned XCredit credentials.
I am grateful to the other alternative pathway workers who shared their
stories—Patrick the certificate earner; Brian Rhodes-Devey, Crystal Acosta,
and Naarai, the apprentices; Robert Gessler, the do-it-yourselfer; and Year
Up interns Ayanna, Anne, and Daisean. And I must make a special call-
out to the high school students who opened up to me during impromptu
interviews about their hopes and dreams, their fears and insecurities. I
want to mention Daniel, Malyah, Sebastain, and Luis, who are featured in
the book, but also the scores of others who spoke to me. Other interviews
that were critical included those with Daniella Ceballos, Malyah and Sebastain's mom, who spoke very honestly about her own journey without a
college degree, and Penny Mickey Smith, who opened up about the challenges to become first in her family to obtain a degree and now guiding
her son, who is on the autism spectrum. And my own relative Joe, who has
tried community college twice but didn't find his community. I want to
thank the college students I featured in chapter 4 on how colleges are
adapting to a skills-based shift, Sofia Cavenaile and Brody Feldberg, who
were earning micro-credentials; Abigail, who was on a "fast-track"
micro-pathway; and Jonathan Mejia, who believes his co-op at Northeastern University helped secure his dream job to become a TV reporter. And
I also leaned on my own class of undergraduates in the fall 2023 section of
Honors College 260_05, Higher Ed Redesign, at George Mason University. They were an excellent sounding board, and it was very useful to be
writing while seeing college through their lenses.

ALTERNATIVE CREDENTIAL PROVIDERS

I salute the alternative credential providers in the book. I mentioned bootcamp entrepreneur Nitzan Pelman, who shared her own story. I also want
to acknowledge bootcamp pioneer Jake Schwartz, who founded General
Assembly; Rob Kingyens at Yellowbrick; and Rebecca Stahelin at Merit

America. Dhawal Shah from Class Central and Nate Anderson from Jobs for the Future (JFF) were very helpful in understanding the nondegree ecosystem. In chapter 7, we met alternative providers who are building a support village for nondegree seekers, Kathryn Harris from ActivateWork and Jason Janz from Cross Purpose, both in Denver. And I want to thank all the providers in Washington, DC, who make up Talent for Tomorrow. Administrators at Year Up DC and national teams were particularly generous with their time, and I want to thank Phoebe Williams, Mary Ellen Matheson, Meredith Jaremchuk, and Elisha Gilliam for openly sharing their thoughts and strategies.

COLLEGES

College administrators and faculty are a remarkable collection of people. They get up every day thinking about ways to support new majority learners. They are not in this work for the money; they share a deep commitment to their students. It was heartening to interview the enthusiastic teams at the five colleges and systems I profiled in chapter 4, which are working toward degrees that provide career experience, certificates, and skills profiles. These include Kacey Thorne and Scott Pulsipher at Western Governors University; Lydia Riley (formerly) and Kelvin Bentley (currently) from the University of Texas System; Claudia Arcolin from the University of Texas San Antonio; Luke Dowden from Alamo Colleges District; Jeff Holm and Robert Warren at the University of North Dakota; Dave Savory from Riipen, who connected me to the University of North Dakota's story; Ian Roark and Dionne Billick at Pima Community College; and Connie Yowell, Esther Chewning, and Karl Reid at Northeastern University. Jenn Dale helped me understand how community colleges are working with state licensing bodies to solve for severe talent shortages. Several administrators at South Carolina Technical Colleges helped me understand their impressive story, including Larry Miller and Rebecca Taylor, as well as Amanda Richardson from Apprenticeship Carolina. Phil Regier, CEO of EdPlus at Arizona State University, gave me a helpful perspective on the world of online education, as did industry consultant Phil Hill. I also am grateful to Paul LeBlanc, who spoke to me as he was wrapping up his presidency at Southern New Hampshire University, and Ted Mitchell at ACE, both of whom gave me a strong sense of the future of the college ecosystem. Amber Garrison Duncan from the Competency-Based Education Network provided critical landscape background as we move to a skillified framework for learning.

WALLET WORLD

Looking at the future of digital credentials and how they will all connect, I want to thank several visionaries who contributed to the book: Pete Janzow from Credly, Ian Davidson from SmartResume, Taylor Kendall from Learning Economy, and Tracy Korsmo from the State of North Dakota.

INTERMEDIARIES, RESEARCHERS, JOURNALISTS, AND INDUSTRY OBSERVERS

Other ecosystem players who gave generously of their time include Maria Flynn, whose organization Jobs for the Future (JFF) plays an exciting role at the intersection of workforce and talent, and Barbara Gellman-Danley and Melanie Booth from the Higher Learning Commission. Investor Jim Shelton from Blue Meridian has inspired me throughout my education reform career, as has Matt Greenfield from ReThink Education. Both provided useful insights for the book. Michael Horn of the Clayton Christensen Institute was very helpful, as was higher ed best-selling author Jeff Selingo, and Louis Soares. Several folks helped me bring the rise of skills-based hiring to life, including Steve Taylor from Stand Together; Joe Farren, formerly from Governor Larry Hogan's office; and Michael Brickman, a former deputy at the US Department of Education during the Trump administration.

The work of the Burning Glass Institute has been very illuminating, and Matt Sigelman provided generously of his time. Byron Auguste and Papia Debroy's awareness campaign on dead-end versus gateway jobs for

STARS (Skilled Through Alternative Routes) workers was eye-opening. Julian Thompson from UNCF was very helpful too. Several funders were helpful with a landscape perspective, including Sean Murphy from Walmart, Andrew Tonsing from Stand Together, and Ryan Stowers from the Charles Koch Foundation.

Researchers were critical to helping me back up my "who needs college" personas and other trends that are changing the landscape. Doug Shapiro of the National Student Clearinghouse was very patient with me, working through the tables and fine print as the 2023–24 enrollment numbers became available. I also relied on Peter Blair of Harvard's Graduate School of Education and Joseph Fuller from Harvard Business School. Anthony Carnevale and his team from Georgetown University's Center on Education and the Workforce assisted, as well as Michelle Van Noy from Rutgers and the researchers and connectors at Strada Education Network, including Jon Furr. Michael Iskowitz, founder of the federal government's College Scorecard, provided a wealth of information. I would be remiss if I did not call out the helpful daily reporting of *Inside Higher Ed*, which I reference in several endnotes, as well as the reporting by the Hechinger Report. Paul Fain's weekly newsletter provided me with several leads, and during his interview near the end of my writing time, he helped me gut-check some of my conclusions. Goldie Blumenstyk, from the *Chronicle of Higher Education*, encouraged me to follow her into the book-writing world.

FAMILY AND FRIENDS

I want to thank journalist Jamie Stiehm, my dear friend, and my cousin Andrew deLaski, who both gave me unfiltered editorial advice. My nephew, graphic designer Dexter deLaski, provided help on the charts in the book. Other chapter readers included education entrepreneur Adam Carter. It might seem odd to thank my British family since I don't tell their story specifically. Married to a British citizen for more than thirty-five years, I have eleven nieces and nephews in the UK, who are now in their twenties and thirties. They are not featured in the book, but watching how this cohort make its way through the British education system helped inform my alternative views. I was always struck by how the narrative about university is different across the Atlantic. About half of my nieces and nephews chose university, and half chose other paths. University wasn't expected. And it didn't feel like there was the same stigma when some went into apprenticeship programs or straight to work.

Thank you to my two brothers on this side of the Atlantic, who helped me crystallize my distant memories of our teenagerhood. I thank my husband, who cooked more than his share during the book process and brought me coffee in bed. I also thank my two children, Amelia and Hawk, who both, in different ways, challenged the status quo system that expected them to aim for top colleges. They helped me think like an outsider, which is essential to reimagining college. And finally, should I acknowledge John Wise, my seventh-great-grandfather, believed to be the first son of an indentured servant to become an American college graduate, who inspired me from across the centuries as I started this book? I am grateful to call him my ancestor. I certainly want to thank Rev. Kenyn Cureton, who made me aware of my relative's humble origins when I Googled Rev. John Wise and discovered Kenyn's blog post about him. Kenyn agreed to an interview and couldn't have been more helpful.

About the Author

Kathleen deLaski spent twenty years as a TV and then digital journalist, including time as an ABC News White House correspondent. This period included a stint in government as the chief Pentagon spokesperson. She then turned her focus to education finance and education reform. She has been involved with founding several nonprofits. The most relevant for this book is the Education Design Lab, which works with colleges to create shorter, more affordable pathways for learners to achieve their economic goals. Stepping down after a decade as CEO of the Lab, Kathleen now serves as board chair there and on the board of Credential Engine. She spends time as a senior adviser to the Project on Workforce at Harvard University and teaches human-centered design and higher ed reform as an adjunct professor in the Honors College at George Mason University, where she also served as an appointee to the Board of Visitors. Kathleen has long played a dual role as a philanthropist, managing the deLaski Family Foundation, which has for twenty-five years been a grant maker in education reform, well-being, sustainable agriculture, and the arts. Kathleen lives with her husband in McLean, Virginia, and has two grown children and a fabulous son-in-law.

Index

Jimmy Carter

Biography

A Life of Peace and Progress

Ashly L Tildenbrowning

TABLE CONTENTS

Chapter 1: Archery and the Race Problem

My life has been shaped inexorably by my forefathers' experiences and decisions, and I've learnt a lot about my family history. My mother's name was Bessie Lillian Gordy, and I knew all of her close family as well as many of her distant cousins. We would sometimes drive to Richland, her birthplace, after church services to eat dinner with her close-knit family, where the table discourse frequently resulted in an explosion of emotions and angry departures. My father's name was James Earl Carter, and I had never met any of his near cousins who resided in the county seat, which was only nine miles from our home in Plains. The Carters did not appear to be interested in each other.

During my first year in office, members of the Church of Jesus Christ of Latter-day Saints visited the White House and presented me with a genealogical study of my Carter family. The data spanned thirteen generations, dating back to the early 1600s, and included birth, death, and marriage records, land deeds, and data from early courthouse procedures including legal issues. I packed everything into a large box and shipped it to our Plains house. I got my first computer after leaving the White House and began entering Mormon research material when I received the first edition of a software program called Family Tree Maker. My wife Rosalynn's family traditionally had three reunions every year (four if two Smiths hadn't married one other), so in 1998 I decided to have a reunion of my great-great-grandfather Wiley Carter's direct descendants on what would have been his 200th birthday. More than 950 people attended, and I repaired and updated errors in my family records. I recently provided the information to our son Jeffrey, who has now written a far more authoritative study, Ancestors of Jimmy and Rosalynn Carter, focusing on our period in America.

William Archibald Carter (1858-1903), his son and my grandpa, relocated to Rowena, a small village approximately fifty miles south, in 1888, where he was a farmer, had two sawmills and a vineyard, and owned a cotton gin. He was petite yet tough. While picking sugarcane, his machete was redirected into his thigh, causing a serious gash. Billy stopped the flow of blood with his belt, went home for a needle and thread, patched up the cut, and returned to work. He was shot and died in a struggle with a man named Will Taliaferro over a desk Taliaferro took from Billy's cotton gin. Billy's family returned to Plains after selling his property and purchasing a farm in nearby Webster County in 1904, which my father, Earl Carter, became responsible for maintaining as a teenager. I can only imagine the numerous skills required to execute all of my ancestors' tasks, and it's possible that my desire to pursue new ideas and design and make things in my woodshop is inherited from them.

In 1920, my mother, Lillian Gordy, left her job as a postal clerk in Richland and relocated eighteen miles to Plains (population roughly 500) to become a registered nurse. When she finished her training in 1923, she married Earl. I was born in October 1924, and my family shared a house on South Bond Street with Edgar and Allie Smith. After serving as a first lieutenant in World War I, Edgar was the sole automotive mechanic in the community, and my father owned and operated a small general store just across the street from his shop. Rosalynn Smith, the Smiths' daughter, was born in August 1927, and my mother subsequently told me that I was escorted to the house next door and glanced into the cradle to see the newest baby on the block. Rosalynn's younger sister was named after Mama, the nurse who nursed Rosalynn's father throughout his final leukaemia illness. When I was four years old, Daddy became a full-time farmer. I grew up on a farm he purchased about two and a half miles west of Plains in the rural village of Archery.

***

My childhood home in Archery was a Sears, Roebuck house built six

4

years before our family moved in. At the time, the Sears catalogue offered homes in a variety of sizes, with three basic options: (1) all the components of a complete house and the tools needed to construct it, loaded into a single railroad boxcar with plans and instructions; (2) everything needed for a house except the lumber; and (3) just the plans and instructions, practically free but requiring Sears-sold doors, windows, hardware, and other parts. We later discovered that our house was one of the second choices, because genetic research revealed that its wooden frame and cladding were made from farm trees.

There was no running water, electricity, or insulation, and the only heat sources other than the cooking stove were a few open fireplaces that were all fueled by wood and only used when absolutely necessary. We peed in "slop jars" at night and emptied them in an outdoor toilet when it was daylight. It was the lone privy on the farm; the other households hid in the bushes. Until 1935, when Daddy constructed a windmill and brought a line from its tank into our kitchen and bathroom, we drew water from a well in the backyard. He created a shower bath by cutting holes in the bottom of a galvanised bucket suspended above a concrete floor, and the used water went through a pipe outside onto the ground. It was particularly frigid in the winter, but it was more convenient than a galvanised bathtub. Electricity was installed on some fields near us in 1939, and after about a year, Daddy persuaded the local cooperative to extend the lines to our house.

Because my room was in the northeast corner, far away from any heater or fireplace, my most vivid and terrible memories are of cold weather. Even under covers, I recall freezing at night, and my bare toes curling up as I slipped out of bed onto the chilly floor and dashed for my parents' room and the warmth of some still-glowing embers in their fireplace. Surprisingly, I don't recall the discomfort of South Georgia's sweltering summer days. The National Park Service presently owns this house and its outbuildings, and the historic site is kept exactly as it was in 1937.

When Mama was on nursing duty, one of the African-American ladies who lived on the farm made our family meals, and my two sisters knew them well. Neither my sisters nor my mother have ever worked in the field. When I wasn't at school, I spent every spare second of my work days around the barn and in the fields, preferably with my father. I had a strong bond with Jack and Rachel Clark, who lived in the house next to ours. Jack was in charge of all the livestock, the equipment, and the barn and its surroundings. He was in charge of milking the cows and rang the large farm bell every morning an hour before daybreak. Jack collaborated closely with Daddy in assigning various personnel to their jobs.

Daddy had many talents, and he used many of them to help the farm become as self-sufficient as possible. He was unwilling to pay someone else to do chores he could learn to do himself, thus he became an accomplished forester, farmer, herdsman, blacksmith, carpenter, and shoemaker. I guess he was still a merchant at heart, and he refined as many of our raw products as he could into retail items. I had to leave for school before dawn some days, but in the afternoons I helped Jack milk eight cows. In our house, there was always plenty of sweet milk, buttermilk, cream, and butter. Some of the extra milk was turned into chocolate and vanilla drinks, packaged in eight-ounce bottles with waxed cardboard covers, and distributed to grocery stores and filling stations within a five-mile radius of Plains. Every Monday, Daddy collected the unsold drinks, which we fed to our pigs. Other milk was separated on our back porch, and the pure cream was sold at the Suwanee store in town. The residual skim milk was dubbed "blue john" and fed to the hogs. We exchanged wool sheared from our sheep for blankets that we sold at our farm commissary, and we collected down from the breasts of about fifty geese and exchanged it for pillows and comforters. The geese also

6

aided in the removal of worms and other insects from our cotton plants. Every year, we transformed around twenty-five acres of sugarcane into syrup, which Daddy marketed under the "Plains Maid" trademark, and he occasionally did the same with catsup prepared from fresh tomatoes. On the coldest days of the year, we butchered roughly twenty hogs, and Daddy cooked sausage and rubbed the hams, shoulders, and side meat with preservation spices, then cured the meat in the smokehouse outside our house before selling it in our store.

He also believed that everything and everyone on the property had to "earn its keep," including my Shetland pony.

We were the only white family in the unincorporated community of Archery, with the exception of the Seaboard Airline Railroad section foreman, Mr. Ernest Watson. The African-American lads with whom I worked or played taught us how to manufacture our own toys. A thick steel hoop from a wooden keg, ten to twelve inches in diameter, was our favourite. We rolled our hoops for miles, even hours at a time, using a strong, rigid wire with a loop on one end for a handhold and a V-shaped notch on the other to fit behind the hoop. We would have felt naked without our rubber-banded flips or slingshots, as well as a stock of little round rocks in our pockets. Other projectiles were equally essential to us, and they had the potential to be lethal weapons. A dart made from a large corn cob, four or five inches long, with a needle-sharpened nail inserted into the pith of one end and two chicken feathers in the other set at precise angles to give the thrown weapon the correct amount of spin before it embedded in a tree or a target on the side of a building was one of the simplest and most enjoyable.

We used the same sharpened points on dog-fennel spears and were astounded at how far we could hurl them using spear throwers called "atlatls," which we invented after reading about them in Boys' Life magazine or one of our Indian books. We hung out at Daddy's shop for days, perfecting our basic design of rubber guns. We installed spring clothespins, wrapped them with rubber bands to strengthen their grip, and then stretched a cross section of inner tube strips over the end of each barrel after cutting out models of long-barreled handguns. A squeeze on the clothespin launched the inner tube loop as a missile. We eventually devised repeaters capable of firing up to a dozen rubber bands. We would wage wars until everyone on either side was "killed" by being hit. We also built popgun barrels out of the pith of American elder limbs and used green chinaberries as ammunition. We learnt how to manufacture kites and competed to see who could design and fly the tiniest one.

Daddy quickly devised a method for me to develop an appealing product and market it. With no tractors on the farm and no need for fossil fuels other than kerosene for lamps and lanterns, we planted maize for fuel and energy, and cotton and peanuts for cash crops. Peanuts ripened shortly after school days ended each summer, and starting when I was five years old, I would walk out into the neighbouring fields each afternoon and pick up the plants, shake the dirt from around the nuts, and take a load to our yard in a little cart. I plucked around ten pounds of the most mature peanuts from the vines, properly rinsed them, and placed them in a large pot of salty water to soak overnight. I boiled them for approximately a half hour in the morning, tested them for proper saltiness, and then split them into about twenty half-pound paper bags. I prepared twice as many on Saturdays, when Plains was packed with shoppers from the surrounding farms.

When cotton hit its lowest price in history (five cents per pound), Daddy suggested that I use my funds to buy five bales of 500 pounds apiece. These were held in one of our farm storehouses, and when the market rebounded, I sold them for eighteen cents a pound. With this money, I bought five houses from the estate of a deceased undertaker and rented two for $2.00, two for $5.00, and one for

$2.50 per month, for a total of $16.50 per month. Whether I worked or not, my residences were making $5.50 every day! Every month, I rode my bicycle from house to house, eventually cornering every renter. Unless a windowpane was missing, the roof was leaking, a door didn't close correctly, or one of the steps was broken, they always seemed to be evasive. I could do all of these fixes myself. My father attempted to collect rent for a few months after I left for college before deciding it was best to sell the residences.

Daddy was a strict disciplinarian, but he only used physical punishment on rare occasions. I recall him whipping me five times, each time with his belt or a switch from a wild peach tree in the yard. In every case, the procedure was like a well-organised trial, with a thorough understanding between him and me about what I had done wrong, his explanation of why the sentence was imposed, and my vow not to repeat my wrongdoing. If I had any resentments, they were quickly forgotten. I never thought about defying an order or even a request from Daddy. I adored and revered him, and one of my life's most important goals was to win his approval. I grew to expect his criticisms, which were always constructive, but his praise was unusual.

My father focused a lot of his attention on me because I was the only boy in the family until my brother, Billy, arrived when I was twelve years old. I followed him around whenever possible, trying to imitate everything he did. This established a beautiful collaboration for me to learn some of the abilities of a craftsman as a kind of apprentice. One of my earliest recollections is chasing Daddy down the path from our house to the blacksmith shop. The small building is still standing, and I recall Daddy occasionally letting me turn the handle on the forge blower as the coals heated up and the inserted iron gradually changed colour from cherry red to white until it met Daddy's expectations and could be moved to the adjacent anvil for shaping. When I was about five years old, this was my first actual job. He would painstakingly explain the fundamentals of the entire procedure to me. Later, when I was able, I would use the tongs to hold the thing on the anvil as he pounded it with a sledgehammer before dousing it in water or oil to achieve the desired hardness and toughness. When I was big enough, I could complete entire blacksmithing jobs by myself.

We did a lot of work with wood on the farm, and the little projects, like manufacturing handles for hammers, axes, hoes, shovels, and rakes, and mending wagon tongues, singletrees, and wooden sections of the ploughs we used for soil preparation and cultivation, could be done inside the shop. We also constructed our own wheelbarrows. Larger wood projects were supported by two or three sawhorses outside, preferably on the construction site. There was always a waiting list for building new hog farrowing pens or storage sheds for cotton seed, fertiliser, and equipment, as well as repairing fences and other agricultural structures. This type of work was done on days when the fields were too wet to work, during the dormant winter months, or during "lay-by" time (after the crops had grown too large to plough but before harvest).

Daddy had a pickup truck, which I learnt to drive as soon as I could see over the dashboard, and which I was occasionally trusted to transport seed or fertiliser to the fields. When I was twelve years old, I was allowed to drive it to Plains proms and church events. We rescued a wrecked and abandoned Model T Ford and removed the complete body before attaching a hardwood seat to the main frame. The auto mechanic (Rosalynn's father) in Plains assisted us in getting the engine functioning, and we used our stripped-down vehicle for off-road adventures.

My principal responsibilities on the farm were all connected to field work. When we were chopping cotton or hoeing weeds, we all walked at the same rate up and down the rows, and adults earned the same income, a dollar a day. As a tiny boy, my regular salary was twenty-five cents per hour, which doubled when I was strong enough to carry two-gallon buckets of water from a nearby spring to the "hands" in the field. Workers were paid on the basis of measured success during harvest, such as how many pounds of cotton were picked from the stalk or how many peanuts were piled on poles after being hauled from the ground and the dirt shook off. All workers, regardless of age, could move at their own pace. Rachel Clark always thrived in the unavoidable daily competition.

One of my natural desires as I grew up was to rise above the company of other children and women hoeing, picking cotton, and shaking peanuts to the high rank of a skillful ploughman who could cultivate a crop. I have to admit that, according to my father, I never fully achieved this aim before leaving the farm for college and the navy at the age of sixteen. My first foray into ploughing was in preparing the area between our house and the workshop in our vast vegetable plot. This was done during the winter, with the help of a particularly docile mule named Emma, and under the direction of Jack Clark. With the reins and my shaky verbal commands, it was impossible to control Emma properly, and the small turning plough made an uneven course through the soil—both horizontally and vertically. At the very least, I didn't cause any serious harm, and I learned from my mistakes.

By the age of twelve, I was allowed to break land in the field, even with two mules and the deeper turning ploughs. This was one of the most dull and difficult tasks I had as a youngster, but it meant a lot to me. The first furrow in a field of several acres was often started before daylight, around the often odd-shaped periphery of the field, as close to the neighbouring woodlands, fences, or hedgerows as possible. Holding on to the plough's unpredictable plunger handles and struggling to steer the mules with vocal commands and rope lines to the bridle bits was a constant battle for my petite frame and poor voice. The mules' gait was better suited to an adult's long steps, and I had to trot at times to keep up with the plough. As vocal orders for my leaders to move to the right or left, loud yells of "gee" and "haw" were useful.

Each lengthy circle would advance a little less than a foot toward the centre of the field, encompassing numerous acres. At first, it appeared that this objective would never be attained, yet progress was steady and pleasant. Because my mind was rather distracted, I had plenty of time for idle thoughts. A honed and balanced steel blade cutting through the soil felt like the ideal tool. I had to be in tune with the mules both physically and psychologically, accepting their quirks and hoping to win most of the inevitable disagreements. There had to be a suitable climate for success, which included the current weather as well as the impacts of prior rainfall and sunlight on the soil. When all of the parameters were in sync, the level of comfort was extremely high. With my weak school maths skills, I would occasionally try to calculate how many miles I would have to travel before finishing this duty and going on to the next chore set by my father. Later, I would double-check my estimate by noting the time required and assuming that the mules and I travelled at a pace of two miles per hour, adjusted for turns and brief rests. A day's ploughing distance ranged between 22 and 25 kilometres. The drudgery was always alleviated by gazing back at the end of the day and seeing how much cropland had been prepared for planting. I felt a sense of success and self-satisfaction knowing that I had done everything humanly possible, even as a boy, and had left visible proof of my work behind me.

I still have comparable feelings while working in my woodshop. Drudgery associated with the repetitive use of a chisel, drawknife, spokeshave, plane, rasp, scraper, sandpaper, or paintbrush fades into insignificance when I can inspect the finished product of my effort. The thrill of creating an original design, the rigorous detail of precise measurements, the adaption of the qualities of the chosen wood, the heft and beauty of the hand tools—some of which are ancient in design—are all wonderful aspects of making furniture. I enjoy seeing what I have imagined and created. The pleasure has not diminished with the passage of time; in fact, my declining physical power has eliminated some of the formerly competing hobbies, making carpentry and painting even more valuable to me.

When we were in eighth grade, all of our farm boy classmates joined the Future Farmers of America, and one of our obligations was to develop the skills we had required and learned on the farm. The school shop was much larger and better equipped than our home shop for the finer aspects of woodworking, such as constructing furniture, with instruction books, a small planing mill, a wood lathe, and glue. We had tests on identifying the numerous trees in our local forests as well as the properties of their wood. We also learnt how to cruise timber to determine the value of trees on a certain parcel of land. I learnt how to manufacture simple chairs, tables, and cabinets in school. My most difficult project, and the one for which I obtained my final grade, was a scale model of the White House!

***

I never considered the social or legal inequalities that existed between our white family and the African-American households that surrounded us in Archery as a child. Of course, I was aware that our house was larger than theirs, that my father gave the commands on the farm, and that we owned a car or pickup truck, whereas our neighbours walked or rode in a wagon or on a mule. I assumed that we got these benefits because Daddy worked harder and was fortunate enough to own the land where we lived. I assumed that having separate schools and churches was merely a matter of tradition, but when I visited St. Mark AME Church in Archery, I saw vitality, honesty, and enthusiasm in their worship services that we lacked at our church in Plains. I had no idea that only white people could vote in elections or serve on juries, and I never heard anyone mention these legal distinctions back then.

The dominating presence in our small village of a prominent black guy, who was the richest and most sophisticated person I knew, muddled my understanding of racial discrimination. Bishop William Decker Johnson owned and managed an excellent school for black children across the railroad tracks from St. Mark AME Church, and I recall him always having a lovely gift for every child who attended the church or school at Christmastime. His duty was all the African Methodist Episcopal churches in five Northern states, and whenever he returned home to spend a few days in Archery, there was a lead article in our county newspaper. Bishop Johnson was always chauffeured in the backseat of a large black Cadillac or Packard, and there was a well-known photograph of him in Paris, with the Eiffel Tower in the backdrop. For myself and many others, he represented the pinnacle of prestige and achievement.

When I was six years old, I attended Plains High School in town, which had around 250 white pupils in classes one through eleven. Our school, despite its modest size, was recognized as one of the best in the state because of our wonderful administrator, Miss Julia Coleman. She pushed us all to write topics, study classical music and art, read a variety of literature, argue, and perform in stage productions. Every day started with a half-hour chapel service, during which we heard announcements, sung hymns, recited Holy Scripture, and listened to a brief religious discourse. A little bus picked up my two sisters and myself in front of our house and drove us to and from school. It had been wrecked previously, and the narrow body sat at an acute angle to the main frame. Some students mocked it as a "cracker box," which it was, but we were proud of the free ride every day. Of course, I made new acquaintances with my white classmates, but I still felt more at home in Archery with my black friends, with whom I spent my late evenings and school vacations. There were no ranks among us other than who caught the biggest fish, plucked the most cotton, played better in the last baseball game, or won a wrestling battle or footrace.

I recall well a seemingly insignificant incident that has had a huge impact on the rest of my life. I had been working in a field north of our house and barn with two pals when I was around fourteen years old. As we approached the "pasture gate," they stepped back to allow me to pass through the opening ahead of them. I was taken aback and immediately assumed they were performing a prank on me, possibly with a tripwire near the ground on which I would trip. Around this time, I started playing varsity basketball, going to Plains weekend parties, and becoming interested in females. I never mentioned it to anyone at the time, but as time passed, I surmised that the first sign of my black playmates' unearned deference toward me was the result of a warning from their parents that the time had come to conform to the racial distinctions that were strictly observed among adults.

During my high school years, one of our favourite persons was a gorgeous teenage black girl named Annie Mae Hollis. She was quite close to my two sisters, with whom she spent a lot of time. After I left for college, she stayed with my family and later worked for a wealthy couple who owned Chasen's restaurant in Hollywood. She kept in touch with us throughout her life, and she returned to Plains in 1953 when she learned that my father was unwell.

My mother was well-known in our neighbourhood even as a child for her reluctance to accept any limitations on her treatment of black individuals as equals. My sister Gloria would later say that some of the other women had made negative remarks, but Mama dismissed them as insignificant. We kids just assumed registered nurses were different, but I believe it is fair to say that all four of us siblings shared this attitude about our black neighbours. My father always treated his African-American clients and staff with fairness and respect, but he was a firm believer in racial segregation. He regarded this as a foundation established by Bible texts and validated by a

15

century of Jim Crow laws that were repealed a year after his death by the Supreme Court finding that racially segregated schools were no longer legal.

Daddy was heavily involved in local and state politics, and Democrats occupied all public posts. The Republican Party in Georgia was made up of some African-American leaders in Atlanta and a few isolated white cliques in the rural areas, and they only dealt with national issues. When there was a Republican president, they managed federal patronage, including postal personnel, tax agents, and U.S. attorneys. Rhine, which currently has a population of roughly 400 people, was the regional centre for South Georgia. This was prior to the Hatch Act, which was enacted in 1939 to prohibit federal government employees from engaging in political action and took several years to take effect. When the Democrats lost a national election, a rural letter carrier or other government employee had to travel to Rhine with a roll of cash in his pocket. He would keep his job if the financial arrangements were successful. My mother's father, Jim Jack Gordy, was a skilled negotiator who worked as a postal and revenue agent for both major parties for the most of his adult life.

My father was a merchant and farmer who was never interested in a political post until he was elected to the state assembly late in life, but he distinguished between two-party national elections and exclusively Democratic local elections. In 1932, he voted for Franklin D. Roosevelt, but later backed Alf Landon, Wendell Willkie, Thomas Dewey, and Dwight Eisenhower. Daddy was a libertarian at heart who despised the federal government's meddling in his personal affairs. During the Great Depression, he was opposed to New Deal agricultural programs that compelled farmers to plough up a percentage of their producing crops and slaughter a portion of their hogs in order to qualify for "government relief" payments. I recall listening to the main party conventions on the radio, sometimes all night. We were still using a battery radio when Wendell Willkie was nominated in 1940, and after numerous ballots, the power was expanded, so Daddy revved up his pickup truck and brought the enormous radio outside, laid it on the ground, and hooked it up to the car battery. He then became a board member of the Sumter Electric Membership Corporation, which serviced our neighbourhood, and we soon acquired electric lights, a kitchen stove, a radio, and a refrigerator. My parents began attending REA yearly meetings in our county seat, Atlanta, as well as national gatherings in Chicago and other convention locations, and our personal lives were revolutionised.

***

I was content on the farm, admired my father, and could have accepted a job in the community as his successor, but my parents had other plans for me. Daddy had finished tenth grade at Riverside Academy, a military school in Augusta, Georgia, before joining the army as a first lieutenant, and I believe this was the greatest educational level attained by the men in his family. He and my mother were adamant that I graduate high school and attend college. Money was tight for everyone, but we knew of two prestigious universities in America that provided free tuition and board: West Point and Annapolis.

Despite Daddy's best efforts, I was unable to obtain an appointment by the time I finished high school in 1941, so I enrolled at nearby Georgia Southwestern College and worked as a laboratory assistant to Dr. L. R. Towson, the science teacher. I received a little salary and the opportunity to learn more about physics, chemistry, mathematics, and astronomy. During the early stages of World War II, Dr. Towson was the commanding commander of the local army reserve unit, and he had drill duties twice a week. As his substitute at the time, I taught freshmen classes.

When the Japanese struck Pearl Harbor in December 1941, I was a freshman in junior college and worried about my uncle Tom, who was stationed on the island of Guam with around eighty other navy men. We found out after a few days that Japanese soldiers had attacked and taken the little and undefended island on December 8, just one day after the war began. The navy personnel were there to relay radio signals between American ships and naval stations in the Pacific military theatre, and they had been ordered not to engage the Japanese in action in order to avoid unnecessary losses among the island's locals. We didn't know what happened to Tom, but his wife, Dorothy, and three small children relocated from San Francisco to live with my mother's parents west of Plains, on a farm adjacent to ours. Dorothy was a lovely lady whom I paid visits to everytime I returned home to see my family, always waiting in vain to hear from her husband. After roughly two years of presuming Uncle Tom was a prisoner of war, Dorothy was formally informed that he was dead, and she opted to return to California to live with her family. We learnt from her letters that her father and four brothers were all firemen in San Francisco. She told us around the end of 1944 that she was going to marry a fireman who was a friend of their family because she needed someone to assist in raising her children.

Chapter 2: Navy Years

I earned an appointment and entered the Naval Academy in July 1943 after finishing my sophomore year at Georgia Tech and completing a year of Naval Reserve Officer Training. My Annapolis class of 1947 was supposed to complete four years of coursework in three years during the war, therefore we graduated in June 1946. I had to master the fundamentals of electrical power, electronics, mechanical design, seamanship, and the construction and operation of ships, as well as the equipment and armaments on board, while studying naval engineering at Annapolis. I could have done much better in my academic work at the academy, but I relied on good grades from my two years of previous college work, including the more difficult academics at Georgia Tech. Except for the option of a foreign language, all midshipmen followed the identical curriculum. My first (plebe) year roommate had already received a bachelor of science degree from the University of Iowa, but this past knowledge was ignored.

There were no African-American midshipmen in my class, but a black student, Wesley Brown, was appointed during my second year at Annapolis. I met him when he joined the cross-country team on which I competed. I felt at ease with him, as I did with my old Archery friends, but I was aware that many of the white midshipmen from all over the country despised his presence and were working together with the upperclassmen to force him to leave, either through harassment or the accumulation of too many demerits. Previously, five African-American midshipmen had been barred from graduation due to similar tactics. The word quickly spread across the brigade that the superintendent would only consider negative conduct reports against Brown from commissioned officers. We assumed that this instruction had come from somewhere higher up, possibly the White House. Lieutenant Commander Brown remembered my relationship and strong support as a fellow runner in his later book, and carried special significance because I was from the Deep South.

Punitive hazing was permissible back then, and I seemed to be the focus of extra discipline by upperclassmen, particularly the Yankees, during my plebe year. As a Southerner, I refused to sing "Marching Through Georgia" or comply with any demands that reflected negatively on my state. Most of the time, I accepted my penalty cheerfully, which undoubtedly fostered more cheerful interactions. There were a few sadists among the senior midshipmen, and we learnt to loathe and avoid them wherever possible. I became adept at running the commando course before reveille and travelling to different rooms at night to do 47 push-ups or 94 deep knee bends (multiples of our class year). Participating in cruise box races was one of the most challenging "games" we were compelled to play. Each midshipman was given a wooden box that we could pack and transport aboard a ship or use to store books or out-of-season outfits. Squeezing into the closed cruise box, changing outfits, jogging across certain predetermined corridors of Bancroft Hall, and then returning to the small place to change back into our original gear was the race. My diminutive stature improved my performance.

We were routinely slapped with brooms or, far worse, the heavy metal serving spoons or ladles at our meal room tables for any real or alleged disobedience of orders. Blisters were frequently the result. One of the purported goals of this mistreatment was to toughen us up and weed out those who couldn't take the punishment. My best friend committed suicide, and his roommate came to live with us. We were told on our first day at Annapolis that either we or the person on either side of us would not survive plebe year, and that the attrition rate was frequently higher than one out of three. If any of us showed signs of weakness, upperclassmen and officials went above and above to promote a resignation or induce expulsion due to multiple demerits. I was relieved to learn that most of the most heinous behaviours were prohibited after the war.

I graduated in the top 10% of my class but did not thrive in any element of academic or military life. Each midshipman's roommate wrote the brief biographies in our yearbook, The Lucky Bag. My dramatisation includes the following words: "Studies never bothered Jimmy." In fact, the only time he opened his books was when his peers needed assistance with an issue. This lack of study, however, did not prevent him from graduating near the top of his class." I am grateful to the academy for providing me with an education and an introduction to military discipline.

***

Even more essential than receiving my naval officer commission, I married a few days after graduation. Rosalynn Smith, my future wife, and I had known each other since she was born. My younger sister, Ruth, spent a lot of time with Rosalynn after we moved to the farm, and she came to our house frequently, so I knew her well as a teenager. I found out later, after we were married, that she and Ruth had attempted to put us together, but I was only interested in girls my own age.

I had spent a month on leave in Plains as I reached my final year at Annapolis and was dating Miss Georgia Southwestern College, Annelle Greene. My last full night at home was spent travelling with a boy who was dating Ruth, seeking a blind date for me. Rosalynn approached us as we passed the Methodist church and promised to accompany us to the movies. When I entered our kitchen the next morning, Mother was cooking breakfast and asked what I did the night before because Annelle was with her family. I said, "I went to a movie in Americus." She inquired, "By yourself?" "No," I said, "with Rosalynn Smith." "What did you think of Rosalynn?" she inquired. I responded, "She's the one I'm going to marry."

Mama and I were both astonished by my response, because Rosalynn and I had never discussed our relationship, let alone a future together. She was stunningly gorgeous, horribly bashful, obviously clever, and yet uninhibited in our conversations on the rumble seat of the Ford Coupe. After I returned from my date with Annelle, she accompanied my family to see me off at the train station late the next night, and I kissed her goodbye. Annelle married a medical student and moved to Macon, which pleased me. Rosalynn and I dated during Christmas vacation, and my parents and Rosalynn visited Annapolis in February for a brief holiday to commemorate Abraham Lincoln and George Washington's birthdays. I asked her to marry me, but she declined, later writing from Plains to tell me that she had promised her father, on his deathbed, that she would finish college and would not marry until then. In the meantime, she was dating other young men from her college. I was distraught and could only keep going through letters and the occasional phone contact. She eventually accepted my proposal, and we married the first week of July, after she graduated from Americus Junior College. We moved in together a few days later in Norfolk, Virginia, where my ship was stationed. We rented a modest upstairs apartment near the navy base.

***

My number was near the bottom of the list of graduating midshipmen who had to draw lots for our first duty station. My duty was to serve on the battleship USS Wyoming, which was commissioned in 1912 and served as a warship in World War I, then as a training ship and for shore bombardment in World War II with her twelve 12-inch guns. The Wyoming then served as a proving ground for the most advanced types of radar, communications, navigation, and gunnery systems. I was required to stay in this position for two years before requesting a transfer to another duty. As a young officer, I had both routine and unusual jobs, including electronics officer. It was a time when just one pre production model of a new gyroscope compass, radar, loran (a long-range navigation system based on radio waves), fire-control system, or weapon could be afforded, and our duty was to test them as completely and affordably as possible. I was also in charge of still and motion image photography of towed aerial targets and shell bursts for assessing anti aircraft missile accuracy. This was during the early stages of colour film creation, which I learned on the ship.

Our regular pattern was to cruise back and forth off the beaches of Virginia and North Carolina for five days to conduct our experimental chores, then anchor on Saturday and Sunday. Our ensigns were onboard duty as watch officers every third weekend and could go home to our families on the other two, unless we had specific obligations relating to our permanent positions. This was the time when new electronic equipment was delivered abroad, installed, and tested in preparation for the next week's work, and as an electronics officer, I was frequently called upon to undertake these duties. I worked on the new equipment and was once violently electrocuted while sleeping beneath a radar power unit that was being repaired. Morale on the ship was really low, and I quickly became dissatisfied with navy life. I completed my necessary responsibilities and was mostly interested in spending as much time as possible onshore, either with my family or producing furniture in the navy base's huge and well-equipped hobby store. SO WHAT? I recall posting a sign over my bunk.

By this point, I realised how fortunate I was to have this job as an electronics officer, since I had unrestricted access to practically every technical advancement being introduced into the armed forces, including the army and marines. For the first time, I decided to devote my entire skill set to my naval career, and I got completely absorbed in learning everything I could about seamanship, navigation, the equipment that came onboard to be tested and appraised, and the ship itself. I was appointed special assistant to the executive officer and volunteered to be the director of the United States Armed Forces Institute, which provided free courses for officers and soldiers to complete or supplement their high school and college educations. When we could get a small group together, I offered classes on topics of mutual interest. One sailor requested a painting class, but he resigned from the navy before his book and art supplies arrived. When they arrived, a few of the sailors and I experimented with watercolours and oil paints, and I started sketching scenes surrounding our flat. I also gathered a few books on notable artists and their works. My library currently houses a sizable collection, including the 1939 version of Jan Gordon's Painting for Beginners.

During those years, I was interested in politics but kept the nominally neutral posture as other officers did. During my final months on the Mississippi, I grew to appreciate President Harry Truman and his political fortitude as he made difficult decisions concerning racial equality and the end of World War II. It was early in the 1948 presidential campaign, and I had heard that Truman's predecessor as Roosevelt's vice president, Henry Wallace, would be appearing as a presidential candidate in Norfolk. I was aware that Wallace was a vocal opponent of racial segregation, that he was the editor of the New Republic magazine, and that he advocated for the end of the Cold War with the Soviet Union. When I told the executive officer about my plans to attend the speech, he was enraged that I would attend a political event, especially one featuring a radical like Henry Wallace. He informed me that this would be a lasting blot on my official record. I didn't pursue the notion, but I did keep an eye on the presidential election.

I'm not sure what prompted me to apply for a Rhodes Scholarship the same year. I received the necessary Naval Academy endorsement and other letters of recommendation, wrote an essay, and filed it as a Georgia resident, where I believed I would have the best chance. My speech stated the hope that, as a navy officer, I would be able to apply my understanding of international affairs gained at Oxford to promote world peace. I was notified that I had been selected as a finalist and travelled to Atlanta for an interview. I stayed with my cousin Don Carter one night and watched my first television set. I recall the screen being approximately the size of a postcard. My primary rival was a small and stooping young man from Alabama who claimed he told Rhodes interviewers that he had focused his study solely on Elizabethan literature and had no interest in anything that happened after Elizabeth I's death in 1603. During the preceding months, I had nearly memorised newspapers and periodicals and had answered numerous questions about history, geography, and current affairs. I was even surprised that the Alabama scholar was picked. He and I exchanged a few letters, and I was saddened to learn from his parents that he died while still a student in England.

As a young navy officer, I had to do everything I could to stretch my monthly income of $300 to cover the cost of uniforms, food onboard ship, apartment rent, and other living expenses for our family, which now included our son, Jack. There was a significant price difference between furnished and unfurnished apartments, and I took full advantage of the complex hobby shops on the main navy bases, which were usually manned by warrant officers who were great cabinetmakers. They taught me how to deal with different types of wood, how to make well-structured joints, how to use correct glues, and how to finish the surfaces. I had a lot of fun designing and creating chairs, beds, tables, and cupboards in the workshops. I left practically all of the furniture behind when I was sent from one duty station to another to save on shipping costs, but we brought some of the bunk beds, tables, and chairs with us when we eventually moved into a small unfurnished apartment in the Plains public housing complex. Our most expensive piece of furniture at the time was a white oak cabinet I constructed while we were stationed at the submarine base in Honolulu. It was meant to store our high-fidelity radio and record equipment and has mitered corners and recessed hinges.

***

I had qualified as a submariner while serving on the Pomfret, but now I was senior enough to meet the qualifications for leadership. I already had the requisite knowledge and skills for submarine construction and operation, but an original thesis was also required. I went over my differential and integral calculus studies and constructed a method for calculating the distance to another ship based on the beat of its propellers and the rate of change of its direction from us. When my idea worked in practice, I was qualified to command.

The K-1 mostly worked in the Atlantic-Caribbean region, spending as much time at sea as feasible. One unusual cruise took place near Nassau, Bahamas, when we were advised to stay submerged for at least thirty days. Unfortunately, after around twenty days underwater, one of my electrician's coworkers developed more severe claustrophobia attacks. To avoid violating our orders, Captain Andrews had the sailor strapped to a bunk in the officers' quarters. The sailor's condition was immediately exacerbated by his confinement, as he began to thrash wildly and foam at the mouth. We had to surface and have him helicopter to shore.

A submarine's interior is packed as densely as possible with equipment, leaving little room for humans to sleep, eat, and move. We slept on bunks packed closely above one another, with a narrow space on one side through which we folded ourselves before extending out, even in the more luxury officers' quarters. There was not enough space on my chest to open a paperback book when I was resting on my back. The K-1 was extremely small, and our modern sonar technology added to the craziness. Air for breathing was either recirculated through filters while we were deeply underwater or replenished when we were cruising on the surface or "inhaling" new air through our snorkel tube (approximately twelve inches in diameter).

A fire might be fatal, especially if toxic vapours from plastic or rubber insulation were released. All submariners had to be taught to battle fires, and while our ships were in dry dock or shipyard for routine maintenance, we were dispatched to special courses to learn how to best combat this ever-present hazard. On one occasion, while submerged, we had a fire in our engine room, and I was the commanding firefighter. I put on the proper clothing and gas mask, found the source of the fires in the main motor, and directed the use of carbon dioxide and dry powder because water or foam could not be utilised. I was wearing headphones and talked to the captain through a microphone, and I reported that the fire was under control. The next thing I remember is lying on a table in the crew's mess room, with a hospitalman's mate attempting to get me to breathe oxygen. I was soon back to normal after a little bout of vomiting.

***

I was on a ship in 1948 when President Harry Truman, as commander in chief, ordered that racial discrimination in the armed forces and the United States Civil Service be abolished. This was seven years before Rosa Parks sat on the front seat of a Montgomery bus and Martin Luther King, Jr. rose to fame. This adjustment was received with equanimity on our ship, and I don't recall any pushback from other crews I was associated with, but there was an uproar from many sources, particularly Southern members of the United States Congress. In the 1948 presidential election, South Carolina Governor Strom Thurmond was nominated as the "Dixiecrat" candidate, and his name replaced Truman's on ballots in Alabama, Louisiana, Mississippi, and South Carolina.

I was on duty when our submarine arrived in Nassau and docked at the Prince George Wharf, and I was the officer who accepted the governor-general of the Bahamas' invitation for our officers and crewmen to attend an official gala honouring the US Navy. A more confidential remark was made that a lot of young ladies would be present with their chaperones. Captain Andrews answered positively, which made us all happy and eager. The next day, we were informed that the non white crewmen would not be involved. When I delivered this message to the captain, he called the crew together in the mess hall and asked for their help in composing a response. We unanimously rejected to participate after many expletives were removed from the communication. The crew of the K-1's choice demonstrated how equal racial treatment had been accepted—and appreciated. I was quite proud of my ship.

Rosalynn, our two boys, and I returned to Plains for a visit with our parents later that year while on leave. My father discreetly left the room as I described the experience, and my mother replied, "Jimmy, it's too soon for our folks here to think about black and white people going to a dance together." I recognized how much difference there was between my life in the United States Navy and my life in Southwest Georgia. When we moved there a few years later, we discovered she was still correct.

***

After serving on the K-1 for two years, I learnt of the planned building of two nuclear-powered submarines. Captain Hyman Rickover, the world's foremost expert on peaceful uses of atomic reactors for generating power, delivering radioactive material for medical purposes, and now steering a ship, was in command of this top-secret initiative. He would be personally in charge of selecting young submariners to command each of two precommissioning crews in developing power plants small, safe, and effective enough to be put in a submarine's hull. General Electric Corporation in Schenectady, New York, would construct one reactor, and Westinghouse Electric Company in Pittsburgh, would construct the other. I applied for one of these positions, and after a few weeks, I was summoned to Washington for an interview with Rickover.

I approached the interview with apprehension and had prepared as thoroughly as possible by reading current events, naval tactics, and other topics that I suspected he would want to cover. When I walked inside his office, I saw him sitting behind a large desk, with a single straight chair in front of it. He motioned for me to take a seat and then startled me by asking what topics I wanted to discuss. I chose topics that I knew the most about at the time, such as current events, naval history, submarine battle tactics, electronics, and gunnery. On each occasion, he asked me increasingly challenging questions until I was unable to respond. He never smiled, always stared me down, and seemed to enjoy my obvious mental—and physical—discomfort. (I later discovered that the front two legs of my chair had been reduced, which explained why I felt like I was sliding off.)

When I told him I read a lot of books, he interrogated me about them. We discussed plays by Shakespeare and Ibsen, novels by William Faulkner and Ernest Hemingway, and a few current bestsellers, including The Caine Mutiny by Herman Wouk. Then he asked what type of music I liked, and I replied brashly that I liked country and jazz but understood more about classical compositions. He inquired what my favourite form was, and I told him I loved piano concertos and opera.

He then turned around in his chair to conclude the conversation and began working on some papers on a table behind his desk. I waited there for a few minutes as he ignored me, then slowly exited the room. On the way back to the submarine base, I was dejected and informed Rosalynn that I had not done well at all. But I was soon informed that I had been picked, most likely because I answered his final question honestly. Jeffrey, our third son, was delivered in the navy hospital in New London before I received my formal orders.

There were few people at the time who were as informed about this new technology as we were, and we all had special security clearances known as "Restricted Data." When a Canadian "heavy water" nuclear power station at Chalk River was accidentally destroyed by a reactor meltdown and associated hydrogen explosions in 1952, Rickover volunteered my group to help with the disassembly so it could be replaced. We took a train to the remote location northwest of Ottawa and were briefed on the condition of the incident. The reactor core was underground and surrounded by high levels of radiation. Even with protective clothes, each of us would take the maximum allowable amount in ninety seconds, so we had to make the most of our time. The limit on radiation absorption was nearly a thousand times higher in the early 1950s than it is today, sixty years later.

On a neighbouring tennis court, an exact replica of the damaged reactor had been built, regularly changed to depict the exact status of the genuine core beneath, including every pipe, fitting, bolt, and nut. Television cameras were trained on the core, so that any changes were replicated on the mock-up.

I divided our staff into threes, and each trio would put on the heavy white suits and masks, sprint onto the tennis court, and remove as many bolts and pipes as they could in ninety seconds. These components were then replaced, and we practised until we were as proficient as possible. Only then did we walk down into the radiative zone and disassemble the true objective. We returned to Schenectady after everyone had spent their allotted time at the nuclear site. There were many jokes about radioactivity's consequences, primarily regarding the prospect of being sterilised, and we had to check our urine until all of our bodies returned to normal. None of us were permanently harmed, and I was relieved to discover that the Chalk River reactor had been restarted several years later.

***

My cousin Don Carter called me in April 1953 to tell me that my father was severely ill and would not survive. He would be taken to

Emory University Hospital in Atlanta for more testing. Daddy had always been in good health, a good athlete, an industrious farmer and businessman, and a member of the state legislature at the time. I was overcome with sadness and worry, especially after my mother informed me that Daddy might have cancer. I had been away from my Plains home since 1941, as a college student and in the United States Navy, and had rarely visited my parents during that time. After a few months, Mama informed me that Daddy was gravely ill with pancreatic cancer and only had a few weeks to live. I got Rickover's permission to leave my post for two weeks so I could be with Daddy, and I drove down to Plains in July. I was eager to get back to my demanding and fascinating career as a nuclear submariner.

My father had been transferred from the hospital to his bedroom at home, and he was being cared after by my mother and our former maid, Annie Mae Hollis. With the exception of a few brief visits from other relatives, I spent almost all of my time at Daddy's bedside, having the longest and most extensive conversations I'd ever had with him. He was becoming weaker and had some brief spasms of discomfort, but he was perfectly coherent and ready to listen to my stories of navy duty and his work in many parts of community life and state administration. What surprised me the most was the constant stream of guests who came to the house, generally not to bother Daddy but to bring him small gifts and express their personal gratitude for things he had done for them or their families. African-Americans made up more than half of the guests.

I knew he was a deacon and Bible teacher at our church, but I had no idea he also served on the board of education, was on the hospital authority, was involved in the Lions Club, and was educating local farmers on better agricultural techniques. He had become a statewide force in the development of vocational-technical schools to supplement the more academic colleges, and he was a champion in assisting rural regions in sharing in Georgia's economic prosperity. Even more crucial than these public involvements were the numerous reports to me of Daddy's charitable actions, which were carried out discreetly and without even my mother's knowledge. He was clearly putting his religious ideas into action every day and having a significant impact on the lives of many individuals.

Annie Mae, who had assisted my family in the 1940s, had learned about Daddy's illness and had returned to Plains from California. When my father took his last torturous breath, Annie Mae was holding him in her arms, and she never flinched when she was coated in his black vomit. Years later, in 1994, a flood wrecked Annie Mae's home in nearby Albany, and Rosalynn and I arranged a Habitat for Humanity crew to rebuild it.

***

My delayed but inevitable contemplation of resigning from the navy and coming home to Plains to inherit some of my father's responsibilities and replicate his activities was one of the weirdest and most unexpected events in my life. I recognized I had one of the most sought postings a military career could provide, and I had the potential for endless progression in the following years. Rosalynn loved being a naval wife because it gave her the freedom to conduct our family matters with relative independence. At the same time, I was burdened by the realisation that I had made a significant investment in my schooling and specialised nuclear training. All of this was balanced against the thought of living in a tiny rural community from which I had been removed my whole adult life, with unknown economic prospects, and with no guarantee of ever achieving the same admirable status that Daddy had.

After my father's death and burial in July 1953, I went back to Schenectady, haunted by lingering uncertainties about my future. I debated the issues for a long time before deciding that I would rather return to Plains. Rosalynn was stunned and upset when I informed her of my decision, but I formally resigned through Admiral Rickover. He never confronted me, and he never brought up the matter with me. His reply was contemptuous; he clearly believed that serving under him should be the pinnacle of life's priorities. Senator Richard Russell of Georgia, chairman of the Armed Services Committee, assisted me in expediting approval of my request. In October, I left the navy with conflicting feelings of thankfulness and guilt.

Rosalynn was not happy with my resignation, and our relationship remained tense. We transported our few possessions back home and drove to Washington to complete my release processes. She avoided me as much as possible and would say to our oldest son, "Jack, tell your father we need to stop at a restroom." We didn't have much money, and I didn't have a steady source of income, so my application to live in one of Plains' freshly constructed government housing units was approved.

We decided to take our boys to the Capitol, and our local congressman, E. L. (Tic) Forrester, agreed to give us a tour. He was an avowed segregationist, and while he was with us, he vehemently opposed the ill-advised public housing initiative supported by racial integrationists, which planned to house undesirable and nasty people alongside nice white people. He used racist slurs to disparage the folks who would live in the units. Rosalynn and I exchanged no comments as we drove to our new home in the Plains public housing unit. While I was in the navy, Rosalynn and I had three sons, the youngest of which was a baby when we returned to Plains. I wanted to try for a girl again, and we had an on-again, off-again argument for the next fourteen years, which I eventually won. Amy was born in late 1967, when our oldest son was twenty.

Chapter 3: Back to Georgia

I had no clue what I would do when I returned to Georgia, other than try to carry on my father's career as a farmer with a small supply business that offered fertiliser and seed to other farmers as well as bought and stored their peanuts during harvest season. Before his death, Daddy had outlined his warehouse activities in broad strokes, but none of us was considering quitting the navy at the time. I assumed that my uncle Alton, nicknamed Uncle Buddy by the family, would be in charge of settling my father's inheritance, so I was surprised when he told me that he would renounce this responsibility and have the local judge appoint me as sole executor. When I objected that I understood nothing about farming or business and knew only a few of the customers involved, Uncle Buddy said that this was the best way for me to learn. He promised to assist me as needed, but reminded me that he was a trader, not a farmer.

Another issue was that the Internal Revenue Service decided to audit my father's income tax returns for several years prior, and they demanded that I substantiate with written proof his claims that much of the income was from the sale of timber rather than earned, and thus subject to lower tax rates for capital gains. Contrary to modern norms, it was common in those days for timber to be purchased by small sawmill proprietors with fewer than 10 employees who saw lumber in the forests. Mules or oxen pulled downed logs a hundred yards to the sawmills, which were shifted on a regular basis. During the years in question, Plains had seven sawmill owners, and several of them had moved away, died, or gone out of business. Their record-keeping procedures were, at best, primitive. It was hard for me to prove the sources of all of the revenue, and the accompanying fines devoured the majority of the funds in my father's estate.

Despite these unexpected issues, I went ahead and assigned my executor duties to other family members. I divided the family holdings into five equal portions using the best estimated valuations that my uncle and I could come up with. My mother, brother, and two sisters joined me at Mama's house one afternoon, and I let them choose their part in reverse order of age. Then I settled for what was left. I was relieved to see 1953 come to an end, and I was now more prepared for the new year. My diverse and expanding responsibilities made my former navy life look simple, even while I assisted in the design and construction of an original nuclear power plant.

Rosalynn and I only had a fifth of Daddy's estate, but I was in charge of the cultivated farmland and a bigger tract of timber owned by most other heirs, including native forests and a few acres of planted pine trees. I had forgotten everything I had ever known about farming, so I spent the winter months before planting season learning everything I could about maintaining woodlands and growing corn, cotton, peanuts, and wheat. I examined booklets published by Georgia experiment stations and travelled to Tifton to attend one-day training courses on the topics of greatest interest at Abraham Baldwin Agricultural College. There were seven families who had been sharecroppers with my father living on all of the combined farms, and I talked to them about the different fields and took soil samples to determine what fertiliser formulae would be best. In addition, I made an attempt to contact some new customers and kept doing business with individuals who had made a good-faith effort to settle their earlier debts to the estate.

With my land and future crops as collateral, I went to the local bank and got a $10,000 loan to purchase farm supplies and sow a crop with high hopes. A fertiliser plant in nearby Dawson agreed to continue selling their products to me, and I added three dollars per ton as profit. The majority of my sales were on credit, with payment due at harvest time. Then calamity struck our farming region, with one of the greatest droughts in recorded history. By the end of 1954, neither I nor many of my customers had made any effort to harvest a significant amount of our parched crops. I had one field of a new peanut variety called Virginia Bunch 67 that received rain the first week of August and produced a decent yield.

Even after deducting the full amount of our unpaid accounts receivable, our annual total income was only $280, with no wages for Rosalynn or me. It helped that our low income allowed us to stay in subsidised housing, with monthly rent of only $31. My application for a new bank loan was turned down unless I also had my mother and uncle sign the note. I didn't want to do this, so I went to Dawson and worked out a deal with the fertiliser firm that allowed me to have a truckload (twenty tons) or a railroad carload (forty tons) at a time, but only on consignment. Any monetary payments were made directly to Dawson, and charge tickets were made payable to them rather than to me. I was still on my own (except for Rosalynn) and had to put all of the fertiliser into my small warehouse by the railroad tracks and subsequently onto customers' vehicles. When a forty-ton freight car arrived, I walked down the street and hired a man to assist me unload it for an hour or two. I was quite grateful when some truck drivers and customers offered to help. The fertiliser was packaged in either one-pound paper bags or two-pound burlap or white cotton bags. I thought the tough workout was beneficial to me and was proud of my new muscles. During harvest season, I hired a number of temporary labourers to assist with unloading peanut and maize trucks. I anticipated selling around 3,500 tons this year, but I recognized I needed to look into some new ideas for improving services to farmers in our area and growing my own involvement in agricultural affairs throughout Georgia.

Producing seed peanuts became a significant source of money for me, and I soon began contracting with other farmers to produce seed on their land for me to process in a shelling facility of my design. I sold my high-quality seed to farmers throughout Georgia, Alabama, and Florida. I also focused on learning everything I could about the seed industry and was elected president of the Georgia Crop Improvement Association, which was in charge of statewide production and distribution of seeds of all varieties, including corn, cotton, wheat and other grains, soybeans, grasses, and even pine trees. I continued to focus on peanuts on my own farm and that of neighbours, and one year I produced sixteen types of this one crop. I later understood that with extra loans, I could have expanded my firm faster and grown wealthier, but I believe growing up during the depression years made me overly careful about being in debt.

My mother and siblings decided to sell me part of their land from my father's inheritance, allowing us to purchase additional farms, including those owned by Rosalynn's family. She and I are the owners of approximately 3,200 acres of land, divided roughly into two plots, one acquired in 1904 and the other in 1833. My mother and brother, Billy, were minor partners in the farm supply business, and our three sons drove trucks and assisted with the handling of peanuts and other commodities when they were old enough. I built enough warehouses to hold around 15,000 tons of peanuts, which were stored from the time they were harvested in the fall until we shelled them for commercial use or seed. I purchased a cotton gin and constructed cotton, corn, and small grain storage facilities. After analysing soil samples, I learned to blend precise formulae of liquid fertilisers and could complete a "prescription" for a certain tract of land to match its demands. By the early 1960s, Carter's Warehouse could provide practically anything local farmers required, and we could buy, prepare, and market commodities grown in our area. It was a family business that grew over the course of twenty-three years, until I was elected president and placed all of our commercial dealings in a blind trust.

I learned farming, forestry, business management, and leadership in statewide organisations connected to these responsibilities. I also attempted to learn as many skills as possible, such as construction with wood, steel, and concrete, as well as equipment maintenance. It was demanding work, twelve months a year, but I relished the challenges, and our various businesses thrived. Meeting obstacles on our own land and collaborating with others piqued my interest in environmental issues.

We left the housing project after the second year and rented what has always been known in our neighbourhood as the "haunted house," which is approximately a mile west of Plains and on the road that leads to the farm where I grew up. Just a few hundred yards from the local cemetery, this was a location to avoid after dark, and residents of our small hamlet would escape the danger zone by strolling down the train lines rather than the dirt road. The home was erected in 1835, when the first European settlers arrived in the area to replace the Native Americans who had been forcibly relocated west to Oklahoma and beyond under President Andrew Jackson's administration. There were accounts of strange occurrences, including multiple sightings of a white-gowned woman strolling around the attic holding a lamp.

While we were there, Rosalynn and the boys reported many unusual incidents and unexplained sounds, but we never had any real encounters with spirit world animals. Our sons discovered a hidden area between the floor and the ceilings of the rooms below one day while playing in the attic, with about six feet of headroom. There was only one chair in the room. We surmised that there had previously been a mentally ill woman housed there by the family, who may have walked around with a lantern.

Rosalynn and I now had time for some leisure activities, which had been unusual throughout my service years. We purchased golf equipment and started hitting balls in the field behind our house. After a few weeks, we got together with some friends and drove to Dawson, where we played on the American Legion's nine-hole course. We learned of a Friday night square dance club and quickly found ourselves enjoying these sessions with about a hundred other members from the neighbouring rural area. Meri Legs, from the American Legion, was the name of the club. Dancing was demanding and difficult, since one or two new steps were added to our repertoire each week. We joined other groups at state conventions wearing distinctive costumes and made many new acquaintances. This membership was going to transform my life.

During my tenure on the Sumter County Board of Education, schools in Georgia were still racially segregated, but I intended to equalise educational opportunities as much as possible within these strong social bounds. I proposed that the five board members tour all of the schools in order to gain a better understanding of the situation in the classrooms, and the other members agreed. Our first trips were to white children and faculty, and we were quite pleased with the two schools that had students at all levels and three others in rural locations that just had elementary pupils. They were attractive brick structures with enough desks, relaxation, music, and art facilities, and current textbooks.

After a few of these excursions, the other board members declined to go on any more. With the emergence of the civil rights movement, the state legislature began to make an effort to demonstrate that the national policy of "separate but equal" was becoming slightly more equal in order to keep the separate. School buses for black pupils were finally approved, but there was a legal requirement in Georgia that their front fenders be painted black so that everyone knew the passengers were not innocent white youngsters. With the first stirrings of racial upheaval in 1955, the Georgia Board of Education fired all NAACP members and declared that no teacher may serve who did not favour racial segregation.

Although the Supreme Court's Brown v. Board of Education ruling came the year after we returned home, "separate but equal" was not challenged or amended in our town. Rosalynn and I supported the evolutionary process of reducing the more onerous components of racial distinctions in our community in a pretty inconspicuous fashion, having watched President Truman's end of segregation in the military. I volunteered to lead an evangelism effort funded by Billy Graham, which used a film that encouraged everyone to work together as equals in our Christian faith. I organised a multiracial steering committee and was not surprised when no white church would allow us to hold race planning sessions. We convened in an abandoned schoolhouse in Americus, the county seat, and followed Billy Graham's rules and procedures, including the employment of radio and newspaper advertisements. Hundreds of black and white people viewed the film together in the local theatre on the final evening of the crusade, and several dozen viewers accepted Jesus Christ as their saviour. Some of the more conservative white men took part without reservation. Other notable persons in the county who shared our more moderate views included the president of Georgia Southwestern College, the county attorney, and the owner of the county's lone radio station.

Rosalynn and I discovered our previously disregarded progressive attitude became more problematic as the racial issue and civil rights protests grew more apparent. When I drove into the sole service station in town one morning, the owner refused to put gasoline in my pickup truck. To service our private automobiles and agricultural trucks, I had to create an underground tank and pumping station. Later, a dozen of my finest clients dropped by my warehouse office, reminding me that they had been good friends of my father, and offered to pay my annual membership dues in the White Citizens' Council. This organisation was founded in Mississippi and officially supported by Georgia's U.S. senators, governor, and all other statewide political officials. I declined to join, and they told me I was the only white male in the village who didn't. COONS AND CARTERS GO TOGETHER was written on our office door one night.

In 1965, our oldest son graduated from high school, and our family took a two-week road vacation through Mexico. When we returned, there was no one in our office, and I eventually learned that members of the John Birch Society had gone to the county agricultural department, obtained a list of our customers, and informed each that I had been away in a Communist training camp learning how to integrate the public schools. I went to each one promptly and explained what we had been up to, and most of our most loyal clients returned. The college president and radio station owner were under such duress that they relocated. I briefly considered leaving Plains and accepting one of the numerous offers I had received from shipbuilders that would have taken advantage of my knowledge of nuclear power and top secret security clearance, but the economic pressures dissipated as we capitalised on the vast geographical area now covered by our seed peanut sales and other business contacts. These racial conflicts today seem like distant memories.

As the years passed, I rose to the position of respected community leader, serving as a Baptist deacon and Sunday school teacher, Boy Scout leader, county board of education chairman, member of the regional hospital authority, and district governor of fifty-six Lions Clubs in our area. I'd also been appointed for statewide leadership positions in my farming and seed company. Unlike in Alabama, Mississippi, Arkansas, and other Southern states, our public schools in Georgia began to integrate peacefully. White parents who were still opposed to racial integration in the classroom sent their children to one of the many private academies that sprouted up across the South. The heated disputes and animosities abated, and practically all of our customers resumed doing business with our warehouse. However, public school integration remained a demagogic topic among Georgia political candidates throughout the 1960s, and Plains High School, like most others, did not enrol its first black pupils until 1967.

***

Although my father had served in the state legislature and our family members were staunch Democrats who publicly supported local and state candidates, I had never considered running for public office and had only participated in politics to support Adlai Stevenson and John F. Kennedy, as did most Georgians. In 1962, after the Supreme Court ruled in Baker v. Carr that all votes must be weighted as evenly as practicable, I decided to run for government. As a result, Georgia's "county unit" system, in which some rural votes equaled one hundred votes in urban areas, was abolished. As part of the state's response, seats in the Georgia Senate that had previously rotated every two years were replaced with permanent seats with far greater power and prestige. I chose, somewhat rashly, to run for the Senate in order to help save the state's public school system, which was threatened with closure if it became racially integrated. Rosalynn asked if I was going to a funeral while I was changing from my khaki work clothes into a coat and tie. It sounds unbelievable today, but I had not informed her of my plans and had replied that I was heading to the courtroom to qualify as a senatorial candidate and to post an advertisement in the local newspaper. Rosalynn was ecstatic about my decision, which she didn't question.

Because it was assumed that candidates elected under the previous system would be picked, only 10 days were permitted for campaigning before the extraordinary election. Our new senatorial district included seven counties and a population of around 75,000 people. I had some posters and business cards produced and started going from county seat to county seat, visiting the local newspaper offices and radio stations and speaking to any civic club that would accept my request. It was a slow season for farming, and Rosalynn and my brother, Billy, operated the office while I was gone.

Our church was hosting a one-week revival, and the visiting pastor was staying with my mother. "Why in the world would you want to become involved in the dirty game of politics?" the preacher questioned when I dropped by to inform her about my ambitions. "How would you like to be pastor of a church with 75,000 members?" I said after a few moments of thought.

Homer Moore, a warehouseman and peanut buyer from my mother's hometown, was my opponent, and I knew and appreciated him as an honest business adversary. Each of us had a natural edge in our hometown, and I was already acquainted with several farmers and Lions Club members. Another important aspect that helped me overcome my late choice was that members of our square dancing group came from most of the same area as the senatorial district, and they were very supportive.

On Election Day, I was running from one polling location to another when I called Rosalynn, who informed me that a relative of hers had reported a severe problem in Georgetown, the county seat of Quitman County, one of Georgia's smallest. We contacted a friend of ours, John Pope, to represent me in court. When he arrived, he was surprised to see the local political leader, Joe Hurst, openly supporting my opponent. He was instructing all voters to mark their votes on a table in front of him and voting for Homer Moore. The ballots were subsequently dropped through a wide hole in a pasteboard box, and John observed Hurst reach into the box multiple times to remove and discard some ballots.

I called the newspaper in Columbus, Georgia's largest city, and told their political correspondent what was going on. Luke Teasley was the one who interviewed me once I became a candidate. I took the car to Georgetown. Hurst didn't seem bothered that he was being watched, even when I insisted that he stop messing with the election. He just said that this was his county, that he was chairman of the Quitman County Democratic Party, and that this was how elections were always held. As the candidate, I was free to speak with his friend the sheriff if I needed to file a legal complaint. Teasley came to Georgetown after Hurst dismissed my accusations, and his attitude was mostly amusement that "Old Joe" was still up to his usual shenanigans. John Pope stayed and documented what happened during the day, while I travelled to visit the other counties.

When the results from the other six counties were in, I was ahead by 75 votes, but in Quitman County, the vote was 360 to 136 for my opponent, despite the fact that only 333 people had voted. The news media proclaimed Homer Moore to be elected. That same week, the state Democratic Convention met in Macon, and I went there to file my protest, which was ignored. Even some of my closest friends thought I was a jerk and recommended me to drop the matter and decide whether I wanted to run again in two years. "Jimmy is so naive, so naive," my mother said to my sister. If I had understood the unusual election regulations, I may have withdrawn, but I was outraged. I had hoped that the recent Supreme Court rulings would usher in a new age in Georgia, based on the worth of individual votes rather than county votes, and possibly including a new generation of legislators who could pave the path toward racial reconciliation.

I went to the law office of Warren Fortson, the county attorney, and we went over the contested election statutes. They were almost entirely focused on a mathematical recount of ballots, not on fraud. In such an unusual circumstance, the county Democratic Committee, of which Joe Hurst was chairman and had handpicked all of the members, should hear the appeal within five days. Our only option was to file an appeal and then request a recount, which would be handled by a regional trial court. We met at my first cousin Hugh Carter's house, and he suggested we phone his older brother, Don, who had been the city editor of The Atlanta Journal. The newspaper quickly sent a suspicious reporter, John Pennington, to the story, and he stopped over to meet me before heading to Georgetown, where he had a very publicised altercation with Joe Hurst. A flurry of eye-catching front-page articles swept the state.

Pennington discovered that 117 voters had purportedly lined up in exact alphabetical order to vote. Many were deceased, in prison, or living in remote locations. Cartoons in the Journal depicted graveyard polling stations with caskets open while their residents exercised their civic rights. We discovered a large number of Quitman County citizens prepared to face Hurst, and we worked tirelessly to compile a stack of certified testimonies corroborating our case. When we came before the Democratic Executive Committee, the county courtroom was packed, but the first item of business was a motion made by my opponent's counsel that the charges be dismissed, and Hurst and his committee voted unanimously to concur with the request. There was no evidence accepted. This left the option of a simple recount of ballots cast, and a conservative judge, Carl Crow, was appointed to preside.

Fortson declined to represent me at this hearing because he was a personal friend of mine and was fairly liberal on the racial problem. Instead, he introduced me to Charles Kirbo, a South Georgia native who now works for the huge Atlanta firm King & Spalding, and he agreed to take my case. We only knew in advance that 496 votes had been reported (360-136) yet only 333 persons had voted when the polls concluded. Even Joe Hurst reported that no absentee ballots were available. The election officials all reported that no voters were swayed during the day, that everything was done correctly, and that all ballots, stubs, and voter lists were in the box. The key question was where the box was and what was inside.

When the cardboard container was finally discovered (behind Joe Hurst's daughter's bed) and placed on the table, the flaps were unsealed and there were no documents present—only a mound of ballots. Over 100 were curled up on top and encircled by a rubber band. Kirbo detailed what had been disclosed in a lengthy speech, speaking slowly and with frequent pauses, and compared the scenario to an anecdote of a chicken thief who dragged a broom behind him to disguise his tracks from the sheriff. Hurst had left no means to assess how many ballots should be in the box because there were no ballot stubs or voter lists. The opposing attorneys chose not to answer, and Judge Crow adjourned the session without remark, except to say that his decision will be announced the following Friday, November 2, in Albany. On page 13, the Columbus Dispatch stated that "Jerry Carter from Plains, who lost to Homer Moore," would lose a recount petition.

On Friday, Judge Crow explained the disparity in votes cast in Georgetown, stating that there were no voting booths or secret ballots, and that the election result could not be determined. All of the Georgetown ballots were thrown out, and the three tiny county precincts had cast 43 votes for Moore and 33 votes for me. This resulted in a district total of 2,811 to 2,746, in my favour. If his choice was adopted, I would be the Democratic Party's nominee, with no Republican opposition! We all agreed to only drink Old Crow whiskey in the future.

The state Party and secretary of state ruled that my name should appear on the general election ballot the following Tuesday, but Homer Moore appealed to our local superior court judge, Tom Marshall, who ruled late Monday night that names should be removed from all ballots and that the election be decided solely by new votes cast throughout the district the following day—beginning in about six hours. I hadn't slept in several days and had lost eleven pounds, but I proceeded to campaign as much as possible on Election Day. Two county ordinaries did not remove all names as required, and the results in most counties were comparable to the first. In Quitman County, however, voters felt liberated for the first time in many years, and I was elected with 448 votes to 23 votes. The aggregate district tally was 3,013 to 2,182.

Homer decided to go straight to the Georgia Senate, whose presiding officer was Lieutenant Governor Peter Zack Geer, a close friend of

Homer and Joe Hurst who had always won Quitman County by a ten-to-one majority. In Savannah, Georgia, there was another contested election, and the lieutenant governor refused to debate either one before the legislature began. We knew he had complete control of the Senate and would allocate freshly elected members to committees and other positions. In essence, Peter Zack would have to choose between Homer and me. The situation was still very much up in the air.

I informed my other school board members that if elected, I would quit as chairman and focus on educational issues as a senator. After a full day of sleep, I began researching senate rules and processes, as well as other district-related topics. In late November, I travelled to Atlanta to meet with the lieutenant governor, and Peter Zack greeted me warmly. He said he couldn't talk about any potential contests, observed that I was the last one to come in, and asked about my committee preference. Homer Moore had previously made his wishes known. He was shocked that I didn't request regulations, appropriations, judiciary, or industry and commerce. He stated that there should be no issues. The top posts were already occupied, but he might make me secretary if I liked to write. I accepted and began to depart, then inquired about a university system subcommittee. There was none, so I inquired if one could be made. He called the incoming committee chairman, who had no objections to my chairing the new higher education subcommittee—if I were a senator.

My two legislative objectives were to enhance election procedures and to establish a four-year institution in Southwest Georgia. Now, with a wealth of knowledge on the voting issue, I collaborated with a small group of judiciary committee lawyers to prepare a comprehensive reform package that integrated the consequences of recent Supreme Court decisions and detailed processes to be followed in situations of fraud. I recall a senator from Enigma (whose name I admired) proposing a floor amendment that would "prohibit any citizen from casting a ballot in a primary or general election who has been dead for more than three years." A lively argument ensued, with allegations that wives or children could fairly correctly predict how their deceased loved one would vote after such a short period. Without the suggested modification, the measures were overwhelmingly supported.

The other issue was far more pressing in my district, because the closest senior college was Auburn University in Alabama, which required our kids to pay out-of-state fees. Georgia Southwestern in Americus (my county seat) and a larger institution in Columbus were the two junior colleges eligible for promotion. Carl Sanders, the newly elected governor, had promised the people of Americus that he would support their proposal, but had backed down under pressure from Columbus. Bo Callaway, our district's representative on the Board of Regents, was one of their supporters. He was wealthy, politically powerful, and chaired the body that determined the academic standing of all colleges. Except that I was head of the panel that had to approve any financing for the university system, I was at a significant disadvantage. I had the suggested law in my pocket since the governor wanted a new dental school in his hometown. Following some quiet but strenuous negotiations between me and the governor, he utilised his clout among the regents to establish the dental school, and Georgia Southwestern was elevated to the status of senior college. Because of this accomplishment, I was re-elected without opposition for another two-year term in 1964. But it strained my relationship with Callaway.

***

As the 1964 general election neared, our state experienced the start of a political revolution. President Lyndon B. Johnson was unpopular in the Deep South as a result of his successful civil rights campaign.

Plains' racial opinions were ambiguous, with the majority of our

48

white inhabitants remaining silent. This began to alter when black activists began to attend churches with predominantly white congregations in order to demand participation in worship services. When black Christians were refused admittance and knelt in front of the church, surrounded by cameras from major media networks, there was a conflict at the Methodist church in Americus that drew international notice. Despite the fact that there had been no conflict at our church, the eleven other deacons voted, against my resistance, to institute a policy prohibiting black worshipers from entering Plains Baptist Church. The matter, like other critical choices in Baptist churches, had to be decided by a vote of the entire church membership. On Saturday, Rosalynn and I were attending my niece's wedding north of Atlanta, and we had to get up early and drive back to Plains before the Sunday morning service. Normally, just about forty members attend a church conference, but approximately two hundred were present for this argument and conclusion. Following the chairman's and my opposing speeches, there was a vote, and 6 persons, including 5 from our family, voted against the deacons' suggestion. Fifty people voted yes, while the rest abstained! Many church members contacted that afternoon to say they agreed with me but didn't want to irritate other members of their families or alienate their customers. This display of opposing viewpoints was a watershed moment for my family, and it reflected the prevailing mindset in Georgia. During the years that followed, the two hundred local school systems accepted the Supreme Court's decision one by one, and none of our governors resisted the federal government by standing in the classroom door, as governors in Arkansas, Mississippi, and Alabama had done.

As my second term as a state senator came to a conclusion, I chose to run against Bo Callaway for reelection to Congress, despite his significant advantage as a wealthy and somewhat popular incumbent who had been lavished with special privileges by the Republican Party. Our personal disagreements were heightened by his status as a

Democratic defector and West Point graduate. I was virtually full-time campaigning when, just a few weeks before the primary, Bo decided to drop out of the congressional race and run for governor, leaving me with no opposition. Former governor Ernest Vandiver, our Democratic gubernatorial contender, withdrew from the contest, citing health concerns. I travelled to Atlanta and tried unsuccessfully to encourage other famous Democrats to run. I was afraid that the main choice would be between Callaway and the archsegregationist Lester Maddox, who had made a name for himself by standing outside the entrance of his Atlanta restaurant with a pick handle, threatening to use it on any black person who tried to enter. He was a fiery orator who claimed that if he became governor of Georgia, there would be no racial mixing.

With the backing of a few young Democrats, I decided to forego my secured seat in the United States Congress and run for governor. Hamilton Jordan and his girlfriend Nancy Konigsmark, both University of Georgia students, agreed to assist me and became crucial staff members throughout my political career. I made rapid progress in my brief statewide campaign, but I failed because I had no prepared organisation and very little money, and Lester Maddox was nominated as the Democratic nominee, with Callaway running unchallenged. In the general election, these two faced off against former governor Ellis Arnall, who ran as an independent. When no candidate received a clear majority, the Georgia constitution empowered the state legislature to select the governor, and the mostly Democratic legislature chose Maddox. They accurately anticipated that they could usurp many of the powers that Georgia's governor had always held. Until then, the governor had appointed the speaker of the house, made final decisions on key committee assignments, and determined when and whether proposed legislation would be put to a vote.

***

I was very disappointed and disillusioned with politics and, more broadly, with life. Ruth Carter Stapleton, a well-known evangelist and author living in North Carolina, came to assist me overcome my bitterness and despair. Using Bible verses to bolster her case, she stated that everyone is doomed to failures, disappointments, embarrassments, and sorrows, and she advised me to forget about myself for a while, strengthen my religious faith, learn from my political defeat, and become stronger, more confident, resilient, and ready to pursue some well-considered alternative life goals.

I followed Ruth's suggestion and agreed to take part in what Baptists refer to as "pioneer missions." I was told to go to Lock Haven, Pennsylvania, where my partner would be a farmer called Milo Pennington from Texas. A group of volunteers from Pennsylvania State University had contacted everyone in the Lock Haven phone directory using a modest budget and a long-distance phone service that could only be utilised at night and on weekends. They identified those who had no religious commitment but were willing to talk about it. We selected around a hundred families and were tasked with visiting each one and talking to them about our faith. Milo had been on similar missions before, but this was my first time.

Some households refused to let us in, some claimed to be Christians, still others seemed amused, while still others appeared to be anxiously expecting our message and invitation. Milo's presentation style made me uneasy at first. He used basic examples from people he knew lives as well as his own religious experiences. As a result, I was astounded by the emotional response of several of the attendees, who were frequently in tears. We would pray with them as they promised to improve their life and accept the faith we had conveyed to them. I sensed the presence of the Holy Spirit. That week, I called Rosalynn and told her about some of the visits. I assured her I had no reservations about our upcoming meetings and, weirdly, no sense of responsibility for the outcomes of our frequently difficult presentations. I said, "I feel that it's in the hands of God." And the outcomes we achieved—the life-changing experiences we shared with those we witnessed—were my first exposure with the extraordinary power of Christian faith.

Not all of our efforts were successful. We once climbed some outside stairs to find a woman living alone in a little apartment. When we started our presentation, she sprang up and said, "Not me! I have not sinned against God, and I certainly do not deserve to be punished." Despite our efforts to explain further, she ordered us to leave her house. We knocked on the front door of a beautiful home owned by a local General Motors dealer, but he refused to let us in or speak with him or anybody else in the house. Another remarkable visit followed later that week, in the city's poorest neighbourhood. When we asked a Salvation Army employee where we could find our desired address, she informed us it was above some stores and then questioned if we were sure we wanted to go there. As we started up the steps from an alley door, we heard a stream of expletives from above—language I'd only heard in the navy, but this time in a female voice. Milo and I exchanged glances before deciding to proceed. A young woman greeted us with delight and soon informed us that she was the madam of a tiny whorehouse, with three other "girls" as her partners.

She clearly enjoyed arguing with us and asking provocative questions, which we responded to as efficiently as possible. We eventually got to talking about her background, and I discovered that she was extremely resentful of her poor parents, whom she blamed for her current predicament. Her father, she claimed, had made inappropriate sexual approaches, and she'd finally found the courage to tell her mother as a teenager. An intense and tearful family argument occurred, and both parents accused the girl of lying and being preoccupied with sexual fantasies. She ran away from home and became a prostitute "to support myself," she added. She has had no communication with her family for eight years. We had been there almost two hours when she announced we would have to leave but offered to come back the next day—our last one in Lock Haven.

Once a woman opened her door surrounded by five or six children. When we told them the purpose for our visit, her husband, who was sitting across the messy room, instantly sought to hide a half-empty beer bottle behind his chair. We assured him that Jesus had no problem consuming wine. As Eloy Cruz told the story, I read from the book of John about Lazarus, Mary, and Martha, three of the closest friends of Jesus. Lazarus had died, and Jesus was ready to restore him to life. This was a compelling story, even with my bad interpretation of the Spanish text. After Jesus cried, and then called to Lazarus, our listeners waited breathlessly. When the dead guy stepped forth from the tomb, everyone broke into cheers. Later, they knelt alongside Reverend Cruz and me and accepted Christ as saviour. I had fantastic experiences every day while I worked with this remarkable individual. He always appeared to know just what to say and struck up an instant rapport with the underprivileged folks whose homes we visited. He could capture their minds and spirits with the most basic phrases.

The reverence with which Eloy Cruz treated me embarrassed me. For one thing, I had a car, which he had never imagined owning. Furthermore, I had served as a state senator and even ran for governor (he appeared to disregard my failure). He saw himself as "just" a Cuban and an exile, but I knew better; he was a tremendous man. As we prepared to say our goodbyes at the conclusion of the week, I asked him what it was in him that made him so compassionate but so successful as a Christian witness, and he was extremely disturbed. He ended by saying, "Pues, nuestro Señor no puede hacer mucho con un hombre que es duro" (Well, our Saviour can't do much with a harsh guy). He observed that, despite being the Son of God, Christ was always gentle with those who were poor or weak. He went on to state that he sought to live by a simple rule: "You only need two loves in your life: one for God and one for the person in front of you at any given time."

Eloy Cruz's comments have had a significant impact on my life, and I frequently remind myself of them. There are moments when bravery is necessary, and genuine humility is difficult to maintain for those of us who have practically every imaginable advantage. Putting myself on an equal footing with a homeless person, a drug addict, a destitute African family, or a neighbour who may be lonely or in need makes me uneasy. But when I succeed, I discover that I am elevating them—as well as myself. This is not an idealistic thought, because I have witnessed it on a few instances in my life.

The combination of my political setback and recuperation taught me some significant and lasting lessons, best summed up by advice provided to us as schoolchildren by our teacher Miss Julia Coleman. She would go on to explain, "You must accommodate changing times but cling to unchanging principles." (I cited her when I was sworn in as president and when I received the Nobel Peace Prize.) I've tried, at least most of the time, to set high goals, accept setbacks and disappointments with grace, admit and strive to remedy my faults and flaws, and then set new, and sometimes higher, goals for the future. I seek as much assistance and guidance as possible, and if these aspirations appear to be desirable and justifiable, I simply do my best and don't worry about the potential negative effects. My experiences in Lock Haven and Springfield have taught me to apply my Christian faith to my secular life much more often, and to overcome seeming problems more easily and consistently.

Chapter 4: Atlanta to Washington

After a little vacation, I returned to my company and community duties, but I also launched another campaign for governor, which I was determined not to lose. At the end of most days, I'd drive around Georgia, giving speeches or taking part in public events until returning home late at night. I took a name-memory course and kept in touch with as many significant individuals as I could remember, and we sent personal notes to many of them. After three years, I was well-versed in our state and the topics that were essential to our people, and I had a long list of possible backers. There were many farmers and others I knew from my seed business, as well as 208 Lions Clubs across Georgia where I was well known. During this period, I campaigned quietly and without notoriety, with no billboards or public announcements. A public opinion poll showed former governor Carl Sanders with an 84 percent favourable rating, which disturbed me.

With planting season ended, we had more time away from the warehouse in the early summer of 1970, so Rosalynn and my sons began campaigning as well. There were many textile businesses and paper pulp mills in Georgia, and we were handing out leaflets at their major doors as people arrived for work early in the morning. Hugh, my cousin, was in charge of funding, and we set a goal of ten cents per inhabitant in each county (which we only met in a few locations). David Rabhan, the owner of a twin-engine Cessna plane, offered to fly me throughout the state. He had many black leaders as friends, including Martin Luther King, Sr., and arranged for me to meet with them and speak at their churches. Many high school and college students offered to assist, including Jody Powell, a former Air Force Academy cadet and current Emory University graduate student. Hamilton Jordan was the campaign chairman.

As my popularity grew, the Atlanta newspapers tried everything they could, both in terms of news coverage and editorial remarks, to portray me as a racist. They forgot to record my numerous interactions with black folks and attributed to me any conservative or news media aspersions thrown on Sanders as a liberal. My campaign ads highlighted my past as a former submariner who is now a full-time peanut farmer, with photos of myself and our sons working in my fields and warehouse. With a widespread slogan: CARL SANDERS OUGHT TO BE GOVERNOR AGAIN, Sanders lauded his successful life, highlighting his elevated social and economic status. I recall extensive TV spots featuring him flying his own plane and a slew of endorsements from Atlanta's political and economic heavyweights. My family's intimate relationships with people in their local neighbourhoods and at work locations were crucial. Because I emphasised my working-class background, it was practically unavoidable that class distinctions would be drawn. I appreciated the support of more conservative Georgians, such as Marvin Griffin, who had been defeated for governor in 1962, but I was never tempted to deviate from the moderate racial convictions I had always had, both in the navy and during my time in Plains.

During the final days of the general election campaign, I was flying from Brunswick to Newnan, Georgia, as Rabhan's copilot. When both engines stopped, he was sleeping and I was flying the plane. I hit him hard with my left elbow while he was still sleeping. He awoke, waited until the Cessna had dropped a few hundred feet, then reached over nonchalantly and flipped a valve to link standby fuel tanks and restart the engines. I was enraged as he chuckled at my discomfort. Finally, I joined in the fun, and we talked about the campaign's imminent conclusion. He had been really generous in his assistance, and I asked David what I could do to repay him. He asked if I had any paper and pencil, so I looked through my belongings for an aviator's map of Georgia with some blank space on it. He wrote, "The time for racial discrimination is over in Georgia," and followed up with, "This is what I want you to say when you are inaugurated."

I worked really hard on my inaugural speech. In eight minutes, I declared that I had probably travelled more throughout Georgia than any prior candidate, "and I say to you quite frankly that the time for racial discrimination is over." No poor, rural, frail, or black person should ever have to endure the added burden of being denied an education, a job, or basic justice." In 1970, several young and progressive governors were elected in Southern states, but this statement made headlines. Time magazine featured a drawing of me on the cover with the heading DIXIE WHISTLES A DIFFERENT TUNE.

***

Dean Rusk, our most distinguished Georgian, called me one morning. He had been Secretary of State under both John F. Kennedy and Lyndon B. Johnson, and was now semi retired in Athens, Georgia, where he taught international law at the University of Georgia. I invited him to the governor's office because he wanted to talk to me. He stated that the topic of his conversation was inappropriate for an official setting, so we scheduled a visit to the governor's mansion for late that afternoon. We sat in rocking chairs on our back veranda, sipping an appropriate Southern beverage. He opened the conversation without introducing himself, saying, "Governor, I think you should run for President in 1976." I was caught aback since I knew him to be a close friend of the Kennedy family and an expert on national politics. I didn't tell him we'd been discussing it, but I listened intently as he explained a meticulously organised, step-by-step approach he thought I should follow.

I didn't respond positively, but simply stated I'd think about his ideas, then took detailed notes and shared them with Rosalynn and the other conspirators. Dean Rusk's support dispelled our last misgivings, and we began to research the new Democratic Party primary rules, the political situations in all fifty states, the names and views of prominent news reporters, potential sources of finance, and potential opponents. Hamilton Jordan produced a seventy-page strategic notebook at my request, containing all of our tentative and highly classified plans. Simultaneously, I resumed my all-out attempt to reform state government.

As the 1974 campaigns for governors, senators, and congressmen loomed in March 1973, National Democratic Party Chairman Robert Strauss came to Atlanta to give a speech and asked if he might speak with me. Charles Kirbo, the state Democratic Party's chairman, had become my closest friend and adviser, and he joined us at the governor's residence. Strauss asked whether I would be interested in overseeing our party's nationwide effort to elect candidates. I listened intently as he outlined how I would be thoroughly educated by professionals in all aspects of conducting a campaign, informed about the most crucial contests, and could send one of my assistants to Washington to participate in top-level Democratic Party planning sessions. I could choose the candidates I would personally assist around my own time. Of course, the national party would cover all of my expenditures.

I quickly agreed, dispatched Hamilton Jordan to Democratic Party headquarters in Washington, and named Frank Moore as my executive secretary in Georgia. I started working as a campaign coordinator whenever I could get away from the governor's office. By November, I had engaged in thirty-seven campaigns across the country, with outstanding results. We Democrats gained four senators and forty-nine congressmen, giving us a two-thirds majority in the House, undoubtedly aided by the Watergate crisis and President Nixon's departure. I learned a lot and established hundreds of useful connections. Just before I announced publicly my intention to run for president, the Democratic Party had a "mini-convention" to adopt a new party charter that made the primary system considerably more transparent and democratic. We printed 1,000 colour campaign booklets for a dollar apiece and handed them to prominent

Democrats. George Gallup had recently released a public opinion poll that included the names of thirty-two probable Democratic nominees. Mine was left out. We had a lot of work ahead of us.

One delightful endeavour I started as governor was a concerted attempt to lure filmmakers to Georgia, which was a huge success. Deliverance, The Longest Yard, and Smokey and the Bandit were among the most well-known of our twenty-six pictures. I travelled to Hollywood and New York to pitch our state to producers, and on one of my travels, I got my first national exposure with an appearance on What's My Line? No one recognized me at first, but after a series of amusing questions, Arlene Francis and the other panellists finally recognized me as a governor. Another time, I went to Radio City Music Hall to see the Rockettes do a dance involving a submarine. They urged me to join their chorus line, and a photographer photographed me standing on one foot with my other leg raised as high as I could. I got back to Atlanta late that night, and Rosalynn asked me what I did in New York the next morning. I replied that I had worked hard all day promoting another film to be made in Georgia. "It wasn't all work," she remarked, showing me a snapshot from the morning newspaper of me in line with the Rockettes and nearly falling over backward!

***

My governorship ended in January 1975, and almost immediately I began travelling around the country with Jody Powell to attend state Democratic conventions and other speaking engagements. We had very little money and just shared a small hotel room when we couldn't find a friend with a spare bed for the night. It was discouraging at first because no one knew who I was and no one was thinking about the presidential race, which was still eighteen months away. Tim Kraft, a young man from New Mexico, was hired as our campaign manager in Iowa, and after a few weeks in the state, we decided to have a press conference and reception in a Des Moines hotel. We leased a large ballroom and purchased soft drinks, sandwiches, and cookies, but only one reporter and three curious potential supporters showed up. I spoke briefly with them before Jody and I walked to the city hall and county courtroom and distributed my pamphlets in every office.

We toured over 120 Iowa communities, held meetings in people's homes and college classrooms, and were ecstatic when as many as twenty individuals showed up. We were always on the lookout for someone with a microphone or even a reporter's scratch pad in the hopes of getting some news coverage. Jody snored loudly, and I generally fell asleep before he arrived in our shared room for the night. He once woke me up and excitedly announced that I would be on television early the next morning. He avoided answering my inquiries, only saying he'd explain later and that we needed to be up at five o'clock. On the drive to the TV station, he asked whether I had a favourite recipe, knowing that I was going to dress up as a chef and be interviewed for a food show. I put on an apron and a floppy white hat and demonstrated one of my favourite ways to prepare fillets of any sort of fish for the audience. I showed how to cut them into strips the size of French fries, marinade them overnight in some kind of steak sauce, flour them, and deep-fry them to serve hot or cold. When I started winning primary elections, the tape of this session was resurrected and replayed, along with reruns of What's My Line?

We were never disappointed by the lack of attention because we were operating on a low budget and didn't face any strong opponents in those early months. Our strategy was obvious, with the only significant change being Kennedy's decision not to run after surveys revealed that too many people recalled his role in the accidental drowning of a girl at Chappaquiddick. In addition to Iowa, we focused on New Hampshire, where Chris and Georgia Brown from New Mexico were in control, and Florida, where Plains native Phil Wise was the state campaign manager. Jody and I travelled to all fifty states during the primary season, accepting speaking invitations whenever available. We recruited a larger and larger circle of young people and relative beginners to politics because most of the other candidates were better known and had garnered the backing of active Democrats. The few people who worked full-time for us received minimal stipends and had to arrange their own lodging, sleeping in their cars or in other's homes, or paying for a cheap hotel room with their own money.

When I mentioned that I had been a submarine officer and was still a farmer—rather than a lawyer—I received acclaim. I went to livestock auction barns in Iowa and other agricultural regions, and the auctioneer would often let me speak to the gathering buyers and sellers of cattle and hogs. I could answer inquiries regarding agricultural issues, including fertiliser costs, seed, and the current selling of corn, soybeans, and pork, to them and interviewers from newspapers and other media. I quickly discovered that my opponents, largely from the United States Senate, would respond to queries concerning poverty, health, education, or transportation by referencing Senate Bill 643 or another number and its proposed impact. I could explain how the same federal laws were assisting or impeding advancement among Georgians.

I provided regular updates on progress and discussed issues presented with some young lawyers who had assisted me in the governor's campaign, led by Stuart Eizenstat and Jack Watson. We investigated Social Security laws, the Farm Bill, health legislation, and, most notably, the contentious issue of abortion. I had to tread carefully to retain the same position in both conservative Iowa and more liberal Northeastern areas. After hearing my thoughts, Hamilton and others planned our week's itinerary. Rosalynn agreed to visit Florida sometime in April, and she campaigned as she had during my governorship. She drove from town to town, stopping at courthouses, newspaper offices, cattle auction pens, and, most importantly, radio stations. She'd find an antenna, walk into a newsroom or broadcasting booth, and tell a reporter or disc jockey that her spouse was running for president and that she wanted to talk about him. If he didn't know anything about politics, as was frequently the case, she offered a printed list of questions he might ask her, and she responded with her perfectly scripted answers. She planned to spend 75 days in Florida, visit 105 communities in Iowa, and expand her crusade into forty other states.

***

When I first started campaigning, it became clear that there was widespread disdain of Washington's senior political leaders. Our eldest son, Jack, had quit his nuclear physics studies at Georgia Tech to serve in Vietnam. When he returned home on leave as an enlisted soldier, his friends and his classmates mocked him for being silly and naive, and he refused to wear his uniform. It was widely known that the White House and the Department of Defense were making misleading statements about the causes that had led to America's involvement in that fight, our large bombing campaign, and our relative accomplishments against the Vietcong. The Watergate revelations and President Ford's full pardon of Nixon, of course, heightened a general sense of alienation.

After a few months, we had seven separate family campaigns going on in different regions of America, with Rosalynn, me, all three of our sons with their wives, my mother, Lillian, and her youngest sister, Emily Dolvin. Rosalynn and I normally met in Plains on Saturdays to share our experiences at our home, then went to church on Sunday and then to Atlanta for strategy meetings that grew steadily in number. Hundreds of Georgians created the "Peanut Brigade" and travelled to critical states on their own dime to knock on doors and explain why I should be elected president. As the other Democratic contenders began campaigning, practically all were still engrossed in Congress or handling the affairs of their own states, campaigning only part-time and focusing on a few crucial primaries where each believed he might do well. I was the only one who sought delegates in every state, expecting to finish top at the very least and get a few convention votes.

Some of my Democratic opponents from Northern states began to bring up race relations, highlighting my origins in the Deep South, where traces of racial segregation remained. On my first campaign trip to Massachusetts, I visited a Revolutionary War site and let several press reporters interview me. The first was a question: "Why should anyone from Massachusetts vote for a governor from Georgia?" I reacted by saying, "Well, when John Kennedy ran for president, he received a higher percentage of votes from Georgians than from the people of your state, and I expect the same treatment." A question was raised during a meeting of campaign leaders in Washington about how well we were including black people in full-time roles on our staff. Most of the others stated that they had one or two qualified employees or were looking for some. When they asked Andrew Young about my campaign, he said, "I don't know how many Governor Carter has now, but there were twenty-two last month." I was regularly questioned on race, and I made a huge blunder when asked about housing trends in big cities, where families with roots to Italy, Greece, Ireland, or other European countries concentrated their residences. I stated that I thought it was fine for individuals who shared the same languages, faiths, and cultures to live near each other in general. There was a media commotion about my support for racially pure neighbourhoods, but it subsided after Daddy King, Andy Young, Benjamin Mays, and others backed me.

We came in front in Iowa and New Hampshire, much to everyone's astonishment except ours, and then focussed on Florida, where segregationist George Wallace was anticipated to repeat his 1972 success and Scoop Jackson was certain to win among more conservative voters and Jewish citizens. To stop Wallace, Andy Young, the Martin Luther King family, and some of the more liberal labour organisations backed me, and I won the state. Then I defeated Senators Lloyd Bentsen, Fred Harris, and Adlai Stevenson III in their home states of Texas, Oklahoma, and Illinois, as well as garnering enough other support to give me a decisive majority at the Democratic National Convention.

**

I concluded that I wanted a vice president who was familiar with Washington and the Congress, so other governors and local officials were out. Before the convention, I met with potential running companions; the majority of them came to my house and toured Plains with me. Senators Ed Muskie, Frank Church, John Glenn, Walter Mondale, and Scoop Jackson were among them. I observed how they interacted with my street neighbours and the customers who congregated in my warehouse office. "Fritz" Mondale was the least well-known, but he was the most compatible with me and had the most comprehensive and ambitious ideas about how the vice president's job should be considerably enlarged. I chose him and supported all of his recommendations, many of which had grown from his extensive conversations with his predecessors in the office, Governor Nelson Rockefeller and Senator Hubert Humphrey.

Fritz and I presented a series of all-day sessions on the most pressing issues of the day before we launched the hectic two-month general election campaign on Labor Day. Groups of the most prominent experts we could find would gather in Atlanta and then travel to Plains in chartered buses, where we would meet in my mother's remote Pond House to discuss taxation, welfare, education, transportation, the military, and relations with the Soviet Union, Israel, China, and other countries. In addition to studying as much as we could, we had the opportunity to get to know these leaders and eventually select cabinet officials from among them to serve with us.

Many of them were aware of our dual objectives, and they were all on their best behaviour.

When I was a member of the Trilateral Commission, I knew Zbigniew Brzezinski, and he helped brief me before the presidential debate on international policy. Later, following my election and during my first months in government, he aided me in developing an ambitious foreign policy agenda. It included the expected problems, as well as a few that had not been at the forefront of campaign topics or highlighted in the national media. I decided to make a major effort for Middle East peace, the abolition of apartheid in South Africa, and majority rule in other countries; the reduction of nuclear arsenals, normalisation of diplomatic relations with the People's Republic of China, open communications with Cuba, and resolution of the Panama Canal issue. This was widely covered since Ronald Reagan had stated strongly during the Republican nomination that we "should not give away our canal." In addition, I determined that human rights would be the focal point of our foreign policy.

***

After President Gerald Ford narrowly defeated Ronald Reagan's right-wing challenge and was nominated as the Republican nominee, he and I engaged in a spirited but mutually courteous campaign, and we both survived three national television debates. Ford had earlier been harmed by Reagan's political attacks and his pardon of Nixon, but I never brought this up. During our discussion of international policy, he oddly asserted that the Soviet Union did not dominate any of the East European countries invaded by Soviet forces. My personal campaign suffered, possibly even more, as a result of an ill-advised interview I gave to Playboy magazine in which I was discussing Jesus' Sermon on the Mount and declared that, like other males, I "lusted" for women. I couldn't think of an appropriate way to explain my goof further and decided to just deal with it. In just a few days, I lost about 15 percentage points in public opinion polls.

Ford and I chose not to raise campaign cash from corporations or individuals, instead funding our general election campaigns with a dollar designated by each taxpayer. (The payment has been raised to three dollars, but presidential nominees have not used it since 2004.) We didn't have the funds or the willingness to buy negative advertising, which have recently become a significant tool in winning elections. I admired Ford for his honesty and encyclopaedic understanding of the federal government and its institutions.

Our family and other close members of our political team gathered in Atlanta on election night to watch as results began to come in from the East Coast and then migrated westward, primarily due to time zone differences. In general, I won the majority of the eastern states, while Ford won the western states. We were practically deadlocked until late returns from Mississippi came in, giving me a narrow popular vote victory and 55 percent of the electoral votes. More than thirty novels have been written about the entire campaign. *Marathon* by Jules Witcover and *Running for President, 1976: The Carter Campaign* by Martin Schram are two of the most comprehensive and accurate.

Chapter 5: Life in the White House

My inauguration address was one of the shortest ever given at a president's first inauguration. It opened with thanks to Gerald Ford for "healing our nation" and addressed two of my administration's primary themes: peacekeeping and human rights strengthening. Despite the fact that I had been preparing to be president, I was taken aback when the Episcopal bishop of Minnesota declared "blessings on President Carter." The title "President Carter" surprised me, but I was ready and prepared to take on the duty, and we were looking forward to living in the White House. My first official act was to pardon Vietnam War draft evaders.

We had a really calm and informal lunch with our family that first night. When Rosalynn visited the White House earlier, some of our staff questioned the chef and cooks if they believed they could recreate the type of meals we had enjoyed in Plains, and the cook replied, "Oh, we've been fixing that kind of food for the servants for a long time." The meals were excellent in general, but we were surprised to learn that our food bill in the White House for the first five days was $600, and that the president pays for all meals for the president's family and special guests.

We went to eleven parties on inauguration night, but we moved quickly, danced a few times for our own fun and that of tens of thousands of other partygoers, met all of our commitments, and arrived back home in time to go to bed around 1:30 a.m. Rosalynn had opted to wear the same evening gown she had worn to my governor's inaugural ball. The news media chastised her for not selecting a new model from a well-known designer, but I supported her decision and was quite pleased with her beauty and grace.

We shook hands with thousands of individuals in receiving lines over the next few days to thank those who assisted us throughout the campaign and to strengthen ties with members of Congress, foreign officials, and members of the military forces. I was very amazed by how many generals and senior enlisted guys came by and mentioned peace, prayed for us, or just said, "God be with you."

In 1942, a modest but luxurious family theatre was created, and many presidents have used it to practise speeches, hold private group meetings, and watch movies. The first movies we saw were One Flew Over the Cuckoo's Nest and All the President's Men, both about the Watergate scandal, which played a role in my election. We could order any movie and frequently acquired new releases before they were released in public theatres. According to the projectionist's records, our family watched 480 movies (approximately two each week), many of which Amy requested to share with her school classmates. On Friday nights, the students would frequently stay up until daybreak, watching one film after another, before going to the swimming pool or bowling alley.

Amy was nine years old at the time, and she was the centre of media attention. It was less commonly known that we had three older kids, two of whom lived with us. Our oldest son, Jack, and his wife, as well as their one-year-old kid, Jason, remained in Georgia. Jeff, our youngest, was with us and attended George Washington University. Chip, our middle son, assisted both me and the Democratic Party with political matters. Our mothers came frequently and stayed in the Queen's Bedroom, which was across the hall from the Lincoln Bedroom.

We arranged to have our family together at suppertime when there was no official White House function, and we ate in a small dining room close to the upstairs kitchen. Our family had open and often heated arguments around the table, just like we did at home in Plains. They all had experiences I couldn't relate to, and it was clear that American individuals expressed themselves far more freely to my family members than to me. Rosalynn and the boys travelled extensively and attended numerous events, while Amy reported on life at her elementary school, which is located in the Foggy Bottom area, about a mile from the White House. She was unafraid to express her views and presented our family with accurate appraisals of life in the public school system. She had close connections among the children of White House staff members who had worked with me when I was governor, in addition to her classmates.

I arrived at the Oval Office early every morning, read the morning newspapers and any personal messages that had been left for me, and received an intelligence briefing from Dr. Brzezinski, who was now national security adviser, at eight o'clock. We were occasionally joined by the CIA director or other professionals. I normally ate my lunch there or in a small adjacent office, and I frequently asked the vice president, cabinet officers, staff people, and congressional leaders to join me. Rosalynn joined me for lunch every Wednesday so we could talk about personal matters and I could answer her persistent queries about official matters.

I was resolved to be fiscally responsible for the country and to set a good example in my personal life. I chose to sell the presidential yacht Sequoia and to reduce the amount of time I spent listening to "Ruffles and Flourishes" when I arrived at public gatherings. I was astonished when some of these reforms proved unpopular, as well as when I learned how much the public valued the pomp and ceremony of the presidency. I also intended to cut back on spending on President Franklin D. Roosevelt's secret hideaway at Camp David. This is a 120-acre enclosed enclave in Catoctin Mountain Park, roughly sixty miles north of Washington. Chip's wife, Caron, began having labour pains during the end of February, and we brought her to Bethesda hospital, where a son called James IV was born. We headed to Camp David for our first visit after holding him for a time. We fell in love with the facility, as did most previous presidents, and I urged my budget director not to alter its funds or tell me how much it cost to run. I also didn't want any more building done there without my permission. As a result, our family and occasionally special guests visited Camp David practically every free weekend.

Collecting Indian artefacts was one of my family's favourite boyhood activities. Rosalynn and our three boys would almost immediately change clothes and go to a favourite field where Native American towns had been when we got home to Plains from the governor's house or the White House during the winter months. I had already identified a half-dozen of these places as productive. A few showers will wash away the topsoil and expose bits of flint stone after a crop has been harvested or the field has been ploughed in preparation for new planting. We'd walk back and forth across the field, approximately fifteen feet apart, meticulously searching the ground. On our best day, we found 26 unbroken points. My collection consists of over 1500 arrowheads and other stone pieces, as well as clay pots, which have been evaluated by professors at the University of Georgia to determine the Indian tribe, type of stone, probable location of manufacture, and estimated date. A number of the arrowheads are nearly identical and appear to have been manufactured in a central site and traded to remote locations. Their ages range from 200 to 6 thousand years. Our forefathers migrated here five years after the Yuchi tribe of Lower Creek Indians were forced to leave our area in 1828. This was exactly one hundred years after the first English settlement was built two hundred miles to the east on the Georgia coast.

I'd been a fisherman my entire life, but it wasn't until I was governor and living near the chilly waters of Atlanta's Chattahoochee River that I learned to fly-fish for trout. On weekends at Camp David, I would often fish in Hunting Creek at the base of the mountain while Rosalynn perfected her casting technique in the pool outside our cabin. Our most enjoyable leisure trips were to Pennsylvania, where we looked for a convenient location to go fly-fishing on weekends. We drove by helicopter as guests of a private hunting and fishing club and landed on the farms of a dairyman, Wayne Harpster, who owned or leased a large stretch of Spruce Creek, about twenty-five miles south of Penn State University. We struck up an instant friendship with him and his entire family, and we began to see him on a regular basis.

My family made my off-duty time in Washington very enjoyable by taking me to museums, theatres, and numerous historic locations, as well as just lounging around the White House playing tennis, swimming, bowling, and watching movies. I spent many enjoyable hours tying trout flies while listening to music. We're all enthusiastic readers, and it was on weekends that I was able to catch up on back reading and prepare for the upcoming week, frequently perusing hefty briefing booklets from my staff. During the first two months, our family and a few staff members attended a speed-reading class every Friday night, which made it much simpler for me to read what my secretary told me was an average of 300 pages of official documents per day.

Rosalynn and I decided that Amy would attend one of the closest public elementary schools, which sparked some debate in the mainstream media because it had been assumed that she would attend one of the more prestigious private schools. As a member of the county school board, state senator, and governor, I had been deeply involved in education and was committed to the public school system. Rosalynn and I wanted Amy to be active in the Washington community and with children from various backgrounds. At Thaddeus Stevens Elementary School, she had classmates from a diverse spectrum of backgrounds, including blacks, Hispanics, and children of foreign embassies' servants.

I was still a mother. In July 1977, I learned that our son Chip was renting a house from a man whose close buddy was scheduled to receive a significant amount of marijuana on a fishing boat in the Gulf of Mexico. I called Chip and asked him to come home without telling him what was wrong. I discovered that he had been invited to go fishing on the boat that would soon be receiving the marijuana. The marijuana was transferred, the bust was carried out, and three tons of marijuana were seized. Chip's contact was revealed to be a federal government informant.

I opted to run the ten-thousand-metre race on Catoctin Mountain, near Camp David, in September 1979. I ran the course twice beforehand to familiarise myself with the challenging terrain, and I timed myself at a few sites along the way. On race day, I chose to shave four minutes off my previous best time, which proved to be a costly miscalculation. The weather was exceptionally warm and humid, and I overexerted myself and had to withdraw from the race due to heat exhaustion. I rapidly recovered and presented the medals during the awards ceremony. I felt a little weak, but there were no side effects. I should have played it safe to ensure my completion, but the mainstream media had a field day with my failure, with photographs of my sagging figure appearing in numerous newspapers.

Amy and I spent a lot of time together, swimming, bowling, and hitting tennis balls. She indicated she wanted a tree home, so we went around the South Lawn for prospective locations. I didn't want to harm any of the ancient trees, so we opted to build the sleeping section in the tree but support it from the ground. She told me what she wanted, and I made the blueprints and purchased the materials, and Amy and her pals were soon spending evenings up in the green foliage, closely monitored by Secret Service agents. Later, when Bob Hope came to visit us, he made a joke about being a Republican, and I informed him that he would be sleeping in Amy's tree house instead of the Lincoln Bedroom.

Jeffrey, our youngest son, was an amateur astronomer who borrowed a good tracking telescope and placed it up on the White House roof. He researched the many constellations and galaxies and was able to describe what we were seeing. Jeff became acquainted with Dr. Carl Sagan, who invited us to the naval observatory close to the vice president's mansion in December 1977. Dr. Sagan provided a slide presentation on outer space, including his prediction about life on distant planets, and the Mondale family joined us. We had a good time stargazing, and I penned a poem about a flock of geese flying above Washington, their breasts reflecting the city lights.

We enjoyed the White House but missed the wide veranda that surrounds Atlanta's governor's mansion. The Truman Balcony, which overlooked the South Lawn, Jefferson Memorial, and the distant Washington airport, was furnished with small glass tables and straight-back seats similar to those found in a soda fountain. We decided to bring some comfy rocking chairs from Georgia and bought six. After that, our family had a wonderful vantage point from which to see a portion of Washington, and we frequented there, particularly in the late afternoons and at night. When I wanted our discussions to be casual and entirely private, I would take key foreign visitors here.

I recall one session with British Prime Minister James Callaghan, who requested an off-the-record talk. We sipped cocktails while admiring the new rocking chairs, and he informed me about Great Britain's economic woes and how the International Monetary Fund was putting pressure on him to cut the country's deficit by extreme measures. I intervened to offer my assistance in lowering IMF demands, and he replied, "No, no! I'd like you to back up their constraints. I want them to put pressure on me and my administration to do what I know is right but is unpopular politically."

Thousands of our friends have spent the night at the White House for South Lawn events, concerts, and official entertainment of foreign dignitaries over the years. Rosalynn and her aides, as well as the State Department, collaborated to compile the guest lists and did an excellent job. We also appreciated having prior presidents' children and grandkids, but for some reason, we failed to invite Margaret Truman, whose father was the president I most admired. We later apologised to her, but I will always be sorry for this oversight.

***

When India's president died after only a few weeks in office, I called Mama to see if she might represent our country at the funeral. She had served as a Peace Corps Volunteer in a village near Bombay when she was seventy years old, and she was widely known throughout the country. I asked her what she was doing when she answered the phone. "How would you like to go to India?" she asked, as she was sitting about the home seeking for something to do. "I'd love to go someday," she replied. Why?" "How about this afternoon?" I suggested. "Okay," she said, "I'll be ready." When I explained the purpose of the trip, she asked if I could have a suitable black dress ready for her when she arrived in Washington, and I agreed. She was accompanied to the event by our son Chip and a few members of Congress with a specific interest in India, and I authorised the funeral party to travel to Bombay (now Mumbai) after the services so Mama could visit her former Peace Corps post. Vikhroli was a town of approximately a thousand inhabitants, and when they arrived, just a few people were waiting to welcome my mother. She was disappointed, but she asked to see the small room where she had been living. When they turned a corner, thousands of waiting villagers erupted out in wild acclaim when they spotted the woman they named Lilly.

Rosalynn, our sons, and my mother saved me a lot of overseas travel by attending the funerals of President Jomo Kenyatta in Kenya, Prime Minister Golda Meir in Israel, and the presidents of India, South Korea, and Algeria, as well as historic birthday events in England, Australia, Canada, and several Latin American countries. Rosalynn went to seven countries for discussions with presidents and other key officials on one occasion when I had a number of serious diplomatic issues in South America and couldn't make the trip myself. She carried personal messages from me urging President Ernesto Geisel of Brazil to abandon his plans to reprocess nuclear fuel for weapons, the leaders of Peru and Chile to reduce their purchases of armaments, and the president of Colombia to inform him that one of his cabinet officers was accepting bribes from drug cartels. Rosalynn was far more forthright and strong in her speeches than either Secretary of State Cyrus Vance or I would have been.

***

Rosalynn went out of her way to prepare entertainment for foreign dignitaries that they would like. She verified with the CIA, State Department, the visitor's embassy in Washington and ours in the foreign country ahead of time, and the performances at state banquets accommodated the interests of our guests. Carmen Romano, the wife of Mexican President José López Portillo, was a concert pianist, so at our supper for them, Rudolf Serkin played many selections, followed by Carmen's performance. Bobby Short sang while we served BBQ on the roof of the West Wing, overlooking the Rose Garden, since Japanese Prime Minister Masayoshi Ohira appreciated informality and popular music. President Anwar Sadat stated that he watched western films every day and asked for the Statler Brothers to play. While King Baudouin and Queen Fabiola of Belgium dined with us, the New York Harp Ensemble performed, and a group of young Suzuki violin students, including Amy, performed. Then, as an unplanned climax, a handful of the more advanced violinists, some as young as seven, joined the US Marine String Band. Rosalynn coordinated a series of Sunday afternoon performances that were recorded and telecast by PBS as a special gift for all Americans.

We were honoured to be a member of the inaugural Kennedy Center Honors program in 1978, which has since continued. I said at the time that the five persons chosen would be recognized, but more importantly, that they would "come here to honour us and all the people of the world." Marian Anderson, Fred Astaire, George Balanchine, Richard Rodgers, and Arthur Rubinstein were named in 1978, Aaron Copland, Ella Fitzgerald, Henry Fonda, Martha Graham, and Tennessee Williams were named in 1979, and Leonard Bernstein, James Cagney, Agnes de Mille, Lynn Fontanne, and Leontyne Price were named in 1980. Andrés Segovia became a close friend, and on a later trip to Spain, he surprised us by performing for us and other guests in a nightclub. Later, he offered us a customised casting of his hands playing classical guitar.

These numerous events took up a lot of Rosalynn's time, but knowing these brilliant people and experiencing their performances brightened the lives of our family and many others.

***

I was determined from the start of my presidency to provide access to members of Congress and news media leaders. I held 41 press conferences for the national press corps during my first two years in government. Special groups of newspaper editors and publishers, as well as news directors and owners of regional television and radio stations, came to the White House frequently for extended luncheon meetings with me. I hired Jerry Rafshoon to my team in May 1978, and at his suggestion, I began hosting intimate dinners with important national media leaders and, on occasion, their spouses. Rosalynn and I thoroughly enjoyed our meetings with news media luminaries like Walter Cronkite, Carl Rowan, Katharine Graham, and James "Scotty" Reston. I would answer all of their inquiries off the record.

My efforts to court the news media were futile. An academic review of presidential press coverage indicated that I received negative coverage in 46 of the 48 months that I served, with the exception of the first two months, when my family and I strolled down

Pennsylvania Avenue. This was a situation we could never grasp or fix, so we just made do with what we couldn't change. Some of the most powerful analysts did not predict my election, and others could not understand the fact that a governor from the Deep South was in office. There was an ongoing dispute about whether I was a liberal or a conservative, with the result that I was being deceptive about my fundamental ideology. An unfavourable attitude toward the presidency was also carried over from the Watergate scandal, with perhaps a perception that we, too, had something nasty to hide. We remember The Washington Post running a whole page of mocking cartoons featuring myself, my mother, and other members of our family with straw coming out of our ears, frequenting outdoor privies, and hanging out with pigs. At the close of my presidency, one of the most distinguished columnists predicted that the Reagans would finally "restore grace to the White House." Charles Kirbo, one of my senior advisers, described my commitment never to lie as a red sign. He declared, "We just lost the liar vote."

Throughout my tenure, we scheduled private meetings with all Democratic and Republican members of Congress, as well as senior members of key committees. During the first two years, I had wide Democratic congressional backing, and Senator Ted Kennedy was extremely helpful. This all changed late in 1978, when he decided to run for president. He became one of my most tenacious opponents, appearing intent to downplay my accomplishments. Kennedy persuaded several of the more liberal Democrats to back him.

The most remarkable instance of Kennedy's opposition to my initiatives occurred in 1979, when it was the culmination of months of work by my cabinet officers, economic experts, White House staff, and congressional leaders. Except for Kennedy, we had the entire backing of the chairmen of the six main House and Senate committees, and all six had been involved in its development. Our plan shielded all Americans from catastrophic illness costs, extended comprehensive health coverage to all low-income citizens, provided total coverage to all mothers and babies for prenatal, delivery, postnatal, and infant care, encouraged competition and cost containment, and laid out a clear roadmap for implementing a universal, comprehensive national health plan. Its whole launch expenses were included in my annual budget proposal, and it was to be fully implemented over a four-year period with guaranteed funding. Senator Kennedy had his own preferred proposal, which was so costly that it had no chance of receiving congressional approval, but his committee members worked with us until the week before the announcement, when he chose to reject the measure. Kennedy's resistance to our idea proved catastrophic; he was a powerful voice, and he and his followers were able to stop it from becoming law. We blew an excellent opportunity to provide comprehensive national health care, and it would be another thirty years before such an opportunity arose again, with only partial implementation.

When my convictions were congruent with theirs, I looked increasingly to moderate Republicans, with minority leaders Senator Howard Baker and Congressman John Rhodes serving as significant allies. These included eliminating government bureaucracy, increasing control over intelligence agencies, implementing zero-based budgeting, beginning free trade agreements, and reducing superfluous weapons systems. Almost every substantial domestic legislative measure was crafted in the White House by Stu Eizenstat, a young Atlanta attorney who had led the committee that analysed issues throughout my campaign. We asked Democratic committee chairs and senior Republicans, as well as their staff members, to attend. Frank Moore, my top aide as governor, handled communications between me and members of the House and Senate. These efforts were effective in getting many measures passed by Congress, with a very high percentage of approval from both parties.

Chapter 6: Issues Mostly Resolved

There were a number of challenges that I confronted at the White House that were not passed on to my successors, whether they were long-standing concerns that I was able to handle or issues that were ephemeral in nature. Everyone urged me not to take on too many initiatives so early in the administration, but it was nearly hard for me to put off things that I believed needed to be done.

***

Chancellor Helmut Schmidt of Germany was one foreign leader with whom I had a fractious relationship. I first met him in 1973, when I was governor and he was finance minister. I was attempting to persuade Volkswagen to create a production unit in Georgia, as well as a trading office in Bonn. We had a productive meeting because he wanted my opinion on the ongoing Watergate hearings. He had recently criticised some of my decisions as president, clearly believing that my insistence on human rights in the Soviet Union was naive and ineffective. I encouraged him to stop providing Brazil with equipment and technology for plutonium production and to stimulate Germany's economy, as other Western governments were doing to solve the global economic downturn. I spoke with his foreign minister in an attempt to resolve these issues before the June conference. We eventually succeeded, but during my presidency, these irritants were always replaced by others, such as the quantity and composition of nuclear weapons in Europe, the level of economic stimulus in the United States, and my forceful reaction when the Soviets invaded Afghanistan. In conclusion, I wrote in my diary in 1980, "He's a strange man and a good German leader." I'm afraid he has an issue with my attitude. He is continuously critical of the United States, of its resolve, justice, commitment, honesty, and so on, in private to the news media and to others. He knocks me, Brzezinski, Vance, Muskie, and others."

The G7 summit (now G20) was both interesting and useful. Among the many topics on our agenda, the two most difficult and time-consuming were human rights and nuclear nonproliferation, both of which we and Canadians were chastised for being too aggressive. I was struck by how eager the other leaders were to meet with me and associate their countries with ours. A lovely luncheon with the British royal family was one really pleasurable event that brought me some grief a year or two later. I sat next to Queen Elizabeth and we had a lovely conversation about both important and personal subjects. She complained about having to wear seven different uniforms on annual events and how difficult it was to fit into them as her weight fluctuated. We felt it would be best to use centimetres for everything except waistlines, which would remain in inches. After supper, I was approached by the Queen Mother, and we talked about how our families had been affected by our involvement in public affairs. I kissed her lightly on the cheek as we said good night, and she thanked me for coming to see her. More than two years later, reports in British newspapers badly misrepresented this episode, claiming that I had greatly embarrassed her with my inappropriate friendliness. These reports upset me, but I couldn't reverse what had happened, nor did I regret it.

***

During the 1976 campaign, Jerry Ford and I both knew that whoever won would have to determine whether or not to build the proposed B-1 bomber. As president, I set a deadline of June 1977 and worked on this matter for months, holding numerous conversations with specialists and interested parties on all sides of the issue. Secretary Harold Brown, the joint chiefs, and I eventually decided that the extremely expensive new bombers were not worth the cost, and that our defence needs could be met for the next fifteen or twenty years by existing B-52s and other smaller planes, combined with new and extremely accurate cruise missiles that could be launched from land, submarines, surface ships, and aeroplanes. We couldn't discuss the top-secret development of "stealth" technology that would make our planes invisible to radar at the time. A few years later, this would be put into fighter planes and B-2 bombers. My decision was endorsed by House and Senate leaders, but defence contractors were dissatisfied. When Reagan took office, he obtained authority to build one hundred superfluous B-1 bombers, each costing approximately $200 million. Although B-1s have seen combat on rare occasions, modified B-52s are scheduled to remain in service until 2040, and B-2s until 2058. Making such long-term decisions about very expensive military products is usually tough for presidents, especially when manufacturing jobs are carefully located or promised to supporters of powerful legislators.

***

The Cold War was raging, and the Soviet Union and the United States were engaged in fierce competition everywhere. There was no country, no matter how little or remote, where we didn't compete for more power than the other. This was frequently advantageous to the local people because we provided them with increased economic relations, some forms of foreign aid, or enhanced military capabilities. My purpose was to show the benefits of freedom and a commitment to human rights above the Soviet system of Communism and persecution. These disagreeable and hazardous practices were on display in Poland, East Germany, Czechoslovakia, Romania, Hungary, Yugoslavia, and Albania—as well as in Afghanistan when the Soviets invaded in December 1979. The dominance of those living within the Soviet Union was the most evident example.

President Ford's denial in a debate that the Soviets dominated any countries in Eastern Europe may have been a watershed moment in my presidential campaign. My first abroad tour after the London Economic Summit was to Poland to convey my empathy for their plight. I began campaigning for the freedom of imprisoned human rights campaigner Natan Sharansky, and my personal contact with Andrei Sakharov and his wife, Yelena Bonner, became widely publicised. Through Soviet Ambassador Anatoly Dobrynin, I made repeated requests to his superiors to allow downtrodden Jews to leave for Europe and America. Later, when I met with President Brezhnev, he was aware that human rights would be on my agenda and prepared a written response, which he simply handed to the translator to read. Although Soviet officials never admitted to denying any rights or that this was a legitimate topic of debate with me, our approach had some practical consequences. The number of Soviet Jews permitted to leave the nation nearly doubled to 51,320 in 1979, and there is no doubt that this boosted Soviet residents' yearning for greater freedoms.

In June 1979, I travelled to Vienna to meet with President Brezhnev and his staff in order to negotiate a reduction and future restrictions on nuclear arsenals. The Soviets were supposed to come to the US for this session, but Brezhnev was unwell and couldn't fly at high altitudes. He was accompanied by Foreign Minister Andrei Gromyko, Second in Command and Future Soviet Leader Konstantin Chernenko, and Defense Minister Dmitry Ustinov. When a more extreme reduction in nuclear arsenal was envisioned, we concluded the SALT II agreement, which had a five-year projected life. SALT II remained in effect after it was not ratified by the United States Senate. The most intriguing occurrence occurred when Brezhnev stated at the outset, "If we do not succeed, God will not forgive us!" Gromyko, as the leader of an atheistic regime, was embarrassed by the subsequent hush, and he finally added, jokingly, "Yes, God above is looking down on us all."

When Soviet leader Mikhail Gorbachev introduced reforms known as perestroika and glasnost (reorganisation and openness) and withdrew Soviet soldiers from Afghanistan in the 1980s, I was overjoyed. In 1991, the Berlin Wall was demolished, the Communist Party lost control, and the USSR was dissolved. Russia remained a significant regional actor, but the United States remained the world's sole superpower.

***

During my 1976 presidential campaign, many Americans inquired about the Middle East, but the majority were only seeking assurances of my good intentions toward Israel. I became increasingly concerned in bringing enduring peace to Israel and its neighbours, and shortly after being elected, I addressed this privately with my national security adviser, Zbigniew Brzezinski. Because there was little information on how Syria, Jordan, Egypt, or even Israel would respond to such a proposal, I resolved to speak with all of their leaders as soon as possible.

On March 7, Israeli Prime Minister Yitzhak Rabin spoke first, and he was shockingly negative about starting peace talks. After his visit, I learned that he and his wife were being investigated for having an illegal money account in America, and that he was facing stiff reelection opposition from Menachem Begin.

On April 4, Anwar Sadat arrived from Egypt, and I found him to be open. He didn't think he'd ever recognize Israel or allow Israeli ships to use the Suez Canal, but he pledged to listen to my future ideas and try to be flexible.

When our family was enjoying Camp David one weekend, Rosalynn mentioned that the solitude and calm setting would be great for negotiating teams. In August 1978, I agreed with her and extended handwritten invitations to Begin and Sadat to join me for thorough peace discussions. They both agreed.

Keeping Faith detailed our thirteen days together, and several other books have been published about our negotiations at Camp David, but I'd like to now explain some of the more intimate ties that evolved there.

I had nearly memorised the maps of contested areas and the enormous briefing materials provided by our intelligence services on Begin and Sadat's histories. Their early lives, political careers, promises and commitments to major political groups, and psychological evaluations anticipating how they would react to pressure while negotiating and after they returned home were all part of this.

I initially imagined I could get both men into a small room in my cabin and have them discuss all of the benefits that a peace accord could bring to their country. But I discovered that this was difficult since both of them would dismiss my suggestions and revert as soon as possible to heated debates regarding events that had occurred during the four wars that had occurred between their countries over the previous thirty years. They would occasionally return to Biblical times. After three days of noisy disagreements, I determined that they should be kept apart, and we retained this arrangement for the rest of our time together. I'd written a single page outlining my vision for a complete peace treaty. I'd take it, normally to the Israelis first, then to the Egyptians, only revising the text when absolutely required. Slowly but steadily, paragraph by paragraph, progress was made.

Tensions were so high that I suggested we take a break and go to the adjacent Civil War battleground of Gettysburg. All officers prepared for military service had thoroughly researched this conflict, as did I and nearly all of Israel's and Egypt's top commanders. Except for Begin, who had never had military training, there were eager comments as we were led from one spot to another. I was concerned about his relative isolation in the group, but then we arrived at the site of Abraham Lincoln's historic address. Everyone fell silent to reflect on the event, and after a few moments, Begin began to recite

Lincoln's words: "Fourscore and seven years ago..." It was an emotional experience, the most unforgettable of the day.

On the ninth day, late at night, I became anxious about Sadat's safety. He was ahead of the rest of his group in agreeing to my recommendations, and we knew that some Egyptians were vehemently anti-Israel. His foreign minister had resigned in protest and returned to Egypt, and several of his other top officials were on the edge of revolt as a result of his concessions. I had sent word that I wanted to meet Sadat late that afternoon, but was told that he had already gone to bed and did not want to be disturbed. I was sceptical of the sincerity of this remark, and I couldn't sleep for one of the few occasions in my life. I finally got security set up outside Sadat's cabin through Zbig Brzezinski, and I was relieved to see him the next morning.

On the eleventh day, I was meeting with Secretary of Defense Harold Brown about some critical budget issues when Secretary of State Cy Vance burst into the room and announced that Sadat had left his luggage on the porch of his cabin and had requested a helicopter to return him to Egypt. This was one of the most difficult times of my life. I knew he was sceptical of our chances after Israeli Foreign Minister Moshe Dayan assured him that Israel would make no further concessions. I walked into my bedroom, knelt, and prayed for a bit, and for some reason, I changed out of my T-shirt and blue jeans for the first time since I'd come. Only then did I travel to Sadat's hut, where we had a nasty fight. I used all of my arguments and threats, and he eventually agreed to give me another chance.

By the thirteenth day, there were just a few outstanding matters that were critical to Prime Minister Begin. The first concerns the status of Jerusalem, while the second involved the evacuation of all Israelis from Egyptian territory. He would not budge on either, and he was furious with me. We all agreed that our only alternative was to return to Washington, admit failure, and plan for future endeavours. Begin had asked my secretary to have me autograph images of the three leaders as keepsakes for his eight grandkids. She had phoned Israel and obtained their names without informing him, so I engraved them with affection to each child. I went to Begin's cabin, and he welcomed me with a polite but cold demeanour. I handed him the images, and he turned aside to scrutinise them before reading the names out one by one. His voice was choking, and tears streamed down his cheeks. He requested me to take a seat because I was emotional as well. We agreed to try again after a few minutes, and after some lengthy arguments, we were successful.

We called Presidents Richard Nixon and Gerald Ford on the way back to Washington to tell them the good news, and then had a press conference at the White House.

***

My first encounter with Panama occurred while I was a student at Georgia Tech, an engineering school that specialised in Latin American affairs. There were numerous students from Panama, which was my first encounter with anyone from another nation, and I was able to practise my rudimentary Spanish with them. They were proud of the Panama Canal, which gave them good jobs and a permanent connection to the United States. As a navy officer operating on ships in the Pacific and Atlantic Oceans, I became increasingly conscious of the canal's importance to international trade in both peace and conflict. During my tenure as a state legislator, I became aware of a severe schism between Panamanians and Americans. My Panamanian colleagues told me about certain Americans' arrogance in the Canal Zone, prejudice toward Panamanians with dark skin, and hiring and pay practices that made local workers feel inferior. As president, I began working on resolving the Panama Canal disputes as soon as possible. This procedure will be described in full since it will be the most difficult political struggle of my life, even if I am elected president.

During the fall of 1975, thirty-eight senators introduced a resolution opposing any changes to the existing treaty, knowing that thirty-four could stymie any attempt. According to polls, only 8% of the American population was willing to give up control of the canal, and conservatives saw this as a major issue. Ronald Reagan and the John Birch Society both launched nationwide crusades with speeches and video and audio records in 1974. This was a task that I was given.

After researching the issues, I judged that Panama had valid claims and began formal discussions. General Omar Torrijos ruled Panama at the time, and I grew to admire his political daring and honesty, as well as consider him a personal friend. Ellsworth Bunker, former ambassador to Argentina and several other countries, and Sol Linowitz, former chairman of Xerox, were my two seasoned and respected negotiators. They found a winning formula in early August 1977. One pact would apply from 1979 to 1999, when the Canal Zone would be decommissioned and the region would be returned to Panama. The other would be a permanent promise that the US will protect the canal and use it first in the event of an emergency. Now I had to persuade 67 senators to vote for a hugely unpopular accord that many had promised to oppose.

My initial endeavour was to enlist the support of Presidents Ford and Nixon, as well as Senate leaders Robert Byrd (Democrat) and Howard Baker (Republican), and then persuade other senators that their most powerful home state political figures would be supportive, if not neutral. We began inviting up to 200 notable residents from various states to the White House, where military leaders, cabinet executives, and I would explain the canal's history and highlight the benefits to our country if the treaties were implemented. My cabinet members and other senior officials made over 1500 appearances across the country, and I persuaded forty-five sceptical senators to visit Panama and see how vulnerable the canal was to sabotage and how capable the Panamanians who provided the majority of the technicians in charge of its operation were. Our Canal Zone commanders and General Torrijos, with the manner and candour of a sergeant, proved to be outstanding marketers.

In September 1977, I invited hemispheric leaders to a signing ceremony of the agreed documents, and eighteen presidents and a number of other top officials attended the emotional event. Torrijos burst into tears as Torrijos and I were about to enter the vast auditorium from a side room, and he sobbed for a few minutes on his wife's shoulder until he regained his composure. Unfortunately, we had to wait until the next year for the Senate to begin real hearings in the foreign affairs and defence committees, followed by lengthy floor debates. Senators Byrd and Baker's public support was a plus, but senators who showed a desire to oppose the treaties were subjected to intense pressure. By this time, polls showed that 34% of Americans supported the treaties.

I kept a notepad on my desk, aided by Frank Moore, with any essential information I could gather about each senator, including twenty or more names of people or groups most powerful with each one. I kept a constant record of people who had pledged to vote for or against the treaties. I was aware of their principal involvements in state or national issues, as well as any personal interests in the canal. President Ford agreed to contact nine "undecided" Republicans, but only one of them voted yes in the end. There was a rush of damaging amendments, and Senators Bob Dole and Jesse Helms loudly and falsely claimed that Torrijos and his family were drug dealers and that high-level US officials had been corrupted. The Senate held private sessions to rebut these claims. The first treaty was to be voted on on March 16, and the second a month later. With one week left, I had been promised 59 votes. Eleven senators were still undecided, and I needed eight of them. Here are some of the major issues that needed to be addressed:

We finally won with 68 votes because I met Nunn and DeConcini's demands with language that didn't change the treaties; persuaded Mansfield to appease Hatfield; agreed with Bellmon on his desalination plant; persuaded Mormon editors (who opposed the treaties) not to condemn Cannon; persuaded the King of Saudi Arabia to intervene with Abourezk; and invited Sasser to the White House to meet a diverse array of stars at the twentieth

This was the most daring vote in the history of the United States Senate. Only seven of the twenty people who voted for the treaties who were up for election that year were re-elected, while eleven supporters—plus one president—were defeated two years later, in 1980. Reagan utilised this as one of his campaign's deciding arguments against me, and the decision remained controversial even later.

American politicians continue to avoid the controversy. When the time came to grant Panama sovereignty in 2000, neither President Bill Clinton, Vice President Al Gore, nor the Secretary of State were available, so Clinton asked me to represent the United States. Later, while President George W. Bush was in office, I received another unexpected request: to represent the US in the start of a significant expansion of the canal's capacity. The plunger was pressed by Panama's President Martin Torrijos (son of Omar) and I to detonate the first dynamite. I was appreciative of the honour on both occasions.

***

Senator Hubert Humphrey has been a hero of mine since I saw him lead the struggle for civil rights at the 1948 Democratic National Convention. The "Dixiecrats" resigned and founded their own party, with Strom Thurmond as their nominee, with the purpose of depriving Truman of Southern votes. Truman prevailed, and Humphrey became Minnesota's first Democratic senator since the Civil War. When I was a state senator, I met Hubert. He returned from an African tour to pay a visit to a fan of mine in Atlanta. He started telling me about his adventures around 9:00 a.m. and was still talking at 2:30 a.m., when I had to leave and drive home to Plains. When Lyndon Johnson ran for president in 1964, he chose Humphrey as his running mate. As I previously stated, Hubert and his wife, Muriel, visited Georgia to campaign, and my mother volunteered to house them.

Johnson decided not to seek reelection four years later, and Humphrey was nominated as the Democratic nominee, with Richard Nixon as his opponent. He had inherited an unpopular war in Vietnam, and he resolved not to criticise or disown responsibility for any of the conflict's actions. This cost him votes from Democrats on the left, while many conservative voters went to independent candidate George Wallace. Humphrey was defeated in a close election. He was re-elected senator in 1970 and served till the end of his life.

Hubert, one of the Democratic candidates who came to see me in 1972, made himself at home in the governor's palace and became our favourite visitor. We have a sweet snapshot of Amy as a four-year-old sitting on his lap, eating him a piece of her brownie with it smeared all over their cheeks. He was defeated in the presidential election again that year, when Democrats nominated George McGovern.

When I appointed Walter Mondale as my vice president, he sought counsel from Senator Humphrey on the nature of the position, and Hubert assisted him in developing a bold and unusual set of recommendations. They included locating his office near mine, having an unrestricted and automatic presence in all discussions, complete briefings with me on nuclear weapons handling, meetings with any member of Congress without prior approval, and the freedom to travel overseas, including meetings with heads of state and an unlimited press entourage. I was startled to find that Vice

President Humphrey had never been awarded these perks and responsibilities. I added a few perks for Fritz, such as the ability to schedule his own vacation periods and the flexibility to visit Camp David whenever he and his wife, Joan, wanted. Senator Humphrey was a steadfast friend and supporter, and he was very helpful in advising me on how to approach other senators when dealing with difficult matters like dealing with Israeli supporters or obtaining votes for Panama Canal accords.

When Hubert was dying of cancer, I discovered that he had never been invited to Camp David and invited him to accompany me for a weekend. I picked him up in Minneapolis on my way back from a trip to the West Coast in December, and we spent a cold and rainy weekend together. We watched a few movies and spent hours in our cabin in front of a toasty fire, which I described in my diary as "one of the most enjoyable and interesting weekends I've ever spent."

***

Mount Saint Helens volcano in Washington State erupted in May 1980, causing the largest natural explosion ever recorded in North America. My science adviser, Frank Press, and other scientists had been watching activity at the site for several months, and people had been warned of the danger, but fifty-seven people were killed when the entire north side of the volcano broke away, causing ash to fall across fourteen states. I decided to go right away, accompanied by Dr. Press, the secretary of the interior, agriculture, and the army, as well as the directors of FEMA and the National Institutes of Health. We discovered that one cubic mile of the mountain had been pulverised, 28 feet of silt had filled the Columbia ship channel, and every tree in a 150-square-mile region had been levelled. As we neared the still-smouldering mountain in a huge helicopter, we could see that nothing but a sea of molten lava remained underneath us, still retaining chunks of ice the size of houses that had been thrown off the peak. Without the early warning, thousands of people would have died, and Dr. Press expressed sorrow that scientists had overestimated the force of the explosion, which was equivalent to a ten-megaton nuclear bomb. Nearby Spirit Lake was filled with 400 feet of ash and lava, raising its surface level by 150 feet. We witnessed some enormous pieces of lava fall beyond our helicopter as we soared around the mountain many kilometres away, and we agreed with the pilot that our observation trip should terminate.

After talking with my advisors, I opted to forego any unneeded modifications and instead let nature heal itself. I couldn't imagine anything growing in the destroyed area, but twenty-five years later, in 2005, I was leading a group of volunteers in building Habitat for Humanity homes in Benton Harbor, Michigan, when a truck arrived loaded with planks appropriate for creating the roof trusses. The lumber was harvested from new-growth trees near Mount Saint Helens' base, and the timber business wanted us to use it for these homes for low-income families.

***

One of the most contentious decisions I took as President was to return the Crown of Saint Stephen to the people of Hungary. It was supposed to have been handed to Stephen, the first king of Hungary, by the Pope in the year 1000 as a symbol of political and religious authority, and it was worn by more than fifty monarchs when they were clothed with power. The twisted cross on top was a distinguishing characteristic. As Soviet troops seized Hungary near the conclusion of WWII, several Hungarians handed over the crown and other royal regalia to American troops, which were then held in Fort Knox alongside our nation's gold. When I proclaimed my desire to surrender the crown, the Soviets still ruled Hungary. There was uproar among Hungarian-Americans and others, and I was accused of accepting the occupied nation's subservience. I saw the crown as a symbol of the Hungarian people's freedom and sovereignty. In January 1978, I returned it, specifying that the crown and insignia be handled by Hungarians, thoroughly guarded, and made available for public display as soon as possible. In March 1998, a replica of the crown was presented to The Carter Center as a gift for me, and it is now on exhibit in our presidential museum.

Rosalynn and I led volunteers to build Habitat houses in Vác, Hungary, in 1996, and we were received as distinguished guests by the government and escorted to the Hungarian National Museum to see the crown and the stream of residents passing by, many of whom were chanting a prayer. We were told that almost 3 million people pay their respects to the crown each year. After a few years, it was relocated to its permanent location, the Hungarian Parliament Building.

***

During my presidency, there was another major disagreement over an environmental issue that had been pending for a long time. This could be my most major domestic achievement in my political career. When Alaska became the forty-ninth state in January 1959, a discussion erupted over how part of its huge federal properties should be shared among indigenous Indians and Eskimos, deeded to the state government, or preserved as national forests, parks, and wilderness areas. President Dwight Eisenhower and his successors skirted the contentious topic, and the discovery of oil and the expansion of commercial fisheries had added an essential factor: the battle over vast money. I decided to start talks to try to resolve the issues, but I quickly discovered that the Alaska congressional delegation was deeply invested in the oil industry and other commercial interests, and senatorial courtesy prevented other members from disagreeing with Senators Ted Stevens (Republican) and Mike Gravel (Democrat) over a matter involving their home state. Former Idaho governor Cecil Andrus, my secretary of the interior, and I began researching the history of the conflict as well as maps of the contested areas, and I flew over several of them.

Environmentalists and the majority of indigenous peoples were my allies, while professional hunters, loggers, fishermen, and chambers of commerce were allies of the oil companies. All odds were stacked against us until Cecil discovered an ancient law, the Antiquities Act of 1906, which allowed a president to set aside land for "the protection of objects of historic and scientific interest," such as Indian burial grounds, artefacts, or an ancient church building or the site of a famous battle. We decided to use this ability to set aside significant sections of Alaska as national monuments for preservation, eventually including more than 56 million acres (bigger than the state of Minnesota). This provided me with the necessary bargaining power, and I was able to triumph in the future disputes.

My actions were quite unpopular in Alaska, and I had to travel with extra protection. I recall a state fair where people threw baseballs at two targets in order to sink a clown into a tank of water. My face was on one target, and Iran's Ayatollah Khomeini's face was on the other, and just a few individuals hurled at the Ayatollah's.

The Alaska National Interest Lands Conservation Act (ANILCA) was passed by Congress in December 1980, expanding the extent of our national parks, tripling wilderness areas, and safeguarding twenty-five free-flowing streams. At the same time, we clarified ownership of remaining properties and opened all offshore regions and 95 percent of land areas to oil development, with the exception of the Alaska National Wildlife Refuge, which is a pristine area. After several decades, the ruling has gained traction throughout the state.

***

My final year in office was the most difficult and stressful of my life. Since November 4, 1979, American hostages have been held hostage by Iranian terrorists backed by Ayatollah Khomeini and his government. This crisis was critical to me, so I limited my travel and visited frequently with relatives of the captured ambassadors to give any information we had. During the first month, I warned the Ayatollah that if a hostage was hurt, Iran's access to the outside world would be cut off, and that if one was murdered, Iran would be attacked militarily. He took my warning seriously and was concerned about the safety of the Americans. When one of them appeared to have a paralyzed arm, he was swiftly released and returned to his home in Maine.

Our intention was to liberate the captives through negotiation, but we felt we needed to be prepared for other options. After roughly two months in captivity, we began strategizing how to free the hostages. In the American desert, our special troops practised and polished the method. The final plan was to fly seven large and long-range helicopters from an aircraft carrier to Desert One, an isolated location in the Iranian desert, where they would be refuelled by a C-130 plane. The rescue team would then fly into Tehran at night, use night-vision technology to overwhelm the captors with as little violence as possible, and the hostages and rescuers would helicopter to a neighbouring airport, where a huge passenger plane would land and deliver them to safety. Our regular space observations showed the captors' tendencies, so we knew who was on duty at any given time by the parked cars. A cook from Greece had been working in the embassy, and he told us where the hostages were and what they did on a daily basis. We needed six helicopters to haul out all of the hostages and the rescue crew, because anyone left behind would be executed. Everyone on my national security staff agreed to these measures after we examined and improved them in the White House's classified "situation room" sessions.

When the rescue squad had been trained, the desert landing site had been scouted by sending a small plane to land there, and the weather was favourable, so we were ready to go. When the Iranians failed to follow through on an agreement to transfer the hostages in early

April 1980, I gathered my advisers together and we resolved to proceed with the rescue effort on April 11. My final recommendation was to add another helicopter, giving us two more than we needed. Secretary Cy Vance and everyone else had helped us arrange the rescue procedure step by step. Cy, on the other hand, was on vacation when the final date was decided, and upon his return, he communicated his displeasure. I called another meeting to discuss the matter. He presented his concerns, we had a long discussion, and all other participants voted to go once more.

Everything went according to plan, except that one helicopter mysteriously returned to the aircraft carrier and another crashed in a sandstorm, leaving us with the required six at Desert One. Following refuelling, one of the helicopters veered on takeoff and collided with the C-130, injuring both and killing eight crew members. I was forced to tell the rescue squad to call it quits. After a few hours of sleep, I reported on television about a tragedy and a deep letdown.

After the initiative failed, Vance resigned from our government. Although Cy was closest to me in terms of overall policy toward peace and human rights, he was fiercely protective of the State Department and had threatened to resign three times before when he felt the White House staff wielded too much power or that I did not implement his recommendations. He said that he was opposed to the rescue attempt because it constituted an enormous risk of armed confrontation and loss of life, but I suspected that his resignation was the consequence of unresolved complaints. We kept in touch, and after leaving the White House, I spent several nights in New York City with the Vance family.

The unsuccessful rescue attempt had disastrous political ramifications for me. During the Democratic primary campaign, Senator Ted Kennedy made a serious challenge to me, and Ronald Reagan highlighted the matter extensively in the general election. Because I refrained from using military force to punish the Iranians, my failure to achieve the release of the hostages exposed me to their accusations that I was an inadequate leader.

While the international sanctions put on Iran as a result of their unlawful deed weakened them, they were invaded by Saddam Hussein's forces in Iraq. I hated the invasion because it hampered my efforts to liberate the hostages, but it also produced further issues because significant oil exports from both countries were cut off, resulting in rising oil prices and global inflation, as well as high interest rates.

***

During the hostage crisis, we dispatched a number of secret delegations into Iran, which was rather straightforward since Iranian leaders wanted to preserve as normal an environment as possible and loved all the favourable press that came from international news media visits. Ayatollah Khomeini himself granted personal interviews to American journalists. We had a few CIA spies in Tehran on one occasion who were travelling with fake German passports because many Iranian leaders had been schooled in Germany. As our group was leaving, one of our members had his credentials checked and was waived through by customs officers. However, he was called back, and the official stated, "Something is wrong with your passport." I've lived here for almost two decades, yet this is the first time I've seen a German document that used a middle initial rather than a full name. I don't understand why your name is Josef H. Schmidt." "Well, when I was born, my given middle name was Hitler, and I have special permission not to use it," the quick-thinking agent explained. The official approved his exit with a smile and a nod.

***

Many Republicans and some foreign officials criticised my

dedication to human rights as naive and a show of weakness. One of my main concerns was with Latin American military dictators and their ardent American allies in the commercial sector, as well as congressional lobbyists and key figures in the State Department and other sectors of our government. For centuries, the official US policy had been to defend these regimes against any challenge posed by their own citizenry, who were instantly labelled as Communists. For decades, US troops had been deployed in Latin America to defend our military partners, many of whom were graduates of the US Military Academy, spoke English, and sent their children to our country to be educated. They were frequently involved in profitable trading deals involving pineapples, bananas, bauxite, copper and iron ore, and other precious commodities.

Military juntas ruled Argentina, Bolivia, Brazil, Chile, Ecuador, El Salvador, Guatemala, Haiti, Honduras, Nicaragua, Panama, Paraguay, Peru, and Uruguay when I became president. I resolved to back peaceful movements toward freedom and democracy across the hemisphere. Furthermore, our government utilised its influence in financial institutions and public declarations to put extra pressure on the regimes that were most abusive to their own people, like Chile, Argentina, Paraguay, Nicaragua, and El Salvador. Rosalynn and I visited the region and met with religious and other leaders seeking peaceful political change, and we refused dictators' requests to defend their regimes from armed revolutionaries, the majority of whom were poor, indigenous Indians or descendants of former African slaves. All of the Latin American countries I mentioned above had become democracies within ten years, and The Carter Center had watched early elections in Panama, Nicaragua, Peru, Haiti, and Paraguay.

***

I had a varied group of senior advisers in the White House, State Department, Defense Department, and CIA, and I wanted to ensure that we were all on the same page. Most foreign policy decisions I made were never seriously hampered by Congress, but I saw the need to avoid misunderstandings and potential disagreements among my National Security team by gathering them on a regular basis. When I was in Washington, I started having breakfast meetings with Vice President Mondale, Secretary of Defense Brown, Secretary of State Vance, National Security Adviser Brzezinski, Hamilton Jordan, and occasionally Jody Powell and CIA Director Stansfield Turner. We went over an agenda that was made available to all of us ahead of time. Brzezinski took notes, recorded our joint decisions, and met with Brown and Vance the next week to ensure that my decisions were carried out. If cabinet officers were unable to attend, their deputies were occasionally included. This approach worked quite well for us, ensuring that we were working as a team and resolving challenges in the same manner. This is an unavoidable difficulty for American leaders, because prominent people in every department seek to make policy that impacts the rest of the globe, and this desired unity is not always realised.

***

After dealing with multiple natural disasters, I found that there were numerous federal entities responsible for dealing with local community catastrophes, with no effective method to coordinate their actions. In June 1978, I submitted to Congress a reorganisation plan to bring together the primary groups responsible for weather forecasting, federal housing assistance, crime control, insurance, and a variety of other federal, state, and local services. This process was completed about a year later by my Executive Order, which included a guarantee from me that the new Federal Emergency Management Agency would have a director who was competent and experienced, would have complete control over the disaster area, and would be adequately funded. The new body would also be tasked with coordinating the operations of our military forces, including National

Guard units if needed. Except for a setback during Hurricane Katrina on the Gulf Coast in 2005, when none of these pledges were met, FEMA has operated admirably.

Chapter 7: Back Home

When I was elected president, our agricultural supply business and farms were thriving, and I placed them in a blind trust, not allowing my trustee to even provide me annual reports. When I was about to leave the White House, I discovered that we had accumulated a very huge debt due to bad administration and three years of severe drought, with no commercial assets to pay it off. I was terrified we would lose our acreage and even our home, but Archer Daniels Midland Company decided to enter the peanut business and purchased Carter's Warehouse for nearly as much as we owed. We kept the farmland, which still grows peanuts, cotton, soybeans, grain, and pine trees. I gradually reduced my responsibilities as an active farmer, relying instead on partners or renters with modern equipment for planting, growing, and harvesting the crops. We continue to appreciate caring for the forest while talking with a qualified forester.

Before leaving Washington, I decided to write a memoir on my presidency. I glanced over the extensive journal notes I had dictated in the Oval Office and discovered that they were twenty-one volumes long and contained over a million words. My first year was spent reading them and writing down the most important events. Keeping Faith, the subsequent book, became a best-seller.

When we returned home, I had no idea what I was going to do with the rest of my life. I was fifty-six years old and one of the White House's younger survivors. Our first duty after unloading our goods in the garage was to add more storage space in our home. Rosalynn and I chose to construct a floor in our huge attic, which proved difficult because the roof trusses and joists were rough lumber that needed to be sanded and levelled as a preparatory step. This kept us occupied for the first two weeks, until I purchased a word processor and began writing my presidential memoir. It was nothing like current computers, but it was better than my small portable typewriter.

***

I received several offers to assume an academic job, either as president of a university or as a professor, and I eventually accepted an offer from Emory University to become a "distinguished professor." I was promised unlimited freedom of expression and that I would not be required to teach individual pupils for a semester or deal with their grades. My job was to give lectures to large and small groups of students on topics determined by me and the professors and deans. During the academic year, I lecture in a variety of schools and departments at Emory, including history, political science, environmental studies, theology, African-American studies, business, medicine, nursing, and law. Every September, I do a town hall meeting with thousands of students, where I address their unanticipated questions. So far, I have not avoided answering a question because it might be politically or personally controversial, and I adhere to the same philosophy in smaller-group presentations. In my academic capacity, I have enjoyed this independence, although I occasionally cause a brief flurry in the news media by commenting candidly about judgments made by public authorities in the United States or other countries.

Rosalynn and I spend at least a week each month in Atlanta, where I work on The Carter Center's affairs, meet with foreign leaders, have supper one night with about twenty-five family members in the area, have extended discussions on mutual interests with a few Emory professors and deans, and Rosalynn and I have breakfast with the university's president and spouse, as well as the CEO of The Carter Center.

***

My father was 59 years old when he died of pancreatic cancer, and my doctors at Emory University were concerned when, in 1983, my sister Ruth, 54, died of the same disease, and five years later, my brother Billy, 51, died of the same disease. The National Institutes of Health began routinely screening all members of our family, and my last surviving sibling, Gloria, 64, was diagnosed with pancreatic cancer and died in 1990. There was no record of another American family losing four members to this condition, so I've had regular X-rays, CAT scans, or blood analysis since then in the hopes of being detected early if I acquire the same symptoms. Cancer of the pancreas has frequently metastasized to other major organs by the time it is identified and is usually fatal within a few months. A worldwide investigation turned up a few other families like ours, and it is most likely that a genetic flaw is at work, possibly triggered by cigarette smoking. Being the lone nonsmoker in my family could have contributed to my longevity.

***

My most difficult task was to secure approximately $25 million in private contributions to construct a presidential library. This endeavour was challenging and time-consuming for me as a failed Democratic candidate with no chance of returning to public office and few rich friends or supporters. I ultimately decided to start building using the architectural drawings we had approved and go into debt for the remaining funds. I didn't just want to construct a museum or keep my White House archives and mementos; I wanted a place where we could work.

I awoke after a few hours of sleep one night and contacted Rosalynn, saying, "I know what we can do for the future." We may set up a location in Atlanta near our presidential library and museum and welcome people to visit, much as Anwar Sadat and Menachem Begin did at Camp David. I am available to serve as a mediator to assist prevent or resolve conflicts inside or between nations. I can travel to their country if they wish." The Carter Center was born in this manner. We broadened my vision for our Center by hosting conferences on critical problems in which I had been involved as president, such as Middle East peace, international security and arms control, business and the environment, education, and global health. We legally founded The Carter Center in 1982, working with Emory, and for the following five years I spent much of my time soliciting funds from individual contributors to pay for the presidential library, as well as accompanying structures to house the Center's operations. Emory gave me an office on the top floor of their library, and I began to formulate more detailed plans with the assistance of Dr. Steven Hochman, who would be my only assistant for the next year or two.

We established a few fundamental principles: Our Center would be nonpartisan; we would be as innovative as possible, not duplicating or competing with existing groups that were successfully addressing issues; we would not be frightened of failure if our goals were good; and we would always operate with a balanced budget. The Carter Center expanded its operations into eighty countries, promoting peace, human rights, democracy, and freedom, as well as better health care. We now have a $100 million annual financial budget, with an equal amount of in-kind contributions of medications and other supplies provided in our health projects, particularly in Africa and Latin America. Our regular staff of 180 is occasionally reinforced by several hundred skilled professionals on our payroll, as well as thousands of unpaid volunteers whom we train to work on our projects in target nations. We have stayed true to our founding values and achieved our objectives over the last three decades, and I am still at Emory University.

***

The most unexpected outcome has been that global health has become our most important commitment, including the majority of our workers and spending. We focus on malaria as well as five "neglected tropical diseases" that are no longer recognized in the developed world but continue to affect hundreds of millions of people in Africa and Latin America: onchocerciasis (river blindness), schistosomiasis, lymphatic filariasis (elephantiasis), trachoma, and dracunculiasis (guinea worm).

In the early stages of a project, I would travel to a country and meet with the president, prime minister, and ministers of health, transportation, education, and agriculture. I would notify them of our intentions, define what was required of them, and we would sign a "memorandum of understanding" outlining our shared duties. Our health programs are now well-known and respected throughout Africa, as well as in the Latin American and Caribbean regions where we work. Whenever I meet with groups of international students at Emory University, I am thanked for our contributions to health in the students' home countries. We offer the locals as much credit as possible for their efforts. I spend a lot of my time at celebrations, commemorating the accomplishments of hardworking local health workers and volunteers. Our Carter Center personnel, together with those we train, travel to the most isolated settlements in the jungle and desert to explain our goals, recruit volunteers, and train them, as well as a few paid supervisors. Then we distribute donated medicines, water filtration cloths, and insecticide-treated bed nets and ensure that individuals understand how to use these items appropriately. Every year, we treat around 35 million people. Over half of these are now for river blindness, and we have been able to eliminate the illness in four indigenous Latin American countries and demonstrate in Uganda and Sudan that the same aim can be achieved in Africa. In 1986, an estimated 3.5 million cases of guinea worm were found in around 26,000 villages across twenty nations. In 2014, there were less than 130 cases worldwide. We hope that this disease will be the second in history to be eradicated from all nations. (The last known case of smallpox occurred in 1977.)

We are responsible for over one-third of the world's trachoma surgeries, the leading cause of blindness other than cataracts, and have helped build more than 3 million latrines to lower the population of flies that carry the disease. In Ethiopia and Nigeria, where malaria occurs, we assisted in the installation of two bed nets in each home. The mosquito nets have been sprayed with a pesticide that kills them on contact. Malaria and lymphatic filariasis are transmitted by these insects. One of our most recent efforts is to eradicate the two illnesses from the Caribbean island of Hispaniola, and the governments of Haiti and the Dominican Republic, which are not always friendly, are working together to achieve this aim.

Our Center's one-of-a-kind International Task Force for Disease Eradication has taken on the ongoing mission of examining every human ailment to decide which ones may be eliminated from a specific region or country, or eradicated entirely.

***

In 1985, Nobel Laureate Norman Borlaug, Japanese benefactor Ryoichi Sasakawa, and I met in Geneva, Switzerland, and decided to launch Global 2000, an agricultural program aimed at increasing food grain production in a number of African countries. We started our effort in Ghana, Sudan, Zambia, and Zimbabwe and finally taught 8 million African families how to increase or triple their production of maize (corn), wheat, rice, sorghum, and millet. We taught them how to use the best seed, plant in contoured rows to minimise erosion, use necessary fertiliser, control weeds, harvest at the right time, and store and market crops properly using Japanese funding, Dr. Borlaug's knowledge of agronomy, and our help with organisation and implementation. We normally started with forty farmers in a country as demonstrators and grew to approximately sixteen thousand in three years. In Ethiopia, the number of farms implementing our simple but productive agricultural practices reached several hundred thousand, thanks to Prime Minister Meles

Zenawi's government funding. I would travel with Borlaug to verify compliance with our instructions after meeting with national leaders to finalise agreements on how we would share responsibility.

I was resting in a Western-style hotel in Addis Ababa when I was awakened by extreme itching in my left knee. I walked into the bathroom and noticed two little perforations, rubbed some ointment on them, then returned to bed and fell asleep. The next day, Dr. Borlaug and I drove about 150 kilometres south to see some farm plots, slept the night, and returned to Addis with my knee inflamed. I went to the US embassy, where a doctor handed me antibiotic medications to consume. He put me to bed with an IV after my entire leg swelled to nearly twice its normal size. The following morning, he determined that my life was in danger and arranged for me to be transferred to a U.S. military hospital in Wiesbaden, Germany. The doctors there raised the strength of the medication, determined the probable kind of spider based on the puncture scars, and returned me to Atlanta. My body was covered in a rash by that point, and I was admitted to Emory University Hospital for five days as a team of doctors tried various treatments to minimise the swelling and acute itching. I gradually recovered, but I still have an exacerbating rash that requires daily treatment with prescription salves and lotions. According to dermatologists, the condition is permanent but managed.

***

Although The Carter Center and I have collaborated on conflict resolution efforts with the United Nations and the United States, we have mostly dealt with dangerous circumstances on our own. These options are not always popular because they expose us to undesirable persons or groups. Maoists in Nepal, Communist dictator Mengistu Haile Mariam in Ethiopia, Mobutu Sese Seko in Zaire (now the Democratic Republic of Congo), Radovan Karadi in Bosnia and Slobodan Miloevi in Serbia, Kim Il Sung and his successors in North

Korea, the Castro brothers in Cuba, Omar al-Bashir in Sudan, and Hamas leaders in Gaza and elsewhere have been among them. On every occasion, we keep American officials up to date on our goals and the outcomes of our efforts.

On behalf of The Carter Center, I have addressed various dangers to peace. Let me use some events from 1994 as examples. For three years, North Korean President Kim Il Sung had asked me to come to Pyongyang to assist resolve some of the tensions between him and the US administration, but I had an initial objection to accepting his request because of the Korean War. I was eventually persuaded that my skills could be useful, but my standard requests to the White House for permission to visit North Korea were denied.

In the spring of 1994, there was a crisis. North Korea renounced their commitment to the Nonproliferation Treaty, kicked foreign inspectors out of their nuclear site, and began converting spent uranium rods into plutonium. The US government declined to negotiate with North Korea and instead petitioned the UN Security Council for a condemnatory resolution. Some Chinese acquaintances informed me that if their government was labelled an international outlaw and their revered leader a criminal, North Korea would launch an attack on South Korea. I chose to leave after devising a strategy that I was confident would defuse the problem. When President Bill Clinton turned down another request to sanction my trip to Pyongyang, I wrote to him to tell him I was going anyway. Vice President Al Gore intercepted my message and persuaded me to change the phrasing. He then transmitted the message to Clinton, who was in Europe, who approved it. My one request to Kim Il Sung was that we bypass Beijing and enter North Korea directly from South Korea. He answered that even the UN Secretary-General passed through China, but he eventually relented. Rosalynn and I became the first people in 43 years to go directly from Seoul to Pyongyang over the Demilitarized Zone.

I was able to discuss the difficulties adequately due to my expertise in nuclear engineering. Kim Il Sung was pleasant and surprisingly knowledgeable about all of the issues we discussed. During a long boat ride from Pyongyang to the sea, we reached a dozen important agreements, including the nuclear issue and the return of international inspectors, summit talks with South Korea, troop withdrawal from the DMZ, and the recovery of the remains of buried Americans.

I informed the White House of these agreements. Kim Il Sung died soon after I arrived, and I received a message from his son, Kim Jong Il, promising to keep his father's promises. Official talks in Geneva resulted in both parties' ratification of what we had agreed, and Secretary of State Madeleine Albright visited Pyongyang in October 2000 to reinforce mutual pledges. President George W. Bush disavowed the US-North Korea deal in 2002, calling North Korea an "evil empire," and since then, Kim Il Sung's successors have expanded their development of nuclear weapons and long-range missiles. The US currently avoids practically all interaction with North Korea, and tough economic sanctions continue to be placed on the often-hungry population.

Later that year, in 1994, Haiti experienced an emergency. Jean-Bertrand Aristide, the elected leader, had been pushed into exile in 1991. He was replaced by General Raoul Cédras, and both leaders asked me to act as a go-between. I knew a lot about Haiti and had a long-standing personal relationship with both men. For years, Presidents Bush and Clinton wanted to attempt different methods of restoring Aristide's power, but none of them worked. By September 1994, President Clinton had chosen to deploy 30,000 American troops as an invasion force. Meanwhile, I had encouraged former Georgia Senator Sam Nunn and General Colin Powell to join me in a peace endeavour, and we had proposed it to President Clinton. He agreed to our proposal to go to Haiti and try one last time to negotiate before sending in the military.

We talked for two days with the gathering generals in Port-au-Prince, and Cédras was hesitant to accept any of my offers. "I have been informed that Cédras's wife, Yannick, is extremely influential," Rosalynn stated when I called to tell her about our failure. Why not approach her?" I followed her advice, and the general's wife was truly the key to his changed demeanour. We recognized Cédras to be a capable and outstanding leader. He had been Haiti's universally renowned military leader, who had kept security in place while Rosalynn and I led Carter Center monitors who had supervised Aristide's previous election, and he had protected Aristide from an assassination attempt when he was removed.

Cédras was finally willing to accept our offers, ready to stand beside the American general and welcome US forces if their entrance was calm and Haitian military men were handled with dignity. I pledged to find him and his family a suitable spot to live in another nation. At this apparent point of agreement, one of his subordinates, Brigadier General Philippe Biamby, hurried in and said that President Clinton had sent fifty-two planes loaded with paratroopers from US military sites on their way to invade Haiti. Biamby had gotten this information from a Haitian who worked at Fort Bragg in North Carolina. Thousands of irate protesters surrounded the building where we were gathering at the time.

Both negotiating teams dashed out a back door and drove to the president's office, which was occupied by Emile Jonassaint, an elderly former chief justice. General Powell dialled a phone number and eventually connected to the White House, while Cédras and I presented the president with our signed agreement. "I understand and agree," he remarked after reading it, "but it will have to be translated into French before I sign it." This was completed quickly, and both he and I signed the document. The American planes were halfway to Haiti at this point, but Clinton ordered them to return to their base, and the situation was over. General Cédras and his family relocated to Panama as arranged. Aristide returned to Haiti and proved to be a disastrous leader, forcing him into exile in Africa once more, this time under duress from Washington.

My final assignment as a mediator that year was to mediate the Bosnian-Herzegovina war with Serbia, following the country's declaration of independence from Serbian-controlled Yugoslavia. Radovan Karadi initially contacted me, expressing a wish to amicably resolve issues between the Bosnian Serbs, whom he led, and the Bosnian Muslims and Croats, the two other major ethnic groupings. If I agreed to come to Sarajevo, he offered a series of promises about peace, human rights, and a complete cease-fire. I told President Clinton and UN Secretary-General Boutros Boutros-Ghali about the expedition and received their assent. I had Karadi repeat all of his commitments on CNN. Slobodan Miloevi, the president of Serbia, requested that I meet with him on my tour, and I accepted. My objectives were to arrange a cease-fire with human rights guarantees and a clear demarcation of geographical control, as well as to explore some crucial constitutional concerns.

On December 18, I met with Croatian President Franjo Tudjman in Zagreb, who backed the mission, and then flew to Sarajevo, donning and sitting on flak jackets since snipers were firing from both sides. I was grateful for Karadi's commitment not to attack me during my visit. I had a lengthy conversation with Alija Izetbegovi, the president of Bosnia and Herzegovina, which was seeking independence from Serbia and whose small territory was encircled by Serbian armies on three sides. He supported my assignment but stipulated that any cease-fire be limited to three months. I awakened early the next morning, scribbled out my most hopeful offers, and then Rosalynn and I drove nearly two hours to Pale, a distance of only nine miles via a gorgeous mountain area that hosted ski racing competitions during the 1984 Winter Olympics. There seemed to be a military roadblock around every bend in the road. Karadi visited us, joined by prominent Serb authorities, including Army Chief of Staff General Ratko Mladi, and they gave me a formal welcome in front of a big news media contingent. In our private talks with Karadi, he insisted on a twelve-month cease-fire, which I eventually reduced to four months in order to please Izetbegovic. I agreed to propose that the United States and the United Nations withdraw economic sanctions against Serbia, but I could not guarantee any favourable results.

Karadi and Mladi signed my document in front of me. Its basic terms were a cessation of hostilities on December 27, 1994, UN forces stationed along the front lines for four months or longer if mutually agreed upon, both parties negotiating a comprehensive peace agreement, unrestricted movement of relief convoys, unhindered use of Sarajevo's airport, and protection of human rights. The White House was delighted with the draft accord but insisted on Izetbegovi's approval. When I contacted Sarajevo to inform him that all of his conditions had been met, he refused to speak with me.

We drove back to Sarajevo and reviewed the difficulties with Vice President Ejup Gani before returning to Pale the next morning with a few minor changes. After numerous heated debates with his subordinates, Karadi consented to a final statement that now had the approval of Izetbegovi, Karadi, Mladi, the US, and the UN. We arrived in Sarajevo and boarded our jet, which was protected from ground fire by a massive UN truck. Four bullets had gone through the left side of the prior plane. We took off wearing our flak jackets, but I also wrapped an extra one around my hard disk, paperwork, and signed documents.

We met with Serbian President Slobodan Miloevi in Belgrade after passing through Zagreb, who, like everyone I met, had to first narrate a history of the region. I was relieved that he began with World War I rather than the eleventh century. I handed him a copy of the agreement, which he endorsed, but he was harsh in his criticism of Karadi, his rival for Serbian leadership. I continually asked him what it would take for them to reconcile, and he finally responded that if the parliament voted for the "Carter Plan," that would suffice.

The cease-fire went into force the following week and lasted four months before being terminated. When the conflict flared up again, the international community backed Bosnia and Herzegovina while condemning Serbia. Both sides committed war crimes, the Serbs most heinously, and NATO sent sixty thousand troops and launched more than 3,300 bombing flights against Serbian forces, largely with American planes. In December 1995, Miloevi, Izetbegovi, and Tudjman signed another more permanent cease-fire in Dayton, Ohio. The International Criminal Court charged Miloevi, Karadi, and Mladi with war crimes after they surrendered defeat. Miloevi was arrested in 2001, and his trial lasted five years, until he died in 2006. Karadi was arrested in 2008, and Mladi was arrested in 2011, and both are currently on trial for war crimes. I've often wondered what would have happened if the international community had truly supported the basic conditions of the 1994 cease-fire agreement.

***

Since becoming president, one of my top foreign policy priorities has been to bring peace to Israel, which inevitably entails peace for the Palestinians and its neighbours. This became a crucial commitment for The Carter Center, which has full-time offices in Jerusalem, Ramallah, and Gaza and has been monitoring the three Palestinian elections. The first election took place in 1996, when Yasir Arafat was elected president and members of the Palestine National Authority were appointed. Following Arafat's death, Mahmoud Abbas was elected president in 2005, and another election was held in January 2006 to select new members of parliament. Fatah, the Abbas party, and Israel all opposed the election since Hamas candidates were expected to win up to 35% of parliamentary seats.

However, the US insisted on holding the already late election. The issue with Hamas was that it had not agreed to the terms of the Oslo Agreement, which established the Palestinian Authority.

It was a fair election, and Hamas fared far better than predicted, taking 74 of the 132 seats. Doctors, lawyers, educators, business executives, and past local officeholders were among those elected. I delivered a plea from Hamas to President Abbas to stay in office and assign Fatah members to some of the most important cabinet positions. While eager to stay in power, Abbas refused to include Hamas in a unity administration. I returned to Plains, changed my clothes, and flew back to London to attend a conference of the International Quartet, which included the US, the UN, the European Union, and Russia. They permitted me to make a brief appeal in support of the election results before voting without debate to invalidate them by imposing demands that Hamas would not accept. Nonetheless, President Abbas accepted a Hamas-nominated cabinet in March, and there was movement toward a unity administration during the summer. Eight Hamas cabinet members and twenty members of parliament who lived in the West Bank and East Jerusalem were detained by Israel, and several of these leaders were imprisoned for several years.

I wrote a book that evaluated the situation in the Occupied Territories and outlined a feasible strategy for comprehensive peace in the region that was compatible with long-standing official US and UN policies. Without a "two-state" agreement with the Palestinians, Israel would inevitably resort to a one-state solution, according to Palestine Peace Not Apartheid. This was a potentially disastrous scenario, according to Israeli prime ministers. With Israeli control over the land from the Jordan River to the Mediterranean Sea, Israel would have to either grant Palestinians equal voting rights and eventually relinquish Jewish control of government affairs, or treat non-Jews as second-class citizens with no equal rights. My book was slammed by the pro-Israel lobby, AIPAC (American Israel Public Affairs Committee), and a number of notable political figures, principally because of its title, in which I avoided mentioning Israel. Within a few days of its publication, I got 6,100 responses, the vast majority of which supported my stance, with many authors identifying as Jewish. Despite my efforts at book signings and other public occasions to reaffirm my long standing support for Israel and her security, this incident has been excruciatingly unpleasant for me. The book tour was turned into a feature-length film, *Jimmy Carter: Man from Plains*, directed by Jonathan Demme.

The political consequences have not subsided. When the Democratic National Convention convened in 2008 to select Barack Obama, I planned to attend and deliver a speech, as is usual for previous presidents. I was approached by his advisers, who informed me that neither Bill Clinton nor I would be speaking, but that we would be making twenty-minute documentary films to be presented to the delegates, with each film structured to be most helpful to the current contender. They wanted me to go to New Orleans and the Gulf Coast, where Rosalynn and I had built Habitat houses in the aftermath of Hurricane Katrina, and show how Republican leaders had failed to respond appropriately to the disaster. I spent a day in the area to complete this project, but when we got to the conference in Denver, I was told that the film would only be four minutes long and that I would not be allowed to speak, even to meet the delegates. (Clinton and his wife, Hillary, were key figures in the convention.) Obama's top assistant, David Axelrod, indicated that the president did not want to jeopardise his Jewish supporters. Unfortunately, this "estrangement" has endured during his presidency, but our Centre has continued to support US and international policy and to promote the Middle East peace process in every manner we can.

From 2010 to 2012, the Carter Center watched Egypt's parliamentary and presidential elections following the fall of President Hosni

Mubarak. I was in charge of our group of observers. During my conversations with candidate and then-President Mohamed Morsi, I urged him to fulfil all of the parameters of the Egypt-Israel peace deal that I negotiated in 1979 and that both countries have faithfully followed. During his tenure in office, he kept this promise.

When Rosalynn and I visited Washington in January 2013 to attend President Barack Obama's inauguration, John Kerry and his wife, Teresa, came to our hotel room and spent two hours that morning discussing his ambitions as the prospective Secretary of State. He told us that he would make every effort to reach a compromise between Israel and the Palestinians, and that President Obama will visit the Holy Land early in his next term. Secretary Kerry has done everything possible to achieve this goal. For months, there had been anticipation that the United States would submit a concrete plan based on international law and our country's long-standing policies, and that this public proposal would be examined by the disputants and the international community. It would be difficult for either the Palestinian or Israeli leaders to reject this all-out effort with President Obama fully involved. These hopes have not been realised in the absence of overt White House help and direct involvement by the president. The critical connections between Israel, the Palestinians, and the US have deteriorated, and the Palestinians are now attempting to refer the conflict to the United Nations.

***

In my mediation of civil disputes, I quickly discovered that opposing military leaders would refuse to negotiate even through an intermediary, so I decided to depend on the assumption of "political self-delusion" that motivates practically all candidates who believe they will be chosen. I began by proposing an open election, overseen by The Carter Center, and encouraging both opponents to convince themselves that they would be the victor. Following this method, we began monitoring elections in Latin America and were soon invited to work in countries all over the world. Our role is to assist nations in developing democratic societies through citizen empowerment. We are also pioneers in raising election standards. Our standard procedure is to deploy four to six long-term observers into a nation for a prolonged length of time before an election to study everything they can about the country's history, geography, government, and politics, as well as to become acquainted with political parties, candidates, and issues. They evaluate voter registration as well as the central election commission's integrity and competence. We deploy between forty and eighty short-term observers several days before the election, and they receive a crash course from the long-term observers before being dispersed to key voting districts in pairs, each with an automobile and driver, an interpreter if needed, and a radio or cell phone. We go to as many polling places as possible, and the observer teams report back to me, Rosalynn, or our other leaders in the capital city.

The Carter Center has created a handheld electronic tablet, similar to a Kindle, that allows each observer to provide real-time updates on the situation at each location. The equipment is known as ELMO (election monitor). We make a pronouncement regarding whether the election process was fair and free, appropriately representing the will of the people who voted, after we consolidate and review information from all observers. The presidential election in Tunisia in December 2014 was the ninety-ninth we had observed, and we usually finish three or four of these projects each year.

***

Our involvement with Habitat for Humanity has been challenging, unpredictable, thrilling, and rewarding. Rosalynn and I have led volunteer groups for a whole week of hard labour, building and refurbishing homes for low-income families who have never had a good place to live. Families are forced to pay the full purchase price for the houses over a twenty-year period with no interest charges, and payments are invariably less than rental costs in the same broad neighbourhoods. Families are also asked to put in hundreds of hours of work on their own or neighbouring homes. This has allowed us to work with these ambitious and industrious individuals, understand their struggle, and treat them as equals.

About a year in advance, Habitat leaders and I agree on the site location and general design of the homes, and we try to simplify the proposed plans. Our typical project consists of roughly a hundred dwellings, and the goal is to finish construction in five days, commencing on a Monday with only the foundation in place. To accommodate this schedule, we alter the number of the work crews, which range from twelve to thirty-five individuals depending on the size of the dwellings and the type of construction. We have completed projects in many American states as well as in Hungary, South Africa, three cities in Mexico, South Korea, Canada, the Philippines, Haiti, China, Vietnam, Laos, Thailand, Cambodia, and South Korea (including in the Demilitarized Zone). In 2015, we intend to construct 100 homes in Pokhara, Nepal.

***

I discovered that I enjoyed writing after authoring Why Not the Best? in 1974-75 for use in my presidential campaign and Keeping Faith: Memoirs of a President in 1981-82 to explain aspects of my leadership. My novels have done well in the market and have offered a much-needed source of money for my family. An unexpected bonus has been the opportunity to convey my political ideas and describe our work at The Carter Center. Talk shows and interviews on television, radio, and in newspapers have given me far more possibilities than teaching at Emory University or giving public speeches on occasion.

My next major project, The Blood of Abraham, was published in 1985 and was based on my extensive travel in the Middle East, where I met with key leaders, took careful notes on their personal perspectives on the prospect of a comprehensive peace, and compiled this information from Israel, Egypt, Lebanon, Jordan, Syria, Saudi Arabia, and the Palestinians.

In 1984, we held a large consultation at The Carter Center called Closing the Gap. This looked at the gap between what medical experts and individuals knew how to perform and what they really accomplished. Following that, Rosalynn and I decided to coauthor a book, Everything to Gain, concentrating on personal health and how a person's own habits and success or failure in embracing universally accepted health information were frequently the determining factors. Writing this book together turned out to be the most serious challenge to our marriage we'd ever faced. We split up the chapters, and each was responsible for writing the content and submitting it to the other for editing. Rosalynn considered my chapters as rough drafts because I write quickly. She writes slowly and deliberately, and she considers the final sentences as if they were etched into stone on Mount Sinai. It hurts her to see them changed in any manner. Another distinction was that we did not always remember or treat experiences in the same manner. We were always arguing and could only converse via scathing emails. When we decided to quit the project and return the advance money to the publisher, our editor came to Plains and suggested that he divide the contentious paragraphs between us—as unilateral authors with no participation from the other. Each of these paragraphs is labelled in the book by a "J" or a "R," and our marriage survived.

My second book, which came out in 1988, was a labour of love. An Outdoor Journal chronicled my encounters with nature, beginning with my childhood on our farm and extending to trout streams and mountains in Alaska, Argentina, Japan, and Nepal. In 1992, my first political attempt was chronicled in Turning Point, when an election was taken from me by a dishonest official who packed the ballot box, voted dead persons, and browbeat other local officials. That same year, Dutton asked me to develop a book that could be used as a textbook regarding conflict causes and resolution approaches. To illustrate the arguments I made in Talking Peace: A Vision for the Next Generation, I used some of my own experiences.

Soon after leaving the White House, I met Miller Williams and other Arkansas poets, who urged me to prepare some of my poems for publication. I worked on this for several years, and Always a Reckoning was released in 1995. My poetry advisers were harsh critics of my submitted lines, but we agreed that they could not make precise word or phrase suggestions. The book's success has shocked both the publisher and me.

Amy, my daughter, enrolled in the Memphis College of Art in 1994, and one of her tasks was to illustrate a children's story. As a submarine officer with small boys at home, I made up stories about an imagined sea creature named Little Baby Snoogle-Fleejer, which I told them after returning from sea cruises. Amy painted thirteen scenes in the book, and I wrote one of the stories as a narrative.

Every Sunday, I taught Bible lessons at my local church and decided to write about my religious beliefs and experiences in two books, Living Faith and Sources of Strength, which were released in 1996 and 1997, respectively.

By 1998, I was approaching my seventieth birthday, and reflecting how wonderful and fulfilling my experiences had been since my "retirement" from politics, I decided to publish The Virtues of Aging. Some remarked that it would be the shortest book ever written. The book has been fairly popular, describing how much unprecedented flexibility we have to embark on new initiatives once we are no longer required to adhere to a normal work schedule.

After having groups of black and white older folks come to our home to share their own recollections of Christmas in Plains, I finished another book in 2001 that focused on how we spent Christmas over the years of my childhood.

I decided to write a book about my childhood on a farm, where practically all of our neighbours were African-American, and I was thrilled when it was named a Pulitzer Prize finalist in 2002. An Hour Before Daylight has elicited more written and vocal comments than any of my other novels, particularly from people who grew up as farm children, whether in America or elsewhere.

I earned the Nobel Peace Prize in 2002 and shared my acceptance speech with Simon & Schuster ahead of time so that the compact book could be released at the same time as the award. This book has sold more copies than any other I've published because of the content and the inexpensive price.

I was always concerned about the scarcity of history books or historical novels that provided a balanced and factual portrayal of significant military battles during the Revolutionary War. Knowing my own relatives' histories, I spent seven years conducting comprehensive research, using personal testimonies of individuals in the American and British military services. This was before Google, and I could have dozens of library books on my shelf at once. Readers from all over the world have expressed their astonishment and delight at this view from the Southland, where practically all of the main conflicts took place.

Many people questioned Rosalynn and me if we worked all the time or if we ever had time for fun and leisure, so in 2004 I authored Sharing Good Times. I mentioned the many activities we tried for the first time as adults, such as downhill skiing, mountain climbing, bird viewing, and fly-fishing in various locations.

I was particularly concerned about some of our government's policies and wanted a public forum to discuss them, so I wrote Our Endangered Values in 2005 to express my views on unnecessary wars, derogation of women and girls, excessive incarceration and the death penalty, unwarranted invasion of citizens' privacy, the rise of fundamentalism in government, and the intrusion of religion and excessive money into politics. It criticised various federal government policies as well as worrying violations of the Universal Declaration of Human Rights, the Geneva principles of warfare, and other international standards that we claim to uphold.

My most controversial book, Palestine Peace Not Apartheid, was published in 2006, not because of its substance, but because of its title. Beyond the White House, a book on the work we did at The Carter Center, was published the following year. In 2008, I published a book on my mother, who, at the age of seventy, was a registered nurse, a dedicated political activist, and a Peace Corps volunteer in India. When I was growing up in the Deep South, she never observed the notion of white supremacy, which helped define my devotion to the protection of human rights.

We Can Have Peace in the Holy Land was published in 2009, and it suggested a precise strategy for peace between Israel and its neighbours.

I created a fairly comprehensive volume of highly personal remarks from my daily diary while serving as president. Published in 2010, White House Diary includes many insights that were too delicate or intimate to put in Keeping Faith some decades earlier.

By 2011, I had taught over 600 Bible classes, which I had captured in audio and video format and kept in a refrigerator in my presidential library. I chose 366 of them, and each tape was summarised by a Zondervan editor. For Through the Year with Jimmy Carter, I cut them down to page-length versions with a religious statement for each day. I also contributed over 200 remarks to a New International Version of the scriptures titled NIV Lessons from Life Bible: Personal Reflections with Jimmy Carter, which was published in 2012.

My most recent book, A Call to Action: Women, Religion, Violence, and Power (2014), is the most important, in my opinion. We have hosted two Human Rights Defenders Forums on the subject at The Carter Center, and a third will be held before the publication of this book. In my book, I detailed the horrifying abuse of women and girls that occurs in practically every country and presented twenty-three recommendations for action that might be taken to ameliorate this violence.

Writing and promoting the sale of these books has allowed me to study a wide range of subjects in depth, analyse what I've learned, and offer my findings to the general public in America and many other nations. This has also given me the best possibilities for media interviews and answering questions from students and those who attend my seminars. As I write this in November 2014, I have recently delivered speeches to overflow crowds at the John F. Kennedy Presidential Library, to ten thousand members of the American Academy of Religion in San Diego, to a larger assembly sponsored by the Islamic Society of North America in Denver, and to students and faculty at Harvard Divinity School, Yale, and Princeton. All institutions are grappling with allegations of excessive sexual assaults on campus, with rapists operating with relative impunity. I summarised A Call to Action, addressed audience questions, and then autographed copies of the book.

Since leaving the White House, the books I've authored have provided the majority of my family's income. Although my time in Plains is limited due to active involvement in The Carter Center, Emory University, and Habitat for Humanity issues, I try to make the most of my days at home. I visit our fields on a regular basis, consult with our forester and the row crop farmers, and handle normal housekeeping. Every Sunday when I am at home, I give Bible classes, and Rosalynn and I are involved in local community issues. On a somewhat free day, I get up early and spend as much time as possible writing on the computer. When I'm tired of writing paragraphs and staring at the screen, I go out to my workshop and design and create furniture or paint images.

***

I discovered a great wood shop at Camp David, which I used frequently on weekends, usually to produce small objects as gifts for friends and family members. Many people were aware of my passion, and my farewell gift from the White House staff and cabinet members was an order to Sears, Roebuck for all the power tools required to construct furniture. I installed the equipment in our former garage because we no longer owned an automobile, and throughout the past 35 years I have updated the lathes, jointers, drill presses, planers, and various saws as needed. I also have a complete collection of hand tools that I purchased in different nations, particularly Japan.

During our first year at home, I limited my travel to a transition office in Atlanta, where our presidential library and The Carter Center were being planned. Our house and property had deteriorated significantly over our four years in Washington, giving us much to do. We bought half of twenty-one acres in the North Georgia highlands and erected a little wood cabin beside Turniptown Creek. I planned and built all of the beds, chairs, tables, storage cabinets, and other small fixtures for our "second home." I created green wood stools and dining room chairs using Colonial-era techniques that used just hand tools and no nails, screws, or glue to hold the pieces together. In October 1983, four ladder-back hickory chairs were auctioned off at Sotheby's for $21,000 each to help fund The Carter Center.

This started a lengthy trend of me donating a piece of furniture to our Centre to be auctioned off practically every year. In subsequent years, I have donated either an original or a copy of one of my paintings for the same purpose. Bids ranging from $50,000 to $1 million have been accepted. Furthermore, I have donated much of my furniture to my children and grandchildren, with cradles being used multiple times. Many years ago, I understood that I have no exceptional aptitude as an artist or craftsman, but with a lot of study and effort, I have become quite proficient. More recently, I wrote an explanation of techniques and materials used, as well as my reasons for painting specific subjects, and these texts will accompany approximately sixty-five of my paintings in a high-quality coffee table book, with proceeds benefiting The Carter Center.

Woodworking and art have been particular delights for me, and I anticipate that they will take up a larger portion of my time as I get older and have fewer interests away from home.

**

When I was elected, Richard Nixon and Gerald Ford were the two living presidents, and I was resolved to treat them with respect, to keep them as up to date on current events as possible, and to call on them to assist me with difficult matters that required bipartisan cooperation. As a result of the Watergate events and his forced resignation, President Nixon was in a position of partial dishonour, and he maintained a high level of family secrecy. I appreciated him for his achievements while in government, particularly on environmental concerns and his efforts to improve relations with China. From our fought race, I knew President Ford to be a fierce political competitor, exceptionally informed about legislative matters, and a thoroughly honourable and dedicated public worker.

I started giving them both regular briefings on internal and international matters, either from National Security Adviser

Brzezinski or one of my other senior assistants. They responded by offering to assist me with contentious matters, which they continued to do during my time. On March 24, 1977, I made the following entry in my diary:

"President Ford arrived, and our thirty-minute meeting lasted three times as long." I share his concerns about budget imbalances. He also met with Dr. Brzezinski and arranged for regular briefings on world events."

After roughly six months, Nixon informed me that the briefings were excessive and that they should only be presented when he needed additional information on certain themes. President Ford enjoyed the visits, and we agreed that anytime he was in the area, he would spend some time with me in the Oval Office.

When Anwar Sadat was assassinated by militant terrorists in October 1981, President Reagan and Vice President George H. W. Bush chose not to attend his funeral. Instead, we three past presidents were honoured and flown to Cairo on a government plane. Nixon remained in the area, so Ford and I returned together. We shared a small compartment and spent the majority of the ride talking in an increasingly personal manner. Surprisingly, we developed an intense connection that extended to our wives and children. When we gathered in the White House in 2000 to commemorate the White House's 200th anniversary as the president's residence, historians remarked that the relationship between Jerry Ford and Jimmy Carter was closer than any other president, at least in recent history, who had served there. During the summer of 2006, I had a routine phone call from Jerry, and after exchanging greetings, he said he had a particular favour to ask of me. I agreed ahead of time. He requested that I deliver the eulogy at his funeral. After a few moments of stammering, I responded that I would do so if he would make the same commitment. I was saddened yet honoured to fulfil my pledge a few months later.

Unfortunately, my relationship with President Ronald Reagan was fragile, and on several early journeys abroad during his presidency, I learnt that US ambassadors had been told not to assist me or even acknowledge my presence. This occurred in Turkey, Argentina, and a number of African countries. My initial requests to the president for briefings on major topics were turned down or disregarded, and when I threatened to convene a press conference on the subject, I received a briefing that was entirely based on current news reports. I did, however, get along well with Reagan's five national security advisers, as well as Secretary of State George Shultz. During my repeated trips to the Middle East, I was frequently asked to deliver messages or queries to leaders and was also called to come to the State Department to provide a personal report on my observations.

My best and most delightful presidential encounters were with George H. W. Bush and his secretary of state, James Baker. Throughout their tenure, they made the best use of our Center's resources, encouraged our involvement in politically delicate areas, and even dispatched an aircraft to fly me right to the White House following several of my international visits for a report.

President Bill Clinton never requested collaboration with The Carter Center, but he did reply to several of my offers. I valued these possibilities for us to help reduce international tensions by accepting requests to resolve conflicts from disputing parties.

We decided to attend the January inaugural ceremonies after the contentious election in 2000, in which the Supreme Court blocked a recount of all Florida votes and ruled that George W. Bush was the elected president. There were few "voluntary" Democrats present, and the Bush family was cordial to us. The new President Bush asked if there was anything he could do for me, and I just asked that he try to finalise the peace accord between North and South Sudan, which our Center had been working on for many years but had been stymied by prior White House policies. He agreed and maintained his word. As I pushed the ideals of peace and human rights in my publications, classroom lectures, public pronouncements, and forums, it was inevitable that some disagreements would arise. After my visit to Cuba, President Bush asked me to the White House for a comprehensive report to him and his national security adviser.

Because I had been out of government for more than three decades when Barack Obama became president, there were few possibilities for The Carter Center to have a direct relationship with the White House. During this time, I have had pleasant and appropriate interactions with Secretaries of State Hillary Clinton and John Kerry. Because we continue to play an active role in the Holy Land, this is especially vital to us now that Secretary Kerry has revived the US effort to bring peace to the region. Another reason for the Carter Center's weakened engagement with the White House is that The Carter Center's major activity has evolved over the years from peace discussions to managing and eliminating tropical illnesses and monitoring difficult elections.

Rosalynn and I have attended most national Democratic conventions and, of course, all presidential inaugurations. In fact, it was on one of these occasions, twelve years after I left office, that I met my first Democratic president: the inauguration of Bill Clinton.

***

The development in economic and political might of China, India, Brazil, South Africa, and other nations will inevitably reduce the United States' relative global influence. My goal is that our leaders would recognize and capitalise on our country's most admirable characteristics. When people in other countries encounter a struggle or an issue, they should look to Washington for help or as a shining example.

Our administration should be known for its opposition to war, commitment to peaceful conflict resolution, and eagerness to achieve this aim whenever practicable. We should be seen as the unwavering advocate of human rights, both among our own population and throughout the international community. America should serve as a rallying point for those nations concerned about challenges to the quality of our shared environment. We must be willing to set an example by sharing our enormous wealth with those in need. Our own society should ensure that all citizens have equal opportunities and have access to fundamental essentials of existence.

There would be no cost to exhibiting these characteristics. Instead, regaining the trust, admiration, and goodwill that our country formerly enjoyed among other peoples would benefit our country's well-being. Simultaneously, all Americans may be united in a common resolve to revitalise and nourish the political and moral ideals that we have advocated and sought over the last 240 years.

***

In retrospect, it appears that all phases of my life have been tough, but also successful and joyful. My early youth on a farm in Archery during the Great Depression, primarily isolated with my own family and black playmates, was relatively deprived in comparison to modern-day existence. Even though there was no running water or electricity and I had to work as hard as anybody else, I still have great recollections of those days. There was a nice and safe atmosphere that was embodied by my parents and siblings, and it is difficult to recall any discomforts or negative family ties.

My college and naval years were very rewarding, as Rosalynn and I settled down and embraced our growing family. The difficulties I experienced with my classmates were offset by my wonderful experiences, and I accomplished every goal that a young officer could want for. My submarine service provided excellent training for dealing with obstacles, and it was a selling point for voters when I campaigned for public office.

For seventeen years as a farmer and businessman, I built a solid financial foundation for my family, learned how to deal with hundreds of clients, and forged a long-overdue collaboration with Rosalynn in all facets of life.

I've already mentioned my time in public office, and I'm grateful for the experience. I am content with my achievements, mourn my missed goals, and plan to use my former governmental position to improve everything we do in our senior years.

The existence we have now is the finest of all possible worlds. We have an expanding and harmonious family, a rich life in our church and the Plains community, and a diverse range of adventurous and interesting work at The Carter Center. Rosalynn and I have travelled to over 145 countries and are as active as we have ever been. We are fortunate with good health and look forward to the future with excitement and confidence, but we are prepared for difficulty when it comes.

Printed in Great Britain
by Amazon